SCHOOL TIES AND
LESSONS LEARNED

The words engraved on the Mace of the Scottish Parliament are:

Wisdom, Integrity, Compassion, Justice

They seem to me to apply equally well to a life in education

FOREWORD

When I drove home at the end of the Summer term in June 2012, my feelings were all familiar. As in any year, the end of term had arrived almost too quickly. There were last minute references to complete, interviews with potential members of staff, checks on the new timetable and its operation, and preparations for the end of term Community Mass and staff concert for the pupils.

Once the school buses had been waved off with echoes of "Have a good holiday!", "Take care!" and just plain "Hooray!", there was the final tidying of the desk, a late phone call or two, a parent with a last minute enquiry, and then the task of arranging with office staff to drop in during the next week to tie up any loose ends. Then the computer was closed down, the bag was grabbed, good wishes exchanged with colleagues, and out into the sun of the car park.

I think all teachers will recognise the feeling experienced on the drive home at the end of the session. In fact, it's not all that dissimilar to the feeling felt by the pupils. I always think of it as an extended exhalation of breath that's been held in for too long. It comes with the realization that, for the next six weeks, the thousands of details, plans, checklists, bits of information, and worries and concerns, can be let go, at least to the back of the mind. As is the case with many similar professions, teaching is not a task that can be put away in evenings or at weekends. It's a linear occupation and the knowledge and information gained and used each day has to be carried on week to week, month to month. The need to 're-boot' over six weeks is a vital part of the ability to operate at the high level of intensity needed when working with young people and their futures, and one which is perhaps not understood by those who criticize 'long holidays' for the profession.

So driving home in the sunshine, breathing came easier, the world seemed brighter, the limbs lighter. It's the kind of mood where you could find yourself singing!

For me, though, this end of session was unlike any of the previous thirty six starts to summer. This time, I would not be coming back in August to start it all again; in August, I would be retiring from the job. I wasn't driving towards the summer holidays, I was driving towards the rest of my life!

I'm not sure how I had expected to feel on this journey. The emotion had come days before at a formal retiral lunch and in individual moments with friends on the staff over the previous few weeks. There was also the convenient fact that, strictly speaking, I was not retiring at the end of term, but at the start of the new term; driving home, I was still Deputy Headteacher, and would be for another six weeks.

However, it was more than that.

All through my career I had intended to retire when I was sixty. Initially, I had thought I might go on my birthday, in January – one helluva party! Then I got to thinking that perhaps the end of the Spring term might be better. However, as I came closer to retirement age and was still enjoying the job, it seemed best for all if I continued to the end of the session and made the natural break in the Summer.

From that point of view, driving into retirement on this date was something I had known about for years, so there was no upset or any of the adjustment needed by those who are not expecting to stop, who are desperate to escape, or who have it thrust upon them.

I knew I was ready to go, it was time. I had been privileged to do a job I loved, in the way I wanted to do it, with staff, pupils and parents who had made coming to work a joy. I felt I still related well to those around me and had the energy and vision to embrace change and to motivate and encourage.

However, I was also the oldest member of staff, and teaching is a young person's career – whether that youth is in chronology or thought; the world of education was very different to that which I had entered in the mid 70s, and each time I observed a young teacher's lesson I marvelled at the ingenuity, the flexibility, and the sheer scale of what they could achieve in the classroom. The baseline of teaching – relationships – hadn't changed, in fact it was more important than ever, but all that surrounded it – in terms of paperwork, the qualifications sought in leaders, the approach to the job by officialdom – all was different. It wasn't necessarily worse, just changed, and matching the times. These weren't my times, they belonged to the young, and I was happy to be leaving before I became the grump in the corner, reminiscing about 'the olden days'.

It was great to be leaving on a positive note: I had done my time, to the best of my ability, and enjoyed it thoroughly. Now there were other things I wanted to be doing.

Perhaps it was best summed up, unintentionally, by one of the bright eyed newly qualified teachers with whom I loved working as mentor. After a chat in my office shortly before the end of term, she said, innocently, I'm sure:

"It's so good to be able to come and get your advice, Sean. After all, you've got a whole lifetime of experience!"

It was true, and it meant I was right to move on and let others gain that experience.

So as I drove home that June day I wasn't overwhelmed by the moment; it was more like a feeling of accomplishment: I had completed what I had set out to do and now I would be looking for new challenges and approaches to life.

There was one question floating about at the back of my mind, though. After thirty seven years of teaching, as a classroom teacher, a guidance teacher, and a Deputy Head; after working with hundreds of colleagues and thousands of pupils and parents; after school shows, outdoor residentials, musicals, pantomimes, transit bus driving, sports coaching, column writing, meetings, discussions, presentations, coffee, biscuits, laughter, tears, frustration and joy, what did I think I had been doing?

It seemed to me, only a book could answer the question:

WHAT WAS ALL THAT ABOUT?

OYSTER CATCHERS AND PLASTIC GLASS

If you are fortunate enough to still have a local bookshop, you may well find within it a section labelled with words to the effect of 'bad childhoods'. 'Misery autobiographies' are big business these days, and it seems that the public do enjoy an extended wallow in Monty Pythonesque "You were lucky!" tales.

This gives me a problem as, essentially, my reflections on a life in education are going to be positive and upbeat. Of course, not every day of my education, as a pupil or a teacher, was brilliantly sunny in aspect, but overall I have always classed myself privileged, if not blessed, to have enjoyed a good education myself, and to have gone on to work in a profession I loved, in situations where I felt I could make a genuine difference, and with colleagues and pupils who were overwhelmingly good to be with, and a pleasure to serve.

One reason for writing down these reflections is to offset the largely negative press that our schools, teachers, and young people seem to receive these days. Negative stories about education abound, reporting of the many positives is less common.

However, I want these reflections to be helpful to readers and as accurate as I can make them in content and tone. Furthermore, I don't want them to be a smug recital of a 'glittering career', nor should they suggest that my experience, at school and as a teacher, was universal.

While I will continue to state that I felt lucky to have been where I was, when I was, I am aware that, for some pupils and teachers, education is neither a pleasant nor successful experience, and I don't seek to downplay the struggle of everyday classroom work for many on both sides of the desk.

Naturally I tend to optimism; the glass is always half full, and I'm sure that helped me get through the times and events which were not so enjoyable or successful. Being positive, however, is crucial to education – those involved must offer the brightest hopes and the surest futures to those they teach and support. A recurring theme of my reflections will be that a nation which is not proud of its young people – and of the teachers who work with them – is, at some level, dysfunctional, and is betraying their children's future. Schools have a responsibility to engender this pride, but the community have also a duty of support.

Because of that, as I look back, there will be times when, quite rightly, it is difficult to separate school from community, parents from teachers, and young people from adults. In a memorable quotation, John Dewey said: "Education is not preparation for life, education is life itself." The most successful educators, and schools, remember that, and strive to become part of the community and open to those they serve, in every sense.

Perhaps the best way to illustrate the balance between the positive and the less happy times is to recount two tales from my career which, in a sense, demonstrate education's way of reflecting the highs and lows of life.

For the last sixteen years of my career, I was Depute Headteacher in a school just outside Edinburgh in one of Scotland's 'New Towns'. The school had an enviable location, being situated on a hillside which boasted views to the Pentland Hills and sloped down to a river. The site selected for the building in the early 1990s had been the grounds of an estate dating from the 17th century, and a planning requirement was the preservation of as many of the original trees and grounds as was feasible.

As a result of this, in all the seasons of the year, doing 'lunch patrol' was a greatly enhanced experience. Not only was there fresh air and the chance to interact with pupils on an informal basis, but the 'flora and fauna' was abundant. In the latter years of my career, the school worked closely with "Grounds for Learning" and "Architecture and Design Scotland" to improve the grounds and make them integral to the school's teaching and learning. Spaces were provided for outdoor learning, projects were mounted to enhance the area and encourage more innovative use of the land available. In the process, we discovered the hedge running by the river was up to 400 years old, and realized we also harboured a badger sett.

So it's understandable that using one's lunch hour to 'patrol' the area was little hardship. Under blue skies in Autumn and Spring, the sensation was exhilarating, the cries of young people at play in the distance only adding to the feeling of well being.

Around a decade ago, I noticed an addition to the birdlife on my lunchtime walks. At certain times of the year, three Oyster Catchers would perform a fly past, their high pitched tweep tweep bringing thoughts of the seaside and coastal walks.

A twitcher on the staff said that it was becoming increasingly common for seaside birds to follow the river upstream in search of food, and that was why they had started to visit our campus.

I started to look out for them – they brightened grey days and confirmed the joy of the good days; each time I heard their cry my heart rose and I followed their flight or watched them search for worms on the grass, their distinctive black, white and orange standing out against the green.

Theoretically, they were in 'the wrong place', we were miles from the sea, but they still soared, they still swooped, they still flew excitingly in formation. It made me think of the educators' responsibility to ensure pupils could feel school was 'the right place' for them. It made me think of the pupils who had come to school convinced it was 'the wrong place' for them, but who, through the work of teachers and staff, parental support, and their own efforts, had survived, to 'soar' in the world of education and learning. It made me proud of the work of my colleagues, alert to the importance of our profession, and happy that I was able to contribute, in whatever way, to making that difference.

I love the seaside, I love seabirds, and I loved my job. The Oyster Catchers brought it all together nicely!

"The Wrong Place" could well sum up the point of the balancing tale – this time from the first school in which I taught which was situated in the middle of Edinburgh.

In the mid 1980s, school pupils were less sophisticated than they are these days. Even quite senior students would be happy to attend school discos, organized and run by guidance and management staff.

Having done a spot of DJ work when I was younger, I was more than pleased to 'spin the discs' at these affairs which, though I say it myself, were very popular for a while. In fact, at Christmas time, such was the demand, myself and an Assistant Head would find ourselves running 'disco parties' for year groups from P7 to the seniors. It meant five or six events in eight or nine days, but we enjoyed them as much as the pupils and it certainly gave a buzz to our tiredness in the lead up to the Christmas holidays.

At one of these events, for fourth year pupils, I was taking a break at the front of the school, getting some fresh air, when I became aware of a figure at the bottom of the steps leading up to the front door. A hand was raised rather diffidently, and I realized it was a boy I'll call 'Ally'.

His background was difficult for him. His mother was not on the scene, his father worked all hours at his own business to make ends meet, and he didn't really get on with his older brother. It was not a particularly unusual set of circumstances, but Ally's reaction was very mixed up. He constantly sought attention and affection. Having originally attended a private school, he could be extremely articulate and sociable – with adults as well as his peers. However, he was emotionally very immature and from time to time would fly into rages which were alarming to teachers and pupils alike. Apart from himself, I don't recall him actually hurting anyone physically, but when he was 'on a downer', he was extremely difficult to reach and often out of control.

As a school we tried hard to support him. These days I suspect there would have been more external support available from organizations dealing with mental health such as SAMH. Then, however, we were limited to in-school supports, followed by work with social services and youth groups, till eventually Ally ended up being referred to the Children's Panel. At a meeting where everybody in the room struggled with their emotions, it was felt that, for Ally's sake as much as anyone's, he should spend time in 'secure accommodation'. This meant, in essence, he would be in a boarding school environment where he would not be allowed to leave the building – except, perhaps, for home visits, to be arranged at weekends. The idea was that some stability and consistency in his lifestyle might help him deal with the temper tantrums and swings in mood which were making his life so difficult.

So, on this particular Friday night, obviously home from his school, Ally had turned up at the Disco for Fourth Year pupils. Inside were the students who had been his classmates until three or four months previously.

"Hi, Sir. How are you?" he said, slurring his words a little, a shape suspiciously like a beer can in his jacket pocket.

He came up the steps and I shook his hand.

"How ye doin? What's the school like?"

Eyes cast down, he muttered words to the effect that it was ok and he was getting on well.

He looked up.

"Any chance I could go into the disco, sir? It's 4th year isn't it? All my pals, like."

I reflected that Ally had had precious few pals in his year group but that in any case we had a solid rule that only pupils could attend school functions. I told myself, in his case, it was probably for the best anyway.

"I'm sorry, Ally. You know the rule – pupils only."

"Aye, right enough, sir."

It would have been easier if he'd started to argue.

He stepped down to the bottom of the stairs, and turned back, looking up with a smile.

"Thanks anyway, sir. Good to see you. Have a happy Christmas."

He turned to walk away and then threw one last comment back over his shoulder.

"The place is ok actually. They look after you. It's got plastic glass in the windows."

With that he waved and meandered down the street towards the Meadows, blond hair under the weak street lamps, "Merry Xmas Everybody" from Slade vibrating through the front doors of the school behind me.

I never saw or heard of Ally again. I still don't know why the glass was plastic: to stop them getting out, or to prevent them hurting themselves. The comment still haunts me nearly thirty years later. At times like that you would need that oyster catcher feeling to provide the balance.

WISDOM

The only true Wisdom is in knowing you know nothing

Socrates

BEGINNINGS

There is little success where there is little laughter

Andrew Carnegie

How would I define 'Wisdom', particularly in an educational sense?

I believe it is the ability, gained through experience, to use the knowledge and information at one's disposal to make the best possible judgments and decisions.

In a sense, it's the job of teachers to help young people to gain that knowledge, and the perspective to use it wisely. Knowledge for its own sake, is of limited use; the capacity to use it to gain understanding, and to use it alongside one's fellows in a positive fashion, is emblematic of a sophisticated and civilized society.

We shouldn't be learning facts merely to qualify us for employment; we should study as widely as possible: to find out about who we are, where we come from, and why we do what we do, and so that our learning informs our decisions. Learning, as well as life, contributes to experience.

However, having established such an approach, one is bound to wonder: where does it come from? How do we establish or choose approaches to things like teaching and learning?

The obvious answer is: in the home and in our own education. So, though this isn't intended to be an autobiography, it seems to be sensible to look back on my family and educational origins in an attempt to try and trace the genesis of my views on education. For,

17

surely, education and learning exists in a context, and we need to know and understand that context before we can really reflect on those things which affect our educational journey.

If I look at my grandparents, a pattern emerges.

On my father's side, my grandfather, John, was brought up on a farm in County Leitrim in the north west of Ireland. His dad was a tenant farmer who couldn't read or write. Grandad was one of six siblings – all of whom emigrated: the three girls to America, and the three boys to Scotland – although my grandad and his elder brother came to Edinburgh via Brooklyn.

Having worked as a tram driver in Brooklyn, grandad joined his brothers in running grocery shops in Edinburgh, and later one brother moved to do the same in the Gorbals in Glasgow, and another died. My grandmother, Katie, was Liverpool-Irish and had met John when she was 'in service' in Brooklyn.

On my mother's side, my grandfather came from a long established Lancashire family – who reached back to John and Richard Duckett, listed among the Catholic Martyrs in the Reformation. He served as a Gunner in the First World War and was a postman and, eventually, a postal supervisor. He also enjoyed a brief career as a music hall stand up comedian. His wife, Rose, was Liverpool-Irish, and, after a brief stint as a nanny in New York, came home to Liverpool for the sake of her health, and became a respected seamstress.

Both sides of the family, then, by the inter-war years, had just about achieved a kind of bourgeois, 'higher' working class, respectability, but close enough to poverty to fear for the future, particularly having witnessed the recession in the late 20s.

This fear, I suppose, most impacted on my parents in terms of their own parents' respect for education – in an age when free education for all at secondary level was not available.

My father attended Holy Cross Academy in Edinburgh – the Catholic Senior Secondary, and when he left worked in the family shop and then the St Cuthbert's Co-operative grocery – the "Store" as it was known to generations of Edinburgh folk. For his siblings, again, Holy Cross was the schooling, and one joined the Post Office but died young after being a Prisoner of War in the Great War, one played football for Hibs before becoming a Franciscan Priest, two became salesmen – one in England and the other with Sears Roebuck in New York, and the only girl, as was often the case in Irish Catholic families, became a nun, and spent most of her life in Australia, working with young people and then with the aged.

My mother took accountancy exams after secondary school, her sister went to Art and Commercial College and spent her whole career as manager of a bridal store in Liverpool. After working as a book keeper, my mother did youth work and eventually, when widowed, became a priest's housekeeper.

There are some clear parallels and themes running between both sides of my family: Catholic Faith, a respect for education, and an intention that children be well prepared for employment and a place in society; service to others and working with people also seems to feature. I can also identify in myself a certain facility with words and a love of music, though, sadly, my uncle's footballing ability doesn't seemed to have trickled down!

The relevance of this slice of genealogy, becomes clear when I examine my own educational experiences.

I started school at St John's Primary in Portobello, Edinburgh's seaside suburb. That I would attend a Catholic school was a given, but St John's wasn't the nearest denominational primary to where I lived; I was sent there because it had the best record in the city of preparing pupils for senior secondary education at Holy Cross Academy. A letter I still possess, written by my dad to his sister in Australia, enthuses about my first day at school and particularly notes that I was the only one in the class who could read and write my name.

So, right from the start, I had the benefit and advantage of parents who had thought carefully about my education and made positive choices based on their hopes for my future. This is, perhaps, the basic lesson of education: that parents must be involved and make the most of opportunities for their children. The school, likewise, must prioritise its links with parents and carers, and its openness to their wishes and aspirations.

The combination of my parents' positivity and interest, and a good early personal exposure to school, must obviously have contributed to my positive attitude towards education. This was an attitude which persisted strongly even when my actual experiences were not so pleasant.

My first and crucial experience of education, then, backed by my parents' attitude, was positive and supportive.

After such a good start, instability took over. The year I started school my father died suddenly. In another year we had moved to the north west of England and, ultimately, in the first three years of my primary education I attended five different schools – in two different education systems.

The consensus would be that so many schools would lead to problems in my academic and social progress. It's impossible, of course, to suggest how things may have been different in other circumstances. My father's death not only changed the emotional, family, and social landscape for me, but also the geography of my life. All experiences guide who we are and who we become, and it may be that the variety of teachers and styles I experienced at such a young age helped me become more adaptable to change. It's safe to assume there were pluses and minuses, and that how I reacted to my experiences was more formative than the experiences themselves.

Stability returned when I entered the primary department of St Mary's College to begin what would be a successful ten years of academic progress.

Again, my mother's foresight was on display. St Mary's College was a Catholic direct grant Grammar School (the English equivalent of a senior secondary in Scotland), run by a religious order called the Irish Christian Brothers and based in Crosby, a northern suburb of Liverpool. It had the excellent academic reputation one would expect from such an institution, and admitted pupils from an area stretching south of Liverpool city centre to the seaside town of Southport where I lived, a catchment of around twenty miles, covering a wide demographic from docks to stockbroker bungalows.

As was the system in those days, admission to the secondary school was by passing the "Eleven plus" examination and an 'Entrance Exam'. My mother's obvious conclusion had been that if I attended the primary department of the school, my chances of admission to the secondary were increased. Again, this was another decision based on educational opportunity, and, though my Edinburgh school had involved a ten minute bus journey from Piershill to Portobello, the travel involved now – and for the next ten years, was a twenty five minute train ride followed by a twenty minute walk. Those of us who travelled on that train – to St Mary's and several other schools in the area, formed our own 'commuter community', and some remain amongst my best friends, but it is interesting to note that I hardly ever had the benefit of a local community school during the majority of my education.

I don't want to pursue too much detail about my education at St Mary's, but I need to outline its approaches – if only to contrast them later with my own attitudes as a teacher.

Two major pieces of background knowledge might be helpful – regarding grammar schools of the time, and the Christian Brothers. Both provided a major input into the education of the baby boomers and, therefore, are responsible for much about the way the country looks and acts today, for better or worse.

Grammar schools were established by the "Butler Act" of 1944. The intent behind the Act was to provide, for the first time, free secondary education for all. In this aim it was successful and it also provided access to high quality secondary education to many who previously could not have afforded it – in terms of fees, but also, particularly in large families, in terms of family financial needs.

However, like other 'one nation' Conservative measures, its practice was not entirely as successful as its intent.

Secondary education was to be divided into different sections – for those who were deemed by the 'eleven plus' examination or other measures, to be best suited to 'academic', 'vocational' or 'technical' education. In Scotland, this translated largely into 6 year Senior Secondaries, and 3 or 4 year Junior Secondaries.

In some cases, this met needs admirably, but in many ways, the judging of pupils at the age of eleven, and the subsequent 'labelling' of their educational potential, was ineffective and

22

counter productive – even if you agreed with the somewhat dubious contention that pupils were possessed of 'types' of ability, or that they were all 'measurable' at the same age, regardless of individual developmental stages.

Eventually, and probably inevitably, despite brave individual efforts by some schools and teachers, those who attended 'secondary moderns' or 'junior secondaries', often came to be seen as having 'failed', and the all important motivation factor was difficult to promote in some areas. Theoretically, pupils could switch from secondary modern to Grammar School – and a number did after their fourth year, to continue with studies, but it became increasingly rare for this to happen, and it seemed horribly like children had been 'told their place' before they even started secondary school. Unsurprisingly, this sometimes impacted on the calibre of staff attracted by the different sectors.

So, politically, and socially, it would seem easy to conclude that this was a 'bad' education system – and in many ways it was. However, it would be foolish to ignore its successes – of which I would count myself as one. One of the motivators for writing this book was the internal debate I have always had between my dislike of the grammar school system and its success in educating me. I cannot deny that it got me to university and on to a career that I loved; at the same time, as an educator, I have to acknowledge the numbers of children that it failed, and the areas of my own development which were perhaps sidelined by my secondary school experience.

My discomfort is hardly helped by the fact that the most accurate quote I have ever heard in this respect comes from the unlikely source of Tory grandee, Kenneth Clark, who stated in a documentary on 'grammar schools' that he had been fortunate to have experienced an education system which was exactly right for him at exactly the right time.

Quite.

It's maybe a selfish take on the situation, but I cannot disagree, as I found myself in the same position. For me, it worked, for many it failed.

The Christian Brothers, as a religious teaching order, like Grammar Schools, reflect this same level of good intent and less successful practice.

They were founded in Ireland in the early twentieth century by Edmund Rice; their mission was to provide education for poor boys. A successful, widowed, businessman, Rice certainly pursued his aims with vigour. Indeed, both before and after independence, the Christian Brothers made a major contribution to universal education in a country where it was not always resourced or prioritized the way it should have been. Many of the political leaders of the Easter Rising and cultural minds of the Irish literary revival were educated by the Brothers, with their brand of classical education intertwined with a huge respect for Irish history, tradition, and sport – especially Gaelic Games. Up to the present, many members of government in the Republic were educated by the Christian Brothers and it's fair to say that they have had a huge influence on the way the state has developed, for better or worse.

Strangely, as their influence stretched into other places – notably Britain, Australia, and Gibraltar, they tended to have an approach which was not markedly in line with their origins. When I was at school, though many of the Brothers who taught me were Irish, it seemed there was a resolution to be 'more English than the English'. Rugby was promoted as the premier sport, 'Jerusalem' was sung at School Concerts, and any links with Ireland tended to be played down, despite the fact that many of their pupils, like me, would be the children of first or second generation immigrants.

In reality, despite their origins in universal education of the poor, the Brothers in Britain had allied themselves to the Grammar School system. This made sense in as much as the ambitions of many parents, who might well be Catholic and of immigrant stock, were, as we've seen, to seek the most benefit for their children through accessing a high standard of education.

The Brothers' approaches met this requirement, but, as entry to their schools was by academic ability rather than economic capacity, they still ran schools which provided high level education to pupils from all backgrounds and faiths. In that sense, at least, they were still committed to 'universal' education.

The parents of pupils at Christian Brothers' schools generally valued education highly and expected them to provide an ethos which was strong on discipline, academic rigour, and sporting and musical success: the passports to a 'better life' for their offspring.

In a sense, that was what they got.

From the time we arrived at St Mary's College, the secondary school, there was an expectation that we would all be going to university – this in an era when around 8% of pupils went on to take a degree. (The equivalent figure today is around 39%) In fact, you would need to have positively volunteered the information that you had an alternative ambition. So, expectations were very high and we were frequently reminded that we constituted 'the top two per cent of the top two per cent" – whatever that meant.

Such an approach suggests that the school was producing confident individuals, well aware of their abilities. Strangely, this was not the case. For, while the general idea of our high performance destination was promoted at every opportunity, the encouragement of individual confidence, of personal development, of reflection and individuality, was almost completely absent.

It would be an oversimplification to claim that the school frightened us into examination success at the expense of our own development, but it wouldn't be too wide of the mark.

Praise was limited, top marks expected, little attention paid to the reasons for underachievement – which was almost always put down to 'laziness'. There was a regime of two hours of homework every night to be handed in first thing next morning, no excuses accepted. I can remember arriving home from a cross country meeting, at which I had represented the school, around 8pm on a Wednesday evening. I had run 5K and travelled for over an hour and a half without the chance of a shower or anything to eat. I literally fell asleep trying to do a Latin translation and a letter was provided by my mother, explaining why I had been unable to complete the homework on time. No matter: 'two of the belt' was the punishment.

Though I captained both cricket and cross country teams, and sang in the choir, this earned me little approval or praise. In classes where I showed minimal ability – such as art or woodwork – the teachers lavished time on the talented students and left the rest of us to our own devices. Maths and science – both incomprehensible to me for most of the time – merely resulted in increased beltings and punishment exercises.

To those who teach today, or who have attended school in the past thirty years or so, this must be an unrecognizable model. The encouragement, praise, analysis, and individual support -which is taken for granted as the bedrock of the contemporary educational approach – was entirely lacking. "Survival of the fittest" might be a fair description of the education my generation experienced, with corporal punishment a daily occurrence, often without any pretence of justification. One Brother would routinely belt half the class at the start of the lesson "pour encourager les autres"; misdeeds such as a top shirt button unfastened could lead to two of the belt, and many of the teachers were experts in emotional abuse – having those in each class whom they would pick on for the delight of the rest of the class: a subtle and hideous form of control through divide and rule.

However, it is important to me, and hopefully my reader, that this account and reflection is balanced, and I will also continually make the point that education is the product of the society which it serves – its capacity to operate outwith the norms of that society should not be overestimated.

I attended secondary school from 1963 till 1970, starting only 18 years after the end of World War 2. Most of my teachers and my friends' parents had either fought in that war, or lived through the horrors of the Blitz. As they raised their families in peace time, a desire for stability, the 'natural order of things', and compliance, was largely their world view. They had had enough disruption and uncertainty; if you like, they wanted a quiet life with 'everything – and everybody – in its place'.

The birch as an acceptable public punishment was not long abolished, young men had all been through the various humiliations of National Service, and authority – be it political, educational, or religious – was not generally challenged. The fear exhibited by the authorities in the face of the Paris Riots – or even long hair and beat music – demonstrates how repressed and paranoid was an establishment who had lived through the war and were terrified of nuclear annihilation. It's easy to forget that context when we condemn their approaches to education.

From our perspective, whatever the context, they are not defensible, but it is easy to explain their origins.

I don't think that our school was particularly out of line with what was happening generally at the time. Indeed, I suspect from what I have heard that an even more heartless regime may have existed in many junior secondaries or secondary moderns where staff and pupils were operating without the carrot of university education or the benefits of academic successes.

The Christian Brothers, of course, have latterly become infamous, as an Order where abuse – physical and sometimes sexual, as well as emotional, existed to an overwhelming degree. The consensus amongst my friends from school is that, brutal though our time was at school, we seem to have been 'fortunate' that the abuse which took place was largely physical and emotional, and perhaps at the lower end of the horrible spectrum which has now been revealed by so many of those who suffered. Certainly, we experienced, as a common event, focused sarcasm and physical abuse which could range from punching to kicking to pulling hair and sideburns. It was gratuitous and bullying violence, but it wasn't generally hidden, and the response of most parents was along the lines of "You must have deserved it". Different times and different attitudes.

We understand now the dangers of blind trust in religious orders; we know that abusers are attracted to such organizations for the access they offer to young people; we know that there have to be means of reporting abuse and that victims must be confident that they will be supported and taken seriously. We know that each pupil must be treated as unique and precious. None of that was acknowledged then.

There were, of course, Brothers and lay teachers who didn't fit the mould, who were inspirational, kind and compassionate. Their influence stood out all the more against the background of the ethos under which they had to operate.

The Brothers themselves were often victims. Plucked from a hard and sometimes brutal rural life in Ireland, many had not voluntarily chosen to train as Brothers – they had been sent to the college because it would gain them an education. Their own life experience, and sometimes their personal skills and abilities, didn't always suit them to the craft of teaching, particularly not in British conurbations. The community life they experienced outwith the classroom must have been harsh and barren at times. It seems the road to bad educational experiences can often be paved with good intentions.

That then was my educational experience – from the age of five to eighteen. Judged by the expectations of the time, it was successful. Exams were passed, university entrance was attained, the ambitions of my family, and, it has to be said, myself, had been met.

I am trying to focus on 'wisdom' – where it comes from, and how we use it. I wrote that it may be defined by the ability to use our experiences and knowledge to make informed choices. It's unfair, of course, to suggest that 18 year olds leave school overburdened by this wisdom. Indeed, you could argue that it's the lack of fully developed wisdom which leads young people on a voyage of discovery and enlightenment: the willingness to take risks and enter uncharted areas.

However, what we learn and experience at school, for better or worse, helps shape the people we become and the attitudes we adopt – even if that 'school learning' is modified by later, more adult, experiences.

Many of my basic values, formed by family, were shaped and reinforced by my education. Ideas about serving others, counting our blessings, Christian charity, community and politics, Faith, friendship and sport: all were firmly implanted during my school years.

Remarkably, a love of scholarship and the arts, or of literature and music, was largely engendered outside of school rather than as part of the formal curriculum. We learned, often by rote, for the purpose of passing exams; intellectual curiosity was a personal matter rather than part of an educational approach. There was far more stick than carrot, in every area of our school experience. The idea of learning for its own sake – for the joy of discovery and expanding our knowledge - was almost completely absent. Indeed, though school was not unremittingly grim by any means, it would be fair to say that we seldom, if ever, experienced any joy in our education. Our emotional intelligence was hardly acknowledged, and life outside of school was seldom allowed to impinge on our activities. Though I lost my dad at 5, I cannot remember any teacher ever mentioning the fact or asking how I coped with that loss; it wasn't on the agenda at all.

This is all the more remarkable when one considers the percentage of our time taken up by school and its activities.

Sometimes today it appears that there are pupils who struggle to find the time for school between jobs, activities, clubs and social outings, and there are suggestions that midteens may spend three or four hours a day on various types of social media.

For my generation in education, school took up a huge proportion of our time and attention. I left the house at 7.45 and got back between 4.45 and 6.00pm depending on after school activities. There was a minimum of two hours homework four nights a week and around the same at the weekend. If you took part in school sports teams, as I did, that would account for another 6 hours or so on a Saturday, including travel. That's around two thirds of your waking hours.

That certainly led to a focus on study and an involvement with school affairs – but it also reflected a kind of limited view of learning, in a small and heavily proscribed world.

Through the methods employed when we were at school, we learned a lot of facts, and were trained how to pass the exams which would lead us on to more education and high level career prospects. What was less available were the skills we would need to employ that knowledge and to adapt it to the various situations in which we would find ourselves in life.

It wasn't a 'bad' education per se, but it neglected areas such as personal development, self esteem, and critical thinking skills, which we would consider crucial these days. As I've said, it reflected a society which was quite repressive and repressed and largely conformist. It's interesting to note how many former pupils of St Mary's returned to teach there.

Compared to the pupils of today, we had far less choice and input into our life within and outwith school; for better or worse, this diminished the likelihood of us flourishing, but also, I suppose, engendered less confusion in our lives. We were operating on well polished rails – unlikely to crash, but seeing little of the intellectual and artistic countryside.

To illustrate these limitations: I was at a school not ten miles from The Cavern, from 1963 onward; we had former pupils who were stars in Liverpool beat groups, yet the music department never once acknowledged any music other than the classical.

The fact that it was a single gender boys' school was, in some ways, the most crucial element in its ethos. If I formed one early opinion about education it was that all schools should be co-educational. I can accept arguments for certain circumstances where single sex groupings might be helpful, but a school without both genders, to me, faces real difficulties in preparing young people for adult life.

Maybe in my case, as the only child of a widow, the effect was exaggerated, but certainly most of my contemporaries suffered from crippling shyness and awkwardness with members of the opposite sex. However, the most damage was done by the atmosphere in the school.

I've already referred to the barrenness of the Brothers' experience: confined to a male community where it seemed alcohol and tobacco were the only real outlets and, maybe unsurprisingly, a lot of frustration was taken out on the pupils.

For 'the boys', the experience was just 'normal', and as anyone who has been in a sports club or changing room will agree, the 'all males together' atmosphere can be enjoyable – up to a point, and if you are equipped to thrive in such a testosterone-driven environment. However, it's only one small part of most males' make up – and there are a lot more elements of a developing personality which need to be nurtured.

It's perhaps the first and most obvious link between my own education and the manner in which I sought to teach. The acknowledgment of friendships (rather than romances!) between boy and girl pupils was always important to me, and I witnessed many instances of support and kindness which were made possible by both genders being more relaxed in each others' company. It was a whole dimension missing from my own educational experience – and, for me as a teacher, more than made up for the hassle caused in the other direction by the fall out from broken relationships, and distractions caused by teenagers sharing the same co-educational space on a daily basis!

That, then, would be an example of 'wisdom' gained in a negative manner, engendering a determination to 'do things differently', and that, I suppose, would be part of the value of my schooling. It benefited me in some ways and gave me a warning in others. It meant that when I started teacher training, whilst I had a lot to learn and was far from 'wisdom', I was fairly clear about the sort of teacher I didn't want to be and what my priorities would be.

One thing I couldn't know at that stage was the lifelong impression a teacher can leave on a pupil. I am amazed at the influence of some of my teachers, even at this time of my life, and whilst I don't wish to create a stream of anecdotes, this is surely an area where some illustration is helpful.

Step forward, Miss Meredith.

I have said that I went to a number of primary schools prior to starting at St Mary's. I attended one of these, chosen because it was close to my new home, for around six months, and the said Miss Meredith was my teacher. I was 7 years old.

One day she had one of my pals at her desk and was marking his work. She was giving him a hard time, and she suddenly looked up and said: "And there's no need for you to smirk".

As a good pupil, I was getting on with my work, and I didn't know what 'smirk' meant exactly. In addition, she was cross eyed, so nobody ever had any idea to whom she was addressing her remarks. As I worked, I tried out a few facial expressions, wondering if any of them were 'smirks'. The next thing she was shouting at me for being an "impudent brat".

That afternoon the class went on a 'nature walk' – I was left behind in an empty classroom as a punishment. Even as a 7 year old that didn't seem right to me. And it has rankled ever since.

Recently I discovered the school on one of those old pupil websites. I saw, when perusing the pictures, that her face was exactly as I had remembered it – for over 50 years. An example of the power of the teacher. And probably the reason why, throughout my career, the comment from pupils that pleased me most was that I was 'fair' and 'listened to them'. It was an approach based on an understanding of the long lasting effect just one piece of injustice in the classroom can have.

However, I have more positive examples of lifelong influence.

My teacher in the last year of primary was a man called Bill McCann. Tweed of jacket, moustachioed, an RAF veteran, who played rugby, in some ways he was a perfect stereotype of a teacher in the early sixties. However, despite, or maybe because of, his experiences, he approached the job in the most gentle, caring, and understanding fashion.

Routinely called by our surnames in class, Bill usually referred to me as "Mac"; he scarcely raised his voice and encouraged us with humour and a twinkle in his eye. At this distance, it's possible to recognize that he loved his job and that his joy in teaching transferred to the way he performed – another crucial piece of wisdom!

Every Thursday afternoon, we would put our books away, gain some relief from the battery of pre-11 plus "intelligence tests' and "100 sums", and listen, while he would read to us from "The Wind in the Willows".

It's easy, now, to analyse his style and its effect. However, then, it was just a case of the warmth of the class in gathering autumn twilight, the release from the tension of tests, and the joy of listening to his quietly expressive voice, as he brought to life Ratty, Mole, Badger and Mr Toad in their Riverbank adventures.

Fifty years later, I can't read the book, nor even think of its characters, without remembering Bill and hearing his voice. It was, perhaps, less than an hour, one afternoon a week, for a couple of terms, and yet beyond any doubt, it established a reading habit that would last, and indeed grow, over a lifetime. It helped me to love the creation of characters, the setting of scenes, the development of plot – all things which would guide the academic and professional career I would follow.

On a more practical level, it led me to believe, as an English teacher, that, in studying a class novel, it was far more effective, given the teacher had the ability, to read the novel out loud to the class, bringing the characters to life, rather than employing the tortuous method of each pupil reading aloud, no matter their ability. I never accepted that was a good way to build individual pupils' reading confidence and it could certainly ruin any understanding of the atmosphere or life of the novel.

If Bill's secret was empathy, then one of my other 'mentors' could be seen as the opposite, in manner if not in effect.

Jimmy Highton, our head of P.E. at secondary school, was the epitome of a post war 'gym teacher'. A former Army "drillie", he had been a boxing reserve for the GB team at the 1956 Melbourne Olympics, and that background clearly informed the way he went about his teaching.

In common with the contemporary approach, if you weren't talented or interested in his classes, then you were either ignored or treated as 'the enemy'. There's no doubt that, 'the Jimmy' as we called him, made life hell for those pupils he considered indolent or deliberately disruptive. I don't believe he could understand boys who weren't interested in sport, or, much worse in his eyes, those who had ability, but didn't bother using it. He was capable of doling out 'four of the belt' if he felt someone hadn't tried in P.E., and would pick on pupils he felt were 'too timid'. He had a range of post war approaches which appear horrendous to us now, but, as with so many other elements of education, were just accepted at the time.

His influence on me was massive: to the extent that for seven years between September and April, I gave him Saturday mornings and daily training sessions, and ended up Captain of his Cross Country Team.

The 'wisdom' I took from our interaction was all about the complexity of teaching and its proponents. I know that, for many 'non-sporty' pupils who attended St Mary's, Jimmy would be seen, plainly and simply, as a bully. Yet, in an echo of my mixed reactions to my schooling in general, I can also see how positive his presence was for me as a school boy.

I wasn't an 'elite' sportsman at school, though I was desperately keen on many sports and played them with a varying degree of ability. I wasn't even the most committed trainer, I never had the 'dig' to push myself to my absolute limit and become as good as I really could be. Jimmy must have known that, and yet he still supported me, still made me captain as longest serving team member, when there were others far more talented and focussed than I. He recognized, somehow, that I didn't want to let him down, and that I would be there every week, ploughing through mud and ditches, with minimal chances of the medals or recognition that my more successful team mates would garner.

Because of his rough exterior, his relaxed moments were all the more prized: the odd wink in the corridor, the gentle joke shared, references to "Mac" in front of the younger runners, being trusted with various tasks. Even his presence on the sidelines shouting unrepeatable abuse when he spied me playing tennis or cricket – both sports he considered 'unmanly' – constituted a bizarre kind of affectionate good humour.

When Jimmy said: "Well run, Macca!", I felt a million miles tall. Mind you, when he suddenly emerged from the undergrowth half way through a grueling 10k run and shouted "Pick em up! Get a move on, son!" I generally added a couple of miles an hour to my laboured efforts.

I suppose today's language might call it "Tough love", and it's certainly not a manner of teaching I would have wanted to emulate – but it did bring a sort of wisdom.

Jimmy clearly loved his runners; in old team photographs, he sits proudly amongst us, beaming his pride – and quite rightly, as we were a leading school for cross country running for many years. He would defend any one of us against all comers, and in terms of equipment and training support, he was magnificent. We were regularly Northern Schools Cross Country Champions, and each year, when we went to defend our trophies, he would hire a luxury coach, like those used by football teams, with facing seats and tables, and he would make sure we arrived at the venue with all the cups displayed on those tables – Here come St Mary's – Champions! The plethora of cuttings from the local press in those years show how keen he was to show off his lads, something else I learned from him – except, I hope, I was lucky enough to be able to show and share my pride in my pupils, rather than keep it hidden.

The major gift Jimmy gave me was running. Throughout my life, off and on it must be said, I've been a runner and have always thought of myself in those terms. It was years later that I actually realised that most people felt they couldn't 'run', that it was a difficult, if not impossible, task. Jimmy got me into a habit which has contributed to my health for a lifetime – again a huge influence coming from one person. When I competed in the second running

37

of the London Marathon in 1982, twelve years after I left school, one of the first things I did was write to Jimmy Highton and thank him for making it possible. Unknown to both of us at the time, I suspect he supplied some of what I lost when my father died. When school contemporaries rail against him, I am always understanding, but I can't resist uttering the Scottish rejoinder: "Aye. But".

From Jimmy, I learned that there are many ways to inspire as a teacher, and that an overall view of a teacher's temperament might miss some of the more complex elements. There are many ways to care.

So, if Bill was gentle and Jimmy was tough, what other traits 'got through to me' as a pupil?

Cliff Phillips, who at 6 foot 8 inches, was universally known as "Tich", was another teacher with a forces background in the RAF. He drove an old Rover 90, which, according to pupils, he couldn't sell because it was the only car with a roof high enough to accommodate his great height. He employed what would now be thought of as a kind of eccentricity, though, in comparison with his colleagues, just seemed to us to be a kind of humanity. On reflection, it was pretty well controlled, which again was in contrast to some of his colleagues. I wonder how many of his pupils still categorise stalagmites and stalactites according to his red faced dictum: "Down with the tites and up with the mites!"

It took me years to realize that Tich's strength was his enthusiasm for the subject and, even more so, his ability to teach. There are subjects I studied at school which are completely lost to me now. Latin, which was belted into me, almost totally vanished the minute I left the final examination hall. However, even after half a century, I can't go into the countryside without identifying geographical features as taught by Cliff Phillips: drumlins, hanging valleys, interlocking spurs, bergschrund, meanders, ox bow lakes,

38

moraines, soil creep, conical hills, arêtes, corries, cirques or cwms, limestone, millstone grit – all the explanations come tumbling out – to the despair of family and friends. Every time I pass a port, I see red arrows containing 'imports' and 'exports' floating over the water, and imagine all the transport links to their hinterlands. I'll even have a go at podsols and chernozems – although it was probably the scientific elements of geomorphology that put me off continuing Geography after A level and on to degree level.

All of this, Tich gave me by dint of high level classroom teaching skills. It has enhanced my love of the outdoors throughout my life, but it also informed my approach to teaching. It's not all about inspiration and great thoughts and philosophy, the basic nuts and bolts of imparting knowledge, explaining detail, and illustrating effectively and memorably, are immeasurably important in the classroom. Tich used humour and empathy in his teaching but basically, his enthusiasm for, and knowledge of, his subject, and his understanding of what would be accessible and comprehensible to his students, made him a highly effective and well liked member of staff. I have carried the knowledge he imparted through a lifetime, but I never remember it being hard to learn all that detail. The ability to communicate information effectively is a basic, but sometimes overlooked, requirement for successful teaching and learning. Who would have thought glaciation could be so memorable and fascinating!

So. Gentleness, toughness, and classroom skills.

My final positive influence from the teaching staff at school probably combined all of these attributes.

Ernie Spencer arrived at St Mary's as a comparative breath of fresh air. A young Scot, to my delight, he had a modern approach to teaching English, connected well with the pupils and always seemed faintly bemused by the ethos which he had entered at our school. He would say things like "Peely wally" which I would have to translate for my pals, and generally had a wry sense of humour which I appreciated. He also made a habit of calling us by our Christian names which was a bit of a departure for us all, even as senior pupils.

He was clearly enthused by his subject but had also thought carefully about delivery and methodology. He encouraged discussion, set up debate, was not beyond making controversial statements to see if we would challenge him. Occasionally we'd be invited to bring in rock music lyrics for discussion, and then he'd skillfully link their themes to more formal poetry. In short, he was very much a teacher of the late, rather than the middle, 20th century, and, like all talented teachers, he achieved his aims apparently effortlessly; as pupils we weren't aware of the craft he was employing – we just knew we looked forward to his classes and found English enjoyable.

I'm not sure it's possible to point to a moment in time and declare it pivotal in your life: we make so many choices for so many reasons that consequences always seem to come as a result as a long chain of cause and effect. However, I have always been tempted to point to a Thursday afternoon in November 1968 as my own personal road to Damascus.

Ernie announced we would be studying poetry. Cue groans! He then introduced us to a War Poet called Wilfred Owen – who, although dead for 50 years at that point, was certainly a lot closer to us than the likes of Keats and Tennyson. More than that, as Ernie pointed out, such was the urgency of his message – the pity of war – that he wrote his poetry in a style which was new, fresh, and deliberately accessible to all – not just poetry aficionados.

The poem he chose was one of Owen's less celebrated works "The Send Off" – which described not the horror of the trenches but the contrast between men marching off to war and the muted return of those who would survive, a prescient approach if ever there was one.

By the end of that double period, I was absolutely hooked. Ernie took us through the poem line by line, he unpeeled the layers of the poetic onion, revealed the depth of meaning, explained the devices Owen used, brought the content to life in a way that I'd never experienced before.

By 3.30pm I wanted more of this, I was a convert to poetry – and furthermore, it occurred to me how exciting it would be to have a career where you could perform this act for young folk like me. It was the moment I decided I would love the challenge of standing in front of a group of teenagers and saying, as I would often do over the years: "Hate poetry? I'll change your minds!"

So – a double period of English leads to this pupil deciding: "I'll take an English degree and then I'll teach English." I already loved reading – but had not really connected that with the English classes in school, or the possibility of further study or a career. What Ernie sparked was a realization of the possibilities, an increased confidence in my abilities, and a capacity to write creatively and originally that had not been previously encouraged.

As we've seen in discussing 'wisdom', the realization of what is learned doesn't always emerge at the time of the learning, although I was pretty sure in the weeks following my Eureka moment that something important had happened.

However, I don't think it took me more than a term or two as a teacher to realise fully what I'd gained from being in Ernie's classes, and how crucial his input had been to my development.

Then the 'wisdom' kicked in – and it left me with a message which was integral to my teaching career. As a teacher, you are never fully aware of your influence. Teaching and learning is ultimately an amalgam of what the teacher brings to the class and what is brought by each individual pupil. Some of that background you will know, some you will not. Words, activities, references and tone of voice can all trigger a reaction – as Ernie Spencer did with me. As a career progresses and the tasks become more familiar, if not easier, it is important to avoid the temptation to see the classroom as 'routine'. It can never be that for pupils – who have just one go at it, and they deserve that it is treated as better than that by those who teach them.

Of course, if you started each lesson thinking that it could be pivotal in the life of one of your pupils, or that you would be quoted a lifetime later, you would be paralysed. The importance of the realization is that it informs the way you teach and your approach to the process: no lesson is inconsequential, no class is less than important, every pupil is unique. There is no other way to teach and no other way to be professional, no other way to prepare your lessons nor to approach your pupils. It is the emotional intensity of this knowledge and approach which is often not appreciated by those outside the profession who complain about long holidays and short terms.

As it happened, I wasn't quite finished with Ernie Spencer!

He later became an HMI in Scotland and a leading authority on the teaching of English. I cooperated with him on some of his research and then came the day when he was part of the team for a school Inspection.

I rolled out his lesson on "The Send Off" for my class as he sat at the back taking notes. I was delighted to be able to say to the class at the end: "If you enjoyed that lesson, thank that man at the

42

back; and if you enjoy my teaching, or if you don't – he's responsible!"

It was a very good moment.

I wonder if these examples of 'teachers who made a difference to me' suggest that, for all the importance of a school's ethos, the individual teacher, and his or her connection with their pupils, can still send a powerful message. From these people I gained some confidence, an ability to reflect, a sense of my own ability and an enjoyment of elements of learning, which, if I am honest, were not reflected in the school's general approaches to education.

We should remember that, first and foremost, schools are made up of people and they are all different, and, indeed, constantly changing. You can have rules, expectations and a house style; you can prioritise ethos and principles, and you can support in a positive and encouraging fashion. However, ultimately, it remains about relationships, and that connection between pupils and teachers. An effective ethos promotes those relationships in a positive fashion, but even where the ethos may be weak or hard to detect, individual teachers bring their own style to their classrooms and can always make a difference. I know that there are many teachers who have to plough a lonely furrow, unsupported by colleagues or management, but determined to give their pupils the best. They have my respect and admiration because it's a far less challenging task to teach well and effectively as part of a positive ethos and a shared vision, and in an atmosphere of support, than in an atmosphere where support and aims are not shared.

REFLECTIONS

These days, pupils, as well as teachers, are encouraged to review and consider – units, topics, lessons, terms and years. The feedback, if used correctly, is fundamental to planning and adjusting teaching and learning. The Review and Development programme, as part of teachers' continuing professional development, can be an invaluable tool for school and individual, if it is applied correctly and supportively, giving each teacher the opportunity to reflect and plan.

However, looking back on my time as a pupil, it's apparent that to pause for 'review and reflection' was never really an option. I was in an educational tunnel with the accepted light of examination success at the far end of it, and other considerations were cast aside. So, to review it, over forty years later, produces some interesting conclusions.

As is the case with our entire childhood, we only know the education we receive, we have one experience and, mostly, lack the means to compare it with any other model.

The loss of my father has affected me far more keenly in the second half of my life than it did in my childhood, when I knew of no other life. Becoming a father myself has pointed out what was missed. Similarly, becoming a teacher has illuminated the darker parts of my own experience as a pupil and given me a wider context. Wisdom, as I have written, takes time to come to fruition.

In the context of the times, I received a 'good' education. I went to a school with high expectations and teachers who were skilled at helping us, or at least driving us, to pass the necessary examinations. Importantly, I grew up – at home and in school – in an atmosphere which promoted the crucial importance of education and learning. Perhaps, generationally, we were still close enough to the introduction of universal education for people to view it as valuable and transformational. Like universal suffrage, even when something has been fought for with great tenacity and bravery, when it becomes 'the norm' it can lose some of its sheen and become less appreciated. Certainly, my memory of the 1960s contains the popular adage that through education came improvement – no matter your background, and that this could come through academic success or practical training.

So perhaps the most affecting wisdom that I gained as a pupil was that education made a difference and was central to society and its ambitions. I grew up never questioning its importance nor its effectiveness. This, in part, explains my ambition to become a teacher and also my optimism and commitment when I taught.

The slower burning wisdom from my pupil experience, gained as I progressed through my career, exposed the narrowness of my education. As I have mentioned, there was little 'joy' in learning for me in my schooldays. Reflecting the manners of the time, an examination passed, or an essay well written, was the expectation - and elicited little in the way of praise. Our teachers taught to the examination curriculum and encouraged revision or understanding in terms of what would be needed to pass the examination. Part of any teacher's remit is, of course, examination preparation, but when it is the sole motivating force and when the necessity forces out all other approaches, the pupil – and intellect – is being short changed.

To give a practical example from my bête noire subject, Mathematics. I could never understand anything about Trigonometry; I could neither learn the codes nor understand their application. Had someone taken the time to explain that this was a means, for instance, of measuring a structure too high for a tape measure, I may well have gained an interest – but they never did, and I remained ignorant. Likewise, there being no oral content in our foreign language examinations, we were taught with minimal reference to actual pronunciation, leading to scratching of heads, puzzled looks, and incomprehension when we tried out our linguistic skills in France or Spain. Luckily we never had to try out

45

our Latin on any Roman soldiers – nor were we ever told that it was highly unlikely that any Romans in Britain ever spoke that classical language. It was as if education and learning existed in a vacuum, and the advantages of linking them to the world outside, where they had practical application, were ignored.

It's possibly no coincidence that those subjects and teachers I have mentioned as being influential tended to buck the trend in this area. In geography we went on field trips, the topography described and explained by Cliff Phillips was obvious in the countryside, we could make the connection. Ernie Spencer's take on English gave us the language and thoughts to analyse how we were feeling – about ourselves, literature in general, or the songs to which we listened, and the stories and poems we tried to write.

As I started to teach, myself, the need for relevance, the advisability of justifying the content of our lessons – above and beyond passing an examination – became clear to me and became a mainstay of my lessons. Part of the job, it seemed to me, lay in convincing the class of the importance of what we were doing – for each and every one of them, regardless of their ambitions, strengths or weaknesses. The subtext was always, or should have been: "What we are going to do is interesting, useful, will make you think, and you'll be able to take the knowledge away from the class and do something with it." My job was to make sure that I delivered on those terms – perhaps easier in English than in some other subjects, but nevertheless an aspiration, in an age where perhaps some pupils, and parts of society, are less convinced of the intrinsic importance of the educational experience. I never minded being a salesman for my subject: if I couldn't convince the pupils of its relevance and interest, what sort of teacher was I, and who could convince them?

A by-product of this approach was the confidence to go 'off-topic'. Frequently in my career, a pupil would raise a point in

46

discussion which was far more interesting or dynamic than any I had considered. It was both empowering of the class and pupil, and integral to the teaching and learning experience, if I was willing to follow that new and unexpected direction. Likewise, spotting a class was tired or lethargic, a change in lesson – even permission for a 'discussion class' where topics could roam far and wide – often brought a burst of intellectual energy and interest. Part of the craft, of course, was to let the pupils feel they had 'distracted' you from the task in hand and won themselves a 'fun lesson'. The other part of that skill was ensuring it only happened when you judged it helpful or appropriate

The wisdom gained from my schooling, then, or perhaps from this review of it, related to the importance of relationships and relevance in the classroom; the indisputable fact that an education system will reflect the expectations of the society within which it operates; and the need for the teaching and learning process to celebrate knowledge for its own sake and to open up the world to pupils. It also strikes me that, if you fail to treat each pupil as unique, you are letting them down – developmentally and educationally.

My schooling reflected the times in which we lived and the school fulfilled its obligations academically. If I am honest, even this review has failed to crystallize my feelings. I cannot defend the physical abuse and the largely absent recognition of emotional intelligence, and I don't deny that a lot of the time at school I felt stressed by, and even afraid of, unpredictable consequences. At the same time, I enjoyed being at school, and I have an affection for the place, shared by few, if any, of my school mates, and a kind of residual pride in the school. I am unable to deny that it helped me gain the life I have enjoyed, but equally, of course, I cannot know what a life I would have led with more encouragement and nurturing at school.

Perhaps, the lesson, or the wisdom, is that education is such a personal matter, its context so crucial, that generalization is bound to be compromised. I am clear that St Mary's College was central to the person I became. Maybe the crucial point for teachers and parents alike, is to remember how formative schools can be – for better or worse.

A casual perusal of St Mary's former pupils, or "Old Boys" as we are known, reveals John Birt, former BBC mandarin, poet Roger McGough, Cardinal Vin Nicholls of Westminster, Chris Curtis, drummer with Meseybeat icons, The Searchers, and TUC General Secretary, Brendan Barber. Maybe the eclectic nature of that list reflects the impossibility of tying down an educational experience in any singular fashion.

The school motto, in Latin, of course, was "Fidem Vita Fateri." Though as pupils we translated it as "Feed 'em on vitamins and make 'em fat", its actual meaning: "Show your Faith by the way you Live", though not always adhered to by some of the teachers in their classroom approaches, has always seemed to me an excellent motto for life.

Before I leave my own schooling, I realized while writing this, in the back of my mind, St Mary's old school song was echoing away. This was a song, like the school, typical of its times. As pupils we sang it lustily and not without an ironic sarcasm.

Reflecting the school's ethos, the day we left for ever, there were no celebrations, no events to mark the end of our schooling. Once our exams had finished we went in singly to hand back our books, and, if we wished, to say farewell or thank you to individual teachers. A group of us arranged to go into school at the same time, and, farewells complete, gathered untidily outside the headteacher's window. In a mood that hovered somewhere between bravado and defiance we sang, not the school song, but the contemporary chart hit from the England World Cup Squad which commenced:

"Back Home – they'll be thinking about us
When we are far away................"

We were lads and we acted as a group, but it was an interesting moment, and a rather sad ending to our education, whatever our personal reflections.

Looking at the official school song, now no longer used, I notice two things. Its archaic language gives a fairly accurate picture of the school in its own context, and, something which I had forgotten: approaching its climax, it also mentions my topic in this section: Wisdom! Who would have thought it!

When our boyhood days are over
And the broad highway of life
Lies before us still untrodden, still unknown
When our hearts are high exulting
In a future that is veiled
When we reap a golden harvest not yet sown.
We shall sometimes pause a moment
Just to think of yesterday
And our dear old Alma Mater left behind
Then each old association
Every Brother, master, boy
In our hearts will find a place most wondrous kind.
Thoughts will arise
Of friends we made
When hearts were young
Thoughts will arise
Of games we've played,
Of songs we've sung.

Thoughts of that place
Which to its constant praise
Fashioned both words and deeds
In Wisdom's ways.
Come past, come present,
Hearts and voices raise:
Cheer for St Mary's!
Vivat! Vivat! Vivat

(by Frederick R Boraston. 1878-1954)

APPLYING AND ACQUIRING

Education is not preparing for Life, Education is Life.

John Dewey

What I took from my own schooling, then, were positive feelings about education, a desire to study and teach English, and a vague feeling that connecting with pupils would be a better way to go than trying to frighten them into learning.

At University, I briefly considered a more academic career, but even then realized that a large part of my interest in literature, of all kinds, was related to people and their thoughts, rather than the mechanics of writing and creating.

In addition, I have always had a horror of folk who are 'precious' about the Arts – an apprehension which often raises its head during the Edinburgh Festival, especially in Charlotte Square at the Book Festival. It reflects my appreciation of 'connection', I suppose: I would rather see literature as accessible than 'high brow'.

Following that theme, I'm happy to reveal two of my more 'mundane' influences in considering teaching as a career.

In the late sixties, there was a BBC Scotland TV series entitled "This Man Craig". It starred John Cairney as a young and idealistic teacher in a Scottish secondary school. Living in England, I was always pleased when Scotland made a rare appearance of any kind on our screens, and I became hooked on the programme. Its emergence came at the time of the "Orange Paper", the document which introduced the concept of "Guidance" to Scottish schools.

I had no idea whether "Craig" reflected reality in the Scottish schools of the day, but it was the first time I had thought of 'teaching' outside of my own personal experience on the receiving end of it. I suspect his connection with the pupils, and his home visits, and his pioneering support for families, came more from the requirements of television drama than any education philosophy, but it gave me an alternative vision to that which I experienced first hand. For the first time, I saw that there was perhaps a way of teaching which might be appealing to me as a career.

Quite recently, I shared this with Cairney himself, and realized that, unconsciously or not, I had based a lot of my child centred approaches and bolshie attitudes on the character of Craig. He replied graciously that he was pleased that his vocation as an actor had led to my vocation as a teacher!

And it was another media moment which provided a major piece of inspiration when I was at Moray House College of Education.

We were shown Ken Loach's excellent film, "Kes", based on Barry Hines' novel: "A Kestrel for a Knave". Although it had been greeted warmly when it was released three or four years before, I had neither read the book, nor seen the film. Its portrayal of Billy Casper, fighting a disinterested school, and a system hostile to 'disadvantaged kids' like him, was immediately engaging and thought provoking. In particular, Colin Welland, as English teacher, Mr Farthing, emerged as another teaching hero for me.

Like John Cairney's Craig, Mr Farthing was, in every way, a dramatic revelation to me. I had not come across teachers who were interested in your home life, listened to what you had to say, and

52

encouraged you in your out of school interests. For all that, these two fictional characters, and their creators, outlined a path for me which would lead to a different approach to teaching, certainly from that which I had experienced myself, and often down the years, when talking to pupils in challenging circumstances, I heard the voices of Craig and Farthing in my head. You can never tell when a connection will be made, or an idea inspired

I should point out that the year I spent at Moray House was of mixed value. The contrast between the intensity of the final year of an honours degree and the contemporary approach to teacher training was hard to encompass. A lot of the theory was difficult to apply to the practical setting of the classroom, and, as I will suggest later, we would have benefited from more practical experience.

Unfortunately, even our placements were disrupted that year.

My first school was a west Edinburgh secondary, where I felt comfortable, but my experiences were limited due to industrial action. At times the school was only open two or three days a week, and, understandably, staff felt reluctant to hand over their classes to students in the time available. It did, however, give me chance to share a staffroom briefly with one of my writing heroes, Bernard MacLaverty, who was teaching there at the time.

I followed this up with a placement in a school outside of Edinburgh in a mining district. I gained valuable experience in teaching a wide range of pupils but also had to cope with a department which was, to say the least, dysfunctional. Two young teachers gave me great support, but the head of department had serious issues, and I ended up covering all the classes of another staff member who was possibly alcoholic, and told his fourth year class that if they joined his bird watching club he would 'let them off homework for the whole year'. He disappeared shortly after I arrived, and I inherited his classes. It was the preternatural 'baptism of fire' – but surviving it gave me confidence in my classroom ability though, if I'm honest, I'm not sure if that experience, repeated for any length of time, would have persuaded me to remain in the profession.

My final student placement was in one of Edinburgh's major private schools; the College certainly tried to give a breadth of experience! However, it was the summer term, and, with examinations finished, the English department were concentrating on preparations for the end of term shows. Frequently I would reach the door of the classroom to be told there was no point in my staying, as it was just rehearsals, and invited to return to the staffroom. There I had the enjoyable but slightly bizarre experience of sitting in the sun on the patio outside the staff room while an elderly lady came out and served me cups of tea on a silver service. Perhaps not the most useful preparation for a teaching career! When I did teach classes, however, and back in an 'all boys' environment, I found it came easily to me. It was instructional to face classes who, by and large, were quite clear that they felt almost sorry for someone who was preparing to dedicate their lives to teaching. That atmosphere never gave me pause for thought, but it was a further widening of my experience and a little more perspective to bring to the career upon which I was about to embark.

REFLECTIONS

Between leaving school and starting to teach, I had done some growing up – some, I emphasise, but doubtless not as much as I thought I had. Probably the most valuable experiences I had gained from four years at university, and that year at College, related to living away from home with a new set of friends, and a growing appreciation of reading and studying, and how I could apply what I read, and discussed, to my own view of the world. I gained what was, if not a 'guid', then a 'new', conceit of myself, with more confidence in communication, and in writing, and sharing ideas. A stint in a folk band probably contributed as much to this as my academic exploits! I was delighted to achieve a 2:1 degree and felt it an accurate reflection of where I was at: willing to work and achieve my potential, but lacking the madness or originality to be a First Class Honours contender!

On the eve of my first teaching post, I was in a fairly comfortable state of mind. I knew I could do the job, and still wanted to do it – though I was mature enough to decide that I would take time to settle in, and then see if I wanted to make it a lifelong career. I was still faintly surprised to discover that I had ability in the classroom, and, if I am honest, I'm still not sure how that happened.

As to Wisdom: I had realised that it was important to be true to yourself, and that original or dissident thought was not always wrong nor unappreciated. I had discovered that to listen with understanding, it was necessary to not only hear what was being said, but to analyse it and process it through your own thoughts and beliefs.

There were people in the world of different backgrounds, beliefs, and attitudes with whom I could be close and friendly, and, in relationships, openness and honesty were a great safeguard for those times when they didn't work out or when somebody looked to disparage you. Although I could not have realised it at the time, nor indeed been fully aware of those tenets, each of them would come to have a bearing on how I did my job and how I performed as a teacher.

And all of those I had been with: teachers, pupils, lecturers, tutors, and fellow students had played their part in shaping me. I had started on the road to gaining the wisdom and the knowledge that we are shaped by all of our experiences.

Teacher training is vastly changed these days. From working with newly qualified staff, I know it has more focus, more practical application, and more rigour in its assessment and accountability.

Young teachers today have already reflected more when they first arrive in schools than I had by the end of my probationary period. I think part of the reason for that is that they know what to look for, what to consider, and how to self analyse. It is a great step forward and they are well prepared for the classroom from the start.

Generally, they have more confidence and flexibility than my generation, and are more ready to seek advice and act upon it. Better structures exist for their support and high standards are expected. They benefit from a system which now understands that practical experience in the classroom with good support from active teachers is the best way forward. It is a tragedy that fewer career opportunities are open to them.

EARLY DAYS

The Beginning is the most important part of the work

Plato

I suppose the early years of any career are the times when whatever wisdom you have gained must be fully employed, and what wisdom is there still to be acquired must be recognized and welcomed. In as much as this is the case, you would be looking for an environment where you were valued, listened to, encouraged, and supported, but also given role models and clear routes to personal and professional development.

For the first time, but by no means the last, I had good fortune, in that I started teaching in a school where all those conditions were met.

My first stroke of luck was that, in the year I left College, pupil rolls were rising and most of my fellow graduates gained employment in teaching, if not always with the local authority they had chosen. Having waited long enough to return to my hometown, I was clear that I wanted to teach in Edinburgh, where I was familiar with the city and its people.

At my employment interview with the English Advisor for Edinburgh in May 1975, I was naively confident – both in my employability, and the opportunities available. I would like, I said, to join the English department in that west Edinburgh school where I had undertaken my first student placement. He demurred and mentioned that another school were interested in employing me. With the confidence, or stupidity, of youth, I repeated my request.

We batted this backward and forward for a while, but he was a man who enjoyed his lunches, and it was approaching midday. Eventually, he lost patience, and snapped: "They don't want you, but the other school do!"

Reality dawned, and I gratefully accepted the offer. When I left the building, the sun was shining – metaphorically and literally!

These days, whenever I replicate that walk from what was "The Dean Centre" to Edinburgh's West End, I can recall the joy of that day, walking in the Springtime city, thinking: "I'm a teacher!" That was a response which was both presumptious – had I known how much I had to learn – and appropriate, had I known how fortuitous would be that appointment.

All the requirements necessary for a bright start to my career were in place in my first place of employment, had I but known it.

The school was in the centre of Edinburgh, by the Meadows. In fact, I started teaching in a classroom which was around a hundred yards from the ward in which I was born at the "Simpson's", and a couple of hundred yards from the home in which my grandparents had lived. These were to prove happy omens.

It had started out as a convent school in the nineteenth century, and then, with comprehensivisation, had become an alternative secondary for parents who wished their daughters to have a single sex schooling. From 1970 onwards, with the closure of Holy Cross Academy and St Anthony's Junior Secondary, there were two co-educational denominational secondaries in Edinburgh – one for the west of the city and one for the east. For girls, this centrally placed school was another alternative.

The year I joined, however, Edinburgh City had decided to reorganize the provision. The three denominational secondaries would each have their own catchment area – west, east and central city – and the central school would become co-educational. This impacted on me in many ways.

First and foremost, it meant that the headteacher was seeking to recruit male teachers to provide a gender balance in the staffing, thus making my application 'desirable'! It also meant I gained additional experience of different settings in the classroom. As I joined, boys started in first year, but the rest of the school remained girls only. My classes, therefore, in the first couple of years, were largely composed of girls, with only a minority being co-educational. Given my own background, this was a huge, but much needed, learning curve!

This being the mid seventies, in Edinburgh, Bay City Rollermania was very much in evidence. Indeed, I had the younger brother of one of the group in my first registration class. From the earliest time, my experience taught me never to underestimate girl power! I had a small but feisty group of fourth year girls, known as the RoSLA (Raising of the school leaving age) class. They had started school believing they would leave at fifteen but had then learned they would have to stay on for a further year, and, at that stage, without any examinations at the end of it. The year I spent devising courses for them, and keeping them more or less calm, taught me much about classroom skills. To this day, if asked to sketch a scary figure, it might well comprise, a feathered haircut, tartan accoutrements, a long skirt with white patterned tights, and clumpy shoes. I owe them a lot in terms of learning about discipline and control, and, it's fair to say, some basic, dawning, understanding of the group differences between boys and girls!

However, I had fallen on my feet in many ways. As a long haired, moustachioed, hippy-looking young man, joining a previously fairly staid staff, I made an impression of which, thankfully, I was completely unaware. The school, had about 650 pupils which, as the years passed by, I began to think of as the optimum roll for an institution where everyone would know everyone, and its catchment, running from Granton on the shores of the Forth, to douce Fairmilehead on Edinburgh's southern boundaries, was superbly comprehensive. The need for an effective social and academic 'mix' would become one of the major tenets of my approach to education over time, though, in 1975, I suppose I took for granted the warm and friendly atmosphere in the school.

In moving to a catchment based, co-educational model, the school I joined was facing change and challenge, and it meant I became used to both these elements from the start of my career. It brought opportunities for innovation, original thinking, and groundbreaking decisions. I took them for granted, it became the way I operated. Of course, I couldn't know then that the next thirty years of education would, by and large, echo that state of flux, challenge, and directional change. I had gained the best possible grounding for a career based on adapting and progressing, almost by accident.

Most of all, I believe, I was blessed to start my working career with a staff of huge talent and commitment, whose approach made me feel welcome, valued, encouraged and supported – those values, I suggested earlier, that were most necessary for the task of acquiring wisdom and understanding of the career upon which I had embarked. I know a number of my colleagues in other schools were not so lucky, and I have consistently been thankful for my good fortune.

Because the school was changing, and growing, there was a sizable intake of new, young staff in the year I started. It brought energy, innovation and potential to the school, and formed a view which strengthened as my career developed: while stability is important in any school's development, a young staff brings a vitality which is crucial to the teaching and learning experience. It is the task of leadership in the school to maintain the continuity of a school's ethos, standards, and academic challenge, but the driving force is often provided by those coming into the profession with new ideas and few preconceptions. Experienced teachers are crucial, but it is the combination of knowledge and youthful enthusiasm which really makes a school buzz as a learning environment.

In the seventies, staffing and resources were not as tight as later. There was more time to reflect informally and goodness knows how much I learned of the teacher's craft in conversations over coffee in the staffroom with more experienced colleagues

I was lucky that the school and departmental leadership I encountered in my first teaching post was experienced, but young in outlook, supportive, but ready to listen, and provided role models, whilst at the same time promoting our individual confidence. Like any youthful group in the workplace we bonded, worked hard together, bounced ideas off each other, socialized, planned and schemed, reflected and supported. It seemed as if we could do anything, and, hopefully, we passed on that positive message to the pupils we taught.

In looking back, I realize that I flourished in my first years in teaching, largely because I received the kind of encouragement and support which had maybe been lacking in my own education. In those earliest days, from headteacher and my head of department, I learned the importance of the light touch. I was still naïve, of course, and it took me years to recognize how closely I had been monitored. My classroom was next door to that of my principal teacher's; we both taught with our doors open. So, when she praised my teaching towards the end of my first term, without having actually sat in on one of my classes, it never occurred to me that she had been able to hear every lesson I'd taught from the start of term.

Trish Gordon was a perfect department head for me at the time. An attractive English woman, she had babysat for the actress Diana Rigg when younger, and evinced a similar wry, amused, and twinkling approach as the former Avenger. She was somewhere between adored big sister and unattainable older woman and used her style and presentation to make her point in meetings and discussions. Such was the respect I had for her as an effective professional, that, when she let me know she had perfect faith in my abilities as a classroom teacher, my confidence rocketed and I worked even harder to fulfill her expectations.

Her strength was listening, and analyzing her staff till she understood what kind of support they needed, and then supplying it unobtrusively, like a good football manger recognizes which players need an arm round the shoulder and which require a boot up the backside. I didn't even know myself at the time, but I can see now that my confidence was fairly brittle when I started teaching. I was surprised to find I could 'do it', but never let myself believe it was 'easy', or that I'd 'cracked it'. Had I started work under the type of principal teacher who hassled or harassed me, was ultra critical, or demanding of a certain approach, I doubt I would have blossomed. In her later career, as a teacher trainer, she must have been inspirational. Trish gave me the confidence to believe in myself and my abilities. In essence, she set off my career in the right direction and taught me an approach which would be central to whatever leadership skills I sought to exercise for the rest of my career.

This style was echoed by my first headteacher – Jimmy Barbour. In my interview with him, which was conducted in what I would come to recognize was his trademark relaxed manner, we got on well, though this strange wee school, largely composed of pulled together Victorian houses in a side street by the Meadows, was a bit of a mystery to me. My aunt had finished her education there in the 1920s, I had relations who had been pupils, and my dad had been friendly with its one time Head of English, a Miss McIntosh, who we would visit in a gloomy, Brodie-like flat off the Meadows, where the fox's heads on her assorted fur coats would glare at me balefully. However, compared to Holy Cross Academy, I knew little about the school, and it didn't seem like the sort of place in which I would want to work.

So I was pretty relaxed when Jimmy interviewed me. There was one sticky moment when he picked up, from the 'Hobbies' section of my application, that I had an interest in "Celtic history". He pronounced it with a soft 'C' and I pointed out it referred to the countries not the football team. "Actually, I'm a keen Hibs supporter – it's been in the family for generations." Blissfully unaware was I of the keen connection between denominational heidies, especially those from the west of Scotland, and Celtic FC. I still remember his understated reply: "Ah – I see. I'm afraid I don't have that pleasure myself."

For a moment I wondered if I had blown my chances, but, as I found out later, Jimmy remained keen to have me on the staff. I'm still unsure whether he detected something in my demeanour, of which I was completely unaware myself, or if he was just keen to employ more males on the staff. Either way, his decision changed my life.

I've mentioned a couple of times that 'wisdom' is hardly ever acquired or recognized at the time. It establishes itself in the light of further experience and reflection. In my early years as a teacher, my contacts with Jimmy seemed almost haphazard. He would bump into me in a corridor and suggest a quick chat in his room, which would turn out to have been my first year probationer interview; a notice would be brought into class for me to read to the

63

pupils and he would stay and chat to the pupils for a few minutes; there would be a few words at parents' evenings, or a brief stop at a departmental meeting. I never thought about management or leadership in those days; indeed, had anyone asked, I would probably have declared that I loved the classroom so much I would never want promotion of any kind. However, had anyone asked me to rate Jimmy as a headteacher, in my naivete I would have hugely underestimated him.

When he retired early, a few years after I started teaching, he gave the reason as his loss of control over appointments. He felt the role of the authority was increasing, and his skill of moulding together the right staff for the school was becoming more and more difficult to employ. I'm not sure if that was the whole story, but, for the first time, I started to reflect on his style as a leader and manager. Like a magician whose skill is not in the trick but in concealing how he achieves it, Jimmy never appeared, at least to me as a probationer teacher, to be 'managing'. In contrast to today, where headteachers and managers are expected to be visible, high profile, 'in your face' and 'leading from the front', Jimmy's preference was to melt into the background, watch and listen, and act accordingly. Maybe it was his previous experience as a local politician down on the Ayrshire coast, or just his natural personality, but the feeling was always that Jimmy was working with us, and for us, rather than 'managing us'.

There was a period in the early eighties when there was much industrial action in schools, mostly about conditions and funding rather than pay. As has often been the case in my experience, the most radical teachers were also those who seemed to care the most. It followed, then, given the highly committed staff at my school, that we would be in the forefront of the action – even when it became 'unofficial'. A march down in Princes Street was announced one Wednesday afternoon. As it was not backed by the union, we were warned that any staff who left school to take part would receive formal "Disciplinary Warning letters' from the Council. Jimmy ascertained which of us would be joining the march and asked each of us to his office to outline the situation. He was professional and calm about the whole thing.

Later, as we paraded through the east end of Princes Street, a colleague nudged me. There, on the steps of the GPO, head held high, for all the world like a General reviewing his troops, stood Jimmy Barbour. He was supporting his staff – without any fuss or controversy, and we appreciated it hugely. It was another lesson in leadership – and how it can be practised without drawing attention to oneself or over elaborating. I never forgot that moment.

After I retired, I wrote to Jimmy, outlining how his encouragement and example had played a huge part in my career - as a teacher in the early days, and as a manager in later times. He left a typically understated phone message, thanking me for my kind words, and stating that he'd had no idea he'd been such an influence on me. A lifetime of style!

Jimmy's influence continued after his retirement, when the Depute he had appointed, John Dames, became the next headteacher. John was the next generation and had a more hands on, managerial approach, but still with the light touch. When he arrived as Depute Head, nobody on the staff knew anything about him, and the staffroom was agog with the need for information. After a couple of weeks, it became clear that all that anyone could contribute was the fact that whenever they passed him in the corridor he smiled and winked. It became a staff catchphrase; 'Have you had a wink from Damesy yet?"

Long after the laughter had died down and he had become a valued and supportive colleague and leader, the importance of that initial impression occurred to me. It was not a huge declaration, rather an intimation that his style as Depute, and then Headteacher,

65

would be one of approachability, that he saw management as collegiate rather than hierarchical. It was another slice of wisdom – small gestures often have major effects; less is sometimes more, and connecting with people – staff or pupils – makes for a powerful educational tool. My son always claimed that, when I was dressed in my 'Depute's suit', I walked differently – and maybe that too was an understated message of authority, but I always made it a point of importance that I would smile, nod, wink, or speak to any pupil or staff member I passed. To do otherwise would have felt wrong.

I suppose I might have expected to gain wisdom from colleagues and management, but it came as a surprise to discover the energy and strength I received from the pupils with whom I worked. As with so much in my career, it is difficult to discern, especially from this distance, whether I was just fortunate to be in the right place at the right time, or whether other things were at play. Certainly, the mix of pupils in my first ever registration class, whom I also taught English and Religious Education, were a felicitous mix of backgrounds and abilities, who were positive about school and each other and seem to take to me as much as I took to them. We went on a happy voyage of discovery that first term – me new to teaching (though I didn't let that slip to them till nearly Christmas) and they new to secondary. It seemed to me at the time, and, indeed, still does, that if I wasn't happy teaching a class like that, then I shouldn't be in teaching.

By good fortune, a few of that class became parents whose children I taught towards the end of my career. It was tremendously affirming and satisfying to meet them again after all those years, to find that their memories of the mid seventies accorded with mine, and to see how well they had turned out as adults – a privilege which is not always given to teachers.

So, in my first year or so of teaching the sun certainly shone on me. I had everything, I suppose, which a young professional could wish for: a good job, the respect and friendship of colleagues, a good working environment with support from management, and a growing confidence that I had chosen the right career path. It was a blossoming, a dawning of realisation that this might be something I was good at doing. They were formative times and well remembered when I took a role mentoring probationer teachers later in my career. The wisdom was gained in the seventies and employed in the noughties.

As I've said, there was the irony that my starting to work as a teacher gave me some of the affirmation I had lacked when I was at school as a pupil, and just maybe that was one of the reasons why I had considered teaching as a career.

REFLECTIONS

They do say that a baby's first impressions of the world at birth are formative in its development: the light, sounds, human contact - all make an indelible mark which affect the way a child, and its personality, grows. I'm sure that is true to some extent, though you wouldn't want to over emphasise the effect on a whole lifetime of twists and turns.

I suspect the same is true of a career. Those early months are certainly formative, though not necessarily to an immutable extent. It's possible to have a difficult start in teaching but to come through positively and with a resolve to make things better. I understand that had I started teaching in a different school I may have been just as happy or motivated, or, indeed, my career may have developed in different directions. Ultimately, though, I can only relate to my actual experiences, and the wisdom I hope I gained from those early years.

The school was small, welcoming, and built on a hundred years of tradition. It had managed the trick of changing to meet the times while retaining its 'soul' if you like. It translated its denominational status into a caring ethos which valued each pupil and taught concern for others as a priority. It set my professional course on a route labelled 'pupil centred'. In the hundred years of its existence it had had only five headteachers; in the twenty three years since I left its staff, it has had another five. Such is the pace of change in education.

To learn the value of a pupil centred approach in a school where such an ethos was patently successful was a great advantage to me, and, later on, would give me courage and validation in arguing the case against those who saw such an ethos as 'woolly minded', 'not cost effective', or 'difficult to assess'.

The size of the school also gave me an insight into the value of 'small is beautiful' and the advantages such a scale gives to pupils, staff and parents. It remains as a school with around 800 pupils and has some of the best results – examination wise and in pupil destinations – in the city. Nowadays, when the example of Finland's education system is much admired, we find that their schools are seldom bigger than that, and the valuing of individual pupils, and close working with partner agencies makes for successful education.

If the school had a fault it was that it tended to be somewhat insular – perhaps with a high regard for its own individuality, it didn't feel the need to broadcast its successes or link with other schools. It had such a positive atmosphere that the turnover of staff was very low in those days – a factor which was initially in its favour but probably counted against it eventually.

However, when it was challenged to publicise itself in the eighties, with suggestions that it might close because of its numbers, the community certainly reacted positively. At one point over one hundred adults joined examination and leisure classes and worked alongside the pupils. It was a huge success and quite groundbreaking – in the style of what is now seen as the 'Nordic model'. Had the school been better known in the education world, had the authorities or politicians chosen to promote its approach, and had its ethos proved transferable, its contribution to the wider delivery of schooling, in the Capital and beyond, could have been immense. However, for better or worse, its concentration was always on its own pupils, families and staff, its satisfaction sought in serving its community.

The later wisdom for me came from the realization that good practice benefits from being shared widely. Just as the classroom teacher never knows when a phrase or a topic will strike a chord with one of the pupils, so a school can't know when a shared example of its successes might prove inspirational or supportive to colleagues elsewhere.

For a brief time, though, to teach in a small school, where adults and pupils worked beside each other, and the community came into the school, in the same way as the school entered the community, was inspirational.

Long before it was common practice, using parents, friends of the school and the local community, the school established a work experience data base so that all fourth year pupils had a week's work placement, and the senior students had access to work shadowing in professions such as medicine, law and higher education. It involved huge amounts of work for staff but the rewards were there for the whole school community.

It was a time when I learned the wisdom of what is now termed 'learning outdoors'. Being next to "The Meadows", there was the option of teaching Shakespeare sat on the grass under the trees. The central location also meant regular visits to museums, Art College, galleries and historical sites. Teaching 'Burke and Hare', a five minute walk took the class to the sites of the crimes.

This was extended to residential experiences. The school had encouraged European excursions throughout its existence, but in the seventies, every first year class spent an outdoor education week in Dumfries or the Highlands; weekend trips to the Cairngorms or Argyll were a regular event, and staff and pupils benefited hugely from such interaction. It was another lesson which matched my own inclinations and which I promoted throughout my career.

I suppose my early career showed me how much was possible in education, and hopefully instigated a 'can do' approach. It certainly meant that my attitude for the rest of my career was to look at the child's need and to work out how it could be met. It just seemed a more simple approach than trying to fit individual pupils into a pre-conceived pattern.

In looking back to the start of my career, it is tempting to dismiss reminiscences as being tinged with nostalgia for 'the good old days'. However, this would be to miss the point completely.

The years passing don't negate the importance of the wisdom acquired. Fashions may change, trends may come and go, politicians may employ different strategies to seek reflected glory from the work going on in schools, but the basics of education, the importance of connection, the need to value each child, and the requirement for hard work and vision, are all unchangeable, remain crucial, and stand as the least our children and families should expect. As society changes, schools must adapt to meet the challenges produced.

However, the methods may change but the values remain the same.

PROMOTION

No man needs sympathy because he has to work, because he has a burden to carry. Far and away the best prize that life offers is the chance to work hard at work worth doing

Theodore Roosevelt

At the start of a career there are many possible approaches. They vary from those of the entrant who is determined to progress as far as possible as quickly as possible, to the one who is content to gain employment and to whom ambition is not a factor.

Of course, it's not as simple as that.

Ambition can be driven by a need to contribute as much as possible and to maintain job satisfaction, or it can be about accumulating power and influence, and relatively unconnected to any accomplishments intrinsic to the career. Likewise, an absence of ambition can be down to comfort with the level achieved, self knowledge of one's own capacity, or it can simply come from laziness or disinterest. Identifying the motivating forces behind any of these approaches is one of the most taxing elements of interviewing and appointing job applicants.

When I was successful in becoming a teacher, my initial response was one of relief and faint incredulity. When I started the job, I was amazed to find that I seemed able to 'do it', but like many young folk in new careers, also harboured a sneaking feeling that I might somehow be 'found out', and someone would come along and tell me I was doing it all wrong and I would have to leave.

So the early days were spent preparing lessons, getting to know pupils and colleagues and, to a certain extent, getting used to the fact that I was 'a teacher'. I still remember the feeling of liberation when I closed the door for the first time on my first day – and the sudden realization that it was 'my' class and 'my' lesson plan. I wouldn't be compared to the 'normal' teacher; I had earned the right to organize classes and lessons in a way that best suited my aims and abilities.

Newly qualified teachers will tell you that the overwhelming feeling in that first term is one of tiredness, physical and mental. The strain of standing in front of a class, preparing lessons, assimilating workplace information, being creative on a daily basis, marking, and understanding the reality of the job is all encompassing. This is met with a kind of nervous energy which gets you through the day but ultimately adds to the need for sleep!

There is also a sense of excitement – or at least there was for me. It really felt like the job I was doing counted for something, though, of course, the positive response of pupils and colleagues certainly contributed to that reaction.

By the end of the first term, in addition to my teaching duties, I was helping to coach volleyball, playing staff football and badminton, singing in the staff choir, and had written and produced a staff pantomime, as well as volunteering for outdoor education trips and residentials. I had submerged myself in the school completely and without any conscious decision to do so. It was simply that I was enjoying my job and wanted to do more of it. The idea of 'building a cv' or being seen to do the right things was not only far from my mind, but I'd never even heard that approach discussed. Maybe we were naïve or maybe life was simpler then!

However, after I'd been teaching eighteen months, I was at the bar getting drinks after a parents' evening when I felt a tap on the back from the headteacher. If you remember Jimmy Barbour's approach from the last section, you might not be surprised to hear that, as I placed the drinks on the table he said to me: "Have you thought about applying for the acting post in Guidance?"

Modern teachers used to scanning job vacancies on a regular basis may find this hard to believe, but, not only had I not considered applying for the post, I didn't even know it was available. Furthermore, with a background at school in England, I wasn't even sure what a 'guidance' post entailed.

In my first term, a guidance teacher had come into my class with a new pupil. The class had welcomed her and we'd found her a seat, but, as I was about to continue teaching, the guidance teacher muttered in my ear: "She's a climber." And then she'd left.

I was fairly sure I'd misheard her, but continued nevertheless.

Now, one of the most useful, practical points that we had learned at training college was to try and avoid reacting to events in the class until we are fully aware of what is going on.

As I continued reading from the class novel, I was aware that the class, always well behaved, were starting to get a little restless. Out of the corner of my eye I spotted an oddity: the new girl had stood up and was starting to scale a cupboard in the back corner of the class. The pupils, to their credit, were trying to maintain concentration, but increasingly, eyes and heads were turning in her direction. I hadn't misheard the guidance teacher and I worked out that this must be some kind of stress reaction from which the girl suffered.

Looking again, I noticed she was on the top of the cupboard and crouched there looking worried. The advice to delay reaction was one thing, but it didn't really help the decision to be made once you had taken in the event. I've no idea what I would have done next, but luckily, the bell sounded, the class was dismissed, the girl climbed down and fled the class and I never saw her again.

So when Jimmy suggested a post in guidance, I didn't for a minute think it was about 'touchy feely' easy options, as a Director of Education would later memorably describe it to a room full of guidance staff. I was already some way towards understanding the complexities of trying to connect with a room full of thirty young people with different backgrounds and experiences. It seemed to me that working to support these pupils would bring a major increase in involvement, even given the all encompassing classroom work with which I was getting to grips.

However, the Head and Depute explained to me that my interaction with pupils and colleagues, in and out of class, my way with parents, and my commitment to the school had all been noted, and they felt I may well possess the qualities for a role in guidance. They were honest enough to admit also that they needed male figures in the guidance team to reflect the changing gender balance in the pupil roll.

Not for the last time in my career, good fortune had shone on me. By following my instincts and getting 'stuck in' to a job I loved, I had apparently ticked all the right boxes for promotion, though, to be fair to my 24 year old self, I didn't view it as promotion as much as a change of role, even if I was still not fully aware of what it would entail.

The idea of a 'guidance system' had been proposed in a 1968 Scottish Education Department publication, known to all ever since as "The Orange Paper" because of its distinctly colourful cover. Its basic declaration was that every child in a Scottish Secondary school 'had the right to know that there was at least one teacher who knew them well'.

Such a short principle undersells the impact of the paper: establishing a guidance system was to revolutionise Scottish education and make a huge difference to those pupils who most needed support – be it academic, pastoral or practical. It would tackle the biggest problem encountered in the move from primary to secondary – anonymity after the security of the primary classroom, and, in time, would change the way almost all teachers looked at their job and their pupils.

It offered additional support for parents and families, and worked towards levelling the playing field for teaching and learning, which was already becoming notoriously bumpy. The "Orange Paper" took note, in the most prescient way, of the effect on education of the changes in society in the mid twentieth century: increased mobility and relocation, more fractured families – geographically and emotionally, different working practices, and the developing and changing economic environment. In a sense, it helped take education – or at least schooling – out of the vacuum in which it had existed, and placed it in the context of children's – and families' – lives, as well as the society in which it existed.

The formation of a guidance system recognized that 'equality' was worthless unless it meant 'equality of opportunity'. In other words, some pupils would need, and should receive, more support than others, so they were helped to a place where they had equal access to a success based on their individual abilities and ambitions. This founding principle remains crucial – irrespective of governments, trends, styles or fashions – all children should have the same chance of success, and, along with social economics, education – and the manner in which it is delivered – is central to that belief.

Of course, these preceding paragraphs are classic examples of the wisdom which I started to acquire at the time but which I didn't formally recognize for many years, after practical experience and steady reflection.

At the time, my new acting post was seen very much along the lines of 'official' recognition for the manner in which I was already approaching my job. The "Orange Paper" had been insightful on principles but less so on structure, partly to allow for a natural development of the system, and also to facilitate different schools formulating a structure which met their own particular needs. If it was a pupil centred system, it was felt that the needs of the pupils in each school should be central to its development, albeit within a national model.

There were not, in the early days, many training programmes or initiatives for guidance, and schools were very much 'feeling their way'. This led to two notable traits: many of the original guidance staff came from practical subjects like PE and Technical Education – as staff in those departments were often felt to have the most relaxed relationships with pupils; and, in many schools, a system was developed where each year group, or "House" was the joint responsibility of a Principal Teacher of Guidance and an Assistant Principal Teacher. It was a system that worked well on many levels, and its longevity as an approach was evidence of this.

Anyone who supports others will know that they need support themselves. The PT/APT system meant that there was always a colleague to discuss problems or offer advice, that pupils, and parents, had an alternative ear in case of personality clashes, and a uniformity of approach was promoted within the school. The reality in those early days was that each guidance teacher would have responsibility for maybe three classes of pupils in a year group or across a House, somewhere between sixty and a hundred pupils,

78

depending on organization and size of school. This compares with 'caseloads' today of anything up to three hundred pupils.

I was fortunate, then, when I commenced my acting post, that I was assisting an established Principal Teacher who was there to guide my practice and give advice when needed. I quickly learned the lesson echoed in the title of a later paper on guidance, that, as a promoted guidance teacher, you were required to act with "More than Feelings of Concern". A revisionist view of those days of guidance tends to paint a picture of well meaning amateurs wringing their hands and offering cups of tea. That would certainly be a wildly inaccurate picture of what I found when I joined my school's guidance team, where professional standards of confidentiality, accuracy, organization and integrity were constantly reinforced and maintained.

In the days before the internet, email, mobile phones and flexible working hours, the tasks could be difficult. Contacting a parent or social worker might mean three or four days of phone calls going back and forward, wee notes from the Office switchboard in your staffroom pigeonhole. Simply arranging meetings could be fraught with difficulties and many times the easiest solution was to do a home visit or to travel physically to a social work office or Children's Home – all of which was time consuming. Of course, not knowing the computerate wonders which were to come, we just got on with it – and it did lead to good face to face contact with all with whom we worked.

The guidance team shared an office, led by an Assistant Head – of whom more later, and truly worked as a team. Apart from formal weekly meetings, advice was constantly sought and given, problems shared and strategies discussed. It was a formidable learning environment – and, from the pupils' point of view, there was always a failsafe position in terms of no guidance teacher working alone or without supervision of some kind.

If I had quickly become attracted to teaching as a career in my first year in the profession, my six months as an acting guidance teacher caused me to fall head over heels in love with that aspect of education. It was a niche which seemed made for me and I could hardly believe my good fortune at having, more or less, stumbled into it. The phrase I coined in those first months, to try and explain my excitement to bemused friends, was that it entailed 'working with the whole pupil'. It was a feeling that never left me, and I was always aware of the privilege it entailed – in being able, to a greater or lesser extent, to enter a child's family, and I was always mindful of the trust which that implied. It could be an onerous responsibility, but it could bring you to great highs of satisfaction and accomplishment.

After six months, the substantive post was advertised and I had to return to the Dean Education Centre, to be interviewed by the Depute, the Guidance Advisor, and an assistant Director of Education. We were ensconced in a tiny room off the staircase in that huge building, now the National Gallery of Modern Art, originally a Victorian children's orphanage. The interview progressed well, I thought, until the Advisor, a prim and serious woman, fired at me: "As a guidance teacher in a denominational school, how would you advise a pupil who suggested that living together was a good way to cement a relationship?"

While I gathered my limited resources to react, all the lights went out. It was a tense moment. If I had had any idea of the way out of the building I may have run. As it was, I remained in the dark, in more ways than one, listening to our breathing. After about three minutes, which seemed much longer, the lights went up, as did the Advisor's eyebrow, awaiting an answer. Pre-interview practice deserted me, and I found myself blurting out the truth: "I'd say just because you can live together before marriage doesn't mean you'll be able to do so after."

80

I was startled by a loud guffaw of laughter from the assistant Director, Fraser Henderson, an ex PE teacher, who would go on to become an educational hero of mine. For me, he ticked all the important boxes: a people person, not much given to pointless paperwork, promoter of outdoor education and overseas excursions, a man who put the pupils at the centre of everything, and had a huge sense of humour and a matching love of life. Our paths crossed many times later – though possibly not to such startling effect as on that first day at Dean Centre, when he calmed his laughter long enough to congratulate me on being successful in being appointed to the post.

So, as I ended my probationary two years, I was promoted to assistant principal teacher of guidance. It was a rapid ascent which had been achieved almost unconsciously. When I'd started teaching, I was barely aware of the guidance system, let alone set on becoming part of it. It's just as well, perhaps, that it happened in that fashion, as I'm fairly sure it would never have occurred to me to seek promotion at all, and certainly not at that stage.

Now, again, good fortune smiled upon me.

The school was now co-educational in its first three year groups, and, in line with national trends, the pupil roll was increasing rapidly. The council took the decision to extend the school and, with that in mind, we acquired an annexe building, around a mile from the school, beautifully situated overlooking Holyrood Park. The school decided that the best use for this building would be as a 'Junior School'. In other words, years S1 and S2 would attend the junior school, and then switch to the main building from S3 onwards. Some staff would be based full time at the junior building and the rest would travel between the buildings. It was a nightmare for the timetabler, but quite a good deal for the pupils, who, in their first years at secondary would be spared the overwhelming size of a full secondary school and would have chance to settle as secondary pupils before entering third year. Pupils, and staff, on both sites, would have more space and flexibility.

For me, the move was well timed. For my first year in guidance, there would be one year based at the junior school, with myself as its guidance teacher, and an assistant head as 'headteacher' of the building. It was an ideal way to establish your style in guidance, gain confidence and, crucially, get to know the pupils. In addition, the limited number of permanent staff based at the building gave me additional responsibilities.

Of course, there are disadvantages to such an arrangement. Some staff find they have no senior classes, others have a daily journey to make – though a trip across Edinburgh's Meadows, particularly in Summer, is not the worst of commutes! It becomes more difficult to establish a 'whole school' sense in the pupils as they are isolated in their own building, and so events were frequently organized so that they would be familiar with the senior pupils and the buildings they would be attending later in their school career.

However, for me, once again, there was the feeling of "right time, right place" and an opportunity to settle into my new post and get a feeling for the way in which I would want to do the job.

And then there was that assistant headteacher.

Jim Langan was an art graduate who was one of Jimmy Barbour's inspired appointments to the school staff. Popular with staff and students alike, he brought a very human, people centred yet rigorous approach to the work of guidance, and indeed, to teaching in general. It was my good fortune, again, which found me not only having him as my leader in the guidance team, but also, as

82

he was in charge of the 'junior school', having the chance to work closely with him in a focused environment.

Most of the skills I used in guidance, and later in management, I learned from working beside Jim. However, in keeping with the ethos of the school, I can't ever remember him telling me how to do anything. He led by example and discussion. In the early days we would undertake joint interviews with pupils, parents or staff, when there were matters to be discussed. Without realizing it, I understood that humour, empathy, and a calm approach would always gain better results than anger or shows of authority. Of course there were times when there was justifiable use of harsh words or laying down the law – but, being saved for the really serious incidents or concerns, they had more impact and more connection to the matter in hand.

Long before it was a popular mantra, we tried our best to make the junior school a place **where pupils felt safe, parents felt welcomed, and staff felt supported**. Of course, the size of the 'school' – 240 pupils at most, and the limited numbers of staff, certainly helped in these aims, but it was a crucial lesson to me that I learned early and maintained throughout my career that those three endeavours should be central to any school approach. From success in those areas would follow: pupils fulfilling their potential, good examination results, a positive ethos, and enthusiastic pupils and staff. It's an approach which requires a lot of hard work and commitment by all involved with the school, and it needs to be constantly defended against those who maintain that a school's success can be 'measured'. "Safe, welcoming, and supportive" are not elements which can be easily translated into a scatter plot or graph of statistics, but they provide a bedrock for producing figures which can be thus measured.

When the time came to leave the junior school building, I already realized the debt I owed to my time there. In essence, I had developed a style and approach which I would follow, with some adjustments as necessary, throughout my career. I had learned that connecting with people is far more effective than seeking power over them; I had realised that, in dealing with pupils, parents. or staff, you might never know the full detail of what they were carrying in their lives, and you should seek to work with them in a manner where you wouldn't later find yourself thinking: "If only I'd known....".

In the manner of all wisdom, some understanding came to me unbidden and unnoticed. Given permission by our ethos to use humour, in and out of the classroom, I was freed from the mistake of thinking that gravity always equalled gravitas, and, in using humour, I became more relaxed in the job myself, and therefore helped others to relax around me. From the resultant confidence, I never worried overmuch that I might make a fool of myself; if those I worked with, and for, knew I was sincere in my approach, I hoped they would laugh with me rather than at me. Taking oneself too seriously, as opposed to recognizing the seriousness of one's task, can make teaching a difficult endeavour.

The eventual reunification of the whole school on one site, together with some staff changes, meant that, instead of handing on my year group to a senior house teacher for their last two years at school, I had the privilege of being their guidance teacher for their whole time in school, from S1 to S6. It was another learning experience which came to me by accident, but was nevertheless highly valued. The chance to guide pupils from their time as callow youth entering S1 till they left school to go to university, college or employment is rare; it builds a bond and a pride as well as an affection which is never lost. I don't suppose any other group of pupils meant quite as much to me as my first year group, and, even though they are now approaching fifty themselves, I'm still in touch with a few of them. At this distance it sometimes seems that they taught me as much as I taught them. The task of guidance in

84

fifth and sixth year is crucial, challenging, and slightly different in some ways to lower down the school. For a long time many schools chose to have a dedicated 'senior team' to address those challenges; nowadays, as the make up of senior school year groups is changing, there seems to be a return to an 'all through' system – whether based on year groups or vertical house groups. There are benefits whichever structure is applied, but, like all things in education, it's the philosophy behind the decisions and the manner in which they meet pupils' needs, which is the real acid test.

I was lucky to have the same experience of taking pupils from S1 to S6 once more in my first school. It was another pleasure, another learning curve, and another opportunity to gain experience and wisdom. In that time, I was also promoted to Principal Teacher of Guidance. This was more about an equalizing of the promotion structure in the guidance team than to any brilliance on my part, though becoming a principal teacher at the age of 26 led to much slagging from friends along the lines of 'whizz kid'. Once again, it seemed I'd been in the right place at the right time, and I was thankful for it.

Taking my second year group through their school experience, I was lucky enough to be working with a team of people who were innovative, dared to be different, and were, above all, concerned to do their best for pupils and parents at all times. It wasn't a pious atmosphere, we didn't feel we were better or superior, we just knew we were committed to providing the best possible teaching and learning. At this time there was a very low turnover of staff; folk stayed because they enjoyed what they were doing more than they wanted to chase promotion. Despite being heavily politically involved, I studiously avoided any offers to stand for election because I didn't want to leave my job. (I was fooling myself of course: little chance of being selected, even less of being elected!).

Outdoor education was heavily promoted – from the first year classes' residential experience to seniors camping in the Cairngorms. Drama, art and music were central to our ideas, charity fundraising an example of Faith in action. We were open to parents and adult pupils, community education classes and visiting speakers from all walks of life: professors from the universities, politicians, actors, sportspeople, business leaders and local community activists. We had visits from every area of life: from Monty Python's Terry Gilliam to the widow of Christopher Ewart Biggs, British Ambassador to Ireland assassinated in Dublin. Fringe and Festival stars were convinced to visit the school and meet the pupils. Poets like Roger McGough and Robert Garioch were regular visitors. I would have DJ Brian Ford in my senior English class one week and Andrew Greig and Kathleen Jamie the next. Cooperation with the Italian Consulate led to additional opportunities for Italian as a language. Overseas excursions became central to the school year – the only caveat being that they must be affordable for all of our pupils We learned to expect the unexpected and in so doing sought to open our pupils' eyes and expectations. In staff discussions, at all levels, the question was not Can we? But How can we?

I've used the word 'fortunate' a lot in these lines. A lot of the time that was what it felt like. However, undoubtedly, the old sports adage: "the harder I work the luckier I get" applied. A lot of people in the school community, including non-teaching staff and various parent bodies, were hugely committed to the school and its successes, and we were blessed to have pupils who appreciated the staff's care and attention and paid us back with pride in the school and acceptance of our aims.

Today the common consensus of those who were there suggests it was a special time in a special place. Those who weren't there are perhaps more cynical because the school never self publicized, and many of its achievements were unrecognized

86

outside its own community. Perhaps it's a little like the argument about whether the sixties' rock music was the best ever. I guess you had to be there!

However, after sixteen years, I decided it was time to move on.

Mostly the decision was motivated by a sense that the time had come. I had been at the school for more than two whole generations of pupils and was well established as a trusted and competent guidance teacher. Those networks which come with time had been established – generations of families, familiarity with colleagues in partner agencies, instinctive knowledge of what needed to be done, and how it could be achieved. I was comfortable and happy as ever in my job, but.

There was a feeling of repetition; each year, whilst there were always challenges and new departures, nationally and in the school, there was also a familiar pattern. I realized that there was a good chance that if I remained much longer in school I would probably be there for my whole career. That in itself wasn't necessarily a bad thing, and even if I had been thinking of promotion, which I wasn't at the time, there was a good chance that opportunities would eventually arise without the need to move schools.

I did suspect that familiarity can eventually breed contempt. In staff meetings, it seemed to me that half the staff were nodding agreement before I spoke and the rest were shaking their heads. People knew where I was coming from – which was good, and also bad.

I was also curious: how much of what I loved about teaching was about that particular school, and how much was common to all schools? Were there other ways of doing the job? What were staff and pupils like in other schools?

There was only one way to find out, and at Easter 1991, I left my first teaching post and set out on a completely new adventure.

REFLECTIONS

The Scots Makar, Liz Lochhead, has a poem called "The Choosing". It relates to how differing educational opportunities can lead to different lives. She ends by saying:

" and wonder when the choices got made
we don't remember making"

When I started teaching, like most young people, I was nervous about my new career, and focussed on settling in and establishing myself. Anything else would have been a bonus. Far from having an aim to work in guidance, I hardly even knew of its existence. If I had known, I am fairly sure that I would have doubted that I had the qualities necessary to succeed in that area.

Instead, and doubtless as a result of the philosophy with which I had been brought up – that life was a gift, that you did your best, and tried to be true to yourself, I found myself in the area of education which would most reward me.

Nowadays, teacher training covers guidance in some depth, and many of the probationers with whom I worked latterly arrived in school keen to get involved with the pupil support structures from the start, and already seeing it as a possible career path. I always admired their foresight, but I have to admit that I was sometimes nonplussed by the extent of their forward planning. Some newly qualified staff had mapped out their careers in terms of promotions, family breaks, and eventual roles in management. I appreciate that some folks are naturally as organized as that. For
88

me, the most apposite quote was always: "If you want to hear God laugh, tell him your plans for tomorrow!"

It was not that I lacked ambition or aspiration, but I was more concerned with doing a good job to a high standard than I was about the next step on the ladder. I always felt that I would 'know' when I had the wisdom, confidence and knowledge to operate at a higher level – always assuming that anyone with promotion in their gift would agree with me!

During my time in guidance, I did take further qualifications as they became available; one was a year long part time course at Moray House for a postgraduate certificate in Guidance. It was a useful and interesting course, not just for its content, but for the opportunity to meet guidance staff from other schools. In addition, to be in a position of discussing theory and philosophy based on practical experience – my own and others' – was invaluable.

Based on my increasing interest in working with partner agencies, I took a further qualification in groupwork, and again met fellow professionals with a range of ideas on how to support some of the most challenging pupils in school.

When I had the opportunity to move into Guidance, I had asked Trish, my Head of Department, for advice. She had been dead against it; she opined that I would be lost to the English classroom where I had obvious ability, and that would be a shame. Much as I valued her as a leader, I never regretted going against her advice. As my career progressed and I saw the load of administrative duties heaped upon principal teachers of subject, I realized I could never have survived such a career path. Though Guidance could be weighted down with paperwork, there was generally a self evident link to the welfare of pupils, and I could cope with that. In addition, I was lucky enough to continue teaching English, in one form or another, as a guidance teacher and school manager, right up to the final week of my career, and I continued to enjoy the experience thoroughly.

I don't really know if I found guidance, or if guidance found me. What I do know is that the formative experience of those first sixteen years shaped my approach to education, to pupils, parents and colleagues, and gave me a solid foundation upon which to defend my principles and offer them to others as the most effective way forward. I was always happy to lead from the front and explain my strategies, and never asked a colleague to undertake any task I wasn't prepared to do myself.

The strongest wisdom I gathered from those years, thanks to the pupils and staff around me, was that teaching and learning is about respect rather than power, and that understanding pupils, rather than merely controlling them, is advantageous to all concerned. Those who felt that a pupil centred approach was, in some way, 'soft', failed to recognize its genesis – which came from that striving to earn respect, and also the fact that it was a route which was far more difficult and demanding than choosing to seek distance and control in the classroom.

Furthermore, I always believed, in pursuing that approach, that, as an adult with a degree and years of experience in teaching, it was incumbent on me to assess a pupil's needs and then to provide the appropriate teaching and learning, rather than insisting the pupil fitted in with my pre-conceived ideas, and taking dissidence as some kind of personally directed insult.

As I have said, that first school had a catchment area which was as comprehensive as you could wish for. I supported pupils and families with a whole range of difficulties: medical, emotional, behavioural, social, and psychological. I learned never to judge a book by its cover, that problems could affect families from all kinds of backgrounds, and that solutions were seldom obvious. I learned the hardest lesson that sometimes there were problems that could not be solved – by teachers or by any of their partner agencies. Humility was also taught and learned in many situations and in many different ways. Before I was a parent myself, I had to contend with parents asking for my advice, and I gained a true respect for all the hard work that goes into family life, and the challenges so many people face on a daily basis.

I learned, again from practical experience, that listening and understanding were crucial skills, that each problem had its own set of solutions, and that, while often necessary, rules, regulations and paperwork do not always supply all the answers, or those which are most appropriate or effective. Improvisation, innovation and lateral thinking are to be prized if used wisely. We told the pupils that they were each unique, and precious, and valued. We understood that, for some, this was something they had never been told, and that, for others more confident or self assured, it was a concept to be slightly mocked. Either way, we believed it, and we acted with that as our major principle – whether with the pupils or their parents or carers. This reflected the theme and ethos of mutual respect.

Importantly, I learned that supporting pupils can only be fully effective if staff also feel supported. A united and consensual approach to school ethos makes this possible. Where people don't buy into the 'respect agenda', it becomes much more difficult. I was always happy to state that schools were for pupils, but also to recognize that pupils were best served by competent, supported and confident staff, who were happy in their work. The respect, as I have said, has to be mutual, and, to achieve that, much hard work, leadership and commitment is necessary.

I was in the last year of my thirties, and I had found a career I loved and an approach to which I was well suited. I had learned from my colleagues and pupils, and perhaps been inspired by those distant heroes "This Man Craig" and "Mr Farthing". I was also putting into my teaching many of the elements I perceived had been missing from my own school experience.

All we do adds to our understanding – and our Wisdom!

OUTSIDE MAINSTREAM

I took the road less travelled by, and that has made all the difference

Robert Frost

I had decided to move on out of curiosity to see what education was like in a different setting and also in an attempt to further my knowledge of supporting pupils – especially those who faced most challenges.

In my last years in my guidance post I had started to work closely with a number of partner agencies. One of these was a facility in central Edinburgh which had a long history of supporting young people with family or school based difficulties, or frequently both. I had enjoyed working with their practitioners and when a chance came up to join their team, it seemed ideal.

I joined as Head of Education in their School Support Centre. Its remit was to work with young people who could not maintain their presence in mainstream education, with a view to reintegrating them into their schools. In the wider facility were also community and social workers who worked in schools and in evening groups. Family and group work was at the centre of the strategies, as well as strong and consistent 1:1 support.

The School Support Centre had two groups of pupils, numbering between 8 and 12 pupils, sometimes single sex, more often coeducational, depending on the referrals we had received from secondary schools across a large part of the city. There was a morning group and an afternoon group, each staffed by one teacher and one social or community worker.

The aim of reintegration meant that, ideally, a pupil would be at the Centre for half the day and at their school for the rest of the time, five days a week. In reality, this sometimes took time to achieve, and sometimes never occurred. In other situations, there was sometimes complete success and after weeks with the School Support Centre, the pupil would become fully reintegrated into their mainstream school or another secondary.

The work called for the establishment of a lot of trust – not simply between staff and pupils, but between staff, pupils, home and mainstream school. The half of the day when we weren't with the pupils we would be visiting schools, homes, their social workers or educational psychologists. We sat in living rooms and staff rooms, sharing ideas, seeking to find the best means of support for the pupil and to establish a way forward.

In the Support Centre, we would teach basic education and standard grade subjects to the required level, depending on the pupil's abilities and year group. Schools would provide work schedules and we would assist the pupils and liaise with the school departments. In addition, we had a programme of groupwork which examined pupil's difficulties and shared ideas for overcoming them. There was a premium placed on pupils, and sometimes their families, taking full responsibilities for the decisions they made and the way they behaved. There was also a full programme of outdoor education and sport, though obviously on a smaller scale than that available in a fully resourced high school.

It was very much a development of the ethos of which I had been part. The pupils were central to the challenge, they needed to be listened to, and appropriate action taken for each child and each set of difficulties. This was, of course, far easier in the smaller setting of the School Support Centre than it would be in a large secondary.

I learned the importance of the practical, and received further reminders that small gestures could have a large impact. Always having two adults in the classroom gave a flexibility, not only in pupil teacher ratios and the ability to split into two groups, but also, in any moments of crisis, the troubled pupil could immediately leave the room and be supported by a member of staff. Of course, this is generally not possible in a mainstream high school, but what I learned from the situation was that such a response, a chance for a disturbed or distressed pupil to be given space, and the opportunity to speak to an adult, could very often defuse or even solve potentially serious incidents.

It was also apparent that parents valued home visits, informal communication, and a named person whom they knew had good knowledge of their child and the family situation. Such a structure made them more relaxed and less hostile when worried; they were in a better place to listen and more willing to trust and share. All of this was in the child's interest.

Parents who just couldn't raise their child to go to school were delighted to have a member of our staff arrive at 8.30 to make the point to the pupil and get them into the Centre; pupils who found it difficult to explain a problem they had to school staff appreciated having a key worker to go along to the school to support them, and school based classroom and guidance staff were pleased when a member of our staff could attend the school, sit in the class as support, or share effective strategies with those who taught the pupil. We tried to place words with actions, and to replace reaction with planning, inconsistency with reliability, rush with time, and confusion with information. What we demanded from the pupils and families, we modelled in our own behaviour. We worked with pupils and family who were economically nearly destitute, and with pupils from Edinburgh's leafiest suburbs; there were confident young adults, and bemused immature children, challenging girls, aggressive boys, those with attendance problems, anger control issues, no family ties, or whose parent was loathe to let them out of the house. What they had in common was that they were unable or unwilling either to attend school or to behave appropriately when they were there.

For me, the satisfaction of the job was discovering that an appropriate strategy would work if it were given the right conditions to succeed. These pupils were allegedly some of the most challenging in the city, yet, in most cases, though by no means all, we made good progress. Many returned to school on a full or part time basis, others completed their education at the unit, but ended up with qualifications despite the disruption of their schooldays.

The realization was that these pupils weren't 'different', it was their behaviour or reactions which deviated from what we see as the norm, and seeking to make them conform in mainstream would not work – not without the opportunity for them to examine their behaviour in a safe environment and reflect on why they behaved the way they did. Fundamentally, we approached their education with the same principles of mutual respect, and the value of their uniqueness, as in mainstream schooling – often it was hard to do so, and frequently needed different and more intense resources to achieve such an approach than would be available in the bigger setting.

High expectations are clearly crucial to a young person's development and to their achieving their potential. We challenged these pupils to escape their preconceptions and take part in activities they may not have previously considered. Visits to art galleries and museums, hooked on to their interest in drawing and painting; technical, photographic and computer projects based on shared interests between pupils and staff, health and safety and work experience qualifications; excursions to places like York, and to the Lake District to learn canoeing or hillwalking skills. One group we took to Santander, building up to the excursion with lessons in Spanish, health and safety, geography and maths. We found the bigger the questions we asked of them, generally, the better was their response.

Good communication with parents and mainstream schools also supported the pupils – who knew both their successes and failures would be acknowledged and shared, and realized that the messages they were starting to get from the adults around them were becoming consistent.

If all that sounds like my new workplace was a cross between Boys Town and Gordonstoun, I should point out that it was stressful, hugely tiring and sometimes dispiriting work. The challenges we faced were frequently based in family or societal problems which we were unable to affect in any sustainable fashion; some of our pupils were extremely damaged and would sadly struggle to change the route upon which they had embarked, usually through no fault of their own.

Sometimes, though not frequently, we found both parents and mainsteam schools unwilling or unable to change their attitude towards the pupils: they wanted the young people to change but were unwilling to change themselves. Inflexibility is a major hindrance to supporting and encouraging the young.

There were also tensions within the facility. Working with small groups of pupils, in an environment which housed professionals from different disciplines, was intense and emotional work. All the workers probably gave too much of themselves and often the strain showed. In a small establishment there are fewer opportunities for support and reflection outwith your immediate working situation. Most worked in duos and loyalty to partner rather than to the institution, understandably, could become a feature. As a long standing facility under social work and community education control, the addition of education staff and approaches was a challenge in some areas. Whilst, as a teacher, my instinct was to stretch the pupils to higher expectations and more difficult goals, there were staff who felt their advocacy of the young people should more match their background and expectations. Some felt it was 'imposing middle class values' to refuse cigarette breaks, or to visit galleries or museums. It wasn't a view exclusive to the facility and it's a discussion which still raises its head: what is the difference between 'empowering' a young person and turning them into something they are not? For me, it was a very useful lesson to learn.

There are many approaches to supporting pupils and we should be aware of claiming exclusive rights for our own view. Had there been a clear structure to the centre with an agreed vision and approach, these tensions may have been less important, but it was a new departure for the authorities, and though it was brave and innovative, it perhaps failed to take full account of the need for consistency and a unified approach. Where such arrangements have worked, they have generally been headed up by extraordinary people with strong vision and personality. This facility had evolved rather than been established, and the mix of staff was possibly too great an obstacle to be overcome.

In fact, my feeling was that the place did succeed in most of what it set out to do. Many young people who passed through its doors went on to things which were bigger and better than they could ever have expected had they not had the intervention and support of such a dedicated and committed staff. The problem was that the facility's successes usually came at the price of the toll it took on the workers. It was, in every sense, a hard shift, and with the pupil population constantly changing, and the approach having to be adapted and adjusted, the opportunity for reflection, development and growth – all necessary for workers' mental wellbeing – was limited. However, the Centre has continued to develop and, sensibly, the education facility now operates on a more separate basis from the rest of the provision.

For all that, the experience and confidence I gained, particularly in working with challenging pupils, was highly instructional, and being able to meet and exchange ideas with staff from around fifteen high schools across the city was an opportunity generally available to very few teachers. Viewing systems and approaches 'from the outside', as it were, is a valuable tool for learning. I saw a lot of excellent work being done, often unheralded, in secondary schools, by some skilled and committed guidance staff. Inevitably, I also became aware of a few places where concern for pupils and their development was relegated to second place behind the need to preserve institutional power and staff comfort. Most schools listened, but a few did not seem capable of hearing.

After three years or so, I realized when I was sitting in an overworked assistant head's office, paper piled on every chair, constant comings and goings, and noticeboards hidden behind 'to do' lists, that I actually missed the bustle and scale of the high school. The more relaxed routine and the smaller numbers in the School Support Centre unit had been a relief at first; the opportunity to work as closely as necessary with individual pupils was a boon, but, ultimately, I missed, not just the scale, but the range of challenges in mainstream secondary.

This wasn't a surprise. I had reckoned when I moved to the Support Centre that it was not a post that could be filled for more than a few years. It was too intense and too limited in its experiences, for all the range of schools and agencies with which I worked. I had learned a whole lot in my time with the Centre, and now I felt it was time to employ some of that wisdom in a mainstream setting. I didn't feel I had all the answers, but I felt I had more than I had possessed three years before, and I felt many of them were as applicable to mainstream pupils as they were to school unit pupils.

It was time, I thought, to return to mainstream and seek a position where I felt supported and affirmed, and where I might be given the chance to contribute to a positive, pupil centred ethos with the whole range of pupils. In a sense, I was looking to combine the positivity of my first school with the flexibility of my more recent experience. I wasn't sure how big an ask that was, but I was going to give it a try.

In common with my traditional approach, I felt ready!

REFLECTIONS

From a warm bath into a cold shower: that would probably be the most apposite description for my experiences in the School Support Centre. I had wanted a wider experience and more strategies for pupil support, and I found them.

Working with fellow professionals from different disciplines increased my understanding of their approaches; seeing so many schools in operation at first hand gave me an invaluable perspective; working closely with pupils from all backgrounds and with varying and severe challenges, certainly helped me place education firmly in its place in society, and to start considering more seriously the links between economic, family, social, and academic concerns.

In my first school, the catchment had been truly comprehensive, and this, combined with a strong pupil centred ethos and good leadership had made for a positive working atmosphere. However, focussing on the most challenging and sometimes disadvantaged pupils, I learned that there had to be a harder edge to support than merely 'feelings of concern' and positive encouragement. Possibly, I moved from being an 'instinctive' guidance teacher to a professional with a more considered approach. "Being nice" was not enough; high expectations did not always resonate; even when pupils wanted to conform or learn, sometimes they didn't have the skills or ability to do so.

I gained more insight into the challenges met by families in merely trying to hold together a consistent life for school aged children, and I understood more of the efforts made by various agencies to support these families, and the difficulties they faced.

It was, I suppose, a taste of reality, and a space in which I could reflect on what lay behind school phobia or classroom misbehaviour. I had felt since I started teaching that it was more important to address the reasons for misbehaviour than to merely punish it. Sanctions, employed fairly and consistently, were vital, but were seldom enough on their own to alter or manage behaviour. Widespread observation in schools also helped me understand and accept that, often, school structures or teacher attitudes were unhelpful, or even contributed to dissidence and disturbance in the classroom or playground.

I left the School Support Centre with a number of nuggets of wisdom, most of which echoed my original 'instincts', but were now employed on a more mature basis and with a better perspective.

Blaming pupils for their misbehaviour, and punishing them without changing the causes of that misbehaviour was futile. As respected Educational Psychologist, Alan McLean stated in "Promoting Positive Behaviour in Secondary School":

"If a pupil continues to misbehave despite repeated punishments, the punishments are not acting as a deterrent, but as a reward"

A piece of contemporary research revealed that 'the punishment exercise' was the method of sanction most used by Scots teachers, but also the punishment they deemed 'least effective'. This supported my instinct that there had to be positive ways of guiding pupils towards education – and that classroom teachers needed more support in finding that route and providing the opportunities.

I realized, from chatting to pupils, that they knew well which teachers would disrupt the whole class in reaction to their own misbehaviour, and were capable of choosing to push that particular button. They knew how to get attention and, often being used to negative experiences, were not too bothered if the attention they gained was anger or punishment. Like a gambler enjoys the thrill irrespective of the winning, these pupils would take attention at any price. Positive and listening strategies, addressing why they craved that attention, could have a chance of changing or modifying their behaviour; punishment alone merely reinforced the misbehaviour's effectiveness.

Luckily, I also learned, from talking at length with mainstream teachers, that while many recognized the truth of this approach, there was a big difference between being conscious of the correct approach and being able to employ it while teaching Standard grade to thirty teenagers.

So, ironically, while I learned so much in the School Support Centre about dealing with the most challenging pupils, the most important wisdom I probably acquired related to the need for teachers to be supported, valued and understood. From now on, it seemed to me that an effective guidance system not only supported pupils and families, but it also supported classroom teachers, shared its strategies, and listened to their concerns.

I had missed the understated but strong support of my first school when I moved on; I now understood the practical as well as theoretical importance of every teacher feeling valued and supported, and this would inform my work for the rest of my career.

My time at the Centre also redefined in some ways my view of 'education'.

There remains even till this day a belief that education should be for those who wish to learn, or who find it 'easy' to do so. There are those who would maintain that disruptive pupils hinder the work of the class and that we should be catering only for pupils who are willing 'to conform and to learn'. There should be, unspecified, arrangements for 'the others'. A branch of this belief would agree that a guidance structure which is 'pastoral' rather than focused on examination results and other statistics, is outdated and not part of a school's remit. I've met few poor teachers in my time, thank goodness, but, without exception, they all used the phrase: "I'm a teacher, not a social worker."

That is a sentiment which doesn't really bear much scrutiny.

Every teacher is faced with a class of young people who have each, as individuals, brought their own histories and backgrounds to the class. They all have different starting points, expectations, knowledge and abilities. However, they all have their own unique contribution to make to the class. In a classroom, all, including the teacher, learn from each other. That's one good reason why we have schools rather than a 'school of the air', 1960s rural Australian style, where pupils learned through radio (and now internet) in their own homes. An important part of a teacher's job is to facilitate that dynamic, to encourage the cross fertilization, and to realise and acknowledge that different experiences make for different learning styles and needs. Education is part of society, not separate from it. All who work in support of people are, in some sense, 'social workers'. The alternative is the kind of education which I experienced for much of the time in the sixties – in a vacuum and hard to relate to the world around.

Of course, it is difficult to teach a mixed ability class, or a group where some are less motivated than others, but it is a teacher's remit to accomplish that task. They cannot, in all professionalism and humanity, walk away from pupils who are difficult to teach or reach.

Having said that, it is the responsibility of the state and of parents and colleagues to ensure that these 'social workers in the classroom' have the resources, the training, the support, and the confidence to work with the most difficult pupils. Often that is not forthcoming and one can understand classroom teachers' frustrations.

In addition, there has to be an understanding, from all, that there will always be some pupils who cannot maintain a place in mainstream schooling and will not learn alongside others. They too have a right to the education they need. However, it is important not to brand all disruptive pupils as uninterested or unteachable.

Back in the 90s a television documentary focussed on a 'failing' school in Yorkshire. In one classroom, a teacher was struggling to maintain control and eventually told one highly disruptive and abusive pupil to 'get out'.

With a slam of the door, the pupil complied.

However, a camera high on a building opposite was scanning the school campus. Over the next hour, it picked up the pupil returning again and again to the door of the classroom, no matter how many times he was 'chased'.

I don't know why he kept returning: maybe to annoy the teacher, or to see his friends, or because he had nowhere else to go. The point, well made, was that here was a pupil, with theoretically the freedom to escape school and go anywhere in town that he wanted, but he kept returning not just to the school but to his own classroom. Surely that 'instinct' to 'belong' is something with which we should be working? I found at the School Support Centre that pupils who appeared determinedly against school and what it stood for, and who could hardly summon up a positive word about the subject, were also capable of showing real joy when they achieved a bit of learning or gained some understanding. It wasn't that they didn't want learning, it was that they didn't have the skills, or the confidence, to access it in the manner in which it was offered in mainstream school, and that wasn't always their own fault.

As a final reflection on my period 'outwith mainstream', there is an historical perspective on the way such centres developed and progressed.

In any 'behavioural management' structure, there is the need to be able to transfer the 'modified behaviour' back into the original setting. The challenge of working with pupils in 'small groups' was always to enable them to replicate their newly acquired 'positive behaviour traits' in the larger setting of the classroom.

105

The 'skills transfer' debate was constant. Many of our pupils attended the centre precisely because it was **not** part of a school campus; some pupils actually found it physically impossible to enter school buildings. Others desperately wanted to return to the mainstream setting, but found it very hard to transfer skills acquired in the unit back into the classroom. We worked hard to maintain 'mainstream approaches' in the unit, teachers were treated with respect – as were pupils; acceptable behaviour was demanded on excursions and around visitors. We were quite open with the pupils that we expected them to demonstrate to us that they could comply with 'normal' school rules, that the centre wasn't a youth club or a social setting.

Although such units remain, there has been a move over the past couple of decades to try and set them up as part of mainstream school provision or at least 'on campus' so pupils are still aware of their connection to the mainstream school. This has led to various models being established to suit the needs of individual schools and pupils; it avoids the 'return to the big school' problem and gives more flexibility in usage. Perhaps attendance at the 'unit' is only one afternoon a week – or perhaps for a more limited period. A benefit of this move has been that school staff have the opportunity to interact with these pupils in a different setting, and both teacher and pupil can see an alternative approach in their relationship. Classroom strategies for small groups which apply equally well in mainstream classrooms can be observed and transferred, and there is a welcome blurring between the conforming pupils and those who face challenges in school. The task of education comes to the fore once again.

My time in the Centre gave cause for reflection. I was more aware of technique and philosophy than previously; I had a wider setting and perspective on which to base my views, and I had gained the confidence to want to put them into action

MANAGEMENT

If your actions inspire others to dream more, learn more, do more, and become more, you are a leader

John Quincy Adams

In my final year in the School Support Centre, I had an extended secondment to work with Lothian Region and Moray House College to report on the content and approaches used by schools across the Lothians in delivering Personal and Social Education.

It was another opportunity to widen further my perspective, and discover varying approaches in different schools, and also to sample education outside of Edinburgh. I enjoyed the opportunity of research, discussion, feedback and report writing – especially in working with the Vice Principal of the College, Jim O'Brien. I had always enjoyed writing – but this approach was new to me, and I found it interesting, satisfying and rewarding.

I had extended my remit at the School Support Centre to providing courses and consultation for school staffs on promoting positive behaviour and classroom strategies. I received very positive feedback on these sessions which was a welcome boost to my confidence as an experienced teacher with skills in particular areas.

Just before I left my first school I had been asked to write a regular column for the Times Education Supplement Scotland, best described as a light hearted look at guidance and schools, with a serious intent. In writing my columns, of course, I had further cause to reflect and consider the wisdom I was acquiring and the level at which I was operating.

Around the same time as I joined the School Support Centre, I was invited to join the Lothian Region team of Child Protection Trainers. Though I didn't realize it at the time, this was probably one of the most telling experiences in my teaching career.

To give a little background is not to detour but to provide foundation for the rest of what I wish to write about. As is so often the case, in education, as in life, context is everything.

In the early years of the 1990s, child protection was just starting to be a major concern – for the authorities if not, as yet, in schools. The lurid headlines and details emerging from the Jimmy Savile investigations reflect a little of the contemporary attitudes.

As was probably evident from my discussion of my own education in the sixties, society was only slowly emerging from the Victorian precept that 'children should be seen and not heard'. To suggest even a mild version of 'children's rights' or 'pupil voice' could, and did, produce the response: 'crackpot'.

Although, by the nineties, this attitude had softened to some extent, there were still many major areas in which society was deaf – deliberately or unconsciously – to the needs and concerns of young people. The organization "Who Cares?" worked hard to gain a voice for children in care, and various children's charities sought to support the most vulnerable, but, by and large, it was a world where adults controlled and didn't welcome challenge; neither were they very good at listening. When Erin Pizzey established the first 'battered wives' refuge', as it was known, in 1971, a lot of 'well meaning' folk opined that it was a bad move 'because it will encourage marriage break ups'. From today's standpoint, it is a

108

bizarre take on the initiative, but it gives a sense of how an older generation, the one still in positions of power in the eighties and nineties, viewed the world. (As I write this, news comes that Westminster Council are considering banning soup kitchens 'because they encourage people to live on the streets' – a reminder that some attitudes are very slow to change)

In the early nineties, it was becoming clear that abuse was a major problem and could only be tackled if victims felt supported and listened to. Part of the reason their voices weren't heard was ignorance, or attitudes as mentioned above, and the other was an understandable but inexcusable refusal to believe the facts as they were being revealed. One of the greatest advantages to perpetrators was that unwillingness to believe there could be so much evil in the world.

The ignorance affected all of us. Only when I had received my own training was I able to look back over nearly twenty years of teaching and recognize which pupils had been exhibiting signs of abuse or of wanting to reveal their situation. We didn't know, and we didn't realize. Therefore we were powerless to help.

However, as I've noted, attitudes change but slowly.

My first training session was spread over two days and involved every secondary headteacher in the Lothians. It was a salutary experience.

First of all, to stand in front of a room filled with around eighty headteachers and realize that you were looking at a gathering which was composed overwhelmingly of middle aged men in dark suits, was to gain a new insight into the gender imbalance in senior posts at the time.

The body language was interesting as well. Almost half of these heads didn't want to be at this training session and had needed to be 'encouraged' by the authority. Many were openly saying it was a 'waste of time' and that they had 'better things to be doing in school'. Some even went as far as to sit with folded arms and crossed legs turning away from the speakers.

However, the training leader and Child Protection Manager for the Lothians was one of my education heroes: Sue Hamilton, and she delivered a lesson, not only in child protection and its relevance to all who worked in schools, but also in communication.

I don't think she would mind being described as a feisty, central Scotland redhead, who couldn't have been more in contrast to the sober suited gents in front of her. As she stood before this gathering, one of the few women in the room, apart from those on the training team, she started without any preamble:

"Good morning! I would like each of you to think of your last sexual experience and tell it to the person on your left......."
(Concerned and alarmed grumbling)
"..............detailing where it took place, and who it was with.....if, indeed, it was with anyone....."
(Uproar)

It was one of the most effective verbal hand grenades I've ever witnessed, and it completely changed the atmosphere in the room.

Ripples of laughter, fuelled by relief, moved over the heads, as they realised she wasn't serious, and then took on board the scarcely veiled implications of her final, comedically timed, phrase.

Of course, some were even more incensed by her approach to a subject with which they were already uncomfortable, but, to their
110

credit, most of them relaxed and realized the import of what Sue was saying, and how she was saying it.

She went on more formally to explain that she was highlighting how difficult it was to talk about anything to do with sex, and if confident professionals felt it was embarrassing, they should consider how it felt for children in speaking to adults. The theory that abuse was not widespread related more to the difficulty of reporting it than to its actual incidence. For instance, at that time, there were still no gestures in sign language which would let speech or hearing impaired victims disclose what had happened, thus making them prime targets for abuse, and many mainstream pupils were embarrassed because they didn't know the formal names for various parts of the body, and so couldn't talk to adults about their experiences. It was the job of all professionals working with young people to enable them to talk about what troubled them in a non-threatening and reassuring atmosphere – which, in essence, was a major part of our child protection training routine and the Guidelines which we covered.

At the time, I took on board the effectiveness of Sue's approach in relation to child protection and to an audience who largely remained to be convinced of the importance of the occasion. Later, I realised that it was a wider lesson than that, and impacted on communication and staff meetings in general.

It's a strange fact that there are teachers who can communicate effectively in the classroom but, when speaking to groups of colleagues, fail to connect with them. Sue's tour de force that day had planted the seed in my brain that, if you had important messages to transmit, you had better be well prepared, and employ some strategies to grab the attention and clarify the information. I didn't know at that time that I would take many staff meetings over the next twenty years, a lot of them on the difficult topic of child protection, but I'd received another important part of my own continuing education.

Having decided I needed to return to mainstream, I was fortunate that the education department were willing to recognize the situation I was in, and I found myself in another guidance post – originally an acting position and then, after interview, a permanent post, in a high school in West Lothian.

It was another departure for me to be teaching outside of Edinburgh, and I wondered how I would react to different pupils and communities. West Lothian was not well known to those who lived and worked in the capital, and predictable scare stories were thrown my way by well meaning acquaintances.

If it were possible, my second high school post was in a school with an even greater comprehensive mix than my first city centre experience. From detached homes, through council estates in former mining villages, to areas where 'Save the Children' were operating, this school covered half the county and received pupils from all conceivable backgrounds and traditions.

Despite my nervousness, I received a warm welcome from English and Guidance colleagues, and soon discovered that the pupils were different from city pupils - in a positive fashion. Despite only fifteen miles separating the school from the city boundaries, I found the pupils more open and less guarded than their Edinburgh counterparts. There was still a proud community allegiance from the various villages, despite pit closures, and parents had a very supportive approach to education and the school staff. Though the county had a lower than national average third level study statistic, education in general was still highly valued by parents in the community, and this was a huge boost to staff and one which those who had not taught elsewhere did not, perhaps, appreciate.

I have written constantly about varied experience giving me continual cause for reflection. When I arrived at my new school, I found that there was a caring ethos amongst staff, but a guidance system which was not prioritized. I formed the impression that the headteacher was of the opinion that a robust guidance organization was only likely to bring up more problems which would need to be addressed. There was no guidance team office – staff were expected to do guidance work at their classroom desks, and Personal and Social Education programmes were rudimentary. Again, my confidence was boosted by colleagues who sought my support in taking guidance initiatives forward, or by the positive reactions I received from colleagues across the staff. I was happy to be back in mainstream and delighted to have the opportunity to use my experience in helping shape pupil support in the school.

When a new headteacher was appointed, she proved far more pupil centred and was keen to promote guidance approaches. I remember a meeting with her at which I suggested my immediate line manager was perhaps not as 'dynamic' as I would have liked. She replied with an adage which I carried with me for the rest of my career: "Folk always think they can do a better job than the person just above them." Delivered with a twinkle in the eye, I have no idea whether it was approval, warning, or mere observation, but, later on, as a manager, I always made sure that I listened to the views of my team and stayed available for feedback. If there was a better way of doing it, I wanted to hear it! Her words also, on reflection, provided a bit of a challenge to me, along the lines of "If you think you can do better....."

It was a good strategy which got the best out of me, and that headteacher threw initiatives in my direction and had high expectations of my capacity to deliver; it's a ploy which has always elicited my best efforts and I was lucky that I worked with her at this point in my career.

After two years in this post, by which time I was happily and thoroughly settled back into mainstream education, and had gained further perspective on the differences and similarities between schools and areas, an assistant headteacher post was advertised at West Lothian's other Catholic High School. I hope I have never been arrogant, nor over confident, but I had reached a stage in my career where, reflecting the headteacher's comment, I maybe felt I could do some things at least as well, or maybe better than some who were in management positions.

At the age of forty four, I was quite old, I suppose, to be pursuing my first management post, and some may have seen the nearly twenty year gap, since my early promotion into guidance, as a sign that my career had somehow 'stalled'. I didn't see it like that. I felt I now had the experience to do a management job effectively and to the benefit of school community, staff and pupils. I've never had the 'front' to put on a veneer of confidence, and I knew instinctively that to succeed in management I would need not only the confidence of headteacher and colleagues, but also my own conviction that I was 'up to the job'. I thought now I was.

It was an interesting move to contemplate. The school for which I was applying was in 'new town' West Lothian, had been open for only a couple of years, and was in an area which was changing demographically from a mixture of Housing Association and rural, pit village, council houses to the kind of new build, private housing associated with the town's burgeoning status in 'silicon glen', and as overflow from the capital's over heated housing market. As with my other appointments, I would be very much travelling into the unknown, and even the school itself would be unsure of what lay ahead given all the demographic changes taking place.

My first interview for the post was, as it would turn out, at the typically late hour of 6pm. The headteacher was a forceful representation of what could happen if you took a different route to mine. Promoted early, he had become the youngest headteacher in Scotland around twenty years before. Having gained long experience as a headteacher, he was now in a phase of his career where he was on many national committees for examinations and initiatives, and divided his week between these activities and school leadership. Perhaps fortuitously, I knew little of this when I first met him, though he apologized that he had been at meetings in Dundee and Glasgow that day so had had to fit me in where he could.

On some level I think I suspected that my curriculum vitae, with its emphasis on guidance, youth strategy, off campus initiatives, and generally quirky side routes, would not impress him. Apparently, I couldn't have been more wrong.

I would later realize that two things were in my favour. He had the experience to trust his instincts, and though we were temperamentally very different, he saw that as an asset rather than a disadvantage. He was confident enough to want a management team composed of different rather than similar characters. In addition, as would soon become obvious, though he perhaps lacked some of the skills to be an effective guidance teacher himself, he was fundamentally and immovably supportive of guidance and its role in the school. I think he saw from my career history that I operated with a similar, consistent commitment, and recognized its worth in school leadership. I hope so, anyway.

I learned of my promotion to management from a phone call in the strange late night surroundings of a local golf club, where my current school were having an end of session party. It was perhaps an intimation that life in management, far from predictable and staid, was going to be an interesting roller coaster. After the summer, I would be an Assistant Headteacher.

Very little about promotion in my career was straightforward, at any stage. The complication here was that local government was being reorganized and Lothian Region would be de-aggregated back to West Lothian Council in the near future. All appointments were therefore deemed to be 'acting', and at some point in the future I would need to be interviewed again for this assistant headship. After nineteen years in teaching, I found myself a 'probationer' again.

A cliché I have never been afraid to use, and one which, indeed, lies at the heart of this book, is 'the more you teach the more you learn', and it was certainly the case when I became a member of a management team.

Throughout this account, I have emphasized how fortunate I have felt at each stage of my career, and in so doing, I may have erroneously given the impression that it was all 'easy'; it wasn't, and I'll reflect on that later. However, I would have to say that, perhaps predictably, moving into management was a huge step and one which took a lot of effort, understanding and fortitude.

The headteacher with whom I was now working had firm ideas on his management team being respected by staff. When I was appointed to the post, I was lined up to attend a Child Protection conference in Dublin, one of my favourite cities, which would cover the first few days of the new session. He made it very clear that my absence from the school, at the beginning of term, and in my first days in post, would be a bad start in the eyes of the staff – and certainly from his point of view. I bowed to his perspective. It was also part of this approach that he expected his assistant heads to be classroom teachers. As I've written, I was always happy in the classroom, and agreed that staff needed to see that managers

116

had classroom as well as leadership skills. However, a half time commitment to classroom teaching did put a huge burden on management time and tasks, and was a further challenge in my adjustment from principal teacher to assistant head.

I had to get used to my new management team colleagues and to a perspective which was whole school focussed. I had had some experience of this in guidance, but my remit was not at first in guidance but as head of third and fourth years. Areas of curriculum and timetabling became more crucial and I was now having to meet parents on a basis that might not be seen as solely supportive. Although my approach never wavered from the pupil centred, there are obviously times as a manager where the needs of discipline and sanction take precedence, and when parents may not approach the school in a positive frame of mind. My guidance background was invaluable in this area, and I discovered, to my surprise, that I had an ability to calm irate parents and negotiate ways forward. This was a mixed blessing, as I was often called in to do the 'blue helmet' peacekeeping job as it was termed!

More difficult was getting used to the fact that I was now 'Management' with a capital M. I had spent my career thus far as definitely one of 'Us' – as a union rep and activist, now I had to accept I was seen as a 'suit' by many of the staff and had become one of 'Them'.

This is a crucial area in 'leadership' and one which is difficult to cover in management training or qualifications simply because it depends so greatly on individual personalities, schools and context.

All my instincts and history told me that, as a school leader, my job was to serve the school community – pupils, staff and parents. That may sound overly 'noble', but, for me, it was certainly preferable to seeing my new post as a position of 'power' or 'authority'. However, like a teacher in the classroom, there needs to be clarity in the situation. If you are paid as a manager or leader, then it is your responsibility to exercise the remit of that job. Coming into management, I had to work out how I would 'lead' and how I would demonstrate my 'authority' in the school community.

I knew from my own experience that those managers who had been overly forceful, authoritarian, or unreachable had generally transmitted an aura of insecurity rather than certainty. The least effective managers I ever came across were hard to contact, not visible round the school, and always aware of their 'position'. All of these traits are understandable in one who is not confident about their own abilities or their role with staff and community.

I realized if I was to execute my duties effectively and show leadership, whilst maintaining a closeness with staff, I would have to act in a way which reflected my skills as a leader, but also as a listener, and someone whose first priority was pupils and staff. My door would always be open, and walks around the school building or campus would be a major part of my day. I didn't have the political skills to present a 'front' or follow a 'strategy', nor did I have the energy for pretence or contrivance. My strengths were my commitment, my enthusiasm, and my support for the school community. I hoped that if I led from the front, eschewed cynicism, and, as with the pupils, expected the best from the staff, I would gain their support.

In a way, I was instinctively going back to my first teaching experience with the management styles of Jimmy Barbour, John Dames and Jim Langan. I would be fierce in commitment, ever ready to listen and support, friendly in demeanour, enthusiastic in my tasks, and understated in my 'management style'. There would be nods, winks, and smiles in the corridors too!

Of course, these might have been my own intentions, but they required a certain reciprocation on the part of the staff – and my management team colleagues, for, even more so than when I had been part of a guidance team, I now had a 'corporate' responsibility as part of 'senior management' – another learning curve for someone who had always seen himself as slightly 'agin the government'!

School leadership skills, to an extent, replicate classroom teaching skills. It's important to remember that a staff of around eighty teachers and the additional non-teaching staff, are all individuals with their own concerns and with differing personalities and working styles. Any effective leader needs to show flexibility and understanding in his approach to whole school matters.

As with a class, I found staff members who were enthusiastic, some who were more diffident but open to ideas, and a small number who simply mistrusted 'management' on an instinctive basis.

This last group were most difficult to work with because they 'second guessed' anything a manager said, on the basis that there was some kind of hidden agenda. I never operated in that style, but was well aware that the more you protest your openness, the more defensive you may sound, and the more suspicion is raised.

Ultimately, the only means of working through these problems was to demonstrate transparency, and hope, in time, they would appreciate that I might be 'one of Them', but that I was trying to operate in support of all of "Us".

The scale of the new post was daunting too. I recall, on my first day, standing on duty whilst 90% of the 1100 pupils filed past me to the buses, wondering if I would ever manage to learn all their names, especially as I was still taking on board the identities of the teachers and support staff in various departments.

The management team were supportive, but I recognized that the headteacher was wanting me to contribute more to meetings and to come up with ideas and initiatives. It took time to gain that kind of confidence, based on a better knowledge of staff, pupils, and school.

The reader will be pleased to discover that I don't intend to cover my years as a manager in any great depth; most of the 'wisdom' I acquired, will be reflected upon in the second half of the book under "Integrity", "Justice" and "Compassion". However, it is perhaps worth covering the major areas in which I progressed as an educator and the additional understanding I gained from being in a position of school leadership.

REFLECTIONS

I knew, of course, from being a teacher, and being a member of staff, that **communication**, as in any workplace, was of the essence for school leaders. I am old fashioned enough to believe that 'vision' is important and that part of what a manager is paid for is to have the vision, and also to possess the skills to explain it to staff, and to enthuse them into sharing it. It is vision which gets us through the bad days and which provides the extra energy when motivation is low. A shared vision binds a team together and gives a sense of purpose and an ability to gauge progress – the old mantra: Where are we? Where do we want to go? How do we get there? How will we know when we are there?

Those who commenced a teaching career in the past three decades or so will certainly recognize the approach of these questions. Assessment, evidence and accountability – for pupils as well as staff – has taken the limelight in these times. Undoubtedly, the ability to self assess and measure progress is crucial. However, overemphasis of these components of success can lead to a diminished sense of vision or perspective.

For too many in modern education the manner of the journey and proof of its existence, rather than its ultimate academic aim, has become central to their means of operating. Education – or the act of educating - is the most human and interactive of processes. The preponderance of forms to fill in – at all levels of education – has produced the inevitable effect. Many teachers are reduced to doing what they need to do to fully complete the forms – which is not educating, because it doesn't, and can't, take into account individuals, context, and specific requirements. It encourages, and ultimately produces, a kind of lowest common denominator in the teaching and learning process: as long as we can tick all the boxes we can't be criticized.

Modern school leaders are required by their political masters to operate their schools in this manner. Like driver instruction, which sometimes teaches you how to pass the test rather than how to be a good driver, the current approach enables tables and statistics to be issued which may, or may not, indicate 'progress made' towards the latest initiative. However, in so doing, it minimizes vision and diminishes school leadership's authority to match provision to school population. Many recently appointed managers are comfortable with this approach because they have become heads after passing the Scottish Qualification for Headship, a formula which operates in much the same manner.

The SQH came about from a desire to ensure that those who became headteachers possessed the requisite skills to run a school in the 21st Century. The position of headteacher is increasingly complex and progressively more scrutinized, and it seemed fair to seek a means of ensuring a consistent and basic level of ability in management skills and approaches. Previously, there existed some brilliant 'mavericks' in the ranks of headship, but also those who lacked the competencies to lead a school. There needed to be a more measured means of selecting heads.

Involvement of school and local community, extended probationary periods, specific training for identified areas of leadership: all these would have been a good way forward in achieving this. Indeed, I often thought that the areas covered in the SQH course would have been better accessed by headteachers once they had been appointed, rather than as a prerequisite for being able to apply for such posts.

I saw lots of evidence of newly promoted headteachers approaching established heads for advice on various matters – and it seemed to me a formal mentoring system would be valuable.

Generally speaking, what has happened is that, in the absence of middle ranking principal teacher posts which largely disappeared after the "Teaching in the 21st Century, 'McCrone' Review", ambitious teachers apply early for Principal Teacher Curriculum posts, and start to apply for the SQH course as soon as they reach that level or the equivalent. Entry to these courses can be highly competitive, and acceptance suggests headteacher and local authority are impressed by the candidate.

A successful application gives teachers confidence, refusal can demotivate them. The decision for the ambitious staff member lies not in considering when he or she feels 'ready' for senior leadership, but in aiming to gain acceptance to the SQH. It has become, in the absence of the former APT > PT > AHT > DHT route, the 'next step' on the career ladder. Furthermore, because nowadays Deputes are seen as the pool from which headteachers will be selected, the need for SQH qualification when applying for

Deputy Heads' posts has emerged, which causes a problem for those, such as I, for whom a Depute's job is the main ambition.

Has the introduction of the SQH made for better leadership in our schools? It's all a matter of perspective and I suspect the answer varies from area to area. It has certainly failed to address the paucity of applications for many headships, and, by extension, kept many suitable candidates out of Depute posts for which they would be well suited.

Like many questions in education, the answers are complex and uncertain. It is true to say that previously in the ranks of school leadership one found many idiosyncratic figures – some of whom were good for their pupils and staff, and some who were not. On the other hand, I fear we now risk a generation of headteachers who have the basic competencies, or at least are able to pass the SQH, but lack the sense of vision, perspective, and personality to dynamise their establishments and inspire the community.

And, without that vision or the ability to communicate it, schools will be worse off.

None of this is to criticize those who have sat the SQH and passed it, nor those who have taken that route to Headship. You can only operate within the structure available to you. I'm just not fully convinced it is the right structure.

However, communication is not all about the ability to hold or energise a meeting, and many differing personalities make for successful leadership. Indeed you would want a leadership team to contain contrasts of approach. Communication of vision and ethos can be as much about the content and style of meetings, and of paperwork, which needs to be produced with an understanding of staff fears and their varying levels of comprehension..

I'm not naïve enough to believe that we can run schools without paperwork and in-service meetings – in fact, where the communication skills are high, both these elements can be very positive and empowering to staff. The fact remains that, for many teachers, they both bring a sense of doom and boredom – "death by powerpoint" is a comment much used before in-service meetings.

School leaders owe it to their communities to take such 'information opportunities' seriously, but to develop means of transmitting what needs to be heard in a positive and clear manner. Setting is important – and that doesn't necessarily equate with a visit to a luxury hotel. A change of style or scene within the school can be just as effective. The use of visiting speakers and effective multi-media presentations has an effect also. Perhaps most crucially, good advance notice of what will be happening at the meeting or on the day, with the aims clearly set out, can be the most effective communication tool – so, like pupils to class, staff arrive with knowledge of what will be expected of them and what outcomes are being sought. If they can see how their tasks are linked to the clearly communicated vision, they will at least acknowledge that there is a point to the event.

Because teachers have so many deadlines and so much paperwork, a badly organized meeting or in-service day leads immediately to an attitude which says: "I've got better things to do with my time." Of course, for some teachers, for a variety of reasons, that will always be the default position, but most will react positively to a well run and engaging event with clear outcomes and an opportunity for feedback and discussion.

Even carefully created paperwork can have a positive effect.

In my last school, we had a teacher who was really skilled at producing clear and easy-to-complete forms which gathered the required information smoothly and in a comprehensible manner. If we needed an update on departments' progress, we would explain what was needed and she would design the form.

On the in-service day, she would issue the form with simple instructions, and departments would be asked to meet, discuss the answers, and fill in the detail. Usually, that would take no longer than an hour or ninety minutes. At the end of that session all parties had a sense of accomplishment. The management had a snapshot of progress, and the departments had gone through an extended, directed, and focussed opportunity to discuss where they were at, complete the return, and reflect on their progress. More often than not, this exercise revealed they were doing 'better' than they thought they were, which produced a positive outcome. The brevity of the exercise meant that time was freed up during the rest of the day for other activities or personal development time: a 'win win' for all concerned.

It was achieved by the realization that clear communication removes misunderstanding and can empower a whole staff, and that every element of communication should be carefully considered, with consultation and feedback on its effectiveness.

The reverse is true, of course, when there is poor communication. Along with an education officer, I once spent the best part of two weeks of the summer holidays trying to translate and enact instructions received from the authority for a 'first day back' meeting. The paper was almost impenetrable in its demands and, when the day was a shambles, the frustration of its author was only matched by the anger of staff, who had no idea what they had been doing or what was the aim of the day-long event. Without clarity of communication, it was impossible to judge achievement. A clear vision was paramount because that was what you had to share, and in sharing and consulting with staff, you could take them forward. The collegiate carrot always tasted better than the authoritarian stick, and I will come back to 'vision' in its own right, later on.

Whilst considering 'in-service opportunities', it is worth referring to one of the saddest experiences of my career. I had always been aware of the importance of the mental well being of staff as well as pupils, and eventually, one of our in service days became devoted to 'staff mental welfare'. It was innovative and different and soon copied by other schools.

We would have a motivational speaker, or exercise and fitness guru, to speak to the whole staff – someone who would get staff thinking and moving – and then the rest of the day would be given over to positive pursuits arranged by staff themselves – a chance to partake in – and share – their favourite relaxing pastimes. We had river walks, golf, fishing, skiing, quiet reading and spa treatments, physiotherapies, Wii Keep Fit, Irish Dancing lessons, music, and drama as part of the many options.

The feedback was hugely positive and the overwhelming majority of staff used the day appropriately and benefited from the relaxation it engendered.

However, after two or three years of successful operation, the opportunity was cut to half a day – out of fear that the authorities would see the exercise as 'a waste of time' when so much work was required to prepare for the new curricular changes. Of course, this completely missed the obvious point that supporting staff's mental welfare equipped them even more effectively to deal with the changes and demands being made upon them. Predictably this sent a message to staff, and, before long, we had teachers asking to be 'excused' from the 'mental welfare in service' because they had 'too much work to do' and needed the time.

Having cut the time available for the exercise, it was difficult to insist upon its importance, and gradually it was removed from the in service agenda. Given my concern for staff support and awareness of the pressure they faced, it was one of the few moments of my career when I felt seriously discouraged. For the first time, my early days in teaching seemed a long way away. The winds of change were rattling my classroom door.

If 'vision' was an inextricable part of 'communication', that is, if you were to connect effectively with staff, *what* you had to say was as important as the way in which you said it. I also quickly realised, at least given my own personality, that **humour** was a crucial part of communication.

As any comedian will tell you, laughter is a serious business, and is at least as dependent on the audience as it is on the 'perpetrator'. I have mentioned that, on becoming a member of senior management, one of the things with which I had to come to terms was that my self perception in the post might not match the perception of those with whom I was working.

It never occurred to me, when I was appointed assistant head, to operate as if there was a military style 'hierarchy'. My remit had changed, and I had whole school responsibilities; from that point of view, I could ask members of staff to perform tasks, and I could represent the school management view on various issues. However, if I thought of a graphic representation of my role, it would be towards the centre of a circle, rather than towards the head of a pyramid.

I discovered though that there were teachers who, deliberately or unconsciously, had a view of management which was at best cautious and at worst suspicious. They neither expected nor approved of humour from the management team and, if it appeared, in a group or individual situation, tended to assume that they were the butt of the humour, or that it was a ruse to 'catch them off their guard'. To use humour when in their company was to risk being seen as either patronizing or 'sleekit'.

From my point of view, humour had always been a stock in trade – though I concede that it is easier to use humour as a six foot male than it might be for others. I suppose it came naturally in the classroom, where I felt at home, and had an affection for my pupils. When it occurred in the course of communication it could be a useful teaching tool. It would have been the assistant head in my first school, who helped introduce me to guidance, who gave me the early lessons in its careful use outwith the classroom.

Jim Langan would often use humour in tense interview situations – either with parents or pupils. As a lot of my first interviews were jointly undertaken, I had the opportunity to observe his style, and to appreciate the benefits of making what was hard look easy, and what was complex look simple.

I started to realise that there needed to be an understanding of where pupil, or parent, was coming from in terms of their relationship with teacher, school or persons of authority. With pupils, this background might be known, though not always – a fact which needed to be recognized. However, with parents, such background might not be known at all. Had they had a negative experience at school? Were they actually frightened by having to sit in a manager's office? Was their belligerence well founded, or defensive, or merely their normal approach? Were they articulate or struggling to make a point? Were they being totally honest? Had they another agenda?

Reading the situation correctly could make the difference between a successful and potentially supportive interview and a breakdown of trust between school and home.

It is, of course, an area where that acquired 'wisdom' comes into play. Whether interacting with staff, pupils, parents or the wider community, as a teacher or manager, you are dealing with people's lives, and people have differing capacities to see the humour in situations. Get it wrong, and it will seem you are mocking them or lacking in empathy. However, get it right, and the atmosphere improves, some trust is established, and progress is possible – whatever the topic.

I learned to judge folk, initially from those joint interviews alongside Jim Langan. In those far off days, the relaxed seating arrangements, the offer of a cigarette or a cup of coffee, a reference to something outwith the discussion topic – football, the weather, some shared history – all of this could relax an anxious parent and lighten the load of apprehension. In fact, I continued to learn throughout my career from all with whom I worked – about styles, preparation, and reaction – whether in interviews with pupils and parents, in the classroom, or with teachers.

Even as a manager, when a teacher came into my room to see me, the atmosphere might differ. Some were relaxed about coming in to my office. It was, I hope, a welcoming space, the door was always open, there was an eclectic jumble of working papers, books and personal artifacts scattered about, and I was always ready to give my full attention. Some teachers reacted well to a relaxed discussion, others felt more comfortable if we kept things on a more formal basis. It was part of my job to recognize which style was appropriate for teacher or topic, and to understand where humour might be possible, if at all.

I don't think it's possible to overestimate the importance of humour. In surveys throughout my career, pupils consistently said that the most important things about teachers were that they had *strong discipline,* were *enthusiastic about their subject* and had *a good sense of humour.*

129

Of course, humour doesn't exist in a vacuum and we are definitely not talking about teachers who feel they have to be 'funny', or perform stand up routines. Indeed, it is as much about 'being able to take a joke' or to show amusement as it is about the ability to make folk laugh. Pupils, and staff, need to feel a connection to each other; a refusal to laugh at their humour, or to inject humour in to your own interactions, suggests an insecurity, or worse, an arrogance – both of which hinder that connection. Effective teachers are able to use humour in the classroom or school setting in the same way as they use it in other areas of their life. A humour free school is not a good learning atmosphere.

A good piece of advice I received was the importance of smiling at the beginning of interviews. It is difficult not to return a smile, and an exchange of smiles is a positive start. Of course, this is reflected in all dealings in school – perhaps most importantly in the classroom. Welcoming pupils in to your class by being at the door is not only a recommended discipline approach but also sends a message of respect –as does that smile and a willingness to interact and react to the things they are telling you as they enter. Setting the scene is important – even though there may be a thousand things to do to set the lesson in motion – a welcoming atmosphere tends to lead to positive reactions.

It works on a bigger scale as well. We frequently used humour in 'end of term' staff shows – the ability to be self deprecating and indulge in a bit of mickey taking always goes down well as a kind of 'thank you' to the pupils.

In my last school, my fellow Depute and I accidentally discovered another effect of humour or 'positive vibes', if you like. We would frequently be on 'lunch duty' together which, basically, meant being responsible for good order in an atrium where around four hundred pupils were eating and socializing. Though in some

130

places that might have been a poisoned chalice, there was a good ethos in the school and seldom, if ever, any trouble. Visitors commented on this, but also on the low and acceptable noise level – remarkable given the number of pupils and the open nature of the atrium.

To us, of course, it was a natural state of affairs, but the more outsiders commented on it, the more we wondered why the level was so muted. The pupils were happy and interacting, there was no requirement to 'keep it down' – it just seemed to happen. Eventually it dawned on us, with a bit of help from colleagues, that our own demeanour – laughing and joking with each other, chaffing pupils and colleagues – was setting the tone. The pupils felt they were in a safe place and that the atmosphere was somehow controlled; seeing smiling and relaxed senior management, as opposed to angry challenging staff, had a positive effect on their own approach to lunchtime. It was what positive behaviour guru, Bill Rogers, referred to as 'relaxed vigilant' – you were still figures of authority, but you exerted control by setting a calm atmosphere or correcting misdemeanours with a nod of the head or a gesture, which might be as minimal as a raised eyebrow. This was the opposite to a style which involved shouting, pointing and raising conflict – all of which raised the level of reaction from the pupils.

We knew there were schools where 'lunch duty' was hated and the atmosphere was difficult and challenging – and we weren't arrogant enough to believe we had magic powers. What we were doing – and what the use of humour always has to do – was plugging in to an ethos which was already there and had been established by hard work and commitment from all staff. It was only possible because the pupils knew staff respected them, and vice versa. To attempt to relax in any other ethos would have been foolish; we had the confidence to trust the pupils because we had worked hard to earn their trust.

Whenever humour is used, then, it has to be in the correct situation, with the right people and at the right time. If you like, a school with humour is a reflection of a school with clear and high expectations and confidence in its whole community – an atmosphere worth working for.

It is that '**hard work**' which forms the next piece of wisdom which I acquired as a manager.

I have often thought that the public perception of education suffers from an over familiarity with some of its aspects, but not all. It's hard to escape the conclusion that, having attended school themselves, non-teachers, and those outwith the world of education, sometimes feel they have a clear idea of what is involved in teaching and learning. Discussions on 'teachers' almost always come round to a phrase like: "I remember one teacher we had….." or "When I was at school….". Extrapolating from one personal experience to the general is a dangerous business, and I hope I've made it clear in these reflections that I am aware I am writing about one education experience, from a personal perspective, and that others may have very different views.

However, much of the work done by teachers, and indeed by all who work with young people, is, of its nature, not obvious. Although it is a view proclaimed by fewer people these days, there is still a belief that teachers work 'half the day for half the year' and, anyway, if they do work hard, they are well rewarded by long holidays.

The reader might think I would obviously claim that teachers are hard working and that their favourable conditions are to some extent illusory, but the facts back up the argument. I don't think teachers would want to claim that they work harder than anyone else, but rather that the gap in perception between what they do and what some members of the public think they do is large and frustrating. A current survey, organized by no less than Michael Gove's Department of Education and Science in England, finds that teachers on average work between sixty and sixty eight hours a week. Any teacher reading this will be aware that three nights a week, and one day at the weekend of 'out of school work' is not an unusual pattern, and a casual drive past a school an hour or two before or after the official school day is unlikely to find an empty car park.

When one factors in the flexible hours, bonuses, incentives, expenses and salary potential of other similarly qualified professionals, the gap in 'conditions' between teachers and others is not actually so remarkable. For all this, when teachers point this out they are often pilloried as 'whining' and 'ungrateful' and even, incredibly, as 'work shy'.

The problem is, of course, that the teaching profession should not, and need not, become involved in a battle of comparisons. The job a teacher does is, by its nature, incomparable – and those who cannot see that immediately betray a lack of true understanding of the nature of teaching and learning. Teachers are not employed to create wealth – for shareholders or themselves; they don't even serve society precisely in the way that lawyers do, or medics. Their task is unique and therefore invaluable; they are asked to prepare the future. If that sounds grandiloquent, then so be it, because it is an accurate description of what goes on in schools and classrooms. The role of the teacher is, at the end of the day, a vocation – to work with young people, nurture their development and, in so doing, to try to make tomorrow a better place.

It follows, therefore, that hard work must be, and has to be, part of the job, and the motivation is not selfish nor boardroom instigated, it is the knowledge that the young people with whom we work are depending on our skills and craft to give them the best possible chance in the life they will lead.

This sense of responsibility can lead to harsh life styles and damaged mental and physical health for conscientious teachers. In much the same way as junior doctors, teachers operate in the knowledge that the wellbeing and futures of the people they work with may depend on them 'going the extra mile'. Taking pupils for extra classes, coaching or leading extra curricular clubs, organizing and taking residential and overseas trips, sourcing new and fresh material – all of these could be seen as outwith the strict remit of a teacher's contract, but the vast majority of teachers see these initiatives not as 'extras' but as fundamental to building a relationship with pupils, helping their self esteem, and giving them a positive platform on which to learn and develop. To devote this amount of time and thought to the job – above and beyond the high physical and mental demands of teaching in class, marking, and preparation, is seen by the majority of teachers as the only way in which to approach the job. Of course, it is a way of life preferable to unemployment, coal mining, or hundreds of menial jobs, but that doesn't equate with it being an easy experience.

As a member of a management team, one felt exposed – from below to the staff, pupils and families who were depending on you to 'get it right', and from above to the pressure exerted by local and national government to meet their demands as well as those of the school community – and these didn't always form a perfect match! To balance administration, leadership, teaching and support – as well as operating with minimal support, was a tiring and all encompassing task. Unlike executives in similarly regarded posts outside education, management teams tend not to have personal assistants or dedicated secretaries. Largely, in addition to the obvious school management role, a depute head is responsible for his own phone calls, administration, diary arrangements and planning; multi-tasking becomes natural, and meeting the unexpected phlegmatically, and with perspective, is a daily requirement. Again, this is not to claim unique status but to point out that teaching in general, and school management in particular, is no place for those who fancy an easy ride. If it appears so to onlookers, I would tend to suggest, on most occasions, that is down to the skills of the experienced school leader, operating on the swan principle – calm above water, frantic paddling below! Additionally, if school leaders wish their staff to work hard, then they should set that example; nobody should have to work harder then those who are appointed and paid to lead the school community – and, if necessary, the management should take on extra duties to ensure this is the case.

In mentioning 'hard work' I have suggested that comparisons with other areas of employment are not necessarily helpful. However, what is hugely necessary for a school leader is a sense of **perspective**.

It is a timely point at which to refer to perspective. So far, I have used a lot of grand language about the role of the teacher and the place of education in society. There have been words like 'noble' and 'vocation' and 'unique'. While I don't retract any of those words, I do believe it is crucial for teachers, and in particular managers in schools, to keep a good hold on their self awareness. One common quote from those who pontificate on education without necessarily knowing a lot about it is that "back in the fifties teachers were respected as professionals". This is true – but it was a respect which came from the norms of society at the time – which was based on almost automatic respect for authority – rather than something necessarily earned by staff.

Having experienced education close up in six decades, I have no hesitation in suggesting that today's teachers are far more deserving of respect from the community than most of those who taught in the fifties. Today's teachers are generally better trained, more focussed, more understanding of their pupils' needs and far more committed to doing the best for all of their pupils, and they serve a society which provides far more challenges. Just the increased connections between staff and pupils and families reflects how much more demanding the profession is in the twenty first century – not to mention operating in a society where discipline - and even the importance of education itself – is not always automatically recognized.

It was commonplace in my time as a pupil to have teachers who would set a past examination paper as a double lesson task and then spend ninety minutes sitting at their desk reading a novel; pupils were routinely punished for no reason and ridiculed in front of the class as a matter of course; empathy, and a voice for pupils scarcely featured. In those days that was seen as acceptable. These days, though it would be unwise to suggest that there are no teachers whose standards are as low, they are at least seen as unacceptable in terms of successful teaching and learning.

So, when the tabloid press present stories on a 'failing education system', perspective is needed, but it is also needed on a personal level.

There is a constant danger for a teacher that they fall foul of what might be called 'the God complex'. Generally, this danger increases with each level of promotion. It is based on working largely with young people who seek learning through a teacher's knowledge. This can lead to a feeling of power and authority which sneaks towards a suggestion of omnipotence. Teachers may feel they do indeed have all the answers and are seldom wrong – merely based on their ability to set the agenda and share the knowledge in the classroom situation. Teaching and learning requires the flexibility which comes from humility – teachers can get it wrong – and they become more effective teachers if they have the confidence to admit this to their pupils.

However, there is another side to the "God complex", and perhaps a more positive angle. Guidance staff and school management have to recognize that they cannot solve all problems and that sometimes there is not an answer to a problem within a school's remit or reach.

It can be affirming when a child or family approaches the school with a problem that needs to be solved. The greater the trust pupil or family shows in the school or its staff, the more the school will wish to oblige and 'fix' matters. With flexibility, understanding and experience, allied to a commitment to doing their best for each pupil, there are often strategies which may work. Timetables can be modified, classes changed, financial support arranged, exceptions made, circumstances noted and understood, or contact facilitated with local agencies or officials. On occasion, just the fact that someone 'in authority' is prepared to listen, can be a huge help to folk in distressed situations. I have examples of staff and pupils being supported by school advocacy to agencies ranging from social work and health departments to the Foreign Office and Department for Work and Pensions.

On one occasion, a pupil returned to school four years after he had left, asking for help with finding accommodation. He had exhausted every other avenue open to him and felt that the Pupil Support Manager in the school was the one person he felt he could trust to help him. It was an unusual request, but one which we believed affirmed the school's ethos – as well as the great work done by the Support Manager and our team of guidance teachers. She took the matter in hand – and the situation was resolved.

Anyone would share the joy of the team at helping 'one of our own' – whatever the date of his 'leaving' school, but more difficult were the occasions when it was clear that the school was not in a position to help, did not have any answers, or felt an alternative course of action might be in everyone's best interests.

It was then that perspective came into play. I never worked in an establishment which felt its only task was to prepare pupils for examinations; the education and support of the 'whole pupil' was always paramount, and so, when forced to admit that we were powerless to help or support it could be a hard blow. Crucial, though, was the perspective to recognize that we had done our best and to move on. It could be difficult but it was also emblematic of the 'hard edges' needed in management or guidance and the need to be professionally detached no matter how keen we were to support and help. When folk who misunderstood the tenets of guidance talked about it being soft centred, or when they prioritized tracking and monitoring over a pastoral approach, it always seemed to me that they had either never witnessed professionals dealing at first hand with these quandaries, or were in some way scared of such involvement. To be successful in supporting pupils and families, as in any other endeavour, there has to be a full commitment and also a willingness to accept possible defeat.

Perspective is all in such situations. At the end of the day, teachers – at whatever level they operate – are still just teachers, and some things they can't do. To learn from failure, as we teach our pupils, is to turn a negative into a positive. We mustn't be afraid to over reach ourselves, to test our limits – as long as we are prepared to accept the consequences. The real failure would lie in not trying.

I found later in my career that part of that perspective can be gained by **reaching out** and in placing the school on a national stage, and in cooperation with other schools and agencies. In my first school, many lights were kept well hidden under a variety of bushels. The school was fairly idiosyncratic and had a staff and community of which it could be very proud. As a caring school with a high level of educational provision, it was unbeatable, but, as our focus was on our pupils and families, broadcasting our

138

successes was not on our agenda to any great extent. Indeed, there were people even in Edinburgh who didn't know the school existed.

At the time, I was quite content with this approach, but later, especially when I joined the management team in my last school, it occurred to me that both pupils and staff were perhaps not best served by it.

I have developed over the years a philosophy which suggests that a community or society which is not proud of its young people – and by extension its schools, is headed for a dysfunctional future. There is a strong dichotomy between what many teachers witness in schools and the general views proclaimed, again in the tabloids mostly, of feckless, feral youth. Teachers will tell you of young people's commitment to charity fundraising, their willingness to help each other, their awareness of community and their genuine enthusiasm. None of these virtues receive wide attention in the media, particularly in relation to the State sector, and so it is perhaps up to schools to publicise the positive aspects of the pupils with whom they work.

This involves reaching out into the local community, presenting the school as a beacon of learning and support, and encouraging as many links as are feasible. Sadly, the days when schools could operate with an 'open door' policy seem to be gone, but it is still possible for schools to become community hubs – so that local people can have knowledge of what goes on behind the walls of the building, and be familiar with the pupils in a more realistic fashion than that which relates to crowds in local shops at lunch time, and badly parked parental cars at home time.

Community Service for senior pupils in the neighbourhood – visiting old people's homes, anti-litter drives, clearing gardens, redecorating for pensioners and many other   services can strengthen knowledge and connection between school and locality. Invitations to neighbours for school events, pupils serving on local community councils and neighbourhood groups, all promote links, and a national profile, in terms of the school's strengths and innovations, also gives the community something of which they can be proud.

Similarly, the benefits of cooperation with other schools – in the locality, but, increasingly in this electronic age, across the world, impact on the whole school community – and its neighbourhood – in many ways. Initiatives shared, or developed in conjunction with other schools, give a dynamism to staff and pupils alike, and develop that perspective which helps in self assessment and onward planning.

Difficult though self publicity might be for many teachers, as a manager it became obvious to me that trumpets have to be blown. For the pupils, it engendered a sense of pride which raised their own self esteem; for the staff, such publicity showed them they were valued, and enabled them to take extra pride in their achievements across the board, when ranked alongside fellow professionals across the country. For all sections of the school community, the school's national reputation was of great added value for applications to university or college, when seeking employment, and, for staff, in looking for promotion or jobs elsewhere. Increasingly, a reputation for innovation and excellent provision meant a steady stream of visitors - from the inspectorate, other schools, and even other countries. Whilst these visits could be time consuming and nerve wracking, depending on their motivation, they also engendered a sense of worth in the school community, and a determination to maintain standards and continue to improve. This, of course, was to the benefit of all.

That thought brings me to the next piece of wisdom I acquired in my time as a teacher as well as a manager. Pupils, families and staff must have a school in which they can show **pride.**

"Pride" is a difficult concept about which to write. If it is ill founded, an obsession, or used to belittle others, it can be a cancer eating away at individual or institution, and hinder informed decision making or accurate self assessment. However, a positive pride – an understanding of one's true worth, an acknowledgement of success which can be used to inspire and motivate all in the school, is a huge benefit to the school and its community.

The quotation which is often erroneously attributed to Nelson Mandela's inaugural address, but which, in fact, comes from Marianne Williamson, brilliantly explains this approach:
"We ask ourselves: 'Who am I to be brilliant, gorgeous, talented and famous?' Actually, who are you not to be? You are a child of God. Your playing small does not serve the world. There is nothing enlightened about shrinking so that people won't feel insecure around you. We were born to make manifest the glory of God that is within us. It's not just in some of us, it's in all of us. And when we let our own light shine, we unconsciously give other people permission to do the same."

The ethos of the three secondary schools in which I taught was basically the same – and based, though not exclusively, upon a shared Christian approach to living. The value of the individual, the need to serve others, and the encouragement to 'shine' was central to all we did in those schools. Critics of the denominational school will often state that "you can't have 'Catholic Maths'" or that religion should be contained to home and family, but I realised that this shared ethos was found in every part of the school and in the community's acknowledged approach to all areas of teaching and learning, and, far from being exclusive, or insular, it was accepted and promulgated by those of all faiths and none within the school community.

A description of my approach to management, and indeed, teaching in general, might be to state that I was a 'company man'. It's a suggestion with which I would not disagree, and I often described myself in that manner. It was important to me that I could be proud of the institution in which I was working – of its aims, its ethos, its staff, pupils and families. I would have found the job I did very difficult to accomplish had I not felt that pride, and I seldom missed an opportunity to recognize success or broadcast our achievements. This wasn't a hollow pride, nor, I hope, empty boasting. I felt that to work or study in a school of which you could be proud added to the efforts of all to make it that way, and also increased each individual's own self esteem.

This approach takes me back to my own education – and the struggle I detailed in the early chapters between recognizing the failings of my own school, but also being aware of what it helped me achieve. Many of my fellow pupils have, in later life, chosen to highlight its negative aspects, whereas, for me, the positive has always been worth spotlighting. It was this approach which I carried on through my career: I never wanted to hide my job or where I worked, I always felt that announcing what I did and where I did it should be, and happily for me, was, a cause of justifiable pride. One of the 'bonuses' that was available to me as a teacher throughout my career was to hear the response when I identified my place of work: "Oh, that's a very good school!" – whether it came from parents, neighbours, education officials or further afield. Wanting to make that description accurate – for all pupils and staff – was one of my motivations throughout the years I taught.

The connection between all of these strands of 'wisdom' which I acquired in my years in management is clear to see. *Communication* can be sharpened by *humour*, but the right ethos in which that can be used can only be achieved through *hard work*. Crucial though education is, it is important to maintain a sense of *perspective* and a good sense of the school, and one's own, place in the overall scheme of things. This, in turn, would be achieved by eschewing self congratulation and insularity, and *reaching out* to the neighbourhood, to other schools, and to the wider community – on the national education scene and beyond. If all of this is accomplished, then the school, and all in it, will, rightfully, operate with a sense of *pride*. I have long admired the custom in the USA where alumni of high schools continue to connect with the school in adult life, still wearing school hoodies and sweatshirts and supporting their sports teams well into adulthood. This seems to me an appropriate recognition of where they started out, and also a boost to later generations who can pick up on that sense of pride. For those working in the schools, of course, this is an added pressure to be the best they can be. Tradition can be a dead weight, but it can also be used as a springboard to bigger and better things and to continuous development – another target for an ambitious and committed management team.

That would tie in to my support for school uniform or dress code – though some might feel that was an odd position for one who would claim to be 'progressive' in his approach. There were many good reasons for maintaining a formal school uniform. The avoidance of style wars, cliques, or fashion distraction is an obvious starting point, as is the simplicity of an agreed uniform, as against the interminable discussions over what was acceptable in casual dress and what wasn't. In later years, security concerns had to be factored in as well as the capacity for schools to provide cost price deals for most uniform items. I always disagreed with the notion that school uniform somehow smothered individuality. Anyone who has worked in a school will be familiar with pupils' abilities to 'customise' even the most strictly configured outfit, and, even if the argument were true, I would want an education approach which relied on far more than dress to encourage individuality and personal self esteem.

In reality, my support for uniform was based on far more positive motives – and they were linked to pride in the school. From its inception, in consultation with parents and pupils, my last school had had a strict uniform policy. In my last few years, a new head developed the uniform in a more formal, traditional manner – again in consultation with pupils and parents. Our instinct was that, if pupils were happy with the uniform, they would wear it – and this would reflect their feeling that they attended a 'good' school and were indeed proud of it. Again, this challenged management and staff to ensure that the hard work to maintain its status as a 'good' school was maintained – and part of that endeavour was taking the time to check uniform, and discuss with a few individuals their reluctance to wear it. The original naysayers had suggested pupils would become a target for bullying outside of school, and seniors in blazers would give the school a reputation as a 'posh school'.

However, one of the local initiatives was the 'virtual senior campus', where pupils from several schools would travel to join together in one class to widen available subject choices. Before long, those students whose schools did not maintain uniform were lobbying for blazers and smarter outfits after they had shared classes with those who did. Five years later the whole county is awash with blazers and smart uniforms – at pupil request. It was a classic case of folk being prepared to underestimate pupils and assuming they would not want to wear uniform. Though, naturally, there were always some who were unhappy about the rule, the majority of pupils were either neutral and prepared to wear it, as it was easier than choosing an outfit each day, or in favour of it as they thought it made a statement about their school. It was crucial that they were involved in its design and that parents were also consulted and given affordable options for purchase. As I used to

144

say to the pupils, uniform alone doesn't make a school 'good', but the message it sends to the surrounding community about pride and commitment to each other was invaluable when it came to the school's standing and reputation. Like so much else, establishing and maintaining uniform was hard work, but possible within a positive ethos, where pupils and families respected the school and what it provided. You couldn't really 'force' pupils to wear uniform but you could create an environment where they felt it was a reasonable expectation –if you listened to them and took them with you.

When I was interviewed for the substantive post of assistant headteacher, nearly two years after my arrival in the post in an acting capacity, I was asked why I wanted to be part of the management team at that school. It was a question you could view as standard interview fodder, but my reaction, which surprised me, was a statement of intent and approach, which I hadn't really realized I possessed. I answered that, as someone in the middle years of my career, I wanted the challenge of being part of the management team of a school which had the potential and the pretensions to become one of the best schools in the country. This produced a beam from the headteacher, who had similar aims, and raised eyebrows from the education officer, who perhaps felt I was over reaching in my ambitions for the institution. Later on, in a number of areas, the school achieved that description, despite its intake being right on the 'average demographic' for secondaries. It was hugely satisfying, partly to have been involved in that progress, but more so because of what it said about the opportunities we were providing in the education we were delivering to all of our pupils and families.

All of these aspirations ask much of pupils and staff alike, and, also, lest we forget, of the families who are part of the school community. Those who are parents will be only too aware of the demands that schooling makes of the whole family, and not just the pupils themselves. These range from time and commitment to finance and support, and a good school will be well aware of the balancing acts that families have to perform to ensure that all their children are positively supported through the school experience. For some parents, based on their own background, this might be an accepted and familiar routine; for others it may be 'terra incognita' and understanding and reassurance will be required. Schools must involve families in education as well as the pupils, and here again the crucial nature of pastoral support is obvious.

So, if we are asking so much of pupils, staff and families, how can we support them in this? One answer to this question follows on inevitably from the need to generate a sense of pride in the school. If we wish members of the school community to have a sense of self worth and pride, then we need to ensure that **praise** is an integral part of how we operate.

Five or six years after I joined the management team at my last school, the headteacher who had appointed me retired. I have pointed out that, temperamentally, he and I were worlds apart, but for all that I had huge respect for him, especially in the hard work he had put in to establish this new school from scratch, his pride in the institution, and his care for the pupils. In his final speech to the school community he said that now he was retiring he was able to praise the staff and pupils for all of their achievements. He hadn't found it easy before because he feared that they might think he was being patronizing or insincere. It was a common belief in his generation where effusiveness was frowned upon.

It was here that we differed. It seemed to me that people flourish when praised and acknowledged. It was an integral part of my management style to highlight achievement and to give generous praise where it was due. I was happy to take the risk of being seen as patronizing, and if overuse of praise diminishes its effect, well, I was happy to take that chance as well.

I quickly realised as a manager that, often, staff can feel that initiatives or successes which are not commented upon have not been noticed, and this can quickly become demotivating. On the other hand, as a school leader, one quickly became aware of those who continually announced their achievements in an appeal for recognition – whether appropriate or not. Frequently, those who made most noise had least to be praised for, and those who worked away quietly were the ones most deserving of recognition. As in any other sphere of life, the ability to read personalities and strategies was a skill which needed to be acquired and used positively.

In the latter years of my career, the proliferation of social media, and the advances in printing and duplicating, meant that there were increased opportunities to disseminate success and allocate praise – to pupils, families and staff, and it was an element of the job which I hugely enjoyed. Indeed, a congratulatory email to all staff after a successful evening activity became a priority for me whenever I arrived in my office the following morning. My feeling was that having given their own time to the pupils and families till a late hour the night before, their early morning tiredness might be partially assuaged by a message that management had noted their efforts and was appreciative of them.

I also developed a 'praise habit' when involved in formal observation of lessons. The written feedback given to teachers was on a proforma which had space for comment and areas for development. It seemed to me that being observed by management, for some teachers at least, could be a fairly stressful occasion and that they deserved to receive positive comment that recognized their strengths, as well as suggestions for improvement. I developed an approach which included a list of all the positive elements in their classroom style.

Teachers have a tendency to see the things they do well as 'automatic' and not worthy of praise. I would point out the many skills which teachers use in every lesson without being really aware of them – because generally these are the foundation for the 'brilliant' bits of teaching which attract attention. Most teachers were genuinely surprised to realize that they exhibited many classroom skills without being aware of the fact, and, as a school leader, the chance to issue a hard working classroom teacher with comments which listed a couple of pages of positive feedback and appreciation was priceless. I also made a point of highlighting the huge amount of positive and supportive work which was carried out by non-teaching staff – especially the Support Assistants, who for a pitiful wage, regularly reached the parts which teachers and management could not – with families and pupils, and played a full part in the success of the school and the establishment of its ethos.

If praising staff could prove difficult, praising pupils often gave even more cause for concern. Certificates, newsletter announcements, praise at assemblies and in front of the class, pupil or class of the week, 'stars' and exercise book comments, prizegiving ceremonies, colours, social media highlights – there are many avenues open to the school which wishes to recognize success amongst its pupils. All of these formal acknowledgements have their part to play and an effective school will prioritise all of them. However, this approach does have its limitations.

There is a danger that the same pupils – those who routinely perform best in mainstream school activities – receive regular praise, whilst others may be overlooked. Additionally, given teenagers' legendary reticence when it comes to communicating to family what has happened in school, very often parents are unaware of these successes. Most damning of all, whilst adolescents like receiving praise, they can be particular about how and when they are given it. For many pupils, the appearance on the assembly stage, or the publicly broadcast praise for success, was so

148

embarrassing that it almost outweighed the pride in the achievement.

I found a solution to this on a visit to a depute head at Govan High School – another example of what can be gained from sharing and cooperating.

The Praise Postcard system was simple but very effective. Pre-printed postcards were provided for all staff. They stated that the pupil had achieved a 'personal best' in some element of school life which would be filled in by the teacher concerned and then signed by teacher and headteacher. The postcards were then posted home to the parents or carers.

In this fashion, the problems with the more formal systems were eliminated. Pupils didn't feel themselves 'publicly embarrassed', parents got to hear of the praise, and all pupils had a chance of recording a 'personal best' – which may have ranged from an academic, sporting, musical, creative or artistic accomplishment to some kind of contribution to the community or an improvement in time keeping, attendance or behaviour. Teachers were empowered because it was up to them to decide who merited the praise; their relationship with individual pupils benefited as the pupil realised their endeavours had been recognized by that teacher, and parents who may have been at loggerheads with their children over untidy rooms or sulky behaviour realized that in some areas of their lives they were making strides of which they could be proud.

The Praise Postcards succeeded beyond our wildest dreams, and worked well because pupils, teachers, and parents all valued them equally and appreciated the possibilities for recognition that they provided.

They operated in surprising ways. Many pupils had tales of parents framing the cards and hanging them on the living room wall, others reported sudden 'treats', or a melting of frosty relationships when the card dropped through the door. Parents discussed them with their friends and neighbours – generating more praise for the pupils and an extension of good will towards the school. Pupils became motivated by the thought that their smallest efforts and signs of progress were being noted and recognized. Guidance staff had an additional tool with which to support pupils and families. "There could be a Praise Postcard in this for you" became a common encouragement. It was that classic element of successful education – a small thing meaning a lot.

Perhaps the most unexpected pieces of feedback came from a staff member who had been in hospital for an operation. As he came round from the anaesthetic, two nurses were making his bed and speaking across him. One was detailing her delight at the Praise Postcard her son had received from school and the other was saying: "Oh that's lovely. I wish my lad's school would do that."

The progress of the Praise Postcard system really reflected the changes in educational trends. Because it was so successful as a system, the number of cards issued increased over the years. With a young demographic on our staff, we had more and more probationer teachers who were enthusiastic about praise and issued the cards regularly and as part of their teaching approach. Sometimes whole classes received Praise Postcards – which was occasionally appropriate and sometimes not.

Despite all the positive effects of the system, noises were made about the postage costs and the administrative time they took up. We were moving into an electronic era and a focus on tracking, monitoring, and recording. Was there not an online way of achieving the same end? What was the point of issuing the cards if no one had the time or resources to record them in the pupil's file?

As is so often the case in education, problems with the process outweighed the effectiveness of the system in the assessment.

Many hours and pounds were spent with different systems, trying to perfect a tracking, monitoring and recording process which would give statistics at the press of a button. Meeting after meeting discussed how progress could be recognized and pupils motivated. The move from pastoral guidance to monitoring support advanced – but for all that effort, nothing was identified which gave such simple, instant and effective recognition to individual pupils and families as the old fashioned, snail mail, Praise Postcard.

My approach would have been to have resourced an effective administrative process for the cards which could have dovetailed with the various electronic systems. I would have also extended the system so that pupils could issue Praise Postcards to teachers. There may have been some abuse of the system – but I'm willing to bet there would have been a good few cards framed in teachers' houses as well!

The more I reflect, the more I am convinced that praise lies at the heart of motivation – for staff as well as pupils. There is a trend to denigrate what some folk refer to as 'praise for all' or, in the memorable phrase "And all shall have prizes" – but this completely misses the point.

If life is a race, then it's education's job to operate the handicapping system. Not all start from the same place or with the same ability. Part of a teacher's task is to recognize this and reward individual rather than general progress. Knowing each pupil's capabilities, knowing the handicaps – social, academic or physical – under which they operate, is crucial to their motivation. Rewarding them on the basis of that knowledge reinforces their self esteem and signifies that they are unique and valuable and precious as individuals, not just in comparison to others. We all respond

151

positively to praise, and it should be a strong tool in the locker of teachers and school leaders. The more you give praise, the more you tend to receive it. That should tell us something.

If pride and praise are integral to an effective school and to its management, it follows that a school leadership team, like classroom teachers, should operate with **high expectations** of both pupils and staff.

I seldom came across it during my career, but I knew from speaking to friends that schools and establishments existed where the overwhelming approach was one of resignation and acceptance of the status quo, where the school motto may as well have been "What can you do?"

Virtually every piece of research in my lifetime has shown that the most important ingredient in a teaching and learning situation is that there are high expectations. In some ways this is common sense, but it is nevertheless crucial that education professionals remember this and operate by its demands. There is an echo of this in that other research I have mentioned which showed that, again consistently, one of pupils' main requirements is that a teacher shows enthusiasm for their subject. In fact, in chatting with pupils over the years, I discovered that, whilst they expected a level of competence, they were more prepared to accept a teacher who admitted ignorance in certain topics than one who had the knowledge but failed to show enthusiasm.

Reports suggest that pupils from challenging backgrounds start school having heard maybe a few hundred positive messages in their first five years, whereas those from more secure situations may have heard tens of thousands of affirming statements directed towards them. In terms of language acquisition, readiness to learn, and self esteem, these differences speak volumes for the task of the teacher and the need to build confidence before potential can be reached.

As a manager, or in this case perhaps more appropriately, as a school leader, it seemed to me that I had to show and have high expectations of my staff if they were transmit that same positivity to their pupils. It is comparatively easy to state that you have full confidence in a teacher and department, but if they are operating within an ethos which fails to back up that message, then it is meaningless. As leader of the school guidance team, my frequent approach was to ask for their own opinions before making a final decision on a plan or innovation. This wasn't merely window dressing. I truly believed that, as the people working hard on the ground with the pupils on a day to day, lesson to lesson, basis, they were in a position to judge propositions with accuracy and insight. And, furthermore, I trusted them to be honest and to show vision and an acceptance of change – even, perhaps, when it went against their own preferences. In other words, I had high expectations that they were professional and committed enough to make decisions in the interests of pupils, no matter the consequences to them personally.

They were probably less delighted that I had the trust in them to commit them to national and regional developments and to put them forward as innovators and wise professionals. This brought them recognition, but also extra work, but it was a practical way of my showing my expectations of their ability, and of their discovering that my expectations were indeed justified.

The root of the need for high expectations in education reflects the need for respect. Continually we say that respect must be earned and returned, it is a mutual thing. Unlike the fifties, when teachers had, we are told, 'universal respect', my generation wanted to earn that respect because of who we were and what we did, not because of the position we occupied, and equally, we felt it important that we respected those with whom we worked, the pupils, and their families. My favourite statement on high expectations says that often we have high expectations for others because we have high expectations of ourselves – and that fits perfectly with the wisdom I acquired as a school manager: because I wanted our school to be the best for its pupils, it seemed to me that I had to do my best and support the staff in doing their best.

"Be all you can be" was a common phrase, to which needed to be added: "and that is considerable!"

However, referring to the need for *pride, praise*, and *high expectations* brings me to the need for *continuity* in school management and in its approaches. Continuity is not an easy concept to apply to a school community. Every six years there is a completely different pupil population – a population which has also changed partially at the end of each school year. From this, it follows that, despite siblings attending the school, the parent body also continually changes and develops its ideas, desires for the school, and expectations in the contemporary world. It is important too, that staff have the chance to further their own careers, and often this will involve the need for them to move on. As I have suggested previously, a low turnover of staff can be comforting for a school community but if taken to extremes can lead to a certain stagnation, or lack of challenge to the status quo. That is not a good situation for staff, pupils or the wider school community.

However, people are not machines and different personalities function best in varying situations. My cousin worked for his whole career in the one school – for nearly forty years. He became an institution within the institution, as it were, and both he and the school found a happy combination, where his commitment and the school community support for him worked for both of them. Generations of pupils and staff remembered him warmly. Some of the best teachers at the school I attended – before and since my

154

own education – had attended the school and returned as teachers – truly a whole life dedicated to the place.

There are teachers who spend their careers on the promotion ladder, moving on every three or four years. It was not an approach with which I would have been comfortable, but it seemed to suit their philosophy. It was rather like those folk who move house on a regular basis: I always preferred to put down roots and build a home rather than seek regular changes of scene.

Rapid and regular turnover of staff can suggest something is lacking in the school ethos, whilst, as I've suggested, too little movement can lead to a conservative approach to teaching and learning and a certain lack of awareness. Fresh eyes and new approaches are necessary for education to manage the change which is endemic to its success.

Luckily, in most schools, there is a balance between regular movement and long term commitment, and, obviously, a situation where staff are content – whichever approach they adopt – is best for the pupils.

Continuity, though, is not merely about staff or pupils. In my more 'preachy' moods in school assemblies, I used to remind the pupils (and, I suppose, the staff!) that a school is not a collection of buildings, it is a collection of all the people who have been part of its community over the years – pupils, staff and parents. Like graffiti artists of the mind, they have all left their scratchings on the philosophical walls of the place. Some are small indications of their presence, others are more like murals of intent. Contemporary members of the community walk in their shadows and leave their own footprints.

The essence of continuity is to have a school where the ethos continues irrespective of the people involved. Of course, there is change and development to suit the times and needs of the current population, but the school's values and commitment to its pupils, its style of teaching and learning, and its connection to the people it serves should be identifiable through the years. People should know what the school stands for and how it goes about its business. This is sometimes what folk who use private education think they are buying – but familiarity and unchanging routine and uniform is not necessarily the same as continuity of philosophy and ethos. Batons are to be handed on, not to be fixed in the same place for ever.

It is a challenge for all staff – but perhaps particularly for management. They should be aware that they will not be there forever and that they owe it to their successors to leave behind an establishment which can be adapted to change but is based on clearly stated principles and an ethos which stands the test of time.

One approach I used throughout my career to self assess was the 'bus question'. If I went under a bus tomorrow, would the essential philosophy of school or guidance or other parts of my remit be well placed to continue, or was I operating in a manner which was so idiosyncratic that it was impossible for anyone else to run the systems I had established? This was also a reason for tweaking responsibilities on a fairly regular basis – even though it might not be the most popular approach for those who have to adjust to a different remit.

It all involved 'balance' – a slice of wisdom to which I will refer in more detail shortly. In my own case, my career consisted of two blocks of sixteen years in my first and last schools, with five years in between where I worked in a further two establishments. I was lucky in that I moved on from my first school when I felt ready, not because I was unhappy in any way, and I moved to my final school when I felt I could contribute as a manager. Many teachers have neither of these privileges, and, of course, like anyone, I can't know how things would have turned out had I made different choices. I suspect I would have been happy, if a little less fulfilled, had I remained in the same school for my whole career; it's in my nature to support the institution and be proud of its achievements, but I would never have gained the perspective I did from moving on – in particular the valuable experience of working with so many schools during my Youth Strategy days. Perhaps I was fortunate to achieve that balance – long stints in two schools, but shorter times in two other situations. Like so much of my career, it suited me well.

The idea of **balance,** of course, is situated between continuity and change. Anyone who has worked in education will recognize how each generation of children changes, and anyone who is even basically aware politically will know that the demands made on education are modified and expanded as time moves on – for the best of reasons and from other, less justifiable, motivations.

In my own career, I started with 'O' grades and CSEs, and finished with the Curriculum for Excellence, with a number of major initiatives in between. It would be fair to say that most years of my career, over four decades, were characterized by assessing the need for change, preparing for change, or assessing if change had been effective. Many developments were hugely positive, and most of the negatives came from the manner of implementation, rather than the philosophy behind them.

During my time, for classroom teachers a didactic approach was replaced by the less formal, then by group work, then by teacher-led, then by interactive and collaborative learning. The quickly growing development and accessibility of computers and digital technology revolutionised how we approached our tasks. When I started teaching one would often pause to sniff the alcohol on newly copied 'Banda' sheets; when I finished, 'Skype' calls to other parts of the world were commonplace. These were the

157

changes education underwent, largely to keep pace with developments in the society it served.

I always sought to embrace change – as long as I could see its benefits for pupils and staff. What was needed from management was to link these developments and new approaches to the continuity of the school's own approach, and to employ them to support the commitment of staff to providing the best possible education. It was important to balance the changes with what had come before and often our opening remarks in delivering an initiative would be along the lines of: "This looks like major change, but actually it's just a slightly different way of doing what we already do."

The style and structure may have changed over the years, but the basics of good teaching and learning remain constant, and it was important that this was emphasized. A film on a smart phone will still be analysed like one on reel to reel tape; enthusing pupils with coloured chalk was seeking to hit the same learning reactions as using powerpoint or You Tube. The balance is obtained through perspective and remembering the core of the job – to educate, to enthuse, to explain, to listen, and to care. If changes are seen through this prism they become easier to implement and less difficult to understand. Pupils, parents and staff have to be listened to, their fears understood and met, and that 'old vision thing' employed to explain the why and the how of any changes. Staff have to be supported and the authorities have to be made aware of the stress and strain engendered by teaching one system while preparing for another. The majority of staff I taught with over the years weren't against change, they just wanted the resources to be able to employ it effectively.

The task of management was to understand all of this, to reassure staff and to support them in their approach to new structures and approaches. Change should never be seen as something being 'done' to staff or pupils – rather as a joint venture in a new direction which could be achieved with mutual support and a positive approach. In brief, the tenor of the in service meeting had to be: "How are we going to do this?" rather than: "Here's something you have to do!"

The balance came in the need to apply national directives alongside the duty of understanding and support for staff and pupils. As in everything else, where the ethos of the school was already good, where there was trust between staff and management, and home and school, change was more easily achieved.

That word **"vision"** appeared again in that discussion of balance, and before completing this section of reflections, it's crucial to stress again its importance, but perhaps also to illustrate its practical application: managers should have dreams, but they shouldn't be dreamers.

The way I saw 'vision' employed many times was as follows. A teacher or manager would have an idea for a development or support initiative, based on an informal chat in staffroom or office; the idea would be fleshed out – either by manager, or teacher, or both. It would quickly be transferred from idea, to plan, to consultation through feedback, to implementation. For the process to be most successful, it needed to operate within a reasonable timescale, had to be finessed by way of whole staff consultation, and needed to be proposed and delivered by its original author. When this was a member of management, it reflected their commitment to school and staff; when it was a classroom teacher, it reflected the school as a listening institution and empowered teachers to believe that they could all influence the school's progress and ideas. The difficult part of all this was, of course, the 'vision' in the first place – the remainder of the process merely required a willingness on the part of the staff at all levels to make it happen.

You could see this operate more formally when it came to the School Improvement Plan. Teachers will know that, if handled incorrectly, this could be a frustrating paper chase, with many pages of boxes, charts and initials – all in the name of progress and development. Often the template for the Plan was dictated by the local authority – who wanted a common format to all schools and to ensure that weaker schools filled in the necessary sections. This could be demotivating for schools who were 'getting it right'.

The positive way to consider development or improvement planning was to approach the whole exercise from the other direction. If your school is in touch with national and local expectations, and has a motivated staff and a positive ethos, the improvement plan becomes a prioritising exercise, rather than a process to check omissions.

If the school knows its mission and has a clearly shared and understood ethos, then everybody in the community already knows what should be in the Plan. The exercise can then be completed by management issuing the major points for improvement planning and staff agreeing which are the priorities. The departmental or faculty plans will be a reflection of the school plan with reference to their own specific areas. Responsibilities will be allocated by remit or relevance. If approached in this way, the whole exercise becomes a formalisation of the school's overall shared 'vision', it details progress and priorities, and it makes clear to all involved their particular role and responsibilities. In other words, it should be seen and delivered as an opportunity to focus on 'big ideas' rather than an administrative box ticking exercise; a chance to celebrate the journey on which the school will embark for the next three years, rather than an expenses form for the fuel.

Ineffective schools operate without vision; the work of educating becomes reduced to a kind of civil service administration of clerical duties. It is incumbent on managers to produce that bigger picture, to think big, dream big, and talk big – and by so doing to remind their staff of the great enterprise of which they are a part – the formation of the future. From such an approach comes the joy of teaching and learning; to diminish the vision is to eliminate the greatness of the task. Fear, caution, and limited ambition should be no part of a child's education. On the other hand, converting vision to reality takes strength, knowledge, skill, and focussed responsibility. It's a brave task and not for faint hearts.

Schools, I believe, are special places, and often it's not enough to compare them to other places of work – they have to be more than that. However, many of the pieces of wisdom I acquired as a manager would apply in other settings where a small group of people were responsible for leading a community – listening, valuing, reflecting, and delivering a vision are traits everyone would like to see in their workplace, but they are crucial to a successful learning community. It's impossible to place these pieces of acquired wisdom in any kind of hierarchy – **communication, humour, reaching out, perspective, praise, high expectations, continuity, balance, vision** and it is not an exhaustive list – the ability to listen, plan, convince, organise, and inspire are all in there somewhere too – but they all feed off each other and the possession of any one of these strengthens the operation of the others – communication is aided by humour, vision by balance and perspective and so on.

In my conclusion to this reflection, I would add one more requirement which, personally, I felt was of huge importance. No matter how talented, committed, experienced or reflective a management team is, unless they **lead by example**, their efforts are liable to be undermined or at least limited in effect. Pupils very quickly spot if a teacher is recommending one approach but not following it themselves, and staff are just as skilled at making the same assessment of a management team.

The issue of nomenclature comes into this. For most of my career, the team of headteacher, deputies and assistant heads, was known as the Senior Management Team. This was fair enough, as, at least a part of their role was to 'manage' the school community, its staff and pupils. The term attracted little notice as far as I recall, often being shortened to 'SMT'. In the later years, there developed a trend to call it the 'Senior Leadership Team' – and again this was reflective of another role they have to perform – that of 'leading' the community and motivating progress. As a lifelong union person, I generally felt a little happier with 'leader' rather than 'management'. To be honest, as far as I was concerned, I preferred people to call me 'Sean' and generally referred to the headteacher as 'The Boss'. As I've repeatedly mentioned, throughout the world of education, I have always been of the opinion that respect and authority has to be earned and should be based on your actions rather than on your job title.

It was for this reason that I came to realise that demonstrating by 'doing and being involved' was a crucial method of earning the respect and trust of the staff, pupils and parents. On one level, especially as head of pupil support and guidance, this meant that my door needed to be always open to pupils, staff and parents. There are, of course, all kinds of 'management reasons' why this is not advisable, but I could never quite compute how I could expect those groups to be available to me if I was not available to them. Inevitably, when I find it difficult to meet with someone, I wonder if they are disrespectful towards me or my position, or if they are acting out of insecurity. None of these messages were ones which I would have wanted to give as a deputy head. The open door and listening ear gave me an authority to expect the same in return, and that was what I experienced throughout my career. I wanted folk to know I was either happy to see them, or, in more negative

162

circumstances, keen to support in any way I could – whatever the reason for our meeting.

Practically, to lead by example could mean a range of things – from serving tea and moving chairs on parents' evenings, through teaching difficult classes, and being available to support staff and pupils in the most challenging situations. It was a given: I was there for pupils, staff and parents – anything less would be a dereliction of duty. More than that, I couldn't think of any other way of fulfilling my role.

I suppose it would be an integral part of authority in any situation – to lead by example, to share the load - but I felt it was especially important in teaching. My emphasis on 'sharing vision' is partly a recognition that classroom teachers – who perform at the sharp end of the education system and whose effectiveness is at the root of any success – must often feel that they are submerged beneath a whole load of policies, strategies, initiatives, requirements, assessments, reviews and observations. It seemed to me that part of a senior team member's duty was to remove some of that weight rather than adding to it, and to try and illuminate the way forward by explaining the strategies and philosophies – or, even better – by choosing the route in consultation with the staff and school community.

To that aim I saw my role as much as a co-ordinator as anything else – unless major challenges or negative situations were to be faced. At that point leadership, management and authority all became important components of what I was there to do, and I wasn't naïve enough to believe that leadership could always be about pleasant and positive experiences. I could be harsh if I needed to be – and all the more effectively as it was such a rare situation in which to find myself. A good senior team operated the school in such a way that the teachers were helped teach to the best of their abilities and were encouraged to stretch their potential. It seemed to me, harking back to high expectations, that I should help to establish the optimum ethos for the best possible teaching and learning to exist in the school.

When the "McCrone" recommendations meant that I "transmogrified" from 'Assistant Head' to 'Depute Head' overnight, all that changed was the title on my door and, perhaps, the acquisition of an even fiercer commitment to do my best for the school community.

To be in the senior team was as much about serving as leading, as much about listening as managing, and as much about parents, staff, and pupils as it was about position or hierarchy. On the occasions when staff had let down themselves or their pupils, the establishing of my authority was based on that wisdom, and exercised, I hope, with understanding and perspective. It's maybe a slightly unusual description, but, for me management was an opportunity to encourage joy, allow enjoyment, and ensure the best possible experience for all in the school community.

It was a weighty responsibility, but one which I sought to exercise with a smile on my face. When I was fierce it was in defence of pupils or staff, when I was calm it was in the interests of the whole school, and when I was busy it was because I had elected to serve as a manager.

I still can't think of a better job.

Confucius said: :

"By three methods we may learn wisdom: First, by reflection, which is noblest; Second, by imitation, which is easiest; and third by experience, which is the bitterest."

He was right, more or less. In my case, I like to think I acquired wisdom in each of these ways, but I was lucky that my experiences were not bitter but sweet.

INTEGRITY

A little integrity is better than any career
Ralph Waldo Emerson

When I decided to base this memoir on the words on the Scottish Parliamentary Mace, I realised I was setting the bar high. Each of the four words has resonance and portent – for a country, a philosophy, a career or a book, the employment of such words as guidelines foreshadows a tricky path.

A 'word cloud' of these pages would generate much 'noble' and 'grandiloquent' language, as I've already pointed out. I am well aware of the danger of writing a reflection which could fall somewhere between precious and self serving. My twin defence against any such accusation is firstly that I have repeatedly underlined that I am conscious that I had a 'blessed' career in terms of good fortune and the people and pupils with whom I worked - a privilege that many teachers do not enjoy, and, secondly, that the whole basis of what I am writing is that education – teaching and learning – is not 'just another job' but is special in many ways, and deserves, in fact, demands, the grand language that I allot to it.

Indeed, it is my strong feeling that if we attempt to downplay the role of education, or the language we use in its description, then we narrow the vision and understanding of its role. A graphic illustration of such an impoverished understanding and approach is to be found currently in England, with their government seemingly happy to sell off 'academies' as a 'business opportunity'. Neither should we become too smug in Scotland where there are those who claim we 'cannot afford free education'. Leaving aside the case that 'free' education is paid for by all of us, as an investment in the country's future, such a statement calls into question the priorities of such a philosophy. As has often been suggested, if you think education is expensive, you should try ignorance.

Having said all that, if ever a word was fraught with danger for the writer, it surely must be 'integrity'. Apart from anything else, it is a concept that cannot be claimed for oneself, it is rather one that must be spotted by others. At the outset, then, I should explain that I am making no claims for my own integrity in these pages, but rather setting out why I believe it is crucial to successful teaching and learning, and is a bedrock of education, and a teaching career.

The Emerson quotation at the top of this section would reflect my view that career building and integrity are not always easy partners. Note that I did not claim they were mutually exclusive, and some of the most ambitious people I have known – within and outwith education – have been driven by the highest integrity and a selfless attitude to what they wished to achieve for others. However, the first point has to be made that, especially in areas where a certain ruthlessness is needed for progress, integrity can well find itself endangered. One of the greatest philosophical dilemmas known to man is surely whether the means can ever be justified by the end. I would suggest, in education, that the answer is pretty constantly 'No'. The main reason for this being that, for a teacher or an educator, the requirement is not just to pass on information, nor even merely to generate an interest in learning or discovery, it is also to be a role model.

It is easy to claim that teachers are the last people that young folk seek to emulate while they are at school. Whilst they may be impressed by the style and enthusiasm of some of the younger staff, in general they seem to view teachers as old, out of touch, and ignorant of what it is like to be a teenager. However, as I have pointed out repeatedly, the impact of a teacher should never be underestimated. My own experience is that the demeanour of my teachers, as much as what they said, has stayed with me for a long time, and I am also lucky to have the perspective of a whole career behind me. Much more than references to individual lessons or events, former pupils consistently tell me that it was the attitude of teachers, the way they presented themselves, in class and around the school, which has remained with them into adult life. Some even say: "I found myself wondering what Mr X or Mrs Y would have done in that situation."

This is a huge responsibility and not one which I am convinced many teachers fully take on board when they sign up for a career in the classroom. It frequently involves courting unpopularity from youngsters who may see a strong moral standpoint as old fashioned or out of touch with current trends.

It is a dilemma which perhaps came closest to the surface in discursive subjects such as Religious Education, Personal and Social Education, or even English. In these areas it was possible to discuss practical scenarios as an illustration of integrity. A favourite definition was: 'Integrity is doing the right thing, even when nobody is watching.' The practical illustration we would often discuss was as follows: "You find a £10 note in the street; nobody is about. Do you hand it in to the police or put it in your pocket?"

Undoubtedly, most teenagers feel they are 'on stage' all the time, particularly in this age of social media, so the idea of 'nobody watching' was the initial difficulty. Indeed, even as they were preparing to vote on the issue, eyes would be sliding around looking to see how others were deciding. Some sought to sidetrack the discussion with comments such as: " Oh – there would always be a cc tv camera watching, sir!" – a slightly sad reaction in itself. Additionally, the concept of "It's ok if you don't get caught" is far more widely accepted than formerly.

Once we had dealt with the idea of integrity as something which didn't depend on context – which was quite difficult for some pupils, the next red herring to appear would be relative to the amount of the money. "Aw, sir, but if it was only a fiver, you wouldn't have to hand that in, would you?"

This, of course, was a fine introduction to the concept of integrity being 'flexible' and most classes were sharp in their appreciation of this. When you pointed out that it wasn't a case of 'how much' but of 'the right thing to do', the next question would not be long in coming. "But, sir, if you find a 2p in the bus park, do you hand it in to the police?"

This was a classic practical reference. Most days after supervising some eight hundred pupils boarding the school buses at the end of school, there would be a scattering of coins which had been dropped and not picked up. Seldom were they above 20p in value, but, nevertheless, a fair number would be found over the week. The pupil's question was a good one: what did staff do with the money they picked up?

The answer was that we would put all the 2ps, 5ps etc into the school charity box. Any notes that were found would be put into the School office to await a claimant. It was notable that classes who had had this discussion consequently would be watching us intently when we bent down to pick up coins. As was the case in every area of school life, pupils were interested in whether staff's actions matched what they claimed was the 'right way' to do things.

'Integrity', as noted, is a 'big concept' – but its implications could be found in every area of school life. The most angry I saw pupils was when they had a sense of injustice – real or imagined. It was a regular gripe about homework: if I hand it in late, I get punished, but sometimes the teacher takes weeks to return it, or even loses it; why can the teacher be late, but I get into trouble if I am? The teacher swore but I'm not allowed to; the teacher has favourites; that teacher picks on me.

In some cases, these perceived injustices were inaccurate or even made up, but, where they were a fair representation of the facts, they asked all sorts of questions of the teacher concerned and of the school manager who had responsibility for responding to any pupil or parental complaints.

This brings us to one of the major reasons for integrity in education – its need for the establishment of trust between pupils and staff and home and school. The most difficult parental interviews I ever encountered were those which began: "You'll just close ranks and cover it all up – you teachers are all the same!"

Often those uttering such statements would have no evidence for the assertion. Even more frequently, they would be basing the claim on their own child's perception of teachers and the school. Of course, this perception was often wrong or mischievously reported by the child in an attempt to escape discipline, but the problem still remained: if the home didn't trust the school, the child's education was severely affected.

As a manager, such a situation was fraught with problems because of two responsibilities which could often come into conflict: one was the need for transparency and the use of integrity in dealing with such complaints, the other was the requirement to support staff and ensure they were not treated unjustly. While there were parents whose first instinct was to believe there would be a cover up, there were also teachers who believed that management would happily 'hang them out to dry'. It was here that integrity was crucial, and indeed the only way forward.

For me, and I have to say, the vast majority of the senior colleagues with whom I worked, it was a two stage process. Initially: take all possible measures to establish the truth of what happened. Once that had been ascertained: seek the best possible solution for all concerned. Parents and pupils needed to feel their case had been dealt with honestly; staff involved needed to know that their position was understood and they received the support they needed, depending on outcomes. Our old favourite, 'Communication', of course, comes into play here. You could act with perfect integrity, but if the communication was flawed, you would end up with dissatisfied parties. Most complainants were not 'out for blood', they just wanted to get the matter 'cleared up' and wanted a reaction from the school that respected them and reassured them about the school's ethos. Likewise, most teachers who made mistakes did so because of the pressure under which they were operating or through genuine error. In general they were willing to accept when they had been wrong and build bridges with the pupil or parent concerned.

Like ethos itself, of course, it is easy to be aware that an institution is operating with integrity, but not so easy to detail the concrete evidence – it is, after all, a concept, and one which is most easily spotted in its absence. However, I did hear tell of one headteacher who thought he had the answer to that conundrum. He was in the habit of putting five pound notes into empty crisp packets and then dropping them around the school. He would then keep watch to establish, firstly if the pupils were committed to picking up litter, and secondly if, having done so, they would hand in the money. The reports say that it improved the litter problem but cost him a fair bit of cash!

While we are focussing on the practical elements of integrity, it is as well to examine a controversial topic in relation to teachers and integrity. I like to imagine that the overwhelming majority of those who teach would have no problem signing up to the idea that their actions and dealings in school should be beyond reproach, and based on honesty and transparency. As I've said, quite apart from the moral imperative when working with young people, acting dishonestly or without integrity invariably leads to problems and is usually discovered.

It is, though, less easy to assert how far this need for integrity should reach. In other words, is a teacher only a role model in the classroom or school? Is their private life just that – private and distinct from their role as a teacher? I realise this can be dangerous ground, as it depends almost entirely on people's self perceptions and their own view of a teacher's role.

This is a personal reflection, and, though in places I attempt to extrapolate from my own experience and make universal points about education, I have tried to emphasise that these are views based on one person's career and education, albeit with a keen interest in a wider perspective. On this topic, I can only describe my own views and explain how they fit in with my own approach to the job.

When I was at school, though we never thought about it much, teachers were a breed apart – they didn't even dress like other people. They had a sartorial approach in those more formal times which wasn't businessman, nor shopkeeper, nor working man. It was similar though not the same as the dress code of civil servants of a lower grade, I suppose. We seldom, if ever, imagined them outside of school, and never met them, unless they stayed nearby or had some connection to our family. Though it is a surreal notion, for all we thought of them as 'people', they may as well have taken their briefcases and baggy jackets and been hung up in the classroom cupboard overnight.

The two main occasions when I became aware of teachers outside of school activities were quite memorable. On one summer holiday, in the Galway seaside resort of Salthill, two of the scarier Christian Brothers who taught me went cycling past, bringing shadows, quite literally, out of the blue. I think it was the first time my mother ever heard me utter a swear word. Whether in punishment for that or not, I don't know, but when she then spotted them in the Post Office, despite my mute pleadings, she approached them and made an announcement along the lines of: "Look who's here!"

They were possibly the last people I would have wanted to bump into anywhere – let alone on holiday – but thanks to my mother, the die had been cast. They were an awful combination: one was the most vicious teacher, the other the most boring, and the four of us spent a long afternoon sitting on a bench on the seafront making desultory conversation of the most bizarre banality – especially given their normal means of talking to me. The only slight comfort was that they had to endure it as well. I wouldn't claim to be privy to the off duty moments of a Christian Brother, but it's easy to imagine it would have involved horses, drink, and tobacco rather than polite chitchat. I haven't been back to Salthill since.

The other occasion was slightly awkward rather than traumatic. Catching a train in Liverpool for a visit to Edinburgh, we bumped into my English teacher, Ernie Spencer. This was after he had been responsible for my 'Damascus moment', so my mother was well aware of who he was and how highly I thought of him. A brief "hello and have a good holiday" would have sufficed, but, again, my mother felt it necessary to sit by Ernie on the train for the four hour journey. I was older now, I liked Ernie and I think he reacted to the situation with typically wry amusement. Whilst my mother sang Ernie's praises over and over again, I enthused about Wilfred Owen. I'm not sure it was the holiday journey home he had envisaged!

The fact that these incidents are so clear in my memory is testament to their rarity. Teachers were for school and that was that.

These days, however, are different.

As pupils, our relationship with teachers was very formal. It was, literally 'buttoned up'. Our blazers had to be fastened and they weren't allowed to take off their jackets in the classroom. Other than in the teaching situation, there was little or no connection between us. Even extracurricular activities, though more relaxed in atmosphere than the classroom, seldom closed the distance between us.

Now, with a whole different approach to teaching and learning, personality and connection have become far more important in the classroom. Teachers may lend books to interested pupils, or bring in personal artifacts to illustrate a topic, and most will share personal experiences where they are relevant and appropriate. At my last school, one teacher brought in his dog so that the pupils in the 'Nurture Base' could benefit from the experience. Staff partners may be accredited adults on residential excursions, and teachers' children may be at the school meaning that their friends see them in the home situation.. Young people have more social opportunities now and, rightly or wrongly, the number of senior pupils who go clubbing means that there is a strong possibility that younger staff may come across pupils at the weekend. Many more pupils have part time employment now and teachers may often find themselves being served by a pupil in local shops. The added connection brings many advantages, and certainly humanizes the teaching and learning experience, but it also brings with it responsibilities, particularly on the part of the teacher.

Clearly and obviously, in terms of any kind of connection outside of school, the teacher is always a teacher, and, beyond any doubt, is totally responsible for maintaining this relationship in a professional and appropriate manner. This is legally and morally indisputable, and the bedrock of a teacher's integrity.

177

However, my point of view was that the responsibility goes much further than that.

There are those who claim that bringing up a child with a certain moral code is a kind of brainwashing. The child should be left to decide what is 'right' and 'wrong' when they are old enough and competent to do so. I have to say that children I have witnessed who were given this freedom have often turned out to be confused and uncertain adolescents. My own view would be that it is a parent's responsibility to provide a sound foundation for moral decisions – to pass on their own beliefs, as it were – whether religious or secular – but that the young person should be given the security and self confidence – by home and school – to assess those beliefs and make their own choices based on a firm starting point from their childhood.

For that reason, I tend to believe that teachers should try to be role models in and out of the classroom. Obviously I wouldn't suggest that teachers have to have 'perfect' lives – but the skeletons in their closets should not be rattling so loudly as to drown out their teaching. I don't think it is controversial to believe that teachers should not be lawbreakers, for instance. I think their demeanour should suit their position. I wouldn't want to be teaching teenagers who had witnessed me drunk in the pub on a Saturday night, or getting involved with fighting, or recreational drugs. It is difficult to maintain authority or position in such a scenario. Like many colleagues, if I ever bumped into pupils on a night out, I would be perfectly pleasant in greeting them, but would make sure that I spent the evening in a different establishment. As a weekly attender at football matches, even in retirement, I make a quick check around to see if any pupils or families are nearby, and if so, tend to moderate my rants and language!

It is a difficult road to travel. Pupils come from many backgrounds and their families have varying expectations about acceptable behaviour or otherwise. It is not a teacher's task to impose his values on a young person, but I do feel it is important that he or she provide an example which is positive and which the young person can see is based on certain values and self awareness.

Practically speaking, social media has made this whole area even more fraught with challenges. Though most of the press it receives is negative, teachers know there are huge opportunities for teaching and learning if the internet, and sites such as Facebook, Twitter, Tumblr and Buzzfeed, are used inventively and with care. However, like the more relaxed classroom atmosphere, what brings benefits also promotes difficulty.

When Facebook first became popular, many newly qualified teachers were less than vigilant in privacy settings and were thus revealing a whole lot of information, much of it about student days, to anyone, including pupils, who cared to seek out their personal pages. For some pupils this was merely a way of finding out about a favourite teacher, but for others it was a more negative exercise. Either way, it was a release of personal information which probably went far beyond that which the teacher would choose to share appropriately in the classroom. It always seemed to me that, apart from the normal wise security approaches, and a high level of privacy, it was always sensible - for everyone, but particularly teachers, to put nothing online with which they would be unhappy if it was accessible to the public. I could see no good reason for teachers to be 'Facebook friends' with pupils nor for staff and pupils to follow each other on Twitter. For most it would be a completely innocent connection, but I never felt it was worth the risk, nor the minefield of deciding which friend requests you would deem suitable, and which you would turn down. It is easy to set up learning groups and class Facebook pages or Twitter accounts where the teacher can openly connect with a whole class or more without revealing personal information or being involved in one to one contact. Better safe than sorry.

Without doubt, social media will change and develop as years go by. As far as integrity is concerned, however, nothing changes: you are a teacher and should act as one – it is the least your pupils and their families deserve.

I know some would differ and suggest that your responsibilities as a teacher cease when you leave the school each day. I would never claim that such a view leads to less effective teaching, but it was not the approach I took as a teacher, for better or worse.

It is impossible to read, (or write!) this section without reflecting on moments when one might have made different choices or acted in a more responsible or mature manner. It is in the nature of life that we learn as we grow. In suggesting that teachers have a 'vocation' to promote integrity by their own example, I am not seeking to diminish those who disagree, nor suggesting that to fail in this respect is somehow to be less of a teacher. If teaching is about anything it is about humanity, and pupils and families understand these days, thank God, that teachers are human just as they are. The important point is that we are aware of the way we act and that we seek to avoid hypocrisy. We may not always achieve success in this mission, but, as we tell the pupils, if we learn from our failures we are making progress – it's all part of teaching and learning.

As I will discuss in the section on 'Compassion', in the course of my career, I became aware of many young people who were frightened because there was little guidance and few role models in their lives. Teachers cannot fill in for parents, a school is not a home, but it can exist with an ethos that brings some certainty, some sense of a road ahead, to those pupils who most need it. That is why I feel teachers should aim to be role models – to suggest a way forward to those without a clear view, and to reinforce the approach of those who struggle to do what they perceive as the 'right thing', even when it makes them unpopular. Lifebelts don't always save lives but they can give confidence to swimmers in stormy seas.

I have given these practical examples of 'integrity' - and the challenges faced by teachers in maintaining it - on a day to day, very 'ordinary' basis. This doesn't mean integrity is not as important at this level – everyday behaviour lies at the root of establishing an approach to the job that has integrity – but, in truth, the concept is far larger than daily habits.

Again, the language employed has to suit the gravity of the task involved. Pupils get one chance at education, they must not be let down. Even those who blossom later in their lives and return to study as adults will have had the seed sown while they were at school – whether able to react positively or not. All teachers will report that the number of former pupils who tell them later in life that school was rubbish and pointless is far exceeded by the number who come to reflect on its positive value. Even if their own school experience has been negative, even if they were badly served by the education system, it is a minority of adults who don't recognize its importance and the opportunities that it should offer in terms of formation, foundation, and encouragement.

All of this, naturally, demands integrity of all those involved in education. It is not a business - where bankruptcy or incompetence can be covered by administration, close down, and re-establishment. Despite the existence of private education, the vast majority of families have minimal or little choice in where their child is educated. Indeed, there is a strong case for saying that many of those who most need to be able to make a choice to fit their own child's needs, are least able to do so. The so called 'post code lottery' in education is patently unfair and the biggest condemnation of successive political generations and education administration. This being the case, it inevitably lies on the shoulders of the teachers to make their school as successful as possible and to give support, teaching, and learning to the widest range of their pupils. All decisions in education have to be based on integrity, because all of those decisions impact on pupils' futures.

The final sections in my writings – on Integrity, Justice and Compassion – inevitably depend, ultimately, on the context in which teachers operate. Much of the injustice in education reflects similar injustices in society; lack of compassion in the way in which schools operate is almost always down to a shortage of resources – whether in time, training or expertise. Integrity, however, though it can be promoted and facilitated by local and national government and by school leaders, is also something which individual teachers must strive to employ in all their professional dealings.

Going back to the earlier quotation: if integrity does mean doing the right things even when nobody is watching, then teachers face such decisions on a daily if not hourly basis. Do the pupils always get your best effort? Are you fully committed to their progress and welfare? Do you understand and enact fully the requirements and expectations of your post? We expect the best from pupils in terms of effort and commitment, so integrity demands that we provide them with the same and role model our expectations.

One comment I would make would be that, in all of my experience, the most committed teachers were the happiest teachers, and the disillusioned staff tended to be the most cynical. It is, perhaps, a moot point which comes first – but I would suggest to any young teacher that trying the first route initially would be a good way of hedging your bets! The caveat to that, of course, is that schools need to facilitate integrity; commitment has to be recognized and rewarded, cynicism challenged. Integrity is made easy in a positive atmosphere where its rewards are self evident. It brings us back to the earlier points on high expectations and an ethos which values all in the school community. These are nice words, but the result of hard work, and a unity of vision and purpose, which has to be established, nurtured, and maintained by all who work in the establishment.

On a final point, and perhaps this betrays my lifelong socialist and republican approaches, education, at its best, is a public service. I will comment in more depth on private education in the next section, but annual fees don't necessarily buy a better education – they may offer access to better facilities and a social and professional network which will reap lifelong benefits – but they don't guarantee a better education. A 'good' education is provided by skilled and committed teachers working in harmony with families who value teaching and learning, and want the best, in all senses, for their child. It is a partnership, not a business transaction.

Therefore I believe that, as public servants, teachers have a duty to behave with integrity. To behave in any other manner is to undermine the cooperative nature of public service and to let down your fellow citizens – particularly those who are most vulnerable – the next generation. Public service should be a beacon for all that is best about a society, not a political football used by competing parties at election time. The belief that shareholder driven competition can make every endeavour more successful is disproved time and again, though few political figures are brave enough to admit this. At least in education, we should be aware that we work for the good of all in society and that our aims far surpass the blandishments of the profit margin. Perhaps Bob Marley put it most succinctly:

"The greatness of a man is not in how much wealth he acquires, but in his integrity and his ability to affect those around him positively"

Society asks a lot of its teachers, but teachers must ask even more of themselves!

JUSTICE

Until the great mass of people shall be filled with the sense of responsibility for each other's welfare, social justice can never be attained.

Helen Keller

Inevitably, justice and education are inextricably linked. There are many references to this already in these pages. I have already detailed my long lasting sense of injustice felt from the time when I was forbidden to join my primary class on its nature walk – a fire that has hardly been quenched by a recent discovery of a report from that time in which the named teacher has given me 100% for 'Nature Study'! The ill merited and often random nature of punishments from my teachers at secondary school generate as much anger as the ill considered severity of their delivery. Anyone who has taught knows that pupils start school with a clearly established sense of what is fair and what isn't. Some take this to unspeakable heights in their later education, and you would have to ask what they have experienced in school, or elsewhere, for their understanding of natural justice to develop in such a negative manner.

'Fair play' and 'equality for all' are yet more grand statements, but are also the bedrock of justice in education – not only in modelling fairness for young people, but also in establishing equality of opportunity for all pupils. Far back into medieval times, education was always seen as not only a means of developing intelligence and making sense of the world around us, but as a means of offering opportunities and widening choices.

On my grandfather's birth certificate, in 1867, his own father's signature is recorded as "X- his mark". My great grandfather, Patrick McPartland, was a tenant farmer on a piece of boggy hillside in the west of Ireland. Through education, in three generations, his family produced teachers, doctors, accountants, businessmen, clerics and even a Vice President of General Motors

– all made possible by teachers and schools, and the move towards universal education.

As an aspiration towards 'education for all' moved forward in the second half of the nineteenth and the first half of the twentieth centuries, the reformers were quite clear in their reasoning. It wasn't merely a case of education for its own sake, important though that is, it was also a matter of attacking the inequalities of opportunity that existed in contemporary society. It was to address the injustice that saw youngsters working in mines and factories, for long hours and in appalling conditions, or families forced to choose between continued schooling or a desperately needed additional wage, meagre though it might be.

Of course, we are not just talking of a philanthropic approach to education on the part of the politicians. An educated workforce is a valuable workforce; the British Empire, and the state's burgeoning industrialisation, required educated individuals to service it – both in business, but also in the lower middle class and working class areas of civil service and administration. Come what may, universal education was one of the great reforms of the late nineteenth and early twentieth century.

However, revolution and reform seldom cease their evolution when their primary aims are achieved. The world is littered with examples of hope driven revolution being replaced ultimately with disappointment and failure. In a sense, there are areas of education where this is mirrored.

One of the most moving assemblies I ever organized featured some pupils from a girls' school in Africa which our seniors were supporting. In thanking them for their support, one of the African school's pupils told the following story.

The importance of their school was that, apart from basic education, it also prepared the girls for careers after school, and many of them set up small enterprises making use of their creative skills – fashion clothing was a popular choice. She explained that this was vital because the only other alternatives for girls were slavery or prostitution. One of her friends had ended up as a slave and worked as a servant for a rich family. She lived in a shack by the house and the only time she had to herself was four hours on a Wednesday afternoon, when the family all went into the next town. Each week she would walk ten miles to the nearest school. She knew education was important, so she would spend an hour sitting on the ground, leaning against the school wall, under a window, hoping to learn from the words which came out through the glassless gap. Then she would judge the time to leave and hope to get home before the family returned. If she was late she would be beaten, but she felt it was worth it to try and access some education, because it was so important to her. She knew the difference it could make.

It was a perspective which honestly stunned our senior pupils who, not unnaturally, took education for granted, and, on occasions, could be downright dismissive of it. It seems when what is much longed for is finally attained, it can eventually become taken for granted: as would also be reflected in many people's apathy towards politics despite the long fight for universal suffrage.

If that story had a major impact on pupils, a similar tale, a few years later, had a similar effect on staff. A teacher from Africa paid a fact finding visit to our school, and it was my job to give him a tour of the premises. He was clearly fascinated by the scale of our establishment, and, as I prepared to show him the first department, he asked: "Have you a computer in your school?" As he was asking the question, I was opening the door to reveal one of three computer classrooms, each of them with twenty machines. Every other classroom had at least one computer for administration purposes, and many departments had a set of laptops to use in conjunction with the smartboards with which every classroom was equipped. His question was met with an embarrassed silence as we realized the practical gap between the haves and the have nots.

It transpired that he lived some two hours away from the school of which he was headteacher. That, of course, was walking time. Most of his pupils faced a similar walk to school, many being brought by parents. He told us that, should he be unwell or delayed and was late in arriving, many of the parents or pupils would head back home, assuming he wouldn't be there that day. This led to stress on his part and a fair few times when he arrived exhausted through ill health or a particularly frantic 'commute'. He wasn't worried for himself, but for the fact that when the pupils' attendance pattern was broken or irregular it became difficult to work with them. His dream was to buy a motorbike to ensure his relaxed and timely arrival each day – but it would cost £200 which was far beyond his means. You can imagine the further silence of comprehension – and also that it took less than a week for staff and pupils to raise the money to send to him for the bike to be purchased. Even that transaction was complicated and needed to involve a local Mission as monies sent to the school were often misappropriated by local government officials and might not reach him.

Once he had his motorbike, he sent us a picture of him en route to school. It stayed on my office wall – a reminder of what we have and how we can make a difference.

So, you could make the point that, imperfect as it is, our education system is better than some – but to accept that situation as 'good enough' is to deny the natural justice of every pupil getting the best we can offer – mediocrity has no place in the education of young people.

The late Tony Benn memorably stated: "If we can afford to kill people in wars, we can afford to educate people", and the UK's position as the fourth most unequal society in the developed world suggests that, for all our wealth, our priorities are somewhat skewed. Again, as I write this, we are told we cannot 'afford' a 'free' at point of delivery Health Service, whilst billions are being found for the development of the High Speed Train. In writing about Justice in education, we need to be mindful that, despite the brave words of politicians, education only seems a priority when it can be used as 'evidence', and 'major changes' can be produced as 'proof', that the government is 'doing something'.

In the 2010 UK Parliament, 35% of MPs are privately educated – and even at 15% of Labour MPs, this is over twice the national average; 90% of MPs went to university – with three out of ten attending Oxbridge, and over a hundred MPs being Oxford alumni. The Independent reported research from the Sutton Trust which revealed that only 43% of the 2010 Parliament attended Comprehensive schools and that 10% of all MPs came from just thirteen schools, twelve of which were fee-paying. Eton, Highgate and Millfield schools head the list for providing these MPs. Given that the Westminster legislature is theoretically socially, politically and geographically representative of the UK, it is not difficult to see a disconnection between voter and representative in these figures. The oft quoted figure of over twenty millionaires in the current Cabinet, and the gender imbalance, also reflect a law making institution which seems far from reflective of the state as a whole.

Scots Parliament figures are also interesting in terms of balance, with a quarter of members having attended Glasgow University, and around three quarters with third level degree education backgrounds. While numbers of privately educated members are far lower than Westminster, reflecting the general footprint of fee-paying education in this country, the Holyrood legislature could also better reflect the people for whom it legislates.

Of course, it is incorrect to suggest that a private education stymies the ability to make laws for all, but, as far as education is concerned, it is worth noting that a state Parliament which ultimately, at least financially, controls schools north and south of the Border, is legislating for a system of which the majority have minimal practical experience, and, frequently, little personal investment.

Justice demands that equality of opportunity exists for all, and this is patently not the case in our schools. In almost every education authority area there are schools which are designated or labelled as 'failing'. Often millions have been spent on them in varying 'regeneration' packages, which seldom affect the school's image or impact in the long term. This should tell the authorities that the problem is wider than the schools themselves and relates to social problems like housing, health, and unemployment – which in turn lead to disillusion and absence of hope. Even the highest expectations can be defeated in such a scenario.

The concept of 'parental choice' feeds into the cycle, of course. We operate a system where private education, by fees and entrance exams, 'creams off' those of high ability and the commitment and capacity to pay for education. The Parents' Charter then gives many parents the opportunity to 'choose' schools which they regard as more effective. The catchment area system may then leave the 'local' school with pupils who are often less well prepared to succeed. The authority then assesses these schools, largely on the basis of examination results, as 'failing' – without proper regard to the base of pupils with whom they have been left.

Everybody knows how this system works, and its effects. Nobody can blame parents for wanting what they see as the best for their children, and few politicians are brave enough to risk unpopularity through promoting change to this part of the system. The answer, of course, is to prioritise education so that all schools provide an effective, motivating and successful educational experience, and the local school becomes first choice for aspirational parents.

I don't accept for a moment that private schools, by default, provide better teaching and learning. In terms of education, a school is only as effective as the teachers in its classrooms and the support of its community. What private schools do promote, however, is the confidence which comes from high level facilities and the access to a network of contacts.

Facilities are a question of commitment and priority. I noticed in my last school, it being expensively built and only two years old when I joined the staff, that the surroundings were inspirational to both staff and pupils. There was little graffiti, and hardly any vandalism, pupils were pleased to show around the many admiring visitors, and, as a staff, our work in such a 'flagship' school felt valued and noticed. It brought the best out in all of us as we reacted to the high expectations signalled by such resources. Parents and the local community also showed pride in the facilities: "It's a lovely school" was a common comment and a good start to building a partnership to giving pupils the best possible educational experience.

There is currently a re-build programme going on across Scotland's schools – which is good news. The bad news is that most of this is necessary because of appalling build and design in the 1970s. When school buildings fail to last for forty years, it is not a positive message about the priority we give to our children and their education. In many parts of the country there are huge backlogs in terms of school repairs and refurbishment, and even on a micro level, torn shower curtains, chipped paint, dirty windows and broken furniture all send a message about priorities to the pupils and staff who have to deal with them.

We sell off playing field space, restrict the opening hours of school sports centres, allow existing facilities to run down, and tender out 'ancillary' support to private companies. If you want a 'smart business model' for the operation of education, then maybe these decisions make sense. If you want to prioritise the education of young people, raise them with self confidence and belief, and signal to society that our young people are valued, then, I am afraid, that is the wrong way to go about it. As I've repeated throughout these reflections, young folk are not easily fooled; they can see the difference between schools where money is no object and those where 'making ends meet' is a way of life. In the richest parts of Scotland, we have schools, private and state run, of which we can be justifiably proud. In other parts of Scotland there are also schools who serve pupils and community effectively and to great effect, often at tremendous personal cost to those who work there and support the establishment. Sadly, in the poorest parts of Scotland, where education could do so much to make a difference, we are still sometimes letting down our children and our future by the provision which we offer.

There are, then, major changes in spending and priorities which could impact our schools, but it is fair to ask how the system could be changed in other ways to impact on the justice of equal opportunities.

I have mentioned the effect of 'parental choice' – a phrase which deserves to be written in inverted commas as many parents are left, for various reasons, without a real choice in their children's education: the effect of what the papers like to call 'the postcode lottery', but which is actually the result of major inequality in our society.

The idea of a school at the centre of its community, as a kind of social and educational hub, is hugely attractive, but, though it makes a lot of sense in the rural parts of the country, it faces practical difficulties in the urban situation. Because of the way our towns and cities have grown, the idea of a circular catchment with the school at the centre has had an unfortunate reality. In many areas it has led to a 'ghetto' – sometimes 'well off', sometimes 'disadvantaged', which labels the school in a positive or negative manner, and effectively obliterates the philosophy and benefits of comprehensivisation. In leafy suburbs, this has had the desired effect; in deprived inner city areas it has tended to have the opposite effect – with some notable exceptions.

This brings me to the disputatious area of denominational schools. It was never my intention to focus on that element of my experience in these reflections. I respect all opinions and people's right to hold them about denominational education. In the end, I suspect it comes down to one's view of organized religion and one's take on whether parents should pass on their belief systems to their children. I have been fortunate enough to gain teaching experience within and outwith the denominational system. I can, of course, only speak from that experience. I would say that claims that such schools 'brainwash' pupils is totally without foundation – both from the approach in RE classes and from the general ethos.

The idea that such schools 'segregate' their pupils is also false. All three of the denominational schools in which I taught had a large minority of pupils who were either of other religions or no religion at all, and, without exception, pupils all had friends who were from other schools and beliefs. To say that school attendance means young people grow 'separately' is just not true – in denominational schools, any more than it would be where pupils

195

from the same street happen to go to different non-denominational state schools. A cursory look at any teenager's Facebook friend list would show that friendships are not only formed in school. It is also worth pointing out that the very few incidents of bigotry I came across in my career related to football rather than religion, and could scarcely be blamed on denominational education. It only seems to be in certain parts of Scotland that there is an attempt made to link denominational schools with bigotry, whereas in other parts of the world it is not an issue.

There are social issues which impact on denominational education: in parts of the North of Ireland, where housing is segregated, I can understand the desire that pupils be able to meet in a school setting, and the current media and political interest in 'Trojan Horse' schools in the English Midlands is an alert to those who organize denominational education.

We are fortunate in Scotland that our denominational schools are fully a part of the education system, with all that is implied by that, but we should never forget that the task of a denominational school is to expose young people to a particular set of positive values, to encourage them to reflect on them, and to decide, with information and progression, whether they wish to live their lives in that manner. It should never be seen as an opportunity to impose values or enforce rules, nor as a means of highlighting differences. For me, and my colleagues, we believed our schools encouraged basic Christian and human values of respect for others and self, and the responsibility to be an active member of society for the good of all. It was about exposition, not imposition.

On the positive side, I have met many folk who are theoretically opposed to denominational schools but choose to send their children there because they admire the ethos and shared values. These values are not exclusive to denominational schools, of course, but reports regularly commend denominational schools

196

for their ethos, and many of the country's most successful state secondaries are denominational.

There are two non-religious elements that can be identified in the success of denominational schools according to most assessments. One is the fact that they benefit from being a positive choice of all parents whose children attend the school – that is, attendance at a non-denominational school is not automatic, the choice has to be indicated by family. This gives the school, theoretically, 'involved parents' and an agreed, shared, ethos in its community. Both of these facts are valuable to educators, as is seen from the successes of 'over subscribed' schools – be they denominational or otherwise.

The other point to note is that such schools tend to have a wider catchment area than just the immediate locality and this increases the chance of there being a more comprehensive roll, which in turn leads to more effective teaching and learning – for all the pupils involved, and is a far better representation of the comprehensive ideal. Even my own school as a teenager, though based on academic selection, had the advantage of a socially comprehensive mix – to the benefit of everyone in the school community.

Now there can be two reactions to such a state of affairs. Those who are against denominational education will suggest it is 'an unfair advantage' to such schools and is a reason for their abolition. However, perhaps a more positive reaction would be to suggest that, as both these elements of denominational schools seem to operate in the interests of the pupils, there might be a way of duplicating them in all schools.

To encourage parents to make proactive decisions as to the school to which they send their child, the school needs to have a positive image and a successful record – and this goes far beyond examination results. Though anecdotally the consensus is that parents are most interested in examination results when judging the suitability of a school for their children, what I have found, at all times and in all the schools to which I've been attached, is that this is not quite the whole truth.

Of course, parents are concerned that the standard of teaching and learning will encourage their child to reach or even stretch their academic potential, but the large majority of parents to whom I have spoken over the years have placed equally highly a wish that their child be 'happy' at school. All the areas I have highlighted are linked, and 'happiness' comes with a positive ethos, pupils who feel valued, good teaching and discipline, and a pride in the institution. This, in turn, calls for high expectations and top level resources in school and a vision which is shared not only with pupils and families, but with the whole community which the school serves. Teachers, and especially the headteacher and senior management team, have to proclaim the school's successes, interact with the community, and listen to parent, pupil, staff and community needs, as I suggested in the section devoted to 'Wisdom'. People need to 'buy into' their schools and be given reason to do so. Irrespective of whether families have children attending the schools, the neighbourhood should be proud of the learning establishment in its midst. As I have mentioned before, a society which is not proud of its young people is storing up future trouble.

In the early eighties I was part of a committee which organized the 'Meadows Festival' in Edinburgh. The Meadows are a large area of inner city parkland available for relaxation and games, and much enjoyed by the populace. I was interviewed by Muriel Gray on local radio and she questioned me about the idea of the Festival being a 'community festival': "What is the Meadows' Community?" she asked. I hadn't thought of the concept before, but my answer was that, as well as the people who lived around the

198

Meadows, its community also constituted all the folk who used them for relaxation and the thousands who 'commuted' to work, school, college or university by crossing them on a daily basis. I think the same can be said of our schools: their community is not simply the surrounding area but all of the people they serve and all the folk who make use of their facilities, directly or indirectly.

Apart from raising standards in every school, a major contribution to justice in education would be to re-examine the manner in which we set up our catchment areas. As we've discussed, research suggests that well run schools with a strong ethos thrive best when there is a genuine comprehensive mix in their roll. Schools who either focus on academic progress to the exclusion of all else, or who don't rate academic progress strongly enough, tend to fail their communities. The education of the 'whole child' benefits in many ways when the needs of children of different backgrounds and abilities are being met. No child is purely 'academic' or 'non academic', and it is dangerous to suggest that pupils from 'advantaged backgrounds' always find school easier or that pupils from 'disadvantaged backgrounds will always struggle academically. The best schools are set up to meet the needs of all the pupils; 'needs driven' policies are most appropriate and most successful – even though they may sometimes clash with national or local priorities. This puts responsibilities on the shoulders of all teachers, and especially the management team. The school has to know its pupils well to ensure its provision is in tune with their needs – and sometimes this means the head and staff have to fight for resources or initiatives.

One of the reasons I never felt inclined towards headship, nor would have been suitable for the post, was the need for headteachers to promote the corporate approach of local and national government. In terms of the hierarchical structure, of course, this makes a kind of sense: an outward unity must be preserved and a consistent message be presented. However, without

199

a doubt, there are times when the need for headteachers to 'support the party line' clashes with the need to support pupils or promote the school's particular needs. And it isn't quite as simple as that. In my time I saw that headteachers who were conspicuously 'loyal to the system' won concessions for their schools, whereas those who tended to speak out if they felt it was in their pupils' or staff's interests, might find that they were near to the back of the queue when additional support was available. I never felt I would be able to square that particular circle.

I am not sure that 'needs driven, pupil centred' approaches are a good match for the kind of national and local government controls under which our schools operate. It would be nice to think that a more balanced approach – which had room for autonomy, whilst retaining local and national consistency and standards, could evolve. Like most of the topics I have covered, this assumes a high standard of leadership and teaching in each school – and the acceptance that, rather than say "That's not possible, so we have to employ failsafe techniques", we set about finding ways in which we can make it possible. If there is a general fault in education – and perhaps many more of our structures, it is a tendency to plot progress based on examples of weak practice rather than the strongest. In education, we are encouraged to 'share best practice', but often our procedures are predicated on ameliorating 'worst practice'. Children deserve better.

There also needs to be a concerted effort to change the way in which schools are judged. We live in a highly monitored society and the speed of life demands that, rather than through careful assessment and reflection, 'success' is often judged by the ability to meet oversimplified 'targets'. No process seems complete without a 'tool box' to 'measure success' and point the way to 'further development'.

Before my comments generate accusations of 'luddite' or an unwillingness to face inspection, I should make my position clear. Education is so important that it should be as accountable as it is possible to make it; indeed, without accountability, we run the risk of failing pupils through lack of self awareness or substandard approaches. I have no problem with the work of educationalists being monitored and brought to account, it is *how* this is done and *what* is being measured which should be questioned.

It is perhaps naïve to wish that schools were popularly judged by more subtle means than a list of examination results. Whilst it is true that a school's exam results provide an indication of how effectively it performs its primary task of 'educating', they don't really give a meaningful picture of a school's strengths and approaches – unless you believe that the sole task of education is to produce successful examination candidates.

Furthermore, two major research trends during my later career have suggested that, in the future, school leavers will have as many as ten different jobs in their working lifetime – requiring an educational experience which is broader than solely qualifications for a specific career; and, increasingly, adults end up in careers or jobs which are little to do with their ambitions when at school. Both of these trends support the need for a good, broad education experience – one which will prepare the individual to be confident, innovative, and flexible, rather than simply a person who can gather qualifications.

Good examination results tend to suggest a school is operating effectively – but the real measure of its success is finding out *what* it is doing to have such success. Not all pupils are able to gain academic success – so what does the school offer to them and to their families? Not all pupils are ready for examinations whilst still at school: how are they equipped for their future academic development?

I have long believed that parents and pupils are the best advertisements for a school's success and that they have an important role in providing answers to those who seek information about the school. However, I do recognize the pull of easily tabulated statistics in providing some kind of 'snapshot' of a school's effect.

The problem with 'examination league tables' is that they describe what 'comes out of a school' with no reference to what has been 'put in'. A school with a 'positive academic intake' – either from selection or from a catchment in a 'leafy suburb' - might be expected to achieve results which are above the national average – reflecting the demographic of its roll. Likewise, a school in a 'disadvantaged area' may struggle to achieve high level examination results for reasons which extend beyond the level of commitment or teaching amongst the staff – and, indeed, may be providing an excellent education within the bounds of its capability.

If we, reluctantly, accept that, for the purposes of graphs and statistics, tables will need to be formulated, and judgements made, then a far more accurate model is a table based on what is known as 'value added'.

Tests performed in the final years of primary school can provide a theoretical outline of the academic results which may be attained by a particular year group at the age of 16+. It is, of course, a snapshot of a particular group of pupils at a particular time in their education – but, in my experience, it had some currency – especially when applied to a year group rather than individuals. Used carefully, these statistics could give some idea of how much 'more successfully' pupils were performing in examinations than might have been expected when they entered the

202

secondary. Used in comparison with statistics from schools of a similar intake, a further comparison could be made.

I have stated my discomfort with using examination results as indicators of 'success', but, given that they exist and are disseminated, this shaping of the figures seems to me a more accurate representation of what a school is doing than a mere list of examination results. 'Good' schools achieve exam results which are better than might have been predicted, better than the school's intake 'suggests', and better than comparative institutions. In other words, they increase their pupils' chances of success. Indubitably, they do this by concentrating on the 'whole pupil' rather than simply the achievement of examination passes. In so doing they can often offset the injustices foisted on some of our children by the political, economic and social system into which they are born. This, surely, is a major task of our schools, and a criteria for the success of our teachers and their work. School leaders – and politicians at all levels – have a duty to promote this wider image of education in its truest form – whatever the pressures instigated by outside forces.

As educationalists, our only vested interest must be in the development of our pupils, and the maximizing of their potential and their opportunities for success. Crude lists of examination results do a disservice to our teachers, pupils, their families, and the society which they serve – and our young people deserve better.

All of these approaches to 'justice' in education are based on overall approaches to how we deliver teaching and learning, but justice also needs to be provided at an individual level.

Some years before my retirement, came the legislation to integrate most pupils with additional needs into mainstream schools. Such inclusion was welcomed by most – with the caveat that teachers and schools wanted to be resourced to offer the support which each child needed to make a success of their mainstream experience.

What I found amongst the parents of these pupils was an understandable nervousness about a bigger establishment, new staff, and a different way of working, but, also, and frequently, a combative approach which assumed that every support would need to be fought for, tooth and nail. Sadly, for many of them, this seemed to be based on their long experience of dealing with officialdom and the authorities. Many of them brought their children to us with a lack of trust in the establishment in general to understand or listen to their needs, or to provide the basic support which was necessary for their child to flourish. To be frank, it was upsetting to witness their lack of belief in the system – though, to be fair, the majority recognised the efforts of individuals but blamed the structures in place for their disappointments and battles fought.

The way we met this challenge was consistent with our approach to every child and every challenge. We listened, we consulted, we fought for resources, and we tried to put a structure in place which met the differing needs of each individual child. We sought to gain the parents' trust by turning our words into actions.

In most cases we achieved this, as we did with all of our successes, based on the commitment, innovation, and sheer hard work of the staff in the school. Teachers, support assistants, janitors and all associated with the school came forward to support these pupils; the success of the inclusion policy for each child became more important than job descriptions or established practice. The adjustments were pupil led and centred, we discovered 'there was another way' and we built on that. A lot of the adjustments made to welcome additional needs pupils led to better practice across the school for all pupils; staff at all levels became more aware of pupils' needs and the things which impacted on progress and development; we became more thoughtful, more innovative, and more responsive.

In the best traditions of education, no matter how much we gave these pupils, they gave us more back – in terms of reflection, flexible approaches, and understanding. If we gave them more opportunities and a more fully developed potential, they gave us a new understanding of our task as teachers and what we could achieve if we listened, reflected and innovated.

On the title page to this section, I have quoted Helen Keller. It is perhaps ironic, then, that in the case of education, Justice is not blind – it sees, it is not deaf – it hears, and it is not dumb – it speaks out for all who have needs to be met.

This approach was in place for all pupils. In fact, 'additional needs' sometimes seemed like an unnecessary label. All pupils have needs. If there is to be justice in education, a school's task is to identify those needs and do all that is possible to meet them. In doing this, many boundaries are removed – in all directions.

But then, that's often what is necessary when you go in search of justice.

COMPASSION

Anyone can criticise. It takes a true believer to be compassionate. No greater burden can be borne by an individual than to know no-one cares or understands.

Arthur H Stainback

Although the engraving on the Parliamentary Mace has Compassion and then Justice, I have saved Compassion until last in my reflections because I believe it is the thread which runs through virtually everything I have written about my beliefs on education. Without empathy, a willingness to listen, hear, understand, and act on what we discover, our work with young people is diminished in its usefulness and effectiveness. If we fail to prioritise the children's needs, our work is hollow; if we see caring as weakness, we are shallow; if we look for cost effectiveness in our approaches, we are making misdirected judgements; if we adopt structures because they are measurable, our planning is awry. Whenever we prioritise anything above the child's personal development and the pursuit of their potential, we are minimizing our impact and limiting a child's future.

We live in a world where compassion is at a premium. The economic approaches of the 80s and 90s – despite the financial Armageddon which they presaged – are still seen as the norm; 'looking after number one' has become an approved lifestyle, and people are judged very much on their possessions, influence and background. It seems to me that the task of those who educate is to give young people the insight, confidence and understanding to be themselves, and to reject the blandishments of marketing men and social hucksters. This is especially true in an era when even a charitable approach is politicized. For example, the media make much of the work done for ex-servicemen by organisations such as "Help for Heroes" – they seldom make the point that, were the heroes to be treated as such by the political system, they would not need to be supported by a charity. As Dom Camara remarked:

"When I fed the hungry, you called me a saint; when I asked why they were hungry, you called me a Communist."

You may feel that such comments are caricatured and that every individual is different. Of course this is true, but we tend to characterize eras in a cartoon manner: the sixties are referred to in shorthand as 'peace and love', the fifties as 'grey', the nineties as 'greed' and so on. This doesn't mean that everybody was a hippy in the sixties, nobody had fun in the fifties, or that everybody was Gordon Gecko in the nineties – but it does reflect what might be called social trends, and illustrates how we think of the times to which we refer.

In the education system, the guidance structure does not have a superior claim to 'compassion'. Indeed, the point of an effective education system is that the whole edifice is based on compassion, or, as was often put in school terms: 'every teacher is a guidance teacher'. However, just as we discussed 'cartoon terms' for the different decades, so we can illustrate the prioritizing of compassion in our schools by examining the development and treatment of a guidance, pupil support, and welfare system over the past generation or so. An effective school has compassion in its ethos and that ethos will be driven by a committed leadership team and dedicated staff. The guidance team will be charged with putting into place the practicalities of that compassionate approach. The priority given to such an approach is an appropriate measure of the level of compassion in the system.

In the wake of the McCrone Report into Teaching in the 21st Century, I was present at a meeting of guidance teachers, where a high ranking education official promised change was coming and that there would no longer be any room for the old 'touchy feely approaches' of guidance and pupil support. In the ensuing furore in the room, the assembled staff were focussed on the perceived insult in his comment. What they missed was the deeper implications which lay behind his ill considered statement.

His model for the 'future' of guidance was that, in a much reduced senior management team, the responsibility for leading the guidance team in schools would be taken by someone from social work or community education, rather than a deputy head teacher. As one of the perceived strengths of guidance had been the fact that it was a structure staffed by teachers with classroom experience, knowledge of the pupils, and the respect of their colleagues in the school staff, this was a fairly startling change of direction. It may have been worth pursuing as a model of integration between schools and all the partner agencies who work with young people, had it not been so obvious that the real attraction was the halving of salary paid in a senior leadership position. As such, it betrayed either a lack of respect, a dearth of understanding, or an absence of sympathy for the support structures which had been in place for over thirty years. In the end, this particular development was quietly dropped.

Guidance, and its place in school structures, had not featured strongly in Professor McCrone's review of the teaching profession. Nobody knew if this was an oversight, an acceptance of its obvious and ongoing centrality, or a sign that its time was up. When an accountancy firm were appointed to 'job size' the new posts in school staffing structures, there was another heavy hint that expenditure rather than support was driving at least part of the agenda.

I am sure the job they did was professional and thorough – it was just that in places they betrayed a lack of understanding of how schools actually worked. One example would be in the 'weighting' given to the timetabling remit.

Anyone with first hand experience of working in a school would understand the crucial nature of the timetable. For pupils and staff, an effective timetable, which makes best use of school facilities and takes into account all manner of local needs, can drive a school towards success in all kinds of ways. Maths last period every day is not a good idea, Mondays have to be looked at carefully because of frequent holidays, spacing out of subjects through the day and through the week is vital, pupils are better equipped to tackle some subjects in the morning or in the afternoon, individual teachers should have a teaching load which is reasonable and reflects their strengths and those of the department.

In essence, then, creating an effective and workable timetable which meets the needs of the school is a little like fixing a Rubik's Cube – but involving people's daily lives and aspirations – as well as available resources and facilities. In my experience, those who timetabled most effectively spent a huge amount of time on it – anything up to three months - and there was much out of school time employed involving much requisitioning of kitchen tables and family social time.

However, the job sizers saw only a task where the timetabler didn't have 'direct responsibility' for a team of staff and therefore gave the activity very few points in their 'job sizing toolbox'. It must have made sense on paper – but in reality it missed the point that the timetabler, in his or her task, actually had responsibility for *all* the staff and pupils.

You could say this approach was a sign that education structures were moving away from a 'compassion based model' – where empathy and understanding were to the fore. It could perhaps be seen as the start of a trend which has ended up in the present day, where candidates for guidance posts are warned that they will fail their interviews if they come across as "too pastoral". In some places, "pastoral" has become an unacceptable approach to guidance and pupil support – it is now seen, in that familiar phrase, as being 'too touchy feely' – and not amenable enough to measurement, assessment, and cost analysis.

That being the case, maybe it is as well to review what 'touchy feely' meant during the years of guidance and to seek an explanation of why it actually was 'cost effective' and 'measurable' despite contemporary doubts.

We have already seen that guidance was originally constituted on the basis that 'every child should be aware that there was at least one teacher who knew them well' – an aspiration echoed in the quotation at the head of this section which refers to the burden caused by the knowledge that 'no-one cares or understands'.

All the research suggests that pupils who are happy and confident, who are liked by the teacher and who like the teacher, will perform to their best or even stretch that potential. As it is frequently put: pupils learn best from teachers whom they like. 'Liking', of course, should not be confused with 'popularity'. Again, surveys show that pupils 'like' teachers with good discipline, a sense of humour, and an ability to challenge and get the best out of their classes. As with parenting, having affection for pupils does not equate with giving them an easy time, or courting popularity, rather the reverse, in fact. Nevertheless, pupils possess a strong sense of whether a teacher cares about them, and part of a teacher's job is to care enough to make a difference.

The original guidance system recognized that all pupils start from a different position. As became obvious at the start of these reflections, for various reasons, school came easily to me, I felt comfortable there and wanted to connect with teachers – even in a very formal atmosphere. For many pupils, again for varying reasons, school is not an easy place – and for them, and even for those, like me, who take to school, there will be times and

213

situations where additional support and care is needed. The knowledge that there is someone in the school who is there for them, beyond simply teaching and learning, but as part of the education process, is invaluable.

There is a temptation, rather lazily, to equate the establishment of a guidance system with the aforementioned 'Sixties' ethos' of 'peace and love'. The truth, as it often tends to be, is rather more complex.

It is, perhaps, ironic in an age where much energy is devoted to putting in place systems to ensure self assessment and professional reflection, that, without any such formal structures, the teaching profession was far more reflective in the seventies and eighties. Staffing levels, and the prevailing ethos, facilitated discussion, innovation and flexibility. In all of these areas, success was achieved because it came from self motivation rather than external requirement. In 'industrial' terms, the route from idea through discussion, to development, and implementation was smoother, quicker, and more effective.

Any teacher who sought to see beyond the classroom desk to study the whole pupil would be aware of the importance of pupils' backgrounds, and day to day situations, in their learning or development. Similarly, this knowledge was bound to lead to a realisation that, for schools to be effective and successful, all elements of a child's life had to be considered.

However, when considering this need, it was also obvious that children and their families were entitled to their own privacy; help and support should be offered, but there had to be a way in which it could be accepted on the child or parent's own terms. The shadow of Miss Jean Brodie's 'interventions' in the lives of her pupils must have hung heavily over those who compiled the report into the establishment of guidance.

If the support offered were to be equitable, effective, and professional, it needed to be a nationally agreed system which operated in the best interests of child and family – hence the original "Orange Paper".

So, from this angle, we can see that the need for guidance grew out of a change in the way teachers perceived their pupils and the direction in which teaching and learning was developing.

However, if it was not the 'hippy culture' which led to these changes, where did they come from?

In essence, they came from the same stimuli as that 'hippy culture'.

My generation of teachers were the first to be born post war, the first, therefore, with no memory of war. We were the first generation to avoid National Service and to benefit fully from the National Health Service, the Butler Education Act, improved communications, and wider travel opportunities. Generally, the standard of living rose during our childhoods, or, at least, we never felt the cold shadow of rationing. The world looked different to my age group, we had less cause for pessimism and more cause for optimism, especially after Kennedy had faced down Kruschev over the Cuban missiles.

If our parents' lives had been formed by the aftermath of one war and the experience of another, ours had been shaped by the eventual benefits of post war progress.

For all these reasons, innovation and flexibility seemed more possible; new ways of looking at things were praised rather than frowned upon – and whilst this did lead to many obvious pop culture illustrations, in a deeper sense, social relationships and expectations had also changed.

Of course, despite Supermac's suggestion that many of us had 'never had it so good', such progress also brought uncertainty and a change of conditions for many. Faced with a society where there were more broken families, more women working, changing employment patterns, and raised expectations, not to mention less acceptance of traditional authority, and a burgeoning consumer boom, the demands on education, and the way it went about delivering them, were bound to change as well.

All of this fuelled the development of a guidance system, and, perhaps, highlighted the need for compassion to figure more strongly in education than previously. In a society where many are doing well, the fate of the others becomes more apparent. If a society is more prepared to listen, as well as hear, more questions are asked of it.

In responding to these conditions, perhaps the apotheosis of guidance and pupil support came with the development of Youth Strategy in the 1980s.

Initially, in the seventies, as mentioned, guidance was feeling its way as a newly unveiled structure. Pupils appreciated that there was now someone who 'knew them well' and started to make effective use of guidance support. That support could vary from school to school and region to region, but, as training courses were established, and staff gained experience, it became an important part of most schools' approach to their pupils and their welfare.

There was, perhaps, still an echo – from pupils and families – that the teacher could 'do anything' – a respect which attributed powers beyond reasonable expectation. Of course, brilliant teaching could facilitate great academic progress, but there were

216

situations outside the classroom far beyond a teacher's influence, and they were starting to impinge on teaching and learning and the pupil's school experience.

The Scottish Education Department's report on guidance: "More than feelings of concern" (1985) recognised that schools now had to provide more than a listening ear or a word of support, and, around the same time, the development of 'Youth Strategy' in what was Lothian Region, in east central Scotland, attempted to address the need for coordination of support for the most vulnerable young people. Both of these initiatives dovetailed well with the already successfully established Children's Hearing System, whereby children 'at risk' or who would formerly have appeared before a Juvenile Court, were helped to change direction and their families provided with additional supports.

Largely established by the redoubtable Lothian Councillor, Elisabeth McGinnis, and quickly duplicated in other areas, Youth Strategy operated on the grounds of 'early intervention'. It identified young people who were in danger of losing their place in their school, their community, or their family, and sought to put in place measures which would support them in maintaining their position in familiar surroundings and optimize their chances of success, raised self esteem, and maintaining established support systems.

It was driven by a monthly School Liaison Group (SLG) meeting. Pupils could be referred to this meeting by guidance staff, school management, social work, health agencies or, in some cases, at the request of parents, community education, police or Children's Panel – although in these latter cases, a pupil would generally have come to the Group's attention before such a referral was necessary.

The SLG was chaired by a member of the school's management team, and attended by guidance staff, Learning Support, and representatives from social work, educational health, attendance officer, school psychologist, community education, chaplain, outdoor education staff and any other relevant organizations such as local youth groups or support groups. There would be reports from all concerned with the pupil, including their class teachers.

The child's parents or carers would need to agree to the referral and could attend the discussion of their child, or, more generally, would attend a separate meeting with the directly concerned agencies. Guidance staff would have discussed with parents the reason for a referral, the nature of the group and what kind of support might be available. They would also receive a Minute of the discussion about their child and the decisions taken by way of support.

Some referrals came about because of extreme circumstances, but there were also a number of pupils discussed each month on a monitoring basis. Where the risk to their wellbeing seemed to have been removed, they would no longer be discussed, but, for as long as they appeared vulnerable the SLG would discuss their progress on a monthly basis, and review possible support strategies.

There were many advantages to such a system; indeed, it could even be seen as the original 'tracking and monitoring' model – though focused on emotional and social wellbeing which affected performance - rather than on test results and academic progress which tend to be the symptoms of such problems.

Pupils could be referred to the SLG for a wide range of difficulties – from attendance, to health, to behaviour, to home circumstances, to offending in the community.

Whatever the referral criteria, the system had three major strengths: it reflected an 'early intervention' model – the whole thrust being to maintain the pupil in school, family and community; its support decisions were based on pupil needs – and therefore more effectively targeted; and, in its original format, the people round the table largely had the authority to access support immediately, meaning staff, pupils and families could see rapid reaction to their concerns.

Perhaps most pertinently, regular meetings of all the agencies concerned with supporting young people enabled an atmosphere of trust and mutual respect to be built up – which was crucial to effective joint working procedures. Furthermore, pupil, family and school staff knew that there was concern for the pupil's wellbeing, and a body of professionals willing to discuss their progress on a regular basis. They knew, too, that the group would listen to everyone's concerns – including the pupil's – and seek an agreed way forward in support. It wasn't a punitive approach – but it could often be challenging, as in the case of an eight o'clock knock at the door from a youth worker to help an non-attender get into school on time, or participation in outdoor education programmes or local youth projects to raise self esteem.

The nature of the school's roll tended to influence referrals to its SLG, though there was a steady rise in numbers in most schools from a small number in S1 to more in S2 and 3 and a fall off in S4 – although these pupils tended to display the more intractable problems. Boys normally outweighed girls in terms of referrals, but often girls had more challenging difficulties. The majority of pupils would be discussed for no more than two terms, though this obviously varied according to the pupil and the concerns – and some pupils came and went from the agenda at various times during their school career – reflecting family or social crises or health problems, perhaps.

It is difficult to suggest a percentage of school population who benefited from an SLG referral as referrals depended not only on the pupil population, but also on the school's approach to making referrals and the staff and management's view of its efficacy. In a school of around a thousand with an 'average' profile, you might expect around thirty to forty pupils to be on the agenda for a meeting but perhaps only six or seven requiring detailed discussion or action – the rest would be monitored or considered for leaving the referrals' list. It was important that guidance staff consulted pupils as well as family about these meetings and that feedback was accurate, timely, and focused. As well as re-emphasis of targets and aims, pupils and families received positive feedback and congratulations when their progress meant they could be withdrawn from the SLG discussions. The whole Youth Strategy structure complemented effective guidance and pupil support practices.

One of the successes of the SLG system was that it focused on all pupils – a child might be referred for being quiet and withdrawn rather than poorly behaved or challenging. This ameliorated the concern often felt by guidance teachers that their time was disproportionately taken up by pupils who 'acted out', and that quieter, more conforming pupils tended to be overlooked. The range of pupils discussed at SLGs meant that they were less likely to be perceived as being for 'the bad pupils' – and this, in turn, configured a more realistic appreciation of the role of guidance for all pupils and not just those who were challenging.

Regular SLGs meant that professionals shared approaches and ideas and gained more mutual understanding. Many joint initiatives were set up – I was particularly involved in the promotion of groupwork in schools – where teachers would work with professionals from other agencies with small groups of pupils with shared needs – maybe to address anger, or attendance or family

220

difficulties. Self esteem groups for girls were especially needed and successful, as were anti-bullying initiatives and health focussed groups. These were early indications of the importance and effectiveness of peer education – emotionally, as well as academically. Outdoor education and work in the community also featured strongly – and for some pupils, and their families, it was their first exposure to agencies which was positive and child based rather than top down or unresponsive.

I have devoted this space to Youth Strategy because, as stated, in many ways it was the apotheosis of effective guidance and compassion in our schools – as evidenced by its spread from Lothian to other areas. I was overwhelmed by the response I received after giving a speech in Belfast – where professionals from all agencies saw it as a model of best practice of which they could only dream. Over the years, many young teachers attended SLGs as part of their own professional development, or because one of their pupils was being discussed. Invariably they were inspired by the support available to pupils and families – and by the willingness of the professionals to innovate and stretch resources in the interests of the child.

However, like guidance itself, perhaps its positive attributes contributed to its eventual slide down the list of priorities.

It occurred to me quite early on in the life of Youth Strategy that it might be quite discomforting for those in authority to receive demands for resources to support a pupil which were ratified by education, health, child psychology and social services. Such unanimity and shared expertise was difficult to ignore and led to frequent demands for additional resources, which, in turn, put pressure upon education and social services budgets.

In addition, because, quite rightly, the work of the SLG was needs led, according to the pupils it supported, the Youth Strategy approach was quite flexible, and could, and did, vary from school to school. This could be a strength – but also a weakness. Those who were not supportive of the initiative tended to focus on the areas where SLGs were poorly operated as a reason for changing or ending the project. It was another example of policy decisions being based on failures of practice rather than best practice.

That is not to say that those involved were blameless in the demise of Youth Strategy. Once again, in some places, a strength – that it was made effective by face to face liaison between professionals and a building of mutual trust and access – became a weakness. There were schools where there was little mutual trust between professionals, where the meetings were poorly run, and where, ultimately, various agencies decided that an afternoon spent at an ineffective SLG could be better spent elsewhere.

Sometimes this decline was accelerated by budget cuts which meant that it was increasingly more difficult to assign staff to this regular meeting, or where difficult choices had to be made. Where the SLG worked effectively and, as a tool of early intervention, actually reduced workload for agencies, the attendance of professionals tended to keep up, but in other cases, the effectiveness of the forum became weakened in the absence of those who could make resource decisions.

Equally, and still in the area of budget cuts, it was increasingly the case – as it would become for the Children's Panel – that all the detailed joint working which had gone into assessing a child's support needs would be stymied when it became obvious that the resource identified was not available and was unlikely to be so in the near future.

One of the bleakest moments of my whole career came after a Children's Panel Hearing. All concerned, including family and the child, had agreed that for various reasons, an immediate residential placement would be in the young person's best interests. Once the decision had been made, the Reporter made inquiries, only to discover that the nearest available residential place that weekend was in Portsmouth, some five hundred miles away. If you put in place systems of support which ask questions, then you have to be prepared to act on the answers you receive. As Youth Strategy started to uncover the range of needs of our young people and their families, the establishment discovered it was either unable or unwilling to find the resources to provide them.

I spent the best part of a year on a working party of experienced and committed professionals from across all the support agencies, reviewing SLGs and Youth Strategy, with a remit to detail how it could become more effective. Almost inevitably, we concluded that it needed to be heavily backed in its most successful areas – mutual support, access to resources, and adequate staffing to meet pupils' needs. An additional conclusion was that its work should be extended to primary school level – partly in keeping with its motive of early intervention, but also to increase the amount of 'family work' that was done – so that families needing support would receive a continuum of support throughout a child's school days. Experience told us that, in areas such as attendance and behaviour, the earlier the child received support the more effective it was. When the opposite was true, and patterns were established by older siblings, there was a high incidence of their younger brothers and sisters replicating their behaviour when they reached school age. Long term, positive relationships with school and agencies tended to be more effective and be more useful to parents and carers – another example of the wisdom of establishing mutual trust and respect, and building support on that basis.

In the end, as far as I could tell, the report disappeared. I don't think that anyone argued with its conclusions; it was the cost implication which scuppered it. As I've said, an effective care system in schools, working in partnership with other support agencies, will tend to ask questions which have expensive answers. Governments have a tendency to use education as a headline grabbing area, frequently announcing changes in structure, or examinations, providing 'proof' that they care about 'our children's futures'. They also know that the voters' interest in education tends to wane when their own children have left the system and that many of the most influential people choose to pay for their family's education and are relatively untouched by state school configurations.

In truth, supporting all children equally and giving all the same chances in education is only partially the responsibility of teachers. They can offer hope, encouragement, and the materials to offset disadvantage to a degree, but, unless there is the will to address inequality in society generally, the task of teachers will be massive – and will come at a high price. It seems to be a price that governments are increasingly unwilling or unable to pay.

It has also to be said that a high standard of education and support is often listed as an aspiration amongst voters and tax payers, but there is less enthusiasm for the higher taxes to pay for it – and very few politicians brave enough to propose such a measure. In other words, people want schools to be able to challenge inequality effectively, but are perhaps not so willing to fund that work. Would that for all the people who criticize the young, there would be as many prepared to support them into a better future.

The recent announcement by the Scottish Government that they were looking to provide a named 'safeguarder' for every child in Scotland was met with a predictably mixed response.

Whilst some leaders of child support agencies reacted positively, there were other accusations in the media that this was 'the nanny state', an 'invasion of privacy' or 'unwarranted expense and intervention'.

Clearly, if mismanaged, this could be a negative development – but, again, it was interesting to note how much of the reaction was based on a worst case scenario – and how many of the positive reactions came from those with experience in supporting the most vulnerable.

I have already mentioned that, in my career, it was very often the families whose children had most need of support who were least trusting of the agencies tasked with providing it. Sometimes this was based on their own experiences as children, or, on occasion, as a reaction to many hard fought battles which had been necessary to access support which was actually their entitlement. Rightly or wrongly, they felt, strongly in many cases, that the system operated without compassion. It had rules, regulations, criteria and processes – but when it came to empathy or feeling for the disadvantaged, it was found wanting.

The knowledge that there was someone, appointed by authority, whose task was to support families, and help them flourish, would have been enormously helpful to many of these parents. Again, if correctly implemented, the lifelong provision of such a person – in good times and in bad – rather than as a result of some major family crisis, could be extremely helpful to those in need of such support and willing to accept it. It could, in fact, be seen as a token of a compassionate society – where the aim is to help each other rather than the survival of the fittest, and the propensity is to work together, rather than seek 'scapegoats and shirkers'.

Compassion is not an overused word these days; indeed, you are most likely to find it used as part of the phrase 'compassion fatigue' – as if there comes a point when it is simply too tiring to care. I strongly believe that this is not an option for those involved in working with young people – and that they should be supported in their compassionate approach by those who lead them, resource them, and facilitate their careers.

I came across very few teachers in my career who were not compassionate – though there were many different ways of that compassion being shown. Indeed, there were more than a few staff who worked quite hard at presenting a gruff exterior and who would criticize the 'touchy feely' approach, who would also, privately, exhibit huge concern and compassion for their most vulnerable pupils. I have no wish to be critical of those unable to have compassion for their pupils, and indeed their families, but I do question if teaching is the right job for them.

More than anything, I would want to emphasise that compassion is not weakness, nor does it detract from the 'business' of getting examination results. Perhaps the biggest error in the development of education policy in the past decade has been the prioritising of examination results and academic progress over pastoral care – almost as if there had to be an 'either/or' decision. Academic success and pupils reaching their potential in the classroom is an obvious target for every school – nobody would deny that. However, compassion demands that we examine how that is best achieved, and, in so doing, to analyse those elements in a child's life – in and out of school - which can hinder this progress or prevent success. Continual testing or monitoring does not of itself lead to better results. An awareness of failure does not necessarily motivate the changes necessary for success – indeed it is far more likely to demoralize. What needs to be addressed are not the unacceptable results, but the reasons for the low level of achievement or attainment.

In my school days, failure to make progress academically was largely put down to 'laziness' or 'lack of ability'. With the hindsight of a lifetime of teaching, I do wonder how teachers felt they could remedy this – which was, indeed, their job – other than to find a way of stopping the 'laziness'. I have made it clear that I understand my own teachers' approaches as being in the context of the times they lived in and the expectations which society had of them. There is no criticism of their approaches, just a confusion about how they must have viewed their job, and the difficulty of approaching it from such a narrow angle.

The idea of 'educating the whole child' has become so familiar that it has become a little meaningless. However, when analysed, it reflects the need to take into account all of the factors which affect a young person's capacity to develop and grow through the education system. We no longer believe we can 'scare' or 'discipline' a young person into learning, but we have become far wiser in our understanding of the need to equip pupils for self discipline and self motivation, to help them understand how learning works, and the benefits they can gain from it.

'Compassion' comes into this in its ability to place each child's situation in context. We need to listen to what children tell us about the difficulties they face in 'buying into' the positive vision they are given in school.

What if their experience of adults is that they promise much but always let you down? What if they don't have a single role model of employment, success, or stability in their extended family, or in previous generations? What if they have a physical or mental impairment which has meant fighting harder and against additional difficulties to keep up with others of their own age? What if, for some reason, they feel separated from the routes to success and self esteem that they see their peers follow? What if their family background, or previous school experience, has been negative and given them a disinclination to trust, or follow expectations? What if their only means of signifying their existence is to be dissident, recalcitrant, even violent, or withdrawn?

What most teachers generally accept, but what education systems must strive to accommodate, is that schools are for pupils - and that the education structure must recognize their individual needs, the changing contexts of the times, and the flexibility needed to ensure that the whole range of pupils – from the most motivated and talented to the most challenged and overwhelmed – meet an experience in school which is founded on the need to educate them, to encourage their personal development, and to enable them to reach – or even surpass – their potential.

For the most vulnerable pupils, placing emphasis on 'fitting in' or 'being like the others' is a kind of emotional torture. I found very few pupils over the years who found happiness in misbehaviour or failure in school. If we are expecting pupils to conform – and, clearly, if a place of learning is to function successfully there has to be cooperation and acceptance of expectations – we must address their understanding of why that conformity is necessary, but also support them in making that step, by giving them an experience which they can see is beneficial to their development and their future. We should not be looking for all pupils 'to be the same' nor for blind acceptance of everything we say. The most effective education encourages pupils to question and challenge – but to do so from an informed and confident position – rather than as a sign of inferiority or marginalisation.

To reach that position, pupils need to be proud of their school – and it must be obvious to them that the school supports them and wants the best for them. This 'feeling' comes from a strong, positive and supportive ethos – which, in reality, lives in the day to day contact between its staff and all its pupils – in and out of the
228

classroom. The willingness to listen, to make time for each pupil, to understand their fears or concerns, to note their successes – however limited - and to encourage in the face of disappointment, to fulfil commitments, to accept mistakes, to value the input of all members of the community – pupils, families and staff – all of these elements are signs of a compassionate school.

Compassion is a hard and often expensive option. It means not looking away, it means challenging individuals, traditions, and expectations. It can make you unpopular with the decision makers and you can experience rejection from pupils, colleagues and families who may not understand or agree with your approach. There are easier and certainly cheaper ways of approaching education – but they tend to be less successful. There are those who will tell you that a school's job is to qualify pupils for employment and that any widening of that remit is doomed to expensive failure. There are echoes there of the sixties – and a utilitarian system theoretically shaped to fit all pupils.

Pupils are individuals – and, as I repeatedly stated to them, each one is unique and valuable. What they can contribute to the world in their lifetime is vastly beyond what can be measured in their employment or qualifications. Success and happiness comes from being at peace with oneself – whether this leads to high earning careers based on examinations passed, or the contentment of self knowledge.

Perhaps the best lesson we can deliver to them as teachers concerns their own self awareness of the effect they have on those around them, and how they can contribute to a better life for all. And the best way in which we can deliver that lesson is by being role models for that approach – they should look back on their schools and teachers as being the gatekeepers for the road to an assured and happy future. They should remember us as caring and listening and seeking to understand. They should be given the opportunity to learn that each individual is beyond value, and that we each possess the ability to make others feel happy and valued. Gaining the superficial world but losing the spirit and soul should not be on the agenda. Young people need to be nurtured and nourished in knowledge and compassion. Education is far beyond the delivery of facts and the testing of information. Knowledge without understanding is arid, qualifications gained without perspective are pointless. As teachers we work with humanity; it's a huge responsibility.

The 'Compassionate approach' also tends to be downplayed because it is hard to 'measure its effectiveness'. Certainly, one measurement of a school's 'success' would lie in its examination results – and there are authorities and politicians for whom the scrutiny of these results is the major means of judging the education system. As I've said, if we must have statistical judgments, 'Value added' numbers – how much better are the results than the predictions based on pupil intake ability originally in S1 – is a more refined manner of measurement – but still lacks sophistication in examining a school's effect – especially in the area of guidance.

If we look at the areas upon which guidance impacts, we can see that they may all contribute to raising of achievement in the field of examination results, literacy, and numeracy – but are they not about much more than that?

Self esteem, self value, attendance, punctuality, self discipline, acceptable behaviour, concentration, focus, relationships, maturity, planning, self awareness, team building skills, self reliance, responsibility, reflection, judgment, perception, feeling safe, ready to challenge, confidence, inner strength, organization, determination, optimism, care for others, respect for self and others, understanding of other points of view, patience, modesty, commitment – all of these were aims for guidance staff, comments made on reports, encouragements given to young people, successes marked by achievement and attainment.

The problem is: in a world where there seems to be a need for 'toolboxes' to ascertain progress and targets met, how do you assess these accomplishments? Perhaps even more importantly, *when* do you assess them? Given current trends in education management, it is worrying for the future of guidance that much of its most effective work is neither immediately obvious nor easily measured. I have had many former pupils tell me that they themselves were not even aware of the benefit of the supports they received at school until their twenties, their thirties, or forties – and the impact has been such that they have sought out their teachers – guidance and others – to offer a belated thanks.

We no longer think of pupils, in Dickens' memorable phrase, as "little vessels to be filled to the brim with facts". We understand the complexities of teaching and learning far more completely than before, and we accept that children learn in different ways and at different stages in their development – whether in primary, secondary, third level, or post education phases of their lives. We acknowledge a changing world with ever more challenges for the young, and, for many, less stability and consistency in their backgrounds. We know that a child's state of mind and his readiness for learning is affected by every part of his life – and that most of that is outwith the classroom. The right of a child to be heard, to be listened to, to be given basic understanding and support is enshrined in law.

Nobody engaged in education would disagree with that last paragraph – it is self evident; and anyone who has worked in a school with a committed and professional guidance team would agree that the ethos which supports pupils in coping with all of the above is driven by the actions and work of that guidance team.

Theirs is likely to be the first office occupied in the morning and the last vacated at night; they are the ones to whom other teachers turn when a child becomes upset, withdrawn, aggressive, argumentative, depressed, or underachieving. They are on the receiving end of calls and emails and letters and visits from distressed, angry, frustrated, worried, frightened, bewildered and lost parents and carers. They are the bearers of the worst news and the best news to all parts of the school community. When sadness strikes, they pick up the pieces, when innovation is planned, they very often make it possible, when systems fail, it is often the guidance team who cope with the fall out – in every sense.

They can be unpopular with management, as they point out the need for better resources for support, or with colleagues, when they have to dig them out of the consequences of an ill considered or unprofessional interaction with a pupil. They may get little recognition from their pupils as they challenge, harrie, hustle and support them through six years of education, or, sometimes, they receive the gratitude and affection of all parts of the school community when their dedication and commitment is recognized, and their effect is acknowledged.

One thing is certain: few schools with ineffective guidance teams reach their potential as places of teaching and learning; and behind any positive ethos geared for success for pupils, and staff, in personal development and academic success, you will find a dynamic and professional guidance system – working in cooperation with, and with the full support of, the school management.

Of course, none of this is to claim that all guidance teams are highly effective. High level support demands a lot of all involved, not least the understanding and acknowledgement of those with whom it operates – pupils, colleagues, school staff in general and local authority structures. There were teams which failed because of poor commitment, ineffective leadership, lack of support for guidance as a priority in school, and the appointment of the wrong people to the wrong posts. In latter years, there was a tendency amongst the 'reformers' of education to point to ineffective guidance structures as a reason for changing the whole approach. Would that they had looked at the most effective teams and used them as a template!

It was only when I joined school leadership that I fully appreciated the role of management in promoting a child centred, guidance approach. I had been lucky in the support I had received as a young guidance teacher, but perhaps I had assumed that was the norm. As an assistant and then deputy head, I was fortunate, again, to work with headteachers who largely appreciated the crucial nature of the guidance role – either because they had themselves been guidance teachers or because they had worked in schools where the impact of strong guidance approaches was self evident. It was not until very late in my career – and then due mostly to trends outside the school – that I began to feel it was necessary to fight for the role of guidance in school. Until then, it had been obvious and respected.

So what changed?

A general answer to that would be that society's self image and priorities shifted in the lifetime of my career. My lifespan started post war, shortly after the establishment of the National Health Service. It was an era where support for each other and the 'national wellbeing' was a given in public and political life – or at least it was the expected approach in any declarations of philosophy, irrespective of any private motivations. The manifestos of both major UK political parties post war – though far more differentiated than those of today – were underpinned by a sense of the public good, of what would be beneficial to the majority.

Towards the end of the century, profit, private enterprise, the talents of entrepreneurship came to be promoted for their own sake, rather than for what they could contribute to the good of all. The idea of public 'ownership' – either philosophically or economically – became discredited; competition and private enterprise came to be widely accepted as the 'modern' way of doing things. The great national manufacturing industries disappeared – and with them the skills of trades and the pride in accomplishment, and the UK became a state where service industries dominated and the financial sector became the driver of the economy. Taken from a distance, the pitfalls of such a direction, the inevitability of a housing bubble and an economic collapse, seem obvious. In the throes of consumerism, house ownership, and share issues, people chose not to reflect – or failed to do so.

What was left was a place where large areas of employment became 'more flexible' – that is: part time, transitory, or at the whim of overseas investors. Skills training for apprenticeships and lifelong careers was sidelined, and many communities, robbed of their raison d'être
    in mines, mills, heavy industry or technology suffered grievously from a lack of focus or purpose.

The area where I taught for the second half of my career, West Lothian, offers a meaningful illustration of the reality of these shifts in society, and its expectations.

Originally based on shale and coal mining, as well as agriculture and milling, by mid twentieth century, the area was suffering from the erosion of these areas of employment. Government grants enticed companies like British Leyland, Plessey and Lee Jeans to set up in the area – but when the support ran out, or cheaper options became available elsewhere, these factories closed down.

In conjunction with the development of Livingston New Town, the next wave of development came with the optimistically named 'Silicon Glen' – and the area did well to capitalize by attracting a range of high technology outfits – again with government grants and support.

Finally, as the computer industry's needs changed and with cheaper labour available in the far east, these companies too were 'cleared from the Glen'.

The latest 're-generation', in keeping with the times, has been a focus on the consumer market and low paid, part time, retail jobs in a huge 'outlet Mall' in Livingston itself. The 'New Town' has become the centre of the county, the established communities in Bathgate, Whitburn and Broxburn, as well as Linlithgow, struggle to reinvent themselves as commuter towns providing housing, some of which is significantly less expensive than that available in Edinburgh.

This is by no means a story confined to West Lothian or even Scotland, but it is worth reflecting on its impact on education locally.

When I first arrived in West Lothian I was struck by a number of things which clearly delineated it from its Capital neighbour over the county border.

There was a strong and enduring respect for education and what it could provide – which led to a lingering respect for teachers – many of whom had taught current pupils' parents or been at school with them.

Like the strong and proud tradition of brass band music, I took this to be inherited from the proud mining communities – the towns which still had a strong sense of self worth and civic pride, even in the early nineties.

Despite the commitment to education, there was a reluctance for young people to aspire to a university education, based, I suspected, on a lack of tradition, but also on the attraction of, and need for, a steady income as soon as possible.

How did all this impact on education locally?

Two examples will illustrate the results of history and expectation.

When a major overseas computer company set up in the area, it was with great hopes in the local employment pool. After five years, they admitted they were struggling. They had no problem attracting school leaver level applications to work on the production line, but were facing a dearth of graduate recruits. We had to explain to them that the pay levels being offered to school leavers were so attractive that many who were qualified for university courses chose to leave school and go to work for them directly rather than taking a degree and applying later on. It was a reflection in action of the lack of university tradition, and the urge to earn money while it was available.

I have never subscribed to the concept that 'the more people who go to university the better'. While I understand that a rise in university entrance provides handy figures for politicians to announce, I would suggest that it is far more important that young people access the type of third level education which is most appropriate for their skills, aspirations and abilities. By the same token, I have continually been angered by the equally obtuse idea that university should be for the middle classes, and I have worked determinedly to open up access to all who aspire to a degree course or who would benefit from such a step. I have already mentioned

236

that viewing degree courses as merely 'qualifications for work' is limiting of both academics and students, and that attendance at university should be a part of personal and academic development rather than simply a job qualification. That is surely how we produce thinkers, innovators and visionaries?

Nevertheless, as I worked to promote the idea of university in this sense to more of our pupils, I was aware that I was working against both history and currently accepted approaches. In keeping with the trends, and above local statistics, we did manage to more than triple our university entrants in my time as depute, but many were convinced that they should take employment related degrees rather than other options – a decision which seems mistaken given the current employment situation.

In the next wave of regeneration, we also discovered difficulties which impacted on education. The huge expansion of the neighbourhood's retail outlet was obviously good news for local employment, albeit in a somewhat limited manner. However, after some years of operation and with a further huge extension of the facility imminent, we were approached by its management with a particular concern.

The Centre was the main local employment opportunity for young people. With hundreds of retail jobs available, the majority of our senior pupils had a part time job there. Indeed, some worked on Thursday evenings and all day Saturday and Sunday, as well as five days a week during holiday periods. Whilst there had been a major shift in part time youth employment since my own schooldays, the availability of such work locally could cause us problems. In the run up to Christmas, for instance, many firms issued an ultimatum to pupil workers - work every evening or be sacked. The build up to Christmas was, of course, also the build up to Prelim examinations. In addition, pupils who attended after school study classes or sports clubs came under pressure, and weekend school activities became impossible for those who were fully committed to their part time employment.

It was a difficult situation for the school. We were aware that, in some families, the additional wages brought in by such employment made the difference between making ends meet and not. We also knew that there were students who worked merely to fund clubbing and their own car, or indeed because it gave them an alternative social life. The responsibility and expectations of work, and the early appreciation of handling money are, of course, excellent reasons for part time work amongst teenagers. Our concerns were trying to recommend a balance between school and work, study and leisure. We had students who couldn't meet assignment deadlines because they had no time or were too tired from working to complete the schoolwork. Disappointing test results were often attributed to lack of revision time, and it was hard for staff and parents who had committed much time and effort into supporting a pupil in sport, music or other endeavours to be told that they would be withdrawing from an event because 'they had to work that day'.

However, as the Centre management told us, this had also backfired on their own aspirations. In a survey, they had discovered that, while over 90% of their shop floor workers were local, more than 85% of their management staff were from outside the area. When they examined this in more detail, they found the following. The overwhelming number of their workers had been introduced to retail, and the Centre, through 'Thursday evening school jobs.' They saw retail merely as a way of earning 'pocket money' rather than a career. With expansion and development, new outlets were opening all the time, and each time there was a new opening, young people would apply to work in the new shop for a 'change of scene'. From coffee shop, to designer clothes outlet, to computer games, to sportswear: trends oscillated from brand to brand and product to product, and so did the attractiveness of

238

selling them. As a result, the Centre was finding that local employees, rather than establishing loyalty and experience with one particular firm, long into their twenties could be treating employment as they had when at school and flitting from job to job every few months. The pool of experience and commitment, which the various shops generally relied upon to find their management recruits, was absent amongst local candidates.

Together with the companies, we established and later had verified as a national qualification, a course entitled 'Retail Academy' – which sought to work with the various retail firms in providing focussed training for a retail career – from work experience, through modules on health and safety, marketing, customer relations, and design. The idea was to try and help young folk with an ambition to work in retail to see it as a career leading to management and administration opportunities, rather than as a part time means of earning cash.

It was a comment on the times that such an approach was necessary – but at least we were listening to the needs of both pupils and local community and trying to meet them.

Both of these exemplars reflect the changes that came about during my career as a teacher – especially in the last two decades , and how societal changes, as they must do, impacted on the demands made on education.

In broad terms, many certainties had vanished, structures had crumbled and the need for flexibility and self confidence in decision making was ever more paramount.

Thus the need for compassion in education; thus the need for effective pastoral guidance systems.

I worked with many who were whole heartedly in favour of a pastoral guidance system, with some who saw its benefits but were unsure how it could be economically retained or statistically defended, and with some who were so scared of the questions it asked and the challenges it provided, that they were happier to limit support to monitoring and tracking academic progress rather than investigate the causes behind failure or disillusionment.

As a head of guidance, the frustration came from the fact that, when it came down to an individual pupil's immediate needs, I can hardly recall a single colleague who would not have wanted to provide that pastoral support. The challenge was to present to the authorities, and those who set the priorities, that, unless your system was pastorally based – with all the expense and resources which that entailed – it became increasingly more difficult to provide that level of support to individuals, or to work under the early intervention model which had such beneficial effects. These effects, of course, impacted not just on those being openly supported by guidance staff and partner agencies, but on the whole school community, which was spared the hiatus of disaffected, disruptive, and under supported pupils in the classroom and around the campus. Guidance has never been just for 'the bad kids' – it has always been for all; at its most effective it supports not just pupils – but teachers and families as well; if it helps young people adjust to the needs of teaching and learning, then it is a major component of improvement planning and raising attainment and achievement.

That being the case, and considering the challenges which have developed over the past forty years, I find myself asking why we have changed from each guidance teacher being responsible for sixty pupils, to a caseload of around 250, and a fixation with tracking and monitoring. Is this generation of pupils less deserving of our support? Have we given up on the link between disadvantage and poor education? Are the lessons of successful guidance systems to be ignored? Is everything to be reduced to measurable cost effectiveness? Are we happy in a world where 'pastoral' is the word which should not be uttered?

I return to the original quotation. No child should leave school with the burden of never having been heard or understood. Every child should find it obvious in his schooling that someone really cares, and should know that that person is fully supported by the system.

SO WHAT WAS ALL THAT ABOUT?

"Men's memoirs are about answers; women's memoirs are about questions....women want to connect with others here and now; they couldn't care less about legacy"

Isabel Allende

I hadn't seen Isabel Allende's take on 'memoirs' when I started writing, but having digested her views, I hope that I have written something which takes in both gender approaches. I have certainly wanted to ask questions – about what I thought I was doing and why; and how effective were the various systems and structures in which I worked; but I hope that any 'answers' I have provided are clearly set within my own perspective – and reflect a view that, in this most human of occupations, opinions and solutions will be very much based on personal experience, as well as individual goals and philosophies.

Perhaps a better quotation would be that of George Meredith, who said:
"Memoirs are the backstairs of history"

and a driving motivation behind these reflections was the hope that, by telling part of my own story, I could evoke something of the joy, as well as the hard work, that is to be found when one works in education. So many people only experience education as pupils and parents that I felt it useful to give a 'backstairs' glimpse of what teachers seek to achieve and how they go about doing that.

As I am writing these words, the morning newspapers and news outlets are leading on the appalling story of Spanish and RE teacher, Ann Maguire, stabbed to death at Corpus Christi College in Leeds. Thankfully such tragedy is rare in our classrooms, but, as with the deaths of Philip Lawrence in London and Gwen Mayor in Dunblane, apart from the shock, horror and sympathy, there is a common thread to media and public reaction.

245

The phrases used by pupils, staff, and community to describe Ann Maguire have a familiar ring to them. She would "go the extra mile to support you", was seen as "the heart of the school", she was "the school's mother", "gave her life to the school and the pupils" "took us skiing", "wrote all our references". She was only in school on her day off to give her language students extra revision support when she was murdered.

Television news reporters, stationed, as is the custom, outside the school gates, reported these words with a patent tone of surprise. They seemed to be suggesting that this teacher was a unique example of care, concern and commitment. From all accounts, Philip Lawrence, Gwen Mayor and Ann Maguire were all models of excellent, committed teaching, and, like pupils, every teacher is unique, precious and to be valued. However, it is not to demean any of these sadly familiar names to state that such teachers are found in every school in the land. In fact, I would be brave enough to say that, certainly in my lifetime experience, they represent the majority of teachers rather than rare beacons of high level involvement. And it annoys me that the media often misses that point. The tragedy of these deaths is that they were teachers doing a difficult job with great commitment and huge care for their pupils. We see the same, all too frequently, when we receive tales of heroism amongst staff at such unfortunately recognisable localities as Sandy Hook and Columbine. It is what teachers do.

Like most teachers, I have wept many tears in the course of my job – most of joy, but some of sadness, despair or frustration. I have felt guilty as a manager when I have seen the level of concern, involvement, and determination shown by many teachers in support of individual pupils or classes, often to their own personal detriment. I have tried to comfort teachers, and parents, who have been let down by pupils, families, colleagues or school management, and I have marvelled at the ability of teachers to show respect, affection and focus in dealing with the most damaged, difficult, challenging or tragic pupils, families or situations. Most of all I have celebrated the humanity of the profession – its unquenchable desire to care, and its commitment to pupils and families.

The textbooks will tell you of the importance of 'professional detachment' – and, certainly, the most basic respect that we owe to pupils, families and colleagues is that we approach the job with the highest of personal and professional standards. However, that is not a substitute for human connection or interaction. Professional teachers know there are limits to how involved they can become in pupils' lives; they also know there is a limit to how detached you can remain whilst having an effective impact on the young person's development and potential. Perhaps the important point is that our teaching must reflect our personality. In all our relationships – personal and professional – we reflect our own natural approaches; we exhibit friendship, trust, and respect in differing ways, our styles are individual, and that diversity is what makes social interconnection so fascinating.

Were I to list the most effective, the most caring, the most committed, or the most memorable colleagues with whom I have worked, they would all have different personality traits; they would be linked by their commitment to, and concern for, the young people. Some were very relaxed with pupils, others were deliberately formal; some felt able to share an amount of personal information with classes, others were resolutely private; some could be effusive in their dealings with pupils, others were much more reserved. The success of their teaching, the impact of their connection, was that pupils were able to sense that they wanted the best for all whom they taught, that they cared, and that they meant it. It wasn't about popularity or 'giving in' to pupils – it was about a determination to give pupils their best and a commitment to honesty in the way they taught and encouraged.

The most popular were not always the best, and the best were not always the most popular. Pupils were quite able to state: "I really like Mr X – but he's not a good teacher," – or "Miss X is very strict and I don't really get on with her – but she's really good at her job." It may well be true that 'pupils learn best from teachers whom they like, but, as in all relationships, professional or personal, it takes all sorts, and it needs all sorts. Diversity is an important key in all areas of teaching and learning, as are wisdom, integrity, compassion and justice!

So, as I look back over a life in education, what do I see?

It has to be said that there is a satisfaction over being able to view that involvement in a complete sense. I don't mean a smugness, but an understanding that I can now look at a whole experience in its entirety, rather than one which is ongoing with more to come. Some two years after retirement, I feel as if I have a perspective on those years, and perhaps a better or clearer understanding of what I thought I was doing!

I wonder, initially, what was my motivation – and how was it encouraged by family and schooling?

Brought up by a widow and with living and ancestral male role models who were, by and large, 'gentle' men, it is perhaps no surprise that I didn't develop into a 'macho male'. My Faith being an integral part of who I was also taught me to be positive about others and accepting of misfortune. Finally, the zeitgist of the sixties – real or manufactured – promoted a sense of the need to 'change the world' and make it 'a better place'.

All of this, in retrospect, would have driven me towards a career in education – the parts all fit, and, undoubtedly, a lack of drive or competitiveness, certainly in any aggressive sense, would not have fitted me well to industry or commerce.

248

However, there was also the lack of confidence, even in areas where I would now claim some ability, like communication, which didn't obviously fit me to teaching, and I can state without any hesitation that I had no idea of 'changing the world' or making it 'a better place', when I applied to become a teacher. What I like to think became a 'vocation', started off as something which I thought I might be able to do, in a setting with which I was already familiar.

Truth to tell, I lacked the perspective or experience to recognise fully the impact that teachers could have on their pupils. The teachers who inspired me at school affected me more through *what* they did than *who* they were, and I had no idea that I would remember them so clearly for the rest of my life.

As I pointed out earlier, the atmosphere and ethos when I was at school hardly contributed to seeing teachers as heroes or role models; most of them lacked the obvious humanity or personality to inspire emulation. You might wonder about doing their job, but with the few exceptions I mentioned, you wouldn't want to 'be' them. I do read of folk who were encouraged to become teachers because of an inspirational figure in their school, but they generally seem to be of a later generation than mine, and it certainly wasn't the case for me, though, as I mentioned, Ernie Spencer certainly gave me cause to reflect.

However, it is now that the perspective provided by reflecting and writing these memoirs lends additional insight, hopefully.

Like many people, my schooldays have provided me with a fund of anecdotes – some funny, some startling. They have been frequently, probably far too frequently, shared with family and friends – particularly those 'who were there', and they exist as a backdrop to my adult life. However, I suspect that the writing of these memories has been the first time I have deliberately tried to

249

analyse my schooling and its impact on the rest of my life. I perhaps thought that, when I had the opportunity to examine it in such a way, some of the enigma surrounding my reactions to my education would be removed, and I would achieve some kind of clarity. How could I simultaneously 'love' school and have been in an almost constant state of fear? Why would I want to become a teacher when the evidence I had seen suggested that it was a job requiring a kind of toughness and confidence to which I would not want to aspire? And why am I still, despite everything, and in contrast to most of my school friends, proud of the school I attended and the education I received?

However, I have found no clarity, but, as I am totally convinced of the impact of schooling on the rest of one's life, it falls to me to try and make sense of what I have discovered - especially in relation to my later career and my thoughts on teaching.

Some of school's effects – as is the case with every pupil – were personal to me. As a widow's only child, having lost my father at the age of five, having switched countries, and having moved schools regularly, I obviously found, in my final ten years of schooling, a structure, certainty, predictability and community, which filled in areas which may have been riddled with uncertainty, invisibility, or loneliness. As a cross country runner or cricketer or choir member, I had an identity; as one of the lads who got the train to and from Southport, I had a sense of belonging – a commuter gang, if you like. That I am still in touch with most of the lads off that train tells its own story. It seems that, even when some of the certainty was provided by the knowledge you *would* be belted or treated unjustly, the security given by the organization was important to me. This would probably be reflected in my being a 'company man' in the schools in which I taught, always proud of them, keen to promote them, wanting them to be the best. I instinctively knew that such an ethos could prove valuable to the most vulnerable pupils.

I was also brought up to be a conformist and thus the security of high expectations and discipline and a very prescribed way of life at school probably comforted me, despite some glaring injustices.

At the time, and even now, there is a high degree of marketing 'bull' about the sixties and revolution. Yes – like my friends, I was a radical – on Viet Nam, the Six Counties, Civil Rights, the Paris Riots, the housing crisis – but all these were 'somewhere else'. In my own life, I did my homework, kept the school rules, more or less, had a sensible, if appalling, hairstyle, wore conservative, if appalling, clothes, and never tried drugs. It wasn't in my nature to break the rules big time. If ever I had an underage drink, even memorably on the night before my eighteenth birthday, the whole experience was undermined by an overwhelming fear that I would be caught – 'doing something wrong'.

Though I became more outspokenly 'agin the government' as an adult and have adopted a whole raft of unpopular or minority beliefs, I am still more likely to negotiate my way round a difficulty than seek open conflict. Of all the descriptions that folk have laid on me, 'troublemaker' is one I have yet to hear, although, to my delight, an isometric test once summed me up thus: "the kind of person who would paint double yellow lines on the road so he could park on them."

I don't think I was particularly alone in being like this in my youth, and you could put it down to upbringing, lack of confidence, or downright cowardice – whichever description you choose. It meant that much of my schooling fitted in with my willingness to conform and acceptance of consensus. The enigma, from a modern day stance, remains that the school chose not to reward those of us who conformed but rather chose to highlight those who failed to do so. Maybe they were secretly hoping to raise a generation of rebels!

It seems to me that I appreciated the security which school life provided for me but, in my more mature approach, as a teacher, I sought to provide that security rather as a means to encourage young people to take risks rather than as a means of repression. I hope that was the best of both worlds; a rather parental approach – you can go for it, but if it's a mistake, we'll still be here for you. In the words of Apollinaire:

> *"Come to the edge!"*
> *"We may fall!"*
> *"Come to the edge"*
> *"It's too high!"*
> *"Come to the edge!"*
> *So they came to the edge*
> *And he pushed them –*
> *And they flew!"*

In a more negative sense, I suspect that, bizarrely, I also flourished at school because of a lack of real choice.

The task of teachers, and parents, is more difficult these days, because, as a result of gaining rights and responsibilities, young people have also been opened up to far more elements of choice in their lives.

I pointed out that, at school, we weren't encouraged to self assess or reflect. We were told to make decisions with minimal support and then we tended to live or die, as it were, by those decisions. It may have been science or arts, rugby or cross country, cello or viola. Careers were scarcely mentioned and I never embarked, as a teacher myself, on the detailed preparation for university application, without marvelling at the complete lack of input from my own school at that crucial point. We were expected to go to university, but, certainly as far as I was concerned, where we went, and why we went there, was completely up to the pupil with little or no advice from the school.

I chose Edinburgh University because it was my home town and I wanted to return there, then I chose Queen's Belfast and New University of Ulster because I loved Ireland, St Andrew's followed because it was in Scotland, and then, because I had to apply to two more, I think I put Birmingham because I'd heard it was 'good for English' and Exeter because, if I was to be interviewed, I thought that would make for a nice visit. Even at this distance that's a terrifying thought process which nobody thought to question or examine. I only really was interested in going to Edinburgh, and, luckily, that was the only offer I got. Had I been advising a pupil nowadays, with the results I already had and the predictions I carried, I would have been suggesting aiming a little lower. All's well that ends well, I suppose, and, in this case, lack of choice and guidance probably acted in my favour – but it's not an approach I ever wanted to follow as a teacher myself. Another example of my own experience prompting me towards an entirely opposite approach when I found myself in a position of responsibility.

The point remains, however, for whatever reasons, I really don't believe I was equipped to be making lots of choices, I was too immature, too lacking in confidence – so a school which offered few opportunities to choose meaningfully, or to reflect on those choices, not only created those failings, but probably suited me down to the ground! Another element of my schooling which was, to our contemporary eyes, unacceptable, but seemed somehow to work for me at the time.

It seems, then, that at least part of my motivation in my approach to teaching, was concerned with righting the wrongs of my own experience as a pupil. In reflecting on my schooling, the

253

importance of context becomes very obvious. The school I went to was one of the best in the context of its times and society's expectations, and perhaps that is all a school can really aim to be. I keep coming back to the old quote: "School is not preparation for life, school IS life."

As a school manager, I had many a thoughtful discussion on the meaning of 'serving society'. Can a school change things in society – by encouraging pupils to think, question, become involved? Or, ultimately, does it merely reflect the way society operates at any given time?

For a micro-example of that dilemma: if a pupil lives in a house where there is no dining table, should a school be concerned with his table manners at lunchtime? It is an easy jibe to say it is not a school's job to teach or impose 'a middle class ethos', but less easy to detail exactly what that means. Do we abandon the war on litter because perhaps the majority in society have done so? Are manners and politeness, or accurate grammar, or white collar aspirations, to be dismissed as 'middle class' concerns?

"Striving for better" seems to me to be a useful basis. Jean Brodie forever hovers as a warning as to what can happen should one attempt to foist one's own views on youngsters, but there is surely a way to help equip our pupils to survive and prosper in society whilst preserving their own background and individuality?

Maybe such an approach is best reflected in my school's motto: Fidem vita fateri – To show our Faith by the way we live.

From what I can gather, a lot of the dismissiveness, or even anger, felt towards my old school by the majority of its alumni is centred on the fact that, in our time, the school itself patently failed to live up to that aspiration – whether through physical or emotional abuse, lack of respect of the individual, or in other ways.

254

To me, this does not invalidate the motto, though it does expose the weaknesses of those contemporaneously charged with upholding it. Perhaps St Mary's taught me the importance of aspiration, even in the most unlikely of circumstances. Maybe, knowing nothing else, I merely accepted the daily fear, and the lack of approbation, as a type of educational approach.

Looking back now, what I am sure of, is that I left school convinced of the value of education, certain that it could make a difference in some way (though fairly vague as yet on what that might be) and feeling lucky and privileged to have received the education that I had experienced. I suppose I was terrified of academic failure and failing to continue in education – but I was not really equipped to consider why this should be. It also seems clear, despite my lack of maturity at the time, that I was able to discern between those who taught with a kind of savage disregard for the pupils as individuals, and those who worked hard to let their humanity shine through the system.

The most positive outcome of these reflections so far is that I can now see that it was the impact of the latter group, most of whom I have happily named in earlier chapters, who helped make me the teacher I became. They held up the light of a better way - and I spent a career seeking to shine it.

I think, perhaps, the best way to reflect on my career as a teacher would be to divide my thoughts into three sections: on colleagues, parents and pupils. Hopefully such a structure will demonstrate what I learned from all with whom, and for whom, I worked.

A recurring theme – in these words, and during my career, has been my enduring pride in the people with whom I worked. I know there will be people reading this who have a jaundiced view of the teaching profession, some of them may even be teachers, or whose personal stories have been far different to mine. All I can reiterate is that these reflections are based on my own experiences, and as such are a true account of what I found and what I felt. It is a dangerous business to extract the general from the particular, but I feel my lifetime in education gives me at least limited permission to attempt some generalisations.

Like the pupils they taught, my colleagues were individuals who each approached their job in different ways. This, of course, reflected their backgrounds and experiences and often developed depending on their own age and personal circumstances. What teachers bring to the classroom and school is naturally influenced by their own lives – current and previous, and by their own experience as a teacher, or, indeed, in other walks of life. In a sense, it was this flexibility of approach which marked out successful and committed teachers.

In the last year of my career, I had given a talk to Primary 7 parents, whose children would be coming to our school the following August. At the end, a parent approached me and identified herself as having been one of my pupils herself in the 1980s. Apart from the loss of my long haired hippy hairstyle, she said, I "hadn't changed a bit. You're just the same!"

Of course, it was a lovely moment, and I was happy to be able to return the compliment. I knew what she meant, I think, and I was pleased with the implication.

Naturally I *had* changed – in practically every way. I would not have had the confidence to address such a meeting in such a way back in the 80s, neither would I have had the knowledge, nor authority, to reassure parents and children about legitimate concerns about moving to the 'big school'. I probably would have approached the whole exercise in a different way. If I walked the

256

walk differently in my Depute's suit, I had certainly changed the way I talked the talk!

What she meant, I guess, and I hope this is true, is that I was still recognizable as 'me'. The hairstyle, dress and demeanour had an extra thirty years development and knowledge behind them, but the person delivering all of this was still recognizably the same person.

I was lucky in my career that I worked in schools with a relatively low turnover of staff, and I stayed in two of them for sixteen years each.

As I have discussed, there are as many pros and cons to staying put for an extended period, as there are to regular movement. Without a doubt, however, one of the advantages was to be able to see young teachers developing into seasoned professionals and watching how they brought their life experiences into the classroom and their approach to the job.

As in Shakespeare's Stages of Man, it is possible to see the development of a teacher through the years: from the nervous energy and excitement of early years, through the acquisition of confidence which comes with middle years' experience and understanding, to the insight brought by having one's own family, or becoming a confident, independent middle aged adult, to the comfort brought by a tried and trusted philosophy, and a perspective gained over the years on what works and what doesn't.

As in life, things which seemed important at first may fade as the years go by, and elements of the job which were once overlooked may become central to the approach. Each class, and each generation of pupils and colleagues, will bring an opportunity to learn more about the job and oneself. The positive experiences will empower, and the negative will deflate.

I think the best teachers had a life outside of the classroom – whether it was family or hobbies or other commitments, but they also struggled to balance their lives in and out of school. You could always identify a teacher by the way they scanned the television schedules for 'something which might be useful in class', or arranged family holidays to places or regions which would prove helpful in picking up classroom materials. Mostly this was done without complaint, and, indeed, almost unconsciously, though it can't have been much fun for family and friends – though it does reflect the notion of teaching as vocation rather than job.

I would want to debunk some of the stereotypes, though. In my experience, it was not necessarily true that energy dissipated with age, or that cynicism increased with longevity.

In my own case, and something which I witnessed in many colleagues, there was a mutation in energy and involvement. Latterly, I would be amazed at younger colleagues who could spend a weekend in New York, come back to be breezy in the classroom on Monday morning, take an after school class that day and still be alert for an after school parents' night on the Thursday. That kind of energy leaves you sometime in your thirties. However, there is an intellectual energy which comes with experience – and I always thought that staff would have been amazed to see the intensity and enthusiasm with which our leadership team discussed potential developments, changes in directions or improvements in conditions. Arms waving, voices raised, reports produced with frantic speed – all indicated that, whilst physically our energy might have been less, in terms of commitment and reflection, we remained full on. Indeed, I think most of my generation of teachers – when their professional experience had been positive – became even more involved in education and its possibilities as they grew older.

Perhaps the most insulting stereotype held about teachers was that they had an easy lot in life, with short working hours and long holidays, but were always complaining.

To be fair, those with a clear understanding of the nature of the job or its stresses or strains seldom took this angle. Nobody who has taught has ever underestimated the need to clear the head during an extended summer holiday if the following session is to be delivered at full force, nor have they made the mistake of thinking that teachers do no work during holiday periods.

Those who condemn teachers as 'whiners' miss the point. When teachers point to long hours, classroom stress, and difficult working conditions, they are not claiming that such concerns are unique to them or their job. Many folk work long hours to the detriment of their family, many jobs are under resourced, and many workers deal with pressure from the public in their every day working environment. Teachers who highlight their working conditions are merely reacting to those who say they have it 'easy'. There's no claim to moral superiority or a suggestion that teachers work harder or longer than anyone else. What lies behind their complaints often is the fact that many are ignorant of the emotional and physical price teachers pay to be as effective as possible, and the fact that there are others who endure similar pressured conditions but who receive far more in the way of recompense or recognition. When holidays are mentioned, there also needs to be a concern for pupils, their physical and mental needs, and the importance of family time and the opportunity to follow up what they have learned - outside of school and of their own volition – all of that is a crucial part of the teaching and learning process.

It would be interesting to research why so many think so little of teachers. When all is said and done, society trusts teachers with the future – a confident, well supported and respected profession is one of the best investments a nation can make. Sadly, there are those who find it easier to blame an under resourced provision for the nation's ills than to self reflect on political priorities. Teachers can and do make a difference, but, as I keep repeating, they cannot overcome the inequalities generated by governments who have other priorities, or by societies who expect a high standard of education but are unwilling to pay the price in taxes to provide it. To those who have had bad experiences of poor teaching, I would say that part of a fully and adequately resourced system of education would be truly effective supports and mechanisms - either to develop unsatisfactory teachers or remove them from the profession. Nobody, including the teachers themselves, benefits when inadequate teaching is tolerated or goes unchallenged.

However, to move on from that somewhat defensive tone, I would like to reflect on the positives I have witnessed amongst my colleagues, on their classroom presence and commitment.

It was one of the huge privileges of being a depute head that part of my remit was to be visible around the campus, to speak frequently to pupils and colleagues, to drop in to classes, and to be fully aware of what was going on around the school. One of the reasons I knew I taught in successful and effective schools was the knowledge that any unexpected visitor – prospective parent, colleague from elsewhere, parent, or politician – could tour the school and I could be fairly sure that they would not meet with any 'unfortunate surprises'. Some classes would be noisy, others silently focussed; some doors would be open, some closed; some teachers animated and mobile, some more sedentary. For all the diversity of approaches, there was always a purposeful feeling and an atmosphere conducive to teaching and learning. This was a huge tribute to the school's ethos, and the teachers and pupils who maintained it, and it was a source of great pleasure to be able to access that take on the 'whole school' experience.

Similarly, more formal visits to classes for 'observation' were among my happiest tasks. Hopefully I was never threatening in that management role; I tried to be supportive and encouraging – but mostly I just celebrated the opportunity to see so many talented teachers in action, and so many pupils reacting to the experience.

That was why, in common with most who work in education, I regretted that opportunities for colleagues to observe each other in the classroom – particularly from other disciplines – were difficult to come by. There was general acceptance that this was an excellent means of learning the trade and reflecting on one's own practice, but over the length of my career, there were seldom the resources provided to make it possible. Many members of the public, and politicians, seemed to have the somewhat limited view that a teacher who was not actually teaching a class was not 'working' – one of many misapprehensions which would need to be effectively challenged were the philosophy of education in our country to change meaningfully.

Where the ethos was positive, staff were happy to welcome colleagues into their classes – even the dreaded management! An openness and willingness to share was a sign of a sound approach to teaching and learning. In fact, one of the most effective 'tools for improvement' (horrible phrase!) which I observed was the project known as 'the Learning Rounds'.

Basically, a team would be assembled to visit the classes in a year group across a range of subjects. Their remit would be to focus – not on the teaching – but on the learning. They would then compile a report on 'good learning' they had observed – in other words: what had 'worked' in the classroom: what engaged the pupils. This would then be the basis for discussion and application across the school. The innovatory aspect of this exercise lay in the make up of the 'teams'. They would include managers, education officials, colleagues – from within and outwith the school, including associated primaries - parents, and pupils.

The fact that staff would be happy to welcome such an arrangement reflected a certain confidence in the school's approach – and quickly teachers accepted that this was not an assessment of them in the classroom, and that it was the pupils who were being 'watched' – this was reflected in the reports that were produced.

As you would expect, such an initiative needed careful preparation. With the best will in the world, a team of five or six people present in a classroom cannot be ignored – and there would be particular classes or lessons where it would not be appropriate. Staff had to volunteer to take part in the exercise – either as part of the team or as observed classes, and it was a measure of its success, and of staff confidence, that, once it was up and running, volunteers for both parts of the project steadily grew.

There were initial reservations – in particular over the inclusion of pupils and parents in the visiting teams. These doubts were quickly overcome. Parents, as they generally are when they have the chance to see staff in action, were hugely positive – but the major revelation was the part played by pupils in writing up the reports.

Their insight was, of course, invaluable, and they were able to point out positives – and a few negatives – which would have been invisible to adults – and this was crucial in the process. After all, they were the folk for whom the whole project was being run!

It was helpful to primary colleagues to witness the similarities and differences between their approaches and that of the secondaries – and the reverse was true when primary schools were visited. It was also a fine opportunity for some of the primary teachers to see their former pupils in later years.

However, perhaps the core of this approach lay in the participation of primary pupils. Understandably, perhaps, those involved in secondary were a wee bit cautious in involving Primary 7 pupils: would they understand the task, would they have the language to explain their views, was it too high an expectation?

As is almost always the case when you stretch your expectations of young people, they not only reached the mark, they surpassed it. Untrammelled by "edu-speak" or previous expectations, and not aware of current trends or innovations, they merely described, in plain speech, what had worked in the classes they'd seen and what had not. It was a 'Damascus moment' for the adults involved, made all the richer for the self evident truth which it demonstrated: if you want to know about education – ask the pupils!

It also reflected well on their fellow team members who avoided patronizing them, and the professionalism and security of the teachers who were observed, and were willing to listen to the comments of 12 year olds. Praise should also be given to the pupils of the observed classes, who took on board the importance of the exercise and carried on with their learning –despite the opportunity for distraction provided by their classroom visitors.

I like to think that the 'Learning Rounds' also contributed to easing what I have referred to as the 'loneliness' of the classroom teacher, by painting a picture of what was going on across the school and departments and in highlighting their expertise and that of other teachers: providing an opportunity for perspective and reflection.

Inevitably, it should be pointed out that this was in many senses a voluntary initiative and involved staff giving up preparation time, covering for colleagues, and putting in additional working hours to enable it to operate effectively. Even the post visit discussion and compiling of the report took up to a full day's work – and schools are certainly not resourced to allow for that. However, as its efficacy became obvious, colleagues were more than willing to cooperate to make it happen, and to follow up with energetic discussion and planning, based on its findings. The impact it had on teachers, departments and schools suggests it might be a more cost effective way forward than formal Inspections – especially as it would require schools to work towards an ethos which was secure and comfortable with such an approach, thus implying a high standard of teaching and learning. Maybe not so much a case of more money required as a redirection of its use.

I suppose I could review a lifetime's response to my colleagues in the shape of a sequence of vignettes – scenes I may have caught at any time walking about the school or visiting classes: a young newly qualified RE teacher sat on a front desk; she is leaning forward earnestly and her class, an unlikely audience of mostly male fourth years, are riveted by her enthusiasm and classroom skills; a science teacher in white coat, carefully explaining an experiment, pupils around the desk straining to see and understand, hooked by his involvement; an English teacher, under a tree in the Meadows parkland, enthusing pupils with Shakespeare; the Maths teacher making numbers come to life with her enthusiasm and understanding; the drama teacher urging a pupil with additional needs to the performance of his life; the teachers who volunteered to play guitar at the end of term concert with the severely disabled lad who never forgot the moment; a Home Economics teacher welcoming a class, and with a single instruction seeing the pupils prepare perfectly for their cooking, bags and coats away, at their tables, alert and concentrating, inside two minutes; a senior manager, long after 'home time', sitting with an upset teacher, seeking to understand and support; a support assistant, perched on a low wall outside the school, a sobbing boy beside her, she soaking up his distress till he becomes calm enough

264

to talk, and, eventually, follow her back into school; a guidance teacher, near enough to 6pm, at her desk, surrounded by paperwork, as she phones agency after agency to seek support for her pupil – and in a room next door, a young member of guidance staff with a visibly upset parent, trying to reassure her, to offer support and to make a difference.

Sports teachers through the years putting in the work to build confidence and talent – leading to the success that comes – not necessarily with winning trophies, but with driving a minibus full of singing youngsters down the road – happy in their teamwork and friendships. The dinner lady who slips an extra piece of meat on to the disadvantaged pupil's plate, the janitor who ensures there is always a 'special job' for the lad who finds breaktime so difficult. Teachers on boats, on hillsides, on stages, and in department offices, surrounded by preparation and marking. Teachers in staffrooms enthusing about a pupil's progress, or being supported by colleagues after a misfiring lesson; the camaraderie of nights out, the satisfaction of good results; the standing by the door to welcome each class – all of them different, all challenging, all with potential. In addition: the tears, the tiredness, the frustration, the determination, the moments of connection, the thanks from parents and managers; the joy of a pupil's success – at whatever level.

As the well known newspaper used to have it: All human life is here. That's the attraction of the job, surely? However, what I do notice – in these vignettes, and as I think back over my career, is that there is a single trait that was common to all effective teachers – at every level, and however they approached the job, – and that is that they listened to pupils, and heard what they were saying.

I think it is clear from all I have written that I consider relationships to be at the heart of education – obviously between teacher and pupil, but also between colleagues, between school and parents, and between education and the community in which it is based and which it serves. You could say that one of education's prime tasks is to break down isolation by helping individuals communicate, to find themselves in their surroundings, and, in so doing, to strengthen their own sense of worth as well as become effective and contributing members of society.

Of all the tools available to accomplish this task – knowledge, classroom skills, experience, planning, assessment, structure, and reflection – none can be achieved if the teacher is not listening to the pupils and making an effort to understand what they are saying. Imagine a mountain guide who ploughed on with the route, ignoring his party's questions, requests and feedback on what they felt they could do and could not do: it would be a recipe for disaster.

Teachers operate under great pressure – in and out of the classroom, in school and outwith school. (Perhaps it is only when reflecting in retirement that those demands and the pace of it all becomes clear.) This means that time has to be found deliberately for listening and hearing, that we must avoid the temptation to hear comments and questions as a kind of permanent, repeated, backdrop to the vital business of 'getting through the syllabus', 'meeting learning outcomes', or retaining class control while the smartboard refuses to co-operate. Even if we have heard the words a hundred times before, what the child is saying is new to them and important enough for them to verbalise it. If they keep on saying the same things, it could well be because they are not getting, or at least 'hearing', any answers.

Just like in any relationship "We don't talk anymore" can sound the death knell. Teachers who 'talk at' pupils rather than 'with' them, or who fail to make time to listen to their class members, will find it hard to operate effectively. There are, of course, many ways of achieving this, and, as always, each teacher needs to find a style with which they are comfortable. To explain in

266

a physical analogy: there are teachers who are happiest to communicate with pupils by sitting at their level, or squatting down beside them; others would find that awkward and retain a more formal manner, perhaps with the pupil standing by their desk, or a chat in a corridor. The pupils are skilled at reading messages – they are looking for signs that they have your full attention and that you are willing to react honestly to what they are saying to you; how teachers do this will vary according to their own personalities. With experience comes the ability to judge the difference between availability to a pupil and unwanted intrusion, and, like the pupils, an effective teacher becomes practised at reading the signs.

Following the major theme of this memoir, it is obvious that the move away from 'pastoral' approaches in guidance and the predominance of tracking and monitoring, is leading to a situation where the work done by support staff can be more easily demonstrated, but its content may ultimately be of less use to the pupils.

To clarify, it is relatively simple to put a structure in place where every pupil receives a set number of 'tracking interviews' in a school session. The statement can then be made: "every pupil will meet with their guidance teacher at least three times a year", for instance. Two things need to be taken into account, however. One is the inevitability that, if you set such targets, they ultimately drive the approach and the system is run by the need to meet the targets rather than the pupils' needs. The other problem is that the structure is teacher led rather than pupil led.

Guidance works best when the teacher has a good knowledge of the pupils, the time to acquire that knowledge and reflect on it, and the space to let a pupil accept or request support in their own time and in a comfortable manner. These conditions lead to proactive rather than reactive support, help the pupils to see the support system as effective and operating in their interests, and facilitate a listening and hearing model which enables a sense of security and trust amongst pupils, rather than a sense of being 'checked up on'. All of this, naturally, promotes a school where there is excellent teaching and learning, and pupils who meet or even exceed their potential, academically and socially.

'Modernisers' will claim this is a 'woolly and imprecise' structure for support – but, in fact, it is the reverse of that, because it operates on deep knowledge of the pupils and their needs, rather than the ability to fill in pro-formas and provide data for statistics. Of course, it is a more expensive model, but, as I have quoted before, if you think effective education is expensive, try ignorance!

To listen and hear, you need space, and sometimes one should take that literally. It is impossible to overestimate the value of work done by teachers outside the classroom – whether on formal events such as school productions, residential courses or sports training, or more informally in charity events, local involvement in the community and so on. Even the opportunity to 'learn outdoors' is hugely important for pupils, as the different setting and possibilities can stimulate their interest and understanding.

Towards the end of my career, the concept of taking pupils out of the classroom – not just on educational visits, but in the sense of setting up teaching and learning spaces in the school grounds where possible, became popular again, as it had been in my early years of teaching. I have always struggled with the notion that you can help young people learn about the world by keeping them in a classroom, so I was delighted to see this development, and also witness the various innovative ideas promoted by both staff and pupils to make this happen.

Listening and hearing, making space, being flexible, reacting to needs – this, of course, is the language of relationships, and I suppose I have been saying, in different ways, that the connection with pupils, the ability to make them feel valued, and the skill to communicate effectively, are all the signs of an effective teacher. It is a big list, and very demanding, but I worked with hundreds of staff who were brave enough to take that approach and make it succeed.

Ending these reflections on teachers, as a manager, or leader, which I suppose I can't avoid, I recall a motto I once heard which seemed to me to be succinct and accurate and refers to teachers in the classroom as well as to managers in their schools: *"Compliment people. Magnify their strengths, not their weaknesses."*

If the relationship between children and their parents is daunting in its complexities, the connection between school and parents is not far behind in its complicated nature.

I have written a lot about the need for trust in education – between pupil and teacher, management and staff, and also between parent or carer and school. It is, of course, easy to assert that, more difficult to promote it.

Parents have different expectations of schools, reflecting their own backgrounds and experiences, their circumstances, and even their older children's previous interactions with teachers. The school's task is to meet with parental aspirations – varied and contradictory though they may be, whilst at the same time having a clear ethos into which the whole school community is expected to buy. It is a balancing act which requires time, patience, a willingness to listen, and a pride in the school, its achievements, and its manner of operating.

In a parallel to the classroom teacher's approach, a positive relationship with parents does not mean a school always agrees with a parental demand, nor can it be forced into courses of action which may benefit one child to the detriment of others. Part of the establishment of trust is the ability to establish an understanding that the school will do its best for every pupil, within the parameters of its aims as an institution, the resources available to it, and the experience of its decision makers.

In promoting the idea of 'trust', I write as someone who, on innumerable occasions, when in disagreement with a parent, has had to utter the immortal line: "Look – you are going to have to trust me on this one."

That is the cold moment of discovery – do I as a manager, or the school, as an institution, occupy that position of trust in a parent or carer's mind? Will they make what is, in essence, a leap of faith and take my opinion as being a better way forward than their own original wishes'?

So, like so much in education, a high falutin word like 'trust' can be scaled down to some very practical moments.

Is their child happy at school? When they come home and talk about their experiences, do they do so in a positive fashion, reflecting that they feel safe and valued in and out of the classroom, or are they secretive, angry or confused by the educational experiences? Whilst the motif: "Children learn best from teachers whom they like" rings   true, so does the assertion that: "Happy pupils make most progress".

Of course, this does not suggest it is the role of teachers or school to entertain pupils, or merely to make them laugh, or send them home happy - like some kind of scholastic music hall. The happiness to which I refer comes from a sense of progress and achievement, and being valued; an understanding, if you like, that they are in a good school where the right things are happening, and, whilst few pupils are going to wake up each morning dying to get to school, neither should they be dreading the time spent in education. So that element of trust comes from the experience of seeing your child grow – in learning and confidence and understanding. If you like, it is a confirmation to the parent that they have made the right choice in sending their child to that school, that their expectations have been met and it is a positive force in the child's life. No parent likes to think they have made choices which have made their child unhappy.

The first element in building trust, then, is to ensure the school is a positive place of teaching and learning – an obvious point, perhaps, but it is worth remembering that parents do not have to be education experts to assess this: the demeanour of their child will tell them.

Consistency is also crucial in this area of trust. A parent should know what to expect when they approach the school. This applies in the big things: if their children interact with different teachers, will there still be a 'house style'? Are all guidance teachers working in the same manner? Do the management team all sing from the same hymn sheet? Are the structures of communication well used and understood; if they change, is there a real effort to ensure that all parents know this? Many parents dread 'getting it wrong' when they approach the school, well knowing that their children don't always tell them the full story. If they approach the school with this dread, they may well be defensive and more difficult to engage than if they feel comfortable and secure in what they are doing.

Bringing consistency and communication together, perhaps in smaller things, is also important. Is there an approach to communication which is user friendly? Are important messages sent in the same way each time? Are they user friendly and easily understood? Do school communications highlight the positive, as well as sending formal information? Is it made obvious how a parent can contact the school, and is there opportunity for feedback? Are requests and queries handled professionally, timeously and fully – or is there a chance parents will feel 'fobbed off' or ignored?

In my last school, our guidance system operated with a principal teacher and a support assistant attached to each house, as well as a pupil support manager who coordinated work with partner agencies, and myself as head of guidance on the leadership team. Whilst this gave the pupils a range of support, it also increased the chances if a parent or carer contacted the school, they would be able to speak to someone who knew their child, rather than being asked to phone back or await a return call. The ability to make contact when they wanted to was often a means of assuaging their concerns before they grew. It also reflected, in a public way, the priority the school placed on support.

Sometimes in the pressure of school life, the time it takes to be 'on top' of all these issues is hard to find, but, all should be aware that the points of contact with schools - for parents and surrounding communities – can be fleeting and misleading. Imagine the impressions formed – rightly or wrongly – when a parent encounters an unfriendly receptionist, pupils – or even staff – smoking or dropping litter in the school surrounds, poorly maintained property, or pupils or staff dressed informally rather than for education. On their own each of these issues can be dismissed as trivial, and certainly can be addressed fairly easily if the will is there – but if they reflect a certain approach to school life, can lead to a negative view of the school from parents, which may not be merited at all.

To extend the theme, feedback from parents is crucial in understanding their concerns: How was the parents' evening for you? Did you enjoy the concert? Do you find it easy to contact your child's guidance teacher or the senior team? What would make it easier for you to understand the curriculum? We made a point latterly of regularly commissioning a full parental questionnaire about all aspects of school life, on the basis that if we didn't know what concerns parents had it was impossible to address them.

Finally, of course, the mantra of 'hearing and listening' which applies to our dealings with pupils is equally important when it comes to dealing with parents and carers, and more difficult to achieve given the restricted amount of interaction with them.

As I have noted, the concept of 'family life' changed dramatically during my time in teaching. Statistically, in the mid seventies, it would be unusual if more than three pupils in a class of thirty came from disrupted or re-formed family groupings. By the end of my career, no teacher would assume anything when it came to shared surnames or family background.

Obviously, this was far more than just an administrative fact and it was crucial that all staff, and particularly those who had direct contact with home, knew the many different family circumstances that pertained in each child's life. The importance of this could range from legal matters and child protection to an awareness of particularly emotional dates or times of the year. By being aware of a child's individual circumstances, the school reflected how much it valued the child, how professional it was in its treatment of information, and how flexible it could be in meeting the needs of both child and family.

We used to urge pupils not to be dismissive or hurtful to others – partly because they could never know the full circumstances of someone's life, and the same applied to school staff, teaching and non-teaching. Families needed to know that school was aware of the challenges they might be facing, was non-judgmental and was there to support them – another means of building trust.

Most of all, again as in any relationship, there had to be an honesty between school and home. I have already written about integrity and how it affects a teacher's words and actions. Parents have all manner of ambitions for their children, and they are naturally wired to defend them and think the best of them. Personalities and circumstances differ and can be affected by situations – and also by the attitude of authority and officialdom.

I always felt it would be demeaning – to both of us, if I was ever to be less than completely truthful with a parent. Naturally, negative or upsetting news tended to be delivered in as empathetic a manner as possible, but long experience told me that fudging the issue or being 'economical with the truth' only made it worse when the actual truth came out later as it nearly always did. If you sought respect from parents, you had to treat them in the same manner.

Such an approach led to some uncomfortable moments in parental interviews, on a few occasions leading to a high level of hostility – but, with a little reflection and humility on both sides, generally these problems could be overcome.

Some of the most difficult issues in this area arose when parents were unhappy with the performance or action of teachers. As I have said, it was not my job to defend staff no matter what, but neither was I prepared to 'hang them out to dry'. I always sought to see both sides, and attempted to encourage the parent to do likewise. Ultimately, as a manager, I was willing to take responsibility if things had gone wrong, as I expected the teacher to do – and also the parent, if they had got hold of the wrong end of the stick. Sometimes hands have to be held up and a way forward negotiated – it should be no part of education for wool to be pulled over anyone's eyes – pupil, parent or teacher. Honesty, in school, really has to be the best policy; it is another element of trust. And certainly lubricated the strength of communication.

This often meant a proactive approach in contacting home and in working with parents. Most parents appreciated an early indication of possible problems, and, despite initial concern, usually welcomed it as a sign of the school's care for their child. It was one of the great successes of guidance that over the years of my career parents gradually stopped dreading a phone call from the school and appreciated it might be positive, friendly or even containing praise and approval rather than inevitably a sign of 'trouble'.

If you are thinking that communication, consistency, honesty, empathy and understanding are not particularly unusual ideas for how a school best works with its parents, then you are right. They are all obvious elements of a basic humanity which should suffuse all we do in schools.

One of the best feelings as a teacher comes from making the time to compliment a parent or carer on their child, or praise a parent to their child. We all like approval, and nothing counts more, I suspect than the knowledge that someone outside the family thinks we have got it right with our child – or cares enough to want to support us in making things better. (For that matter – words of thanks or appreciation from child or family can make a teacher's year!)

Of all the many foundations on which successful schooling is built, none is more important than having a rock solid triangular bond between school, home, and child. It takes time, thought, and reflection, and makes especially high demands on senior managers and guidance and support staff – but it is an approach which is fulsomely rewarded.

In the ongoing debate over under achievement in disadvantaged neighbourhoods, both teachers and parents are often apportioned blame. The parents are said to be disinterested in their child's education, and the teachers are accused of having low expectations for children from challenging circumstances. In my years in teaching, I found very few parents who showed no interest in their child's education – though I did know some who were sinking under so many challenges that they found it difficult to focus on schooling. As I have been suggesting, a school which has the trust of the home can take some of that strain off the parent or carer, can provide, for both child and family, the knowledge that there is at least one part of their life where they are listened to, valued, and can make some progress. As to the teacher's role: the highest of expectations of each child should be a given – irrespective of their background or potential; anything less severely diminishes the teacher's impact.

Whenever I have talked about the elements which make a 'good school', communication, openness, partnership and trust have featured. All of these must characterise the relationship between school and parents. Just as I was frequently overwhelmed by the efforts made by teachers to support their pupils, the privilege of working with so many families over the years, seeing how they faced challenges, appreciating the mutual support they gave, sharing the joys of success and the anguish of failures and losses, I was able to appreciate the variety of approaches to family life. I realised also that sometimes love was not enough – that fate and circumstances often rocked the family boat, that caring commitment didn't always gain the expected results and that some parents and carers had a lonely, unfulfilling task. Teachers could only support from a distance and show understanding of the demands of the parenting role. On every teacher's mental noticeboard there needs to be a sign saying: "Would I want this for my child?"

And the children, of course, are what education is all about. Such a self evident comment should not be necessary, but it is. Politicians, the media, and big business, as well as teachers, parents

276

and local communities, all have a stake in how schools operate and their own interests in the outcomes of the education process. It would be both naïve and pointless to wish for schools to be unaffected by the trends of contemporary society – they are part of that society and are helping young people gain appropriate skills to exist successfully in it. The problem comes when the needs of others, rather than the children, gain priority – and that would include parents and teachers.

Listening to pupils' needs, assessing which decisions will be in their best interests, taking into account their own preferences, fears and hopes – all of these necessities could be seen as the most difficult parts of education. Providing an education – and a school – which meets the needs of the individual, whilst also reflecting each pupil's role within society, requires knowledge, understanding, many different skills, and a commitment to developing potential and ambition. Many operating requirements – from resources to policy to personnel – can hinder the impact of even the most effective schools.

We are dealing with people – in the provision of education and on its receiving end; it makes the task of teaching and learning unique in many ways – it is not a service industry, its success does not depend on profit achieved or satisfaction reported, but on its lifelong effect on future generations. Often these results are hidden, obscured, or much delayed. Seeking to demonstrate this, I often suggested that teaching was akin to working in a factory, not knowing what the final product was, but still needing to ensure that your role in its development was as perfect as it could be – trusting that, if you did everything to the best of your ability, the end product would be successful. It was one of the reasons that keeping in touch with pupils, or at least hearing of their successes in later life, brings such pleasure to the teaching profession. It is not that we would seek to claim responsibility for the individual's progress, but rather that it brings an opportunity to discover that the boat you pushed from the shore has navigated a safe voyage and has not sunk! You can't control that boat's journey, or its destination, nor would you wish to, but there is some satisfaction in discovering that you have equipped its sailor to navigate successfully.

For all that, I find it difficult to write concisely and meaningfully about pupils – perhaps because I always sought to treat them as individuals, perhaps because I interacted with so many over the years, and certainly because I do not wish to write in a sentimental or patronizing manner. The fact remains that they are obviously central to a teaching career and if I am addressing the question: "What was all that about?", I would hope that they are the major part of the answer.

I have tried to tread the fine line between emphasising the crucial nature of education and writing in a pompous, self important fashion, but it is difficult to overstate the importance of pupils in a teacher's career.

Those who have worked with consistently challenging classes or 'malevolent' individuals will attest to the fact that such experiences can be life and personality changing and become central to everything you try to do, in and out of school. Likewise, if your teaching experiences have been positive, the energy and joy which can be generated from working in an atmosphere which is predominantly peopled by youngsters can be hugely life affirming.

When I am asked what I miss about teaching, my various answers all contain the word 'young'. I miss the company of young staff – a privilege I was lucky to enjoy throughout my career – their commitment, openness, willingness to listen, to innovate, to give of themselves to job, pupils and colleagues. I miss their varied approaches to life, their different backgrounds, their plans, hopes and dreams. All of those things made for a vibrant and happy workplace over the years, and I do realise I was fortunate to have such a positive experience.

But I miss most of all the buzz of being around the pupils– and being in a position to see them and think of them as individuals – rather than as a kind of amorphous mass. For all the paperwork, the daily pressure, the meetings, policies, inspections and disappointments – it was a rare day that a young person did not give me reason to smile, to laugh outright, or to thank my lucky stars for the profession of which I was part – and generally it was an effect they achieved unconsciously which, of course, made it all the more enjoyable.

Writing about teachers, I suggested many of my memories were vignettes, featuring an individual – in front of a class or on the sports field. When I think back to pupils over the years, I find, that though there were a number of classes which were a pleasure to teach and to which I would always look forward because of the dynamic they provided, it is individual moments which resonate.

One of the fascinating elements of teacher pupil interaction is the factor of unpredictability. Often pupils, and others, assumed that teachers most enjoyed working with motivated, 'clever' and successful students – that the "Horace Broons' of this world, the 'swots', if you like, were the natural 'favourites' of the teachers. Leaving aside the fact that effective teachers don't have 'favourites', it was frequently the case that the pupils with whom teachers most enjoyed working were neither 'high performing' nor, in some cases, particularly motivated or easy to teach. A sparky personality, a sense of their own worth, a willingness to listen, interact and challenge – all of these things often provided the content for a successful and positive teacher pupil relationship. I have to say that, when former colleagues and I reminisce, it is not necessarily those who were hyper successful academically who come to mind.

Any teacher will tell you, no matter how experienced or confident they are, to walk through the playground in a strange school, where none of the pupils are familiar, can be a difficult experience. It's a situation which gives a teacher some insight into the views of the general public. A large group of young people who are nameless and unknown can be a daunting prospect – even to confident adults. However, and it is an important point, teaching is not about 'controlling large groups' – it is about connecting with groups of known individuals, so that a class or an assembly is not about a number, but about each of the pupils who make up that number.

It is the individuality of pupils which resonates. There were academic 'high flyers' who really didn't seem to enjoy school or acknowledge their teachers, and were withdrawn and quiet – and others who fairly glowed with their enjoyment of study and progress and community. Whilst, as a guidance teacher, the pupils who faced obvious challenges were most evident to me, as individuals, they too could veer between welcoming and appreciating support, and preferring to keep their troubles private. I always tried to remember that privacy was a pupil's right. Many were happy to make school the one 'normal' place in their life, and that had to be respected.

All a teacher could do was to operate in a way which demonstrated openness and accessibility and a genuine concern for their pupils. If the young people felt able to take advantage of the support on offer, then all well and good; if they could not or would not, nothing was to be gained by trying to force the support on them, although that could be a very difficult call to make, especially if you felt you could make a difference.

Whilst it is nice to recall occasions when pupils could be supported to a better place, perhaps the really sharp memories are

280

based on those pupils who, for whatever reason, could not be helped. The guidance mission was to keep trying, even when success seemed unlikely. You could never tell if, at some dark moment in the future, the fact that, at one time, there was someone who so obviously cared, might make all the difference.

High expectations, the time to listen and hear, following through your promises, and always being truthful – these were the major elements in connecting with young people. There was also that vital need for professionalism and dedication – big words for a big task. The youngsters, and their families, deserved no less. What made the job so rewarding was that, almost without exception, the pupils were worth it. Their enthusiasm, potential, energy, openness to the new, and acceptance of the past – and, yes, their downright unpredictability, as well as their wit and humour, their embracing of the impossible, and their full immersion in life – all of these made teaching a brilliant career, and I can think of no better way to have spent my life.

I have written at length about pupils, and their support, in this memoir – quite rightly, as pupils and their support is at the very centre of effective education. Guidance teachers require strength, experience, skill and empathy to do their job effectively – but, in essence, it is a very simple job remit, especially if you acknowledge that the school is there to serve the pupils.

SCHOOL TIES AND LESSONS LEARNED

"Being a teacher is not what I do; being a teacher is who I am"

Jill Biden

It is tempting to see the completion of these reflections as drawing some kind of line under my career, or vocation, as a teacher. I have looked back, reflected, tried to draw some conclusions, and attempted to offer some insight. As needs be, it has been a very personal and singular look at one person's interaction with the world of education, in particular times and in particular places. I have attempted to walk that line between personal insight and generalisation, and, if I have failed, well, I hope there is enough resonance in these words and ideas to explain, at least, what I *thought* I was doing for those thirty seven years.

However, I find that it does not feel like a completion of anything.

When I was tidying up various areas after my retirement, I came to the profiles on my Twitter and Facebook accounts – and I found I was unable to change them to say 'retired teacher'. In Jill Biden's words, I still felt that being a teacher was what I *was*, not what I *did*.

That maybe a precious or pompous idea, but I have to be honest and say, for me, it resonates. I can still remember my reaction when I heard her make that statement. She was speaking at the Democratic Party Convention and made the point in a speech about the importance of education. It is not a hugely deep or innovative idea, but the way she used it, at, what was, I suppose, a particular time of my life, struck a chord with me.

Of course, it is easy to take on portentous language and ideas in retrospect – and perhaps it is as well that we operate on a day to day basis with a little less self awareness or self regard.

The reality is that, for virtually all of my career, I was concerned, as are all teachers, with getting through from Monday to Friday, not letting down any of my pupils, colleagues, families or associates, and seeking to make the school in which I was working as secure, friendly, happy and successful as was possible.

The philosophy which operates behind a career is one which perhaps develops subconsciously and owes nearly everything to the circumstances in which one finds oneself – the places, the people and the times. I have no doubt these chapters, and, indeed, my life, would have been totally different had I taught in other schools, made different decisions, and been influenced by different colleagues.

However, all of that is speculation, and we can only deal with the reality of what has happened and where we have reached.

So what are my prime feelings in looking back – on my career and on these reflections?

The biggest emotion is one of gratitude.

Anyone who has been involved in education, in any way, knows that there is huge pressure to get things right – for every child, and to support colleagues, as well as families and the wider school community. This can take a toll on those involved – physically, psychologically and socially. As is the case with some other careers, the price of failure is not financial but that of personal regret and sometimes guilt. Furthermore, it is not a life which can be as flexible as some – you can't have a 'paperwork day' in teaching, nor arrive five minutes late, nor organize your day or week to suit your mood, health, or other requirements. Your holidays may be longer than some, but they are proscribed, your working day notionally shorter, but realistically expanded on a regular basis. We are told that a lack of control over our working day is not good for our mental wellbeing. As a manager, I tried to respect and promote the teacher's right to individuality – out of concern for their own interests, but also because pupils benefited from staff who were as free as possible to make their own decisions and choices. However, ultimately, and I do not claim this as being unique to teaching – the classroom teacher marched to the beat of the school timetabler, the curriculum content, and the wishes of management, local authority, and central government – as well as seeking to meet the needs and aspirations of pupils, parents, and community.

I saw many who struggled with the demands of the job, and in many different ways. There is no hiding place in teaching and I often felt that, in some areas or schools, the lack of well resourced, positive measures to support struggling teachers, and even to assist them in leaving the profession, was bad news not just for pupils and colleagues who were affected, but also for the long term good of the individuals themselves. I was grateful, therefore, that throughout my career, I had the support of colleagues, friends and family and that, even in difficult times, I was able to retain my optimism and never doubt that I was in the right profession and that things would get better. Indeed, there were blessedly few occasions when I felt less than positive about my job, and I know that many teachers are not fortunate enough to be able to say that truthfully.

So I am grateful for the chances I had, the support I received, the people I knew, and the places I experienced during my career. I know these reflections may be unbelievably positive compared to the experiences of others, and I acknowledge my good fortune throughout my time as a teacher.

I am grateful too for the support of my family. It is impossible to say whether having another teacher as a partner is a good or bad thing! There is much comfort to be gained from the fact that your other half understands what you are dealing with, but also, in a profession which famously never 'switches off', it means no hiding place from the expectations and concerns of the job, even at home. I hope we managed to be mutually supportive, though it is interesting to note that our son, proud as he was of our careers and of our approach as teachers, never showed any ambition to follow us into education! I certainly could not have survived so positively without the love of son and partner – and the understanding through the times when I was pre-occupied or just plain short tempered or exhausted. Their support was my strength.

Following on from gratitude is a feeling of appreciation. I worked with many brilliant staff, teaching and non-teaching, from whom I learned so much – about life as well as education. I was trusted by so many families – even when it was clear that, while I could be empathetic, I could have no real understanding of the difficulties they had and the challenges they faced. As I have said, I gained a growing insight into the sheer hard work that goes into a successful family life and the sacrifices made by so many parents and carers, of all ages. I fully appreciate that the opportunity to witness and observe so many different types of lifestyle and struggle, as well as success and celebration, has to add to one's own understanding of life and what we are all doing here.

It seems glib to state that it was a privilege to be a part of the lives of so many families – but, nevertheless, it was true. Working with people – of all ages and backgrounds – contributes to wisdom and understanding, and lends a sense of perspective to one's own experiences. Appreciation of such an opportunity is the least a teacher can offer in return. It is part of that partnership which has featured throughout these pages - an awareness of pupil and parent expectations, and an acknowledgement that there has to be trust built up and maintained by all involved. Neither side can choose with whom they will work, but both sides can build a partnership by listening and hearing, committing and trying, and with flexibility and understanding.

All of which brings me to the heart of this memoir: the pupils and young people with whom I worked throughout the years.

How do I remember them?

Are they in a long line filing slowly past me? Are they sitting bowed at desks, playing in playgrounds, nudging each other in corridors, laughing with their heads thrown back, bent over to conceal some private pain, running in the gym or sports field, concentrating in the music rooms, washing dishes in Home Economics, fingers flying over keyboards, shyly bringing out pieces of writing to be marked, scanning my face for approval or disappointment, smiling with exam success, frowning with the difficulty of knowledge? Are they bouncing with hands up, or slumped with last period fatigue, is their school dress smart or casual, conforming or defiant? Are they gathered in a crowd around me, competing for attention, or do they cut singular figures on a lonely walk? Are they smiling or serious, happy or sad, confident or fearful? Do they people the 70s, the 80s the 90s or the last decade? Do they all have names or are some of them anonymous? Are they forever young, or can I glimpse the adults they have become?

All of this, and more, would be accurate. I think of them often and am pleased to have known them all – even those who brought me grief – maybe those in particular. I was luckier than some teachers in that I had to deal with the death of a pupil on only a small number of occasions, but each was devastating and unfair and cutting. And when, on a newspaper announcements page, on a walk around a cemetery, or in a stray post on Facebook, I discover a former pupil has died, the sadness is still there for a life not completely lived. Just as the feeling when a child pre-deceases a parent, it does not seem right that teacher should outlive their one time pupils.

I sometimes wonder about all the lives of which I was a part for such a short time: was potential reached or exceeded, have they met with success or disappointment, did they take the obvious path or has fate given them unexpected journeys and experiences? When I occasionally bump into them or hear news of them, the feeling is comfortable and satisfying – as when a local personality achieves great things: one is pleased at the connection without necessarily feeling any sense of involvement or responsibility. If it is incumbent on parents to let their adult children go, it is even more important that teachers recognise their place. They are important for a very limited time, their job is to help push the boat from the shore; the voyage, its vicissitudes, and its ultimate destination, may or may not depend on the strength and direction of that push – either way, the connection is over once the boat has left the shore.

In writing that, I am aware that, in many places in these pages, I have referred back to my teachers and their life long influence. But, then, I am a teacher – I would say that, wouldn't I? Maybe the fact that my teachers were so important to me is the reason I became a teacher? Maybe for others, possibly the majority, schooldays and teachers fade quickly and are forgotten quite easily. I have many friends who struggle to recall which teachers taught them, their names, or particular incidents from their schooling. It is a good and necessary reminder that teachers should never be full of their own importance and should recognize they are a part of a big team in society – starting obviously with parents and carers – who contribute to the development of a young person. As the African motto goes: "It takes a village" – and teachers have their role to play, as do many others. Teachers should never think they can do it all themselves – but neither should society abdicate total

290

responsibility to those who teach – all have their place in encouraging the next generation.

My pupils were, and are, hugely important to me. I don't write that in any self justifying way; it was simply that the connection with those I taught brought great pleasure to my career and I enjoyed the company of the young – whether in the classroom or, as the years passed, in the staffroom. There is an openness, an optimism and a joy about the young which can inspire those around them – and when those qualities are missing for some reason, can equally inspire adults to support and guide and try to reinstate them: the crucial nature, again, of hearing as well as listening, guiding as well as telling, sharing as well as managing, and always operating with the highest of realistic expectations.

In closing these reflections, I return, inevitably, to Andrew Carnegie's dictum: *"There is little success where there is little laughter!"*

As I have mentioned, when I look back on my career – whether to pupils or colleagues or families – my reminiscences take all shapes and forms – the individuals and the groups, classes and year groups, remote and recent – but a common thread running through the vast majority of the moments I recall fondly is the presence of laughter.

From the most tense promotion interview, to the welcoming of a Primary 7 on their first school visit, I cannot remember a situation where, if it was appropriate, I failed to attempt humour to encourage, settle, diffuse, connect or relax. In all areas of my life, it is in my nature to use wit (though some would say I only ever get half way there!) and I cannot imagine having worked in education without using humour as a lifebelt. On occasion, the humour was very black in desperate situations, sometimes it was sharp, and often it was just plain silly. I like to think it injected humanity into

291

all areas of what could be a very challenging and serious occupation.

In this connection, it is inevitable that I turn to my Depute Head buddy for the last fifteen years or so of my career, George Burns – not named after the well known American comedian, but possessed of a similarly dry and observant wit.

We encouraged each other, sometimes in the most outrageous manner, in the task of pricking what we saw as the pomposity of others with humour and 'witty' observations. From Her Majesty's Inspectors to school janitors, none was guaranteed to escape our verbal buzz bombs. And we were not above a little comic jousting with pupils as well, if we felt it appropriate and helpful.

Growing up in the Sixties, I suppose our role models may have been those disrespectful enemies of authority, Hawkeye Pierce and Trapper McIntyre, from M.A.S.H.

I should point out it was not a deliberate approach, it just reflected who we were and how we approached our lives. Our coming together was a mere coincidence on which we were happy to build.

It is, of course, a high risk strategy, and George, being more daring than I, occasionally misjudged the moment, sometimes with embarrassing consequences, often to cause even more hilarity. Nobody will ever forget the time when he solicitously supported the school chef whose marriage had broken up with the line: "Was it something you cooked?"

By and large, however, I think our approach was appreciated – although the laughter which emitted from the office we originally shared led to us being relocated to separate offices fairly rapidly. I am sure the staff had many names for us as a duet: Stadtler and

Waldorf, Jack and Victor, and Hinge and Bracket were just those of which we were aware. However, I hope and trust that our humour showed our humanity and made us more accessible and trustworthy as school leaders and managers.

I think it proved a sair fecht to some of the headteachers with whom we worked. Neither of us were good at hiding boredom and our 'bull' detectors were always fully switched on at management and other meetings. I have some sympathy for those heads who had important business to cover, or developments to drive through. Whatever their own views, they had to follow the agenda, and wise cracking deputes probably hindered the cause more than they would have liked. On the other hand, we were both hard working and willing to take on any task which we believed to be in the interest of pupils, staff, or school community. I hope the laughter oiled the wheels of progress, and I have to say, I would rather work in a school where the sound of laughter, rather than silence, or anger, escaped through the door from senior management team meetings.

We always took the job seriously, we seldom took ourselves seriously. I think that was the right approach – and I thank George for his comradeship and humour – and for his unfailing support, and affection, for staff and pupils – all of which confirmed and inspired me in my own approach.

We had put our lives into the school for fifteen years or more; we were constants in a changing management team, and we were aware – ourselves, and from the comments of others, that much of the school's pervading ethos had come from the continuity of our approach. Neither of us were by nature self serving or arrogant. However, on good days, when the blue skies were evident through the glass roof of the central atrium, when the steady hum of happy and engaged pupils surrounded us, we would share a look of contentment, and one or other of us would assert, in the words of the old song: "We built this city on rock and roll!"

It all brought its own reward.

In my farewell speech in the staffroom on my final day, I quoted words, albeit uttered in very different circumstances, from one of my heroes, James Connolly.

At the start of the Easter Rising, he turned to Patrick Pearse and said: "Thanks be to God that we have lived to see this day," and, when his wife bemoaned the loss of his life before his execution, he responded: "But wasn't it a full life, and isn't this a good end?"

I am so glad I was a teacher, I can't imagine a life more fulfilling, and I am forever grateful that my career progressed the way it did, and that I was able to end my career so positively – a comfort not granted to all.

I wanted to write this reflection, in part, to answer the question: "What was all that about?" I hope my words have, at least in part, answered that question to the reader's satisfaction.

For myself, for my own answer, I return to that Clintonesque phrase, on the poster on my office wall:

"It's the kids, stupid!"

Printed in Great Britain
by Amazon

The Golem presents a view of science as fallible and untidy, a matter of craft rather than logic. To do this it examines a series of experiments, some famous, such as the proofs of relativity theory, and some not so famous. In each case it shows that scientific certainties do not come from experimental method, but from the way ambiguous results were interpreted.

To explain science the authors display science. Readers should prepare themselves to learn two things: a little *of* science – of the science of relativity, of the centre of the sun, of cosmic forces, of the brains of worms and rats, of the invention of germs, of cold fusion, and of lizards' sex lives – and a lot *about* science – how experiments are really done and how scientific conclusions are reached. The essential fallibility of even so called crucial experiments is displayed.

The Golem: what everyone should know about science

The Golem

what everyone should know about science

HARRY COLLINS

*Professor of Sociology and Director of the Science
Studies Centre at the University of Bath*

TREVOR PINCH

*Associate Professor in the Department of Science and Technology Studies at
Cornell University*

CAMBRIDGE
UNIVERSITY PRESS

Published by the Press Syndicate of the University of Cambridge
The Pitt Building, Trumpington Street, Cambridge CB2 1RP
40 West 20th Street, New York, NY 10011–4211, USA
10 Stamford Road, Oakleigh, Melbourne 3166, Australia

First published 1993
Reprinted 1994

Printed in Great Britain by Athenæum Press Ltd, Newcastle upon Tyne

A catalogue record for this book is available from the British Library

Library of Congress cataloguing in publication data

Collins, H. M. (Harry M.), 1943–
The golem: what everyone should know about
science / Harry Collins, Trevor Pinch.
p. cm.
Includes bibliographical references.
1. Science–History. 2. Science–Social aspects–History.
I. Pinch, T. J. (Trevor J.) II. Title.
Q125.C552 1993
500–dc20

ISBN 0 521 35601 6 hardback

To *the memory of*

SIDNEY COLLINS

and

for **JOAN PINCH**

Contents

Preface and acknowledgements

This book is for the general reader who wants to know how science really works and to know how much authority to grant to experts; it is for the student studying science at school or university; and it is for those at the very beginning of a course in the history, philosophy or sociology of science. In sum, the book is for the citizen living in a technological society. The book adapts the work of professional historians and sociologists for a more general audience. The chapters are of different origins. Some are based on our own work and some on our readings of a selection of the few books and papers in the history and sociology of science that adopt a non-retrospective approach. In these later cases we have relied on the original authors for additional information, and have had occasional resource to archival material. In choosing chapters to represent science we have been limited by the materials to hand. But, given this constraint, we have covered the ground in two ways. We have selected from the life sciences and the physical sciences and we have selected episodes of famous science alongside relatively mundane science and what some would call bad science. We have done this because we want to show that, in terms of our concerns, the science is the same whether it is famous or infamous, big or small, foundational or ephemeral.

Chapter 5 on gravity waves and chapter 7 on solar neutrinos are based on our own original field studies in the sociology of scientific knowledge. The quotations included in these chapters, where not otherwise referenced, are taken from interviews conducted by us with the principal scientists in the areas in question. The interviews concerning the search for gravitational radiation were conducted by Collins between 1972 and 1975. Pinch interviewed solar neutrino scientists in the second half of the 1970s. More complete accounts of this work have been published in other places, notably, Collins' book, *Changing Order: Replication and Induction in Scientific Practice*, and Pinch's book, *Confronting Nature: The Sociology of Solar-Neutrino Detection*.

Chapter 1, on memory transfer, is based on a PhD thesis entitled 'Memories and Molecules' by David Travis, completed with Collins at the University of Bath. Travis was able to read and comment in detail on earlier drafts of the chapter.

The remaining chapters rest on our use of less direct sources of evidence. Chapter 3 on cold fusion is based on Pinch's readings of two books: Frank Close, *Too Hot to Handle: The Race for Cold Fusion* and Eugene Mallove, *Fire From Ice: Searching for the Truth Behind The Cold Fusion Furore*. Pinch also used Thomas Gieryn's paper, 'The Ballad of Pons and Fleischmann: Experiment and Narrative in the (Un)Making of Cold Fusion' and Bruce Lewenstein's paper, 'Cold Fusion and Hot History', and the Cold Fusion Archives held at Cornell University.

For chapter 2 Collins used Loyd Swenson's book, *The Ethereal Aether: A History of the Michelson–Morley–Miller Aether-Drift Experiments, 1880–1930*, and a series of papers. These included Dayton Miller's 1933 publication 'The Ether Drift Experiment and the Determination of the Absolute Motion of the Earth', John Earman and Clark Glymour's 'Relativity and Eclipses: The British Eclipse Expeditions of 1919 and their Predecessors', and H. Von Kluber's 'The Determination of Einstein's Light-deflection in the Gravitational Field of the Sun'. Collins was also helped by personal correspondence with Klaus Hentschel. For chapter 4 Collins used *Louis Pasteur: Free Lance of Science*, by Rene Dubos, and the paper by John Farley and Gerald Geison entitled 'Science Politics and Spontaneous Generation in Nineteenth-Century France: the Pasteur–Pouchet Debate'. (Page references in the text of this chapter refer to the reprint of Farley and Geison's paper in *The Sociology of Scientific Knowledge: A Sourcebook*, edited by Collins.) Collins also referred to the *Dictionary of Scientific Biography*, and consulted some original papers of Pasteur and Pouchet.

For chapter 6, on the sex life of lizards, Pinch relied on Greg Myers's, *Writing Biology: Texts in the Social Construction of Scientific Knowledge*.

The conclusion draws heavily on the last chapter of Collins' book *Changing Order*, on Paul Atkinson and Sarah Delamont's paper 'Mock-ups and Cock-ups: The Stage Management of Guided Discovery Instruction', and on the paper by Collins and Shapin entitled 'Experiment, Science Teaching and the New History and Sociology of Science'.

All the above-mentioned works are fully referenced in the bibliography.

For help and advice we thank David Travis, Lloyd Swenson, Clark Glymour, Klaus Hentschel, Bruce Lewenstein, Gerry Geison, Peter Dear, Pearce Williams, David Crews, Peter Taylor, Shiela Jasanoff, Greg Myers, Paul Atkinson, Frank Close, Eugene Mallove, Sarah Delamont and Steven Shapin. None of them are to blame for the mistakes we may have made in translating their professional work into our words, or in interpreting their findings in our way.

Introduction: the golem

Science seems to be either all good or all bad. For some, science is a crusading knight beset by simple-minded mystics while more sinister figures wait to found a new fascism on the victory of ignorance. For others it is science which is the enemy; our gentle planet, our feel for the just, the poetic and the beautiful, are assailed by a technological bureaucracy – the antithesis of culture – controlled by capitalists with no concern but profit. For some, science gives us agricultural self-sufficiency, cures for the crippled, and a global network of communication; for others it gives us weapons of war, a school teacher's fiery death as the space shuttle falls from grace, and the silent, deceiving, bone-poisoning, Chernobyl.

Both these ideas of science are wrong and dangerous. The personality of science is neither that of a chivalrous knight nor that of a pitiless juggernaut. What, then, is science? Science is a golem.

A golem is a creature of Jewish mythology. It is a humanoid made by man from clay and water, with incantations and spells. It is powerful. It grows a little more powerful every day. It will follow orders, do your work, and protect you from the ever threatening enemy. But it is clumsy and dangerous. Without control, a golem may destroy its masters with its flailing vigour.

The idea of a golem takes on different connotations in different legends. In some the golem is terrifyingly evil, but there is a more homely tradition: in the Yiddish brought from the East European ghetto, a golem (pronounced 'goilem' in that dialect), is a metaphor for any lumbering fool who knows neither his own strength nor the extent of his clumsiness and ignorance. For Collins' grandmother it was good to know a golem if you wanted the garden dug up, but the children were advised to stay clear. Such a golem is not a fiendish devil, it is a bumbling giant.

Since we are using a golem as a metaphor for science, it is also worth noting that in the mediaeval tradition the creature of clay was animated by having the Hebrew 'EMETH', meaning truth, inscribed on its forehead – it is truth that drives it on. But this does not mean it understands the truth – far from it.

The idea of this book is to explain the golem that is science. We aim to show that it is not an evil creature but it is a little daft. Golem Science is not to be blamed for its mistakes; they are our mistakes. A golem cannot be blamed if it is doing its best. But we must not expect too much. A golem, powerful though it is, is the creature of our art and our craft.

The book is very straightforward. To show what Golem Science is, we are going to do something almost unheard of; we are going to display science, with as little reflection on scientific method as we can muster. We are simply going to describe episodes of science, some well known, and some not so well known. We are going to say what happened. Where we do reflect, as in the cold-fusion story, it will be reflection on matters human not methodological. The results will be surprising. The shock comes because the idea of science is so enmeshed in philosophical analyses, in myths, in theories, in hagiography, in smugness, in heroism, in superstition, in fear, and, most important, in perfect hindsight, that what actually happens has never been told outside of a small circle.

Prepare to learn two things. Prepare to learn of little *of* science – of the science of relativity, of the centre of the sun, of cosmic forces, of the brains of worms and rats, of the invention of germs, of cold fusion, and of lizards' sex lives. And prepare to learn a lot *about* science – to learn to love the bumbling giant for what it is.

At the end of the book we'll tell you what we think you should have learned and what the implications are when Golem Science is put to work. The main stuff of the book is in chapters 1–7, which describe episodes (case studies) of science. Each is self-contained and they can be read in any order. The conclusion too can be read at any time, though it will not be convincing outside the setting of the case studies. Whether it is best to read the case studies first, the conclusion first, or something in-between, we do not know; readers can decide for themselves.

We have done very little in the way of explicit analysis of the process of science. Nevertheless, there are common themes that crop up in every chapter, the most important of which is the idea of the 'experimenter's regress'; it is spelt out in chapter 5, on gravitational radiation. The problem with experiments is that they tell you nothing unless they are competently done, but in controversial science no-one can agree on a criterion of competence. Thus, in controversies, it is invariably the case that scientists disagree not only about results, but also about the quality of each other's work. This is what stops experiments being decisive and gives rise to the regress. Readers who would like to go into more detail should refer to the books by Collins and by Pinch mentioned in the 'Preface and Acknowledgements'. The point is that, for citizens who want to take part in the democratic process of a technological society, all the science they need to know about is controversial; thus, it is all subject to the experimenter's regress.

It may be that our conclusions are too unpalatable for some, in which case we hope the descriptions are interesting and informative in their own right. Each case study describes a piece of beautiful scientific work. But the beauty is not the gloss of the philosopher's polishing wheel; it is the glint of rough diamond.

Edible knowledge: the chemical transfer of memory

Introduction

Everyone is fascinated by memory and nearly everyone feels that they would prefer their memory to be a little better. Memorising lines in a play, or memorising multiplication tables, is the kind of hard work that people like to avoid. The slow growth of experience that counts as wisdom seems to be the gradual accumulation of memories over a lifetime. If only we could pass on our memories directly we could use our creative abilities from an early age without needing to spend years building the foundations first.

Between the late 1950s and the mid-1970s it began to look as though one day we might be able to build our memories without the usual effort. This was as a result of experiments done by James V. McConnell and, later, Georges Ungar, on the chemical transfer of memory in worms and rats. If memories are encoded in molecules then, in principle, it should be possible to transfer *The Complete Works of Shakespeare* to memory by ingesting a pill, to master the multiplication tables by injection into the bloodstream, or to become fluent in a foreign language by having it deposited under the skin; a whole new meaning would be given to the notion of 'swallowing the dictionary'. McConnell and Ungar believed they had shown that memories were stored in chemicals that could be transferred from animal to animal. They believed they had shown that substances corresponding to memories could be extracted from the brain of one creature and given to a second creature with beneficial effects. If the first creature had been trained in a task, such as turning left or right in an alley in order to reach food, the second creature would know how to reach the food without training – or, at least, with less than the usual amount of training. The second creature would have, as one might say, 'a head start', compared with one which had not had the benefit of the substance corresponding to the memory.

Worms

The first experiments were done by McConnell on planarian worms, a type of flatworm. McConnell trained them to scrunch up their bodies in response to light. He shone a bright light on the worms as they swam along the bottom of a trough, and then gave them a mild shock which caused their bodies to arch or 'scrunch'. Eventually the worms learned to associate light with shock and began to scrunch when a light was shone upon them whether or not the shock was delivered. Worms that scrunched in response to light alone counted as 'trained' worms. This is how McConnell described the experiments

> Imagine a trough gouged out of plastic, 12 inches in length, semi-circular in cross-section, and filled with pond water. At either end are brass electrodes attached to a power source. Above the trough are two electric light bulbs. Back and forth in the trough crawls a single flatworm, and in front of the apparatus sits the experimenter, his eye on the worm, his hands on two switches. When the worm is gliding smoothly in a straight line on the bottom of the trough, the experimenter turns on the lights for 3 seconds. After the light has been on for two of the three seconds, the experimenter adds one second of electric shock, which passes through the water and causes the worm to contract. The experimenter records the behaviour of the worm during the two-second period after the light has come on but before the shock has started. If the animal gives a noticeable turning movement or a contraction prior to the onset to the shock this is scored as a 'correct' or 'conditioned' response. *(McConnell, 1962, p.42)*

Now this sounds fairly straightforward but it is necessary to go into detail from the very beginning. Planarian worms scrunch their bodies and turn their heads from time to time even if they are left alone. They will also scrunch in response to many stimuli, including bright light. To train the worms, McConnell had first to discover the level of light that was bright enough for the worms to sense, but not so bright as to cause them to scrunch without the electric shock. Since worm behaviour varies from time to time and from worm to worm we are immediately into statistics rather than unambiguous yes's and no's. What is worse, the effectiveness of the shock training depends upon the worm not being scrunched when the shock is delivered. A worm that is already scrunched has no response left to make to light and shock, and therefore experiences no increment in its training regime when the stimulus is administered. It turns out, then, that to train worms well, it is necessary to watch them carefully and deliver the stimuli only when they are swimming calmly. All these aspects of worm training require skill – skill that McConnell and his assistants built up slowly over a period. When McConnell began his experiments in the 1950s he found that if he trained worms with 150 'pairings' of light followed by shock it resulted in a 45% scrunch response rate to light alone. In the 1960s, by which time he and his associates had become much more practised, the same number of pairings produced a 90% response rate.

In the mid-1950s McConnell tried cutting trained worms in half. The planarian worm can regenerate into a whole worm from either half of a dissected specimen. McConnell was interested in whether worms that regenerated from the front half, containing the putative brain, would retain the training. They did, but the real surprise was that worms regenerated from the brain-less rear half did at least as well if not better. This suggested that the training was somehow distributed throughout the worm, rather than being localised in the brain. The idea emerged that the training might be stored chemically.

McConnell tried to transfer training by grafting parts of trained worms to untrained specimens, but these experiments met with little success. Some planarian worms are cannibalistic. McConnell next tried feeding minced portions of trained worms to their naive brothers and sisters and found that those who had ingested trained meat were about one-and-a-half times more likely to respond to light alone than they otherwise would be. These experiments were being reported around 1962. By now, the notion that memory could be *transferred* by chemical means was the driving force of the experiments.

Arguments about the worm experiments

Transplantation versus chemical transfer

The notion that training or memory could be transferred by chemical means gave rise to substantial controversy. One counter argument was to agree that training was being transferred between worm and worm but to argue that it had no great significance. The planarian worm has a digestive system that is quite different from that of a mammal. The worm's digestive system does not break down its food into small chemical components but rather incorporates large components of ingested material into its body. To speak loosely, it might be that the naive worms were being given 'implants' of trained worm – either bits of brain, or some other kind of distributed memory structure – rather than absorbing memory substance. This would be interesting but would not imply that memory was a chemical phenomenon and, in any case, would probably have no significance for our understanding of memory in mammals. McConnell's response to this was to concentrate on what he believed was the memory substance. Eventually he was injecting naive worms with RNA extracted from trained creatures, and claiming considerable success.

Sensitisation versus training

Another line of attack rested on the much more basic argument that planarian worms were too primitive to be trained. According to this line, McConnell had fooled himself into thinking that he had trained the worms to respond to light, whereas he had merely increased their general level of sensitivity to all stimuli. If anything was being transferred between worm and worm, it was a sensitising substance rather than something that carried a specific memory.

It is difficult to counter this argument because any kind of training regime is likely to increase sensitivity. Training is done by 'pairing' exposure to light with electric shock. One way of countering the sensitisation hypothesis is to subject the worms to the same number of shocks and bursts of light, but in randomised order. If sensitisation is the main effect, then worms subjected to a randomised pattern of shocks and light bursts should be just as likely to scrunch in response to light alone as worms subjected to properly organised pairings of stimuli. If it is training rather than sensitisation that is important, the trained worms will do better.

Once more, this sounds simple. Indeed, McConnell and other 'worm runners' did find a significant difference between *trained* and *sensitised* worms, but the effect is difficult to repeat because training is a matter of *skilled practice*. As explained above, to effect good training it is necessary to observe the worms closely and learn to understand when they are calm enough for a shock to produce a training increment. Different trainers may obtain widely differing outcomes from training regimes however much they try to repeat the experiments according to the specification.

To the critic, the claim that a poor result is the outcome of poor training technique – specifically, a failure to understand the worms – sounds like an *ad hoc* excuse. To say that only certain technicians understand the worms well enough to be able to get a result sounds like a most unscientific argument. Critics always think that the claim that only some people are able to get results – the 'golden hands' argument, as one might call it – is *prima facie* evidence that something unsound is going on. And there are many cases in the history of science where a supposedly golden-handed experimenter has turned out to be a fraud. Nevertheless, the existence of specially skilful experimenters – the one person in a lab who can successfully manage an extraction or a delicate measurement – is also widely attested. In the field of pharmacology, for example, the 'bioassay' is widely used. In a bioassay, the existence and quantity of a drug is determined by its effects on living matter or whole organisms. In a sense, the measurement of the effect of various brain extracts on worms and rats could be seen as itself a bioassay rather than a transfer experiment. Yet the bioassay is a technique that has the reputation of being potentially difficult to 'transfer' from one group of scientists to another because it requires so much skill and practice. It is, then, very hard to separate golden hands from *ad hocery*, a problem that has a particular salience in this field. Certainly attributions of dishonesty are not always appropriate.

For this kind of reason the argument between McConnell and his critics was able to drag on, reaching its zenith in 1964 with the publication of a special supplement to the journal, *Animal Behaviour*, devoted to the controversy. At this point it would be hard to say who was winning, but it was clear that McConnell's claim that training worms required special skills was becoming a little more acceptable.

Confounding variables and replication

Sensitisation could be looked at as a confounding variable, and critics put forward a number of others. For example, planarian worms produce slime as they slither along. Nervous worms prefer swimming into slimed areas which have been frequented by other worms. A naive worm swimming in a two-branched alley will naturally prefer to follow the path marked out most strongly by the slime of worms that have gone before. If the alley has been used for training, the preferred route will be that which the trainee worms have used most often. Thus, naive worms might prefer to follow their trained counterparts not because of the transfer of any substance, but because of the slime trails left before. Even in an individual worm it might be that the development of a preference for, say, right turns, might be the build-up of a self-reinforcing slime trail rather than a trained response.

Once this has been pointed out there are a number of remedies. For example, the troughs might be scrubbed between sessions (though it is never quite clear when enough scrubbing has been done), or new troughs might be regularly employed. One critic found that in properly cleaned troughs no learning effect could be discovered, but McConnell, as a result of further research, claimed that worms could not be trained properly in a clean environment. He suggested that worms were unhappy in an environment made unfamiliar because it was free of slime; too much hygiene prevented the experiments working. One can readily imagine the nature of the argument between McConnell and his critics over the effects of sliming.

Eventually, this part of the argument was resolved, at least to McConnell's satisfaction, by pre-sliming training grounds with naive worms that were not part of the experiment. This made the troughs and alleys comfortable for the experimental subjects without reinforcing any particular behaviour.

All these arguments take time, and it is not always clear to everyone exactly what has been established at any point. This is one of the reasons why controversies drag on for so long when the logic of the experiments seems clear and simple. Remember, too, that every experiment requires a large number of trials and a statistical analysis. The levels of the final effects are usually low so it is not always clear just what has been proved.

Whether or not McConnell's results could be replicated by others, or could be said to be replicable, depended on common agreement about what were the important variables in the experiment. We have already discussed the necessity – from McConnell's point of view – of understanding and of skilled handling of the worms. In his own laboratory, the training of 'worm runners' by an experienced scientist was followed by weeks of practice. It was necessary to learn not to 'push the worms too hard'. In his own words:

> [it is necessary to] treat them tenderly, almost with love ... it seems certain that the variability in success rate from one laboratory to another is due, at least in part, to differences in personality and past experience among the various investigators. (McConnell, 1965, p.26).

As explained, to look at it from the critics point of view, this was one of the *excuses* McConnell used in the face of the palpable non-repeatability of his work. The effect of sliming was another variable cited by both proponents and critics in their different ways.

As a scientific controversy develops more variables that might affect the experiments come to the fore. For the proponents these are more reasons why the unpractised might have difficulty in making the experiments work; for the critics, they are more excuses that can be used when others fail to replicate the original findings.

In the case of the worm experiments up to 70 variables were cited at one time or another to account for discrepancies in experimental results. They included: the species and size of the worms; the way they were housed when not undergoing training – was it in the dark or the light?; the type of feeding; the frequency of training; the temperature and chemical composition of the water; the strength of the light, its colour and duration; the nature of the electric shock – its pulse shape, strength, polarity and so forth; the worm's feeding schedule; the season of the year; and the time of day when the worms were trained. Even the barometric pressure, the phase of the moon, and the orientation of the training trough with respect to the earth's magnetic field were cited at one time or another. This provided ample scope for accusation and counter-accusation – skill versus *ad hocery*. The greater the number of potential variables, the harder it is to decide whether one experiment really replicates the conditions of another.

The Worm Runner's Digest

McConnell was an unusual scientist. What people are prepared to believe is not just a function of what a scientist discovers but of the image of the work that he or she presents. McConnell was no respecter of scientific convention and in this he did himself no favours. Among his unconventional acts was founding, in 1959, a journal called *The Worm Runner's Digest*. He claimed this was a way of coping with the huge amount of mail that he received as a result of the initial work on worms, but the *Digest* also published cartoons and scientific spoofs.

Ironically, one of the disadvantages of the worm experiments was that they seemed so easy. It meant that many experimenters, including high school students, could try the transfer tests for themselves. It was these high school students who swamped McConnell with requests for information and accounts of their results. The newsletter, which became *The Worm Runner's Digest*, was McConnell's response.

It is not necessarily a good thing to have high school students repeat one's experiments for it makes them appear to lack *gravitas*. What is worse, it makes it even more difficult than usual to separate serious and competent scientific work from the slapdash or incompetent. It is certainly not a good thing to found a 'jokey' newsletter if you want your work to be taken seriously.

In 1967 the journal split into two halves, printed back to back, with the second half being re-titled *The Journal of Biological Psychology*. This journal was treated in a more conventional way, with articles being refereed. The idea was that the more serious work would appear in the refereed end of the journal while the jokey newsletter material would be reserved for the *Digest* half. (The analogy between the journal and the front and back halves of regenerating worms was not lost on McConnell and the contributors. Which end contained the brain?) *The Journal of Biological Psychology*, refereed though it was, never attained the full respectability of a conventional scientific outlet. How could it with *The Worm Runner's Digest* simultaneously showing its backside to scientific convention in every issue?

Because a number of McConnell's results were published in *The Worm Runner's Digest/The Journal of Biological Psychology* scientists did not know how to take them. To put it another way, any critic who was determined not to take McConnell's work seriously had a good excuse to ignore his claims if their only scientific outlet was in McConnell's own, less than fully attested, journal. In the competition between scientific claims, the manner of presentation is just as important as the content. The scientific community has its ceremonies and its peculiar heraldic traditions. The symbols may be different – Albert Einstein's unruly hair and Richard Feynman's Brooklyn accent in place of gilded lions and rampant unicorns – but the division between scientific propriety and eccentricity is firm if visible only to the enlightened. Much of what McConnell did fell on the wrong side of the line.

The ending of the worm controversy

Around the mid-1960s, as McConnell was beginning to establish that worms could be trained, if not that the transfer phenomenon could be demonstrated, the stakes were changed in such a way as to make some of the earlier arguments seem petty. This was the result of experiments suggesting that the transfer phenomenon could be found in mammals.

Some of McConnell's most trenchant critics had argued that planarian learning was impossible, others that it had not been fully proved. We may be sure that the strong attacks on learning were motivated by the importance of the transfer phenomenon. With the apparent demonstration of transfer in rats and mice, the objections to planarian learning dropped away. Rats and mice are familiar laboratory animals. There is no dispute that they can learn, and there is no dispute that in order to learn they have to be carefully handled. It is acknowledged that the technicians who handle the rats in a psychology or biology laboratory must be skilled at their job. Once the worm experiments were seen through the refracted light of the later experiments on rats it appeared entirely reasonable that worms should need special handling, and entirely reasonable that they could learn. The believers in McConnell's results stressed this, as in the following quotation from two experimenters:

> It seems paradoxical that when we run rats, we handle our subjects, we specify what breeding line the stock is from, we train them in sound-proof boxes, and we specify a large number of factors which when put together give us an output we call learning ... Planarians on the other hand are popped into a trough, given a ... [conditioned stimulus] and ... [an unconditioned stimulus] and are expected to perform like a learning rat. *(Corning and Riccio, 1970, p.129).*

But this kind of *cri de coeur* only came to seem reasonable to the majority at a later date. It only became acceptable when nobody cared very much because their attention had been turned to the much more exciting subject of transfer of behaviour among mammals. This was a much more important challenge to received wisdom about the nature of memory.

Mammals

Early experiments

The first claims to have demonstrated memory transfer in mammals came from four independent groups working without knowledge of each other's research. The first four studies were associated with the names, in alphabetical order, of Fjerdingstad, Jacobson, Reinis, and Ungar. All these studies were being done around 1964, and were published in 1965.

Fjerdingstad placed rats in a training box with two alleyways, one was lit and one was darkened according to a random sequence. The rats were deprived of water for 24 hours, but received a few drops if they entered the illuminated alley. Injections of trained brain extract caused naive rats to prefer the box in which their trained colleagues had found relief from thirst.

Jacobson had hungry rats learn to associate the sound of a clicker with a food reward. The association of clicks with food could, so he claimed, be transferred to naive rats by injection.

Reinis taught rats to take food from a dispenser during the period of a conditioned stimulus – either a light or a buzzer. This expectation, it appeared, could also be transferred by injections.

McConnell's laboratory also began to work on rats in the mid-1960s but, in the long term, the most important mammal experimenter was Georges Ungar. Ungar began by showing that tolerance to morphine could be transferred. As an animal becomes accustomed to a drug it requires greater doses to produce the same effects on its behaviour. This is known as 'tolerance' to the drug. Ungar ground up the brains of 50 tolerant rats and injected an extract into unexposed rats. The result, reported in 1965, seemed to be that the tolerance was transferred. Whether this is to be counted as the transfer of *learning* is not clear. As explained earlier, Ungar might be thought of as doing a complicated bioassay rather than an experiment in the transfer of learning. The significance of this point will become more evident in due course.

Ungar moved on to attempt to transfer 'habituation'. He exposed rats to the sound of a loud bell until they became accustomed to it and ceased to exhibit the usual 'startle reaction'. Habituation too could be transferred, apparently, through injection of brain extract. Interestingly, Ungar transferred the habituation not to rats but from rats to mice.

Early reactions

It is important to get some of the flavour of the early reaction of scientists to these strange and unorthodox results. The following reports of reactions are from 1966, just after the early mammal results had appeared. It is probable that part of the strength of the response was caused by association with the earlier worm experiments.

One scientist reported that after he had given his presentation he found that people 'drifted away from him' in the bar. Other scientists told of similar reactions to the exposure of the transfer results at conferences:

> the nightly private gatherings brought to the surface all the deeply felt emotional objections which, for reasons I have difficulty to understand and analyse, some people have against the whole idea. This was particularly manifest after a few drinks.

> I was stunned. People were really – vicious is maybe too strong a word – but certainly mean . . . It took me quite a while to realize I had trodden on sacred territory. It was 'Why didn't you do this?', 'Why didn't you do that?' . . . it was all accusations.

> . . . it was one of those times when you see the people who are at the absolute cutting edge of a science, all packed together . . . in a smoke-filled room, trying to decide what was right . . . I remember that meeting particularly, because at the end of the evening those people who had gotten positive results were telling the people who had gotten negative results that they were totally incompetent and didn't know how to run an experiment; and the people who had gotten negative results were telling those people who had gotten positive results that they were frauds. That they were faking the data.

Georges Ungar's main work

Ungar's best-known work began in 1967. In these experiments rats had to choose between entering a lighted or a darkened box. A rat's natural preference would be for the dark but on entering the darkened box they were locked in and given a five second electric shock delivered through the metal grid of the floor. The rats learned to avoid the dark box very quickly, but Ungar gave his rats five trials a day, for six to eight days, to make sure that a good supply of the 'fear of the dark' chemical was produced in the rats' brains.

After training, the rats were killed and an extract was prepared from their brains. This was injected into mice, who were tested in the same apparatus. By measuring the proportion of time spent in the light or dark box during a three minute trial it was possible to tell if mice which had been injected with brain extract from trained rats were more likely to avoid the dark than those which had been injected with a similar extract prepared from the brains of normal rats.

Replication in mammals

As explained, all the work on mammals was violently contested and attempts were made both to support and disprove the findings. According to Ungar's rough (and contentious) analysis of published experimental reports between 1965 and 1975, there were 105 positive and 23 negative replications, following the pattern below:

Ungar's analysis of transfer experiments in mammals, 1965–75

	1965	1966	1967	1968	1969	1970	1971	1972	1973	1974	1975
Positive	13	13	13	16	23	17	27	13	23	17	8
Negative	1	6	4	5	1	3	1	1	–	–	1

This is a good point at which to note a feature of science that is often misunderstood. The sheer number and weight of experimental replications is not usually enough to persuade the scientific community to believe in some unorthodox finding. In this case, for example, a single one of the negative experiments, carried out by a number of influential scientists, outweighed the far larger number of positive results. Scientists have to have grounds for believing the result of an experiment – and this is quite reasonable given, as we demonstrate throughout the book, the skill involved. Scientists will demand better grounds where an experiment produces more unorthodox results; one might say that they start with grounds for not believing. Again, among the sorts of grounds people look for in deciding whether or not to believe a result are the scientist's reputation and the respectability of his or her institution. This, of course, militates still more strongly against the unorthodox. Ungar's figures show clearly that experimental replication is not a straightforward business and neither are the conclusions that scientists draw from replications.

Naturally, competing results were supported by competing arguments about the competence and skill of the experimenters. Let us give an example of the 'flavour' of these problems with illustrations from the debate between Ungar and the group at Stanford University.

The debate with Stanford

Stanford attempted to replicate Ungar's work as closely as possible. It was felt that in Ungar's experiments:

> some ... peptide material has evidently been isolated ... if this material – whatever its exact structure or state of purity – is truly capable of specifically transferring a learned behaviour to untrained recipient animals, the discovery ranks among the most fundamental in modern biology. *(Goldstein, 1973, p.60).*

In the event they obtained negative results. Inevitably, this led Ungar to point to residual differences between the Stanford experiments and his own which could account for the failure. In what follows, then, we first see the two series of experiments looking more and more like each other as the Stanford group tried to replicate every detail of Ungar's work, and then the experiments are 'prised apart' again when the unexpected Stanford outcome is reported.

The leader of the Stanford group, Avram Goldstein, first spent three days at Ungar's laboratory to make sure that he could follow the published procedures accurately. In a 1971 publication, the subsequent work of him and his collaborators was described as follows:

In the next three months we carried out eighteen unsuccessful experiments with 125 donor rats and 383 recipient saline and control mice. We then did a blind test on our mice using control and trained donor extracts provided by Dr. Ungar. Next, we sent 100 of our mice to Houston, for testing as recipients concurrently with the local strain. Finally, we selected, from all our experiments, those mice (of both sexes) which seemed to avoid the black box more often after receiving extracts. These animals were bred and the offspring tested as recipients. We hoped to select for recipient capability that might be under genetic influence. The results of all these experiments were negative.
(Goldstein, Sheehan and Goldstein, 1971, p. 126).

These various collaborations with Ungar's laboratories were meant to eliminate any residual differences between the Stanford procedures and those used by Ungar. Stanford, as was clear from the same publication, were trying their best in an open-minded spirit:

We should not dismiss the possibility that acquired behaviour ... can be transferred by brain extracts, merely because the proposed mechanisms ... seem fanciful, especially since confirmatory results have been published by several laboratories.
(Goldstein et al., 1971, p. 129)

After their failure the tone of the debate changed. The Stanford group suggested that their 'rather exhaustive' attempts showed that the conditions for a successful transfer would have to be specified more exactly.

Can the investigators state precisely the conditions for carrying out an assay, in such detail that competent scientists elsewhere can reproduce their results? Our own repeated failure ... could be dismissed as the bungling work of incompetents were it not matched by published experiences of others.　　　　(Goldstein, 1973, p. 61).

The difference between the two experiments began to emerge. With reference to the interpretation of one aspect of the results, Goldstein and his team noted:

Because we were unable to agree with Dr. Ungar on the interpretation of the results they are not included here but will presumably be published independently by him.　　(Goldstein et al., 1971, p. 129).

To this, Ungar replied:

... some of the most important parameters were arbitrarily changed ... This was certainly not done because he was unaware of our procedures.   *(Ungar, 1973, p. 312).*

Ungar also stated that the Stanford group had 'eliminated one of the three boxes of our testing device, trained some of the donors only once instead of five times ... and used a different strain of mice' (Ungar, 1973, p. 309).

Ungar also objected to the measure of dark avoidance that the Stanford group had used. Rather than presenting the results in terms of the length of time the rats spent in the darkened box, they had measured 'latency'. This is the length of time the mouse is in the apparatus before it *first* enters the dark box. Goldstein stated that he had noted that Ungar also recorded latencies, but always published data in terms of dark box time.

> I thought this curious, because if dark avoidance behaviour were really induced by the injections, the latency would be increased. This is elementary logic. Indeed, latency is the common and accepted measure for such behavioural phenomena among experimental psychologists. Yet Ungar has never used latency ...   *(Goldstein, 1973, p. 61).*

Ungar replied:

> ... in his latest comments, he tries to justify one of these changes, the use of latency, as a criterion of dark avoidance, instead of the total time spent in the dark box. We have shown empirically, and showed it to him, that a number of mice run rapidly into the dark but come out immediately and spend the rest of the time in the light ... latency would, therefore, give misleading results.   *(Ungar, 1973, p. 312).*

Goldstein felt:

> Dark box time ... would probably be sensitive to other behavioural effects. A recipient mouse that wanders around more because it is hyperactive would naturally be more likely to leave the dark box than a passive animal.   *(Goldstein, 1973, p. 61).*

As can be seen, Ungar and Goldstein disagreed about whether enough detail had been published, whether certain differences between the original and the replication were significant, and the appropriateness of different measures of fear of the dark. Ungar saw

Goldstein's work as having departed clearly and significantly from his procedures.

Competing strategies

In so far as the memory transfer technique was important to psychologists, it was important primarily because it seemed to offer a tool for 'dissecting' memory. For many of the psychologists the main hope was that the technique would allow them to take apart some aspects of learning. The precise chemical nature of memory transfer substances was of secondary importance to this group. Thus, McConnell remarked, jokingly, that as far as he was concerned the active material might as well be boot polish.

McConnell and other behavioural psychologists worked to find out whether further memory-related behavioural tendencies could be chemically transferred from mammal to mammal. Fear of the dark might be seen as a general disposition rather than something specific that had been learned.

The *specificity* argument paralleled the sensitisation debate in the case of the worms but was even more salient in the case of mammals. The exciting thing would be if there were specific molecules related to specific memories or learned behaviours. For many, this claim was difficult to accept. Much more palatable was the notion that molecules would have a non-specific effect on behaviour that would vary in different circumstances. For example, suppose the effect of the memory molecule was to alter the overall emotional state of the animal rather than providing it with a particular memory. In such a case, placing an injected but untrained animal in the same circumstances that its dead colleague had experienced in training – say a choice between light and dark – should cause it to produce the response that had been induced during the training – choosing the light. In different circumstances, however, the effect might be quite different; for example, if the injected animal was given a choice between pink and blue boxes it might cause it to bite its tail. If this was what transfer was all about, there would never be a *Complete Works of Shakespeare* pill.

McConnell wanted to find out if what psychologists would count as 'grade-A learning' could be transferred. One might say that proving that something like the works of Shakespeare could exist in chemical form was what drove McConnell on.

To show 'grade-A learning' McConnell and other experimenters taught rats more complex tasks such as the choice of a left or a right turn in an alley in order to get food. These experiments were done in the late 1960s. 'Discrimination' tasks such as these seemed to be transferable among rats as well as other creatures such as cats, goldfish, cockroaches and the praying mantis. A degree of cross-species transfer was also found.

Unlike McConnell, Ungar was a pharmacologist by training and was much more interested in a 'biochemical strategy'. That is, he wanted to isolate, analyse and synthesise active molecules. For Ungar the important thing was to find some reproducible transfer effect and study the chemical that was responsible for it, whether or not the transferred behaviour was grade-A learning. Concentrating on fear of the dark, Ungar set about extracting what became known as 'Scotophobin'. To obtain a measurable amount, he required the brains of 4000 trained rats. This was certainly big, expensive, science as far as psychologists were concerned, and even other biochemists could not compete with him. Eventually Ungar believed he had isolated, analysed and then synthesised Scotophobin.

Ungar had hoped that the problems of repeating chemical transfer experiments would be solved by the availability of the synthetic material but, as so often in contested science, there is so much detail that is contestable that experiments can force no-one to agree that anything significant has been found.

There were disputes over the purity of the synthetic material; its stability and the way it was kept by other laboratories before it was used; and the kind of behavioural changes (if any) it induced. In addition, Ungar announced several alterations to the precise chemical structure of Scotophobin. The upshot was continued controversy. A few of those who believed in the chemical transfer effect felt that there was a 'family' of Scotophobin-like chemicals for different species, with similar but slightly different formulae. One experiment showed that the synthetic version of Scotophobin had no effect on mice, but produced dark avoidance in goldfish!

It is difficult to be precise about the numbers of experiments on synthetic Scotophobin that were completed, since different synthetic versions were produced, many results were never published, and some of these were concerned only with testing exactly where the material ended up in the recipient's brain. Several dozens of experiments are known, but there is sufficient ambiguity for both believers and sceptics to draw comfort from the results.

The end of the story

McConnell closed his laboratory in 1971. He was unable to obtain further funding for the work and, in any case, he could see that to prove the transfer effect it would be necessary to adopt an Ungar-like strategy of isolating and synthesising the active agents. Ungar, one might say, had won the competition over experimental strategy. The psychologists had lost out to the 'big science' of biochemistry.

Ungar pressed ahead with his programme of research. Training thousands of rats was too large a project to be done frequently, and he turned his attention to goldfish. Goldfish are good at colour discrimination tasks and are relatively cheap. Nearly 17 000 trained goldfish gave their lives in the production of about 750 grams of colour discriminating brains but this was still insufficient for him to identify the chemical structure of the putative memory substances, 'chromodiopsins'.

Ungar, who was of normal retiring age when he began the work on transfer, died in 1977 at the age of 71 and the field died with him. It was Ungar's very dominance of the field, brought about by his ambitious approach, that had killed off competing laboratories. On the one hand there was never quite enough reliability in the transfer effect to make the experiments really attractive to a beginner or someone short of resources; on the other hand, Ungar had raised the stakes so much that the investment required to make a serious attempt at repeating his work was too high. Thus when Ungar died there was no-one to take over the mantle.

Ungar left behind a number of formulae for behaviourally active molecules that were the result of his work on rats and goldfish. Some scientists tried to synthesise Scotophobin and test it on animals but, as noted above, tests on Scotophobin did not provide any clear answer to the question of whether it really was the chemical embodiment of 'fear of the dark' or something more general such as fear. In any case, if Ungar's heroic efforts did have valuable implications, they were lost to view when the related field of brain-peptide chemistry exploded in the late 1970s. Scientists now had brain chemicals to work on which had clear effects, but effects unrelated to memory transfer.

Scotophobin thus lost its special salience and its historical relationship to the disreputable transfer phenomenon became a disadvantage. Most scientists, then, simply forgot about the area. Like many controversies, it ended with a whimper rather than a bang.

It is hard to say that any particular experiment or set of experiments demonstrated the non-existence of the transfer phenomenon, but three publications seemed decisive at the time. Their *historical* interest lies in the negative effect they had when they were published while one might say that their *sociological* interest lies in the reasons for that effect, especially given that in retrospect they appear much less decisive.

The first paper was published in 1964 and came from the laboratory of Nobel Laureate Melvin Calvin (Bennett and Calvin, 1964); it concerned planarian worms. The paper described a series of experiments – some employing McConnell's ex-students to perform the training – that seemed to show that learning had not taken place. This paper had a powerful effect, and for many years was quoted as undermining the early research on the chemical transfer of memory. Today, its cautious verdict that learning was 'not yet proven' has been superseded and it is accepted that worms not only turn, but learn.

The second paper, by Byrne and 22 others, was published in 1966 (Byrne *et al.*, 1966). It was a short piece in *Science* reporting the failure of the attempts by seven different laboratories to replicate one of the early chemical transfer experiments. Again, it is often cited as a 'knockdown blow' to the field. Indeed, it was at the time. But for Ungar, and other proponents, all of the experiments mentioned in the paper – and the original experiment they attempted to replicate – are flawed because they assumed the transfer material to be RNA rather than a peptide. According to Ungar, the chemical techniques used by the replicators in treating the brain extract probably destroyed the active, peptide, material. On this account, the original experiment, fortuitously, used *poor* biochemical techniques and, failing to destroy the peptide, obtained the correct positive result!

The last paper is the best known. Ungar's five-page report of his analysis and synthesis of Scotophobin was published in *Nature*, perhaps the highest prestige journal for the biological sciences (Ungar *et al.*, 1972). Accompanying it, however, was a critical, fifteen-page, signed report by the referee. The detailed critical comments of the referee, and perhaps the mere fact of this exceptional form of publication significantly reduced the credibility of the memory transfer phenomenon. It is worth noting that *Nature* has used this unusual form of publication subsequently to the disadvantage of other pieces of fringe science and, perhaps, to the disadvantage of science as a whole.

In spite of the widespread demise of the credibility of the chemical transfer of memory, a determined upholder of the idea would find no published disproof that rests on decisive technical evidence. For such a person it would not be unreasonable or unscientific to start experimenting once more. Each negative result can be explained away while many of the positive ones have not been. In this, memory transfer is an exemplary case of controversial science. We no longer believe in memory transfer but this is because we tired of it, because more interesting problems came along, and because the principal experimenters lost their credibility. Memory transfer was never quite disproved; it just ceased to occupy the scientific imagination. The gaze of the golem turned elsewhere.

2

Two experiments that 'proved' the theory of relativity

INTRODUCTION TO PARTS 1 AND 2

Einstein's theory of relativity became widely known in the early part of the twentieth century. One of the reasons for its success among scientists was that it made sense of a number of puzzling observations. For example, the theory accounted for the orbit of the planet Mercury departing slightly from its expected path, and it made sense of a slight shift towards the red end of the spectrum which some had claimed to detect in the light coming from the sun. But the theory of relativity also achieved a popular success; it became the subject of newspaper headlines. This had something to do with the ending of the Great War and the unifying effect of science on a fractured continent. It had something to do with the dramatic circumstances and the straightforward nature of the 1919 'proof' of relativity. And it undoubtedly had something to do with the astonishing consequences of the theory for our common-sense understanding of the physical world. When the implications of Einstein's insight – that light must travel at the same speed in all directions – were worked out, strange things were predicted.

It turned out that, if Einstein's ideas are correct, time, mass, and length are not fixed but are relative to the speed at which things move. Things that go very fast – at speeds near to the velocity of light – would get very heavy and very short. People who travelled this fast would seem to everyone else to age slowly; identical twins could grow old at different rates if one stayed still and one went on a very rapid journey. If the theory is correct, light would not travel only in straight lines, but would be bent by gravitational fields to a greater extent than had been believed possible. A more sinister consequence of the theory was that mass and energy should be interchangeable. On the one hand this explained how the sun kept on burning even though its fuel should have been exhausted long ago. On the other hand, terrible new sources of power became possible, a consequence to be demonstrated later by evidence for which the adjective 'incontrovertible' might have been invented – the explosion of the atomic bomb. In so far as there are facts of science, the relationships between matter and energy put forward by Einstein are facts.

But the explosion of the atomic bomb in 1945 is not what 'proved' the theory of relativity. It had been accepted for many years before then. The way the story is most often told is that there were two decisive observational proofs. These were the Michelson–Morley 'aether-drift' experiment of the 1880s, which we discuss in part 1 of this chapter, and Eddington's 1919 solar eclipse observation of the apparent displacement of stars, which we discuss in part 2.

The conventional story is that the Michelson–Morley observations showed that light travelled at the same speed in all directions, proving the special theory of relativity, while Eddington's expeditions to distant lands to observe the eclipse of 1919 showed that starlight was bent by the sun to the right extent to prove the general theory. The drama lies in the clarity and decisiveness of the questions and the answers. Either light did travel at the same speed in all directions or it did not. Either stars near the sun were displaced twice as far as they should have been under the old Newtonian theory or they were not. On the face of it, nothing could be more straightforward. For many people of that generation, interest in science was fired by the extraordinary nature of relativity and the story of the early observations. But even these experiments turn out to be far less decisive than is generally belived. What is simple 'on the face of it', is far more complicated in practice.

PART 1. DOES THE EARTH SAIL IN AN AETHERIAL SEA?

In 1887 Albert Michelson and Edward Morley carried out a very careful experiment at the Case School for Applied Science in Cleveland. They compared the speed of light in the direction of the earth's motion with that at right angles to the earth's motion. To their surprise, they found they were exactly the same!
(Stephen Hawking, A Brief History of Time: From the Big
Bang to Black Holes, *Bantam Books, 1988, p. 20).*

The tranquil aether sea

Light and the aether

In the latter part of the nineteenth century it was believed that light waves travel through a universal if insubstantial medium called the 'aether'. If this were true, then the velocity of light waves would appear to vary as the earth moves through the aether in its orbit round the sun. Just as when you run fast in still air you create your own breeze, the movement of the earth should create its own 'aether wind' in the tenuous 'aether sea'. Stand on the surface of the earth looking into the wind, and light coming toward you should appear to move faster than it would if the aether were still. The speed of light should be increased by the speed of the aether wind. Look across the wind, however, and light should appear to move at its normal speed. When Albert A. Michelson conducted his early experiments on the aether wind this is what he expected to find; what he actually found was that light seemed to move at the same velocity in all directions.

Michelson and relativity

According to the theory of relativity, light *should* have a constant velocity in all directions, but the theory did not surface until some 25 years after Michelson began his observations. Michelson, then, knew nothing of relativity; he set out to use movement through the aether sea as a kind of speedometer for the earth. Although the experiment is often thought of as giving rise to a problem that Einstein set out to solve, this too is probably false. It appears that Einstein was little interested in Michelson's experiments when he formulated his theory. Einstein's starting point was a paradox in the theory of electrical waves. The link between Einstein and Michelson was forged by others some twenty or more years after the first 'decisive' experiments were completed. Michelson, then, had no idea of the importance his results were later to achieve. At the time he was disappointed, for he had failed to find the speed of the earth. As we shall see, Michelson did not even complete the experiments properly; he went straight on to other things after publishing the initial findings.

How to measure the speed of the aether wind

To measure the velocity of the earth Michelson needed to measure the velocity of light in a variety of directions. The starting assumption was that the maximum speed of the earth with respect to the aether was of the order of the speed of the planet's movement in its orbit around the sun: about 18.5 miles per second. The speed of light was known to be in the region of 185 000 miles per second, so the effect to be measured was small – one part in 10 000. What is worse, direct determinations of the speed of light were too inaccurate to allow such a small discrepancy to be seen, so the only possibility was to compare the speed in two directions.

The method was to use what we now call 'interferometry'. The same beam of light is split into two and recombined. When the split beam recombines it will give rise to 'interference fringes': a series of light and dark bands. The effect is due to the light *waves* in each half of the beam alternately reinforcing each other (the bright bands) and cancelling each other out (the dark bands). This is a simple geometrical consequence of the superimposition of two wave motions: as one moves across the field upon which the rays converge, the path length of each ray changes slightly. For example, the left hand ray (Ray 1 in figure 2.1) has to travel a certain distance to reach the left hand side of the illuminated area. To reach a point a little to the right, it will have to travel slightly further, and to reach a point on the far right hand

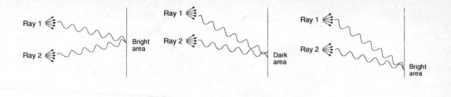

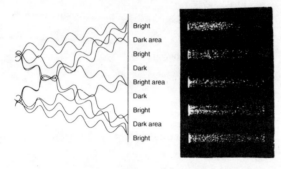

Figure 2.1. Interference fringes.

side of the field it will have to travel still further. Thus the ray will strike the field at various different stages in its undulation; the peak of Ray 1 strikes one point of the field whereas the trough strikes another point a little further along. Since the same applies to Ray 2, both peaks (or troughs) will strike the same point sometimes and they will combine their energies, whereas at other points a peak will coincide with a trough and they will cancel each other out – hence the light and dark 'interference fringes'.

Michelson proposed to transmit the interfering beams at right angles to each other and have them reflected back and recombined near the source. Now let us imagine that the orientation of the whole apparatus is at such an angle to the aether wind that the velocity of light along the two paths is equal (see figure 2.2). Imagine yourself looking at the interference fringes. Now imagine that the whole apparatus is rotated with respect to the aether wind so that the velocity of light becomes faster along one path and slower along the other (see figure 2.3). Then, considering just one path for a moment, what was once the point where a *peak* impinged might no longer be such a point. The same applies to the other half of the beam. The

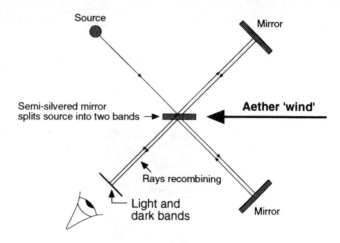

Figure 2.2. Velocity of light equal along both paths.

effect would be that the points of reinforcement and cancelling would shift; that is, that the dark and light bands would be displaced sideways.

In this experimental design, to detect the movement of the earth through the aether there is no need to know which way the aether wind blows at the outset of the experiment, all one needs to do is to rotate the instrument and look for shifts in the fringes. It is possible to calculate both speed and direction once one knows the full range of movement of the fringes.

The above explanation glosses over a very serious point. In Michelson's apparatus the light rays were sent out along a path and then reflected back. Thus, if they were swept along fast with the aether in one direction, they would be slowed in the other; it seems as though the effect would cancel out. Well, the arithmetic shows that this is not quite true. The gain is not completely cancelled by the loss, but it does mean that the effect is very much smaller than it would be if there was a way to recombine the beams without bringing them back to the starting point – which there is not. Effectively this means that, instead of looking for a change in the velocity of light of about 1 in 10 000, one is reduced to looking for an effect in the region of 1 in 100 000 000. It is, then, a very delicate experiment indeed. Neverthe-

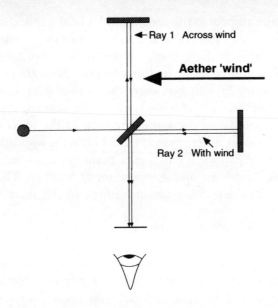

Figure 2.3. One path across aether wind; one path with aether wind.

less, as he developed his apparatus, Michelson expected to see the fringes move about four tenths of the width of a single fringe if the aether wind blew at a speed equal to the earth's velocity in its orbit. This he ought easily to observe.

The elements of the experiment

It is important to note that the apparent velocity of the aether wind would depend on the orientation of the apparatus, and this would change as the earth rotated on its axis; sometimes the wind would seem to blow along the light paths, and sometimes upwards or downwards through the apparatus, when it would have little differential effect on the two light paths. Thus the experiment had to be repeated at different times of the day while the earth rotated so that different orientations could be tested. Further, to understand the movement fully it would be necessary to repeat the experiment at various times of the year when the earth would be moving in different directions with respect to the sun. Should it be the case that the aether was stationary with respect to the sun, so that the whole movement of the earth through the aether was due to its orbital velocity, then the velocity would be more or less constant throughout the year at any one time of day. If, however, the whole solar system moved through the aether, then at some times of the year the earth's orbital movement would be in the same direction as the movement of the solar system, and at other times it would be in the opposite direction. Thus one would expect to find a maximum apparent 'wind speed' at one season of the year, and a minimum at another. The difference could be used to determine the movement of the solar system as a whole.

Note that if the velocity of the solar system through the aether was similar to the velocity of the earth in its orbit, there would be times of the year when the earth's movement in its orbit would nearly cancel the sun's movement. At these times the apparent velocity of the aether wind would be very low or even zero. This would be an unlikely coincidence, but to rule it out it was necessary to make observations during two seasons of the year.

For the experiment to work, the path lengths of the light rays had to be kept constant so that they would be affected only by changes in the direction of the aether wind. The apparent changes in length that were to be observed were of the order of a single wavelength of light. Since the path lengths were of the order of tens of metres, and the wavelengths of visible light is measured in units of a thousand millionths of a metre, it was hard to keep the apparatus stable enough. A slight flexing of one of the arms that supported the mirrors would be more than sufficient to throw the readings out. Michelson was to find that a mass of 30 grams placed on the end of one of the arms of an apparatus weighing tons was enough to upset the results dramatically. As for temperature, it was estimated that differential changes as small as 1/100 of a degree would produce an apparent effect three times that to be expected from the aether wind itself. Magnetic effects on the material of the apparatus caused by surrounding metal or the earth's magnetic field might be sufficient to wreck the results in designs where the iron or steel was used to give rigidity, whereas slight changes in humidity could vitiate those experiments where attempts were made to keep paths stable with wooden distance pieces. The need for temperature and vibration control indicated that the experimental apparatus be heavily built on massive foundations in the cellars of strong, well insulated buildings.

Unfortunately, massive apparatus and careful insulation created an opposite problem. It was thought that the aether might be 'dragged' along by massive opaque materials. Thus it could be argued that a well-insulated room at or below ground level in a large building would comprise, in effect, an aether trap; it would be stagnant pool around which the aether breeze wafted. Worse, hills or mountains, or the surface of the earth itself might carry the aether along with them, just as they carry the air. This way of looking at things indicated that the experiment ought to be performed outside, on top of a high mountain, or at least within a light building, preferably made of glass.

There are, then, six elements in the experiment:

1. the light rays must be split and reflected along paths at right angles;
2. observations of fringes must be made at a number of points as the whole apparatus is rotated on its axis;
3. the observations must be repeated at different times of the day to take account of the earth's rotation on its axis;
4. the observations must be repeated at different seasons to take account of the earth's changing direction of movement with respect to the solar system;
5. the experiment, it might be argued, should be carried out in a light, open, or transparent building;
6. likewise, the experiment should be carried out on a high hill or mountain.

The experimental apparatus

Michelson conducted a first experiment in 1881 and, with the collaboration of Arthur Morley, a second and much more refined observation in 1887. In essence the experiment is simple; a beam is split into two, reflected along two paths at right angles, recombined near the source, and the fringes observed. The apparatus is rotated and the observations are repeated, shifts in the position of the fringes being noted. The practice was to observe the position of the fringes at sixteen different positions while the apparatus was rotated through a complete circle. In practice, the experiment was delicate in the extreme. Of his first apparatus, which was built in Germany, Michelson reported great difficulty with vibration. The experiment had to be moved from Berlin to the more peaceful town of Potsdam, and even then the fringes could be made to disappear by stamping on the ground 100 metres from the laboratory. The experimental runs had to be made at night, during periods when there were few external disturbances. The first apparatus had comparatively short path lengths. In subsequent experiments the path lengths were increased by multiple reflection back and forth, thus increasing the sensitivity to the aether wind, but inevitably increasing the sensitivity to vibration and other disturbances too.

The long history of the experiment can be seen, then, as comprising increases in the path length of the two beams, changes in the materials from which the various parts of the apparatus were made, and changes in the location and housing of the experiment.

The 1881 experiment

Michelson's first experiment had a path length of about 120 cm. According to his calculations, an aether wind having something in the region of the earth's orbital velocity would give rise to a displacement of about a tenth of the width of a fringe as the apparatus turned. Michelson felt he would be able to observe this easily if it were there. In building and using this instrument he discovered the problems of vibration and the distortions produced in the arms when the apparatus was rotated about its axis. Nevertheless, he published the results of his observations, which were that no movement of the earth through the aether could be detected.

After publication, the experiment was re-analysed by H. A. Lorentz, who pointed out that in his analysis Michelson had neglected to take account of the non-zero effect of the wind on the transverse arm of the apparatus; even if you row across a current, it will take longer to get there and back than if there is no current at all! When this effect is taken into account, it halves the expected displacement of the fringes. Michelson concluded that, given the difficulties of the original observation and this new estimate for the displacement, it might be that the effect of the expected aether wind was masked in experimental 'noise'. This led him to design and build an improved apparatus.

The Michelson–Morley 1887 experiment

The next apparatus was much more elaborate. It was built at Michelson's home university in Cleveland. A cast iron trough of mercury rested upon brick foundations in a basement room. A massive block of sandstone, about 5 feet square and 14 inches thick, floated on the mercury. It could be set in motion by hand, and once started it would turn slowly so as to complete a full turn in about 6 minutes and would continue to turn on its own for more than hour. The light, beam splitter, reflectors, and so forth were mounted on the sandstone block. A number of mirrors were mounted so as to reflect the beams back and forth several times before they were recombined on the screen. This gave a path length of over 10 metres, and an expected displacement of about four tenths of a fringe as the apparatus rotated.

After the usual trials and tribulations, Michelson and Morley were ready to observe. At noon on 8, 9 and 11 July, and at around 6 pm on 8, 9 and 12 July, Michelson walked round with the rotating apparatus calling out results while Morley recorded the observations. They were deeply disappointed, for no effect remotely resembling the expected speed of the aether wind was found. Once more, the experiment produced a null result.

Now, we remarked above that there are six components in the experiment: transmission at right angles, rotation of the apparatus, observations at different times of day, observation at different times of year, lightweight buildings and an elevated site. What we have described covers only three of the six elements. Michelson seems to have been so disappointed at the result that instead of continuing he immediately set about working on a different problem: the use of the wavelength of light as an absolute measure of length.

The only way one can understand this is to see the experiment through Michelson's eyes, as an earth speedometer. In that case, it would be expected that the speed would be fairly high and that only by a remarkable coincidence – the cancelling of the velocity of the solar system by the equal and opposite velocity of the earth at the time of the experiment – would a low value result. One also has to assume that he was not concerned with the problem of aether 'drag'. The interferometer, as Michelson had built it, was not much use as a speedometer, that much was clear. If, on the other hand, the experiment is thought of as we·think of it now – a test of the theory of relativity – its theoretical significance is greater, but its experimental significance is much less. To be a test of relativity, the experiment needs to demonstrate not that the earth is not moving with anything like the expected velocity, but that there is absolutely no difference in the velocity of light in whichever direction it is measured. In the first case, the results were sufficiently disappointing to make it not worthwhile to develop the speedometer further. As a test of relativity, however, the slightest apparent shift in the fringes would be of great moment. And, it would be of enormous importance to try the test at different times of the year because a slight difference in reading at different seasons would have significance for the theory. The 1887 experiment was not, then, a very good test of relativity, even though it was adequate as a test of what Michelson and Morley wanted to know. Only after Einstein's famous papers were published in the first years of the twentieth century did the experiment become 'retrospectively reconstructed' as a famous and decisive proof of relativity.

Morley and Miller in the 1900s

In spite of Michelson's own lack of interest in his findings, discussion did not cease. The results were seen as a 'cloud' in the otherwise clear sky of physics. Numerous explanations were put forward in an attempt to show how the existence of an aether was compatible with the null results. These ranged from new sources of inaccuracy in the experiment, such as errors introduced by movement of the observer's eye, to the 'Lorentz contraction' – the suggestion that matter, including the arms of the interferometer, would shorten in the direction of movement to just the right degree to cancel out the effect. The interest was such that by the early 1900s Morley, and Dayton C. Miller, who had succeeded Michelson as a teacher in the university, were building new and improved interferometers. They built an enlarged device, based on wood, to look for differences in the contraction effect, but found results no different from the metal and sandstone instruments.

Still unsettled was the idea that the aether was trapped, or dragged along, by the dense surroundings of the experiment; the next step was to try the apparatus on high ground. In 1905 Morley and Miller tried the experiment in a glass hut atop a 300 foot hill. They again found what could only be counted as a null result when compared with what might be expected from the earth's orbital velocity.

As they completed this work, Einstein's papers were becoming recognised for what they were and setting the scene for the reinterpretation of the 'null' result as one of the most significant findings of experimental physics. It should not be thought, however, that Einstein's ideas were uniformly accepted upon their publication. The battle lasted several decades. Relativity was resisted for many reasons and on many fronts. There was interest in continued re-examinations of the Michelson–Morley result until beyond the end of the Second World War.

Miller claims to have found an aether drift: his 1920s experiments

As the interferometer experiments came to be seen as tests of relativity, rather than measures of the velocity of the earth, what had been done appeared less than complete. Dayton Miller, partly as a result of encouragement from Einstein and Lorentz, decided to test the results with an apparatus built on top of Mount Wilson, at a height of 6000 feet. When the results of the earlier experiments were examined closely in the context of relativity, they revealed their ambiguity. There was a small effect in the earlier experiments, though the fringe displacement was about one hundredth of a fringe rather than the expected four tenths. For relativity, of course, any real effect, however small, was crucial.

In the early 1920s Miller conducted a number of inconclusive experiments on Mount Wilson, experiencing the usual troubles with temperature control, lack of rigidity of the apparatus, and so forth.

He rebuilt the apparatus and took readings again on 4, 5 and 6 September 1924. Miller now found a persistent positive displacement, and concluded that 'the effects were shown to be real and systematic, beyond any further question'.

Miller's experiment was different from the others in that he pressed ahead with the fourth part of the protocol and took further readings in spring, summer and the following autumn. He concluded, in 1925, that he had found an observed motion of the earth of about 10 kilometres per second – around one third of the result that the original Michelson experiments were expected to find. In 1925, Miller was awarded the 'American Association for the Advancement of Science' prize for this work.

Thus, although the famous Michelson–Morley experiment of 1887 is regularly taken as the first, if inadvertent, proof of relativity, in 1925, a more refined and complete version of the experiment was widely hailed as, effectively, disproving relativity. This experiment was not conducted by a crank or charlatan. It was conducted by one of Michelson's closest collaborators, with the encouragement of Einstein, and it was awarded a major honour in the scientific community.

The initial experimental responses to Miller

There were a number of experimental responses to Miller's finding, all of them claiming a null result. The biggest effort was that made by Michelson himself. He built a huge interferometer and ran it in an insulated laboratory, again with null results. He and Miller confronted each other at a scientific meeting in 1928 and agreed to differ. An elaborate German experiment was also completed at about the same time, and this too found no significant effect. Both of these experiments, it must be pointed out, were well shielded, and neither was conducted at significant elevation. The results of these two experiments seem to have quieted the renewed speculation brought on by Miller's positive results even though they were not carried out under conditions favourable for the recognition of an aether wind. A further experiment was flown from a balloon, solving the altitude problem, but necessitating heavy shielding. As is often the case in science, a 'critical mass' of clearly expressed experimental voices can outweigh the objections of a critic however carefully argued.

In 1930 Michelson's huge device was installed at the top of Mount Wilson, in a telescope housing. The housing was made of metal and was, therefore, more of a potential shield than the housings of Miller's Mount Wilson experiments. In any case, nothing seems to have emerged from these Mount Wilson observations. What is more, although Michelson's interferometer was supposed to be made of 'Invar', an alloy not subject to expansion due to heat, a later analysis showed that the material was not properly formulated.

Miller's 1933 paper and the most recent experiments

In 1933 Miller published a paper reviewing the field and concluding that the evidence for an aether wind was still strong. We have then a classic situation of so-called replication in physics. Miller claimed a positive result, critics claimed negative results, but Miller was able to show that the conditions under which the negative experiments were conducted were not the same as the conditions of his own experiment. In particular, his was the only experiment that was done at altitude and with a minimum of the kind of shielding that might prevent the aether wind blowing past the test apparatus. Miller argued:

> In three of the four [negative] experiments, the interferometers have been enclosed in heavy, sealed metal housings and also have been located in basement rooms in the interior of heavy buildings and below the level of the ground; in the experiment of Piccard and Stahel [an interferometer carried aloft in a balloon], a metal vacuum chamber alone was used ... If the question of an entrained ether is involved in the investigation, it would seem that such massive and opaque shielding is not justifiable. The experiment is designed to detect a very minute effect on the velocity of light, to be impressed upon the light through the ether itself, and it would seem to be essential that there should be the least possible obstruction between the free ether and the light path in the interferometer. ...

In none of these other experiments have the observations been of such extent and of such continuity as to determine the exact nature of the diurnal [due to rotation of earth], and seasonal variation.

(Miller, 1933, p. 240).

In spite of this, the argument in physics was over. Other tests of relativity, including the Eddington observations of 1919 (to be discussed below), indirectly bolstered the idea that the theory of relativity was correct and that the velocity of light must be constant in all directions. The sheer momentum of the new way in which physics was done – the culture of life in the physics community – meant that Miller's experimental results were irrelevant.

We have travelled a long way from the notion that the Michelson–Morley experiment proved the theory of relativity. We have reached the point where the theory of relativity had rendered the Michelson–Morley experiment important as a sustaining myth, rather than as a set of results. Results that ran counter to what it was believed the Michelson–Morley experiment demonstrated were largely ignored. Think of it this way. The notion of 'anomaly' is used in science in two ways. It is used to describe a nuisance – 'We'll ignore that; it's just an anomaly', and to signify serious trouble – 'There are some troublesome anomalies in the existing theory.' The interferometry results started as serious trouble for the theory of the aether. The null results passed from anomaly to 'finding' as the theory of relativity gained adherents. With Miller's positive claims, interferometry results became, once more, an anomaly, but this time they were treated as a nuisance rather than a trouble. Miller's results were 'just an anomaly that needed to be explained away'. Miller could not change the status of his positive readings from nuisance to troublesome anomaly even though they were the outcome of the best experiment yet completed, perhaps the only one which could truly be said to have tested what it was meant to test. The meaning of an experimental result does not, then, depend only upon the care with which it is designed and carried out, it depends upon what people are ready to believe.

Postscript

There are, in the scientific community, some with tidy minds who feel uncomfortable even about the anomalies which most think of as merely a nuisance. As late as 1955 a team were re-analysing the whole history of the experiments in an attempt to reconcile Miller's findings with what everyone believed. They concluded that Miller's work had been confounded by temperature changes. Repetitions of the experiment continued after this date. In 1963, experiments were done with a 'maser', the forerunner of the laser, to try to settle the experimental issue. Though, as has been explained, all this was in a sense irrelevant to relativity, it is not irrelevant to the thesis being argued here. Michelson and Morley could not have *proved* relativity, because as late as 1963 the results of the experiments, considered on their own, outside the context of the rest of physics, were not yet clear.

PART 2. ARE THE STARS DISPLACED IN THE HEAVENS?

The gravitational field of the earth is, of course, too weak for the bending of light rays in it to be proved directly, by experiment. But the famous experiments performed during the solar eclipses show, conclusively though indirectly, the influence of a gravitational field on the path of a light ray.
(*Albert Einstein and Leopold Infeld,* The Evolution of Physics:
From Early Concepts to Relativity and Quanta, *New York:*
Simon and Schuster, 1938, p. 221).

The curious interrelation of theory, prediction and observation

The general theory of relativity is a complicated business. It is said that even by 1919 there were only two people who fully understood it: Einstein and Eddington. (This, let us hasten to add, is based on a quip of Eddington's.) Even to this day, theorists are not completely united about what follows from Einstein's theory, while in 1919 there was still substantial argument about what exactly should be expected. It was agreed, however, that according to both Newton and Einstein's theories, a strong gravitational field should have an effect on light rays, but that the Einsteinian effect should be greater than the Newtonian effect. The problem was to find out which theory was correct.

The gravitational field of the earth is far too small to have a measurable effect on light, but the sun's field is much greater. The light coming from the stars should be bent as the rays pass through the sun's gravitational field. To us, it should appear that stars close to the sun are slightly displaced from their usual position. The displacement would be greater in the world according to Einstein than in the world according to Newton. Einstein argued that the stars should appear to be shifted twice as much according to his theory as Newton's theory would suggest, though the shifts in either case were very small. It is as though a star whose light grazed the edge of the sun would appear to be displaced by a distance equivalent to the width of a penny viewed from a mile away. In figures, the expected displacements were 0.8 second of arc and about 1.7 seconds of arc for the two theories, a second being 1/3600 of a degree. The apparent movements that were actually observed would, however, be smaller – about half of these – since no stars could be observed that were closer than two solar diameters from the edge.

Einstein's theoretical derivation of the maximum apparent deflection of light rays is, from a modern point of view, somewhat problematic. At the time it 'caused confusion among those less adept than he at getting the right answer' (Earman and Glymour, 1980, p. 55). As in so many delicate experiments, the derivations, though unclear at the time, came to be seen to be correct *after* the observations had 'verified' Einstein's prediction. Science does not really proceed by having clearly stated theoretical predictions which are then verified or falsified. Rather, the validity given to theoretical derivations is intimately tied up with our ability to make measurements. Theory and measurement go hand-in-hand in a much more subtle way than is usually evident.

It is worth dwelling on the subtle co-operation of theory and experiment. Einstein had said that Newton's theory implied, let us say, a deflection of 'N' and his own theory implied a deflection of 'E'. Others (for what we would now agree were good reasons) were not sure that the 'N' and the 'E' were the right implications of the two theories. One would imagine that one could only test which of the two theories was correct after one was certain about the implications of each of them. To take an extreme example, if, in reality, it were the other way round, and Newton's theory implied deflection 'E' while Einstein's implied deflection 'N', measurements of the displacement of the stars, however accurate, would be in danger of confirming the wrong theory. One has to separate the *theory* from the *prediction* 'derived' from that theory. In the event, Eddington obtained measurements that concurred with Einstein's derived prediction, but the results were taken as confirming not only the prediction but also Einstein's *theory*. In interpreting the observations this way, Eddington seemed to confirm not only Einstein's prediction about the actual displacement, but also *his method of deriving the prediction from his theory* – something that no experiment can do.

The logic of this historical process would seem eminently reasonable under certain circumstances. For example, if Einstein's prediction for the deflection had been very exact, and Eddington's observations had been equally exact, and they had matched Einstein precisely, then the coincidence would force one to agree that Einstein must have been 'on to something' even if neither he nor anyone else was completely sure about the derivation of the displacement. But Eddington's observations, like many measurements in science, were not like this. As we shall see, they were very inexact and some of them conflicted with others. When he chose which observations to count as data, and which to count as 'noise', that is, when he chose which to keep and which to discard, Eddington had Einstein's prediction very much in mind. Therefore Eddington could only claim to have confirmed Einstein because he used Einstein's derivation in deciding what his observations really were, while Einstein's derivations only became accepted because Eddington's observation seemed to confirm them. Observation and prediction were linked in a circle of mutual confirmation rather than being independent of each other as we would expect according to the conventional idea of an experimental test. The proper description, then, is that there was 'agreement to agree' rather than that there was a theory, then a test, then a confirmation. When we describe Eddington's observations we will see just how much he needed Einstein's theory in order to know what his observations were.

The nature of the experiment

What has to be done is to compare the position of stars in the open sky with their apparent position when their starlight grazes the edge of the sun. The stars cannot normally be seen when they are close to the sun, or even when the sun is in the sky, because the sun is so bright. Stars can be seen close to the sun only during a solar eclipse. The size of the displacement – Newtonian or Einsteinian – is so small that the only possible chance of measuring it is by comparing photographs of a region of sky with and without the sun present. For the crucial observations one must await a total eclipse, but the comparison photographs must be taken several months before or after, when the sun is absent from that region of the sky. Clearly, the eclipse photographs must be taken during the daytime, but the comparison photographs must be taken at night, the only time (other than during an eclipse) when the stars can be seen.

In an experiment of such delicacy, it is important that as much as possible is kept constant between the observations and the background comparisons. The trouble is that the observation photographs and the comparison plates have to be obtained at different seasons of the year. This means that lots of other things have time to change. Furthermore, observation plates made in the daytime will use a warm telescope, while at night, the camera looks through a cold telescope. The difference in focal length between a hot and a cold telescope will disturb the apparent position of the stars to a degree which is comparable with the effect that is to be measured. There are many other changes, some calculable, some guessable, some unknown, between observation and comparison due to various sources of mechanical strain on the telescope which will minutely change the focal length and the relationship of the photographic plate to the axis of the telescope.

What makes matters worse is that eclipses can usually be seen only from remote corners of the world. It is not possible to take major telescopes, with all their controlling mechanisms, to such locations. The telescopes, therefore, will be relatively small, with relatively low light-gathering power. This means that exposures have to be long – in this case they were in the region of 5–30 seconds – so as to gather enough starlight to produce well-defined images. Long exposures bring with them another range of problems. Not only does the telescope have to be held steady, but it has to be moved to compensate for the rotation of the earth. Major astronomical telescopes are built with complex and finely engineered mounts to rotate the telescope smoothly with respect to the earth so that it is always directed at the same point in the heavens. Mounts of this sort could not be shipped and set up in the remote locations in which the observations were to be made. Instead the images were kept steady by means of 'coleostats', mechanisms based on a moving mirror controlled by a falling weight which reflects light into the telescope. The coleostat mirrors were a further source of distortion, as were their controlling mechanisms.

On top of all these problems, there are, of course, the contingencies of the weather. If clouds cover the sky then all the preparations are wasted. Earlier expeditions had been thwarted by weather (others had been thwarted by the outbreak of the First World War), and in this case clouds limited the value of at least one of Eddington's telescopes though it did not prevent its use entirely.

The scientists, fortunately, were not completely helpless in the face of these difficulties. The photographs of the field of stars contained some stars that were near the sun and others that were distant. According to the theory, distant stars should suffer no displacement. The effect on the telescope of changed focal length, and so forth, should show up as an apparent displacement of the 'undisplaced' stars. Thus it ought to be possible to measure these unwanted effects and compensate for them in the calculations for the 'truly displaced' stars. It turns out that to control for all the known spurious effects there must be at least six 'undisplaced' stars in the frame. But even this part of the experiment is subject to error. The estimation of the spurious effects depends on assumptions about the statistical distribution of errors in the plates. One can now understand that the Eddington observations were not just a matter of looking through a telescope and seeing a displacement; they rested on a complex foundation of assumptions, calculations, and interpolations from two sets of photographs. And this is the case even if the photographs are clear and sharp – which they were not.

The expeditions and their observations

The Eddington observations were actually made by two separate parties, one with two telescopes, the other party with one. The two parties went to two different locations. In March of 1918, A. Crommelin and C. Davidson set sail to Sobral, in Brazil, while Eddington and his assistant, E. Cottingham went to an island off the coast of West Africa called Principe. The Sobral party took with them an 'astrographic telescope' and a 4-inch telescope. This group obtained 19 plates from the astrographic telescope and 8 from the 4-inch telescope during the course of the eclipse, though one of the 4-inch plates was obscured by cloud.

The Principe group had one astrographic instrument with them. The day of the eclipse proved cloudy but, taking their photographs anyway, they obtained 16 plates. Only two of these, each showing only five stars, were usable. Both groups took comparison photographs a few months later, at the same site in the case of the Sobral group, and back at Oxford in the case of the Eddington party.

The best photographs, though they were not completely in focus, were those taken by the Sobral 4-inch telescope. From these plates and their comparisons, Crommelin and Davidson calculated that the deflection of starlight at the edge of the sun would be between 1.86 and 2.1 seconds of arc (the range being obtained by a calculation of 'probable error'), compared with the Einstein prediction of 1.7 seconds. Though the astrographic plates were less satisfactory, the Sobral party were able to make calculations based on 18 of them and obtained a mean estimate of 0.86 seconds, compared with the Newtonian value of 0.84 (probable error bands were not reported for this instrument). Thus, in very broad terms, one of the Sobral instruments supported the Newtonian theory, while the other leaned towards Einstein's prediction for his own theory. The support for the latter was, however, muddied by the fact that the 4-inch telescope gave a result unequivocally too high and the support for Newton was problematic because the photographs from the astrographic telescope were poor.

The two plates from the Principe expedition were the worst of all. Nevertheless, Eddington obtained a result from these plates using a complex technique that *assumed* a value for the gravitational effect.

At first he used a value half-way between Einstein's and Newton's and then repeated the procedure using Einstein's figures. It was not clear what difference these assumptions made though it is worth noting that, in Eddington's method, Einstein's derivation played a part even in the initial calculation of the apparent displacement. From his two poor plates Eddington calculated that the displacement at the edge of the sun would be between 1.31 and 1.91 seconds.

We can convert the 'probable error' calculations of the two groups into the modern langauge of 'standard deviations', and interpolate a standard deviation for the Sobral astrographic. For the Sobral observations the standard deviations are 0.178 for the good plates and 0.48 for the astrographic, while in the case of Eddington's plates the standard deviation is 0.444. (These are the calculations of John Earman and Clark Glymour.) A modern treatment would suggest that, assuming the measurement errors were distributed randomly, there is a 10% chance that the true answer lies further from the mean measurement than 1.5 standard deviations either side. With this in mind, let us sum up what we have so far, giving the 1.5 standard deviation intervals:

10% Confidence intervals for the observations at Sobral and Principe

	Low bound	Mean	High bound
Sobral			
8 good plates	1.713	1.98	2.247
18 poor plates	0.140	0.86	1.580
Principe			
2 poor plates	0.944	1.62	2.276

If we forget about the theory and the derivations, and pretend that we are making measurements in ignorance of the hypothesis – which is, after all, what we do when we do 'double blind testing' for the effectiveness of drugs or whatever – what would we conclude? We might argue that the two sets of poor plates cancel each other out, and that the remaining evidence showed that the displacement was higher than 1.7. Or, we might say that the eight good plates from Sobral were compatible with a displacement from just above 1.7 seconds to just below 2.3, Eddington's two poor plates were compatible with shifts from just above 0.9 to just below 2.3, while the poor Sobral plates were compatible with shifts from near zero to just below 1.6. In either case, it would be difficult to be able to provide a clear answer. Nevertheless, on 6 November 1919, the Astronomer Royal announced that the observations had confirmed Einstein's theory.

Interpretation of the results

Even to have the results bear upon the question it had to be established that there were only three horses in the race: no deflection, the Newtonian deflection, or the Einsteinian deflection. If other possible displacements had been present in the 'hypothesis space' then the evidence would be likely to give stronger confirmation to one or other of them. For example, if the displacement were hypothesised to be around 2 seconds, then the best readings – the Sobral 4-inch – could be said to confirm this result. There were other contenders at the time, but the rhetoric of the debate excluded them and presented the test as deciding between only the three possibilities: 0.0, 0.8 and 1.7.

Now let all the other horses in the race be scratched at the post. Do the results come down on Einstein's side in an unambiguous way? The answer is that they do not. To make the observations come out to support Einstein, Eddington and the others took the Sobral 4-inch results as the main finding and used the two Principe plates as supporting evidence while ignoring the 18 plates taken by the Sobral astrographic. In the debate which followed the Astronomer Royal's announcement, it appears that issues of authority were much to the fore. On 6 November 1919, Sir Joseph Thomson, the President of the Royal Society, chaired a meeting at which he remarked: 'It is difficult for the audience to weigh fully the meaning of the figures that have been put before us, but the Astronomer Royal and Professor Eddington have studied the material carefully, and they regard the evidence as decisively in favour of the larger value for the displacement' (quoted in Earman and Glymour, 1980, p. 77).

In 1923, however, an American commentator, W. Campbell, wrote:

> Professor Eddington was inclined to assign considerable weight to the African determination, but, as the few images on his small number of astrographic plates were not so good as those on the astrographic plates secured in Brazil, and the results from the latter were given almost negligible weight, the logic of the situation does not seem entirely clear.
>
> *(Quoted in Earman and Glymour, 1980, p. 78).*

Eddington justified ignoring the Sobral astrographic results by claiming that they suffered from 'systematic error' – that is, some problem that meant that the errors were not randomised around the mean but that each reading was shifted systematically to a lower value. If this was true of the Sobral astrographic and not true of the other two sets of readings, then Eddington would have been quite justified in treating the results as he did. It appears, however, that at the time he was unable to educe any convincing evidence to show that this was the case.

In the end, Eddington won the day by writing the standard works which described the expeditions and their meaning. In these he ignored the 18 plates from the Sobral astrographic and simply described the 1.98 result from the 4-inch and the 1.671 result from his own two plates. When one has these two figures alone to compare with a Newtonian prediction of around 0.8 and an Einsteinian prediction of around 1.7, the conclusion is inevitable. But there was nothing inevitable about the observations themselves until Eddington, the Astronomer Royal, and the rest of the scientific community had finished with their after-the-fact determinations of what the observations were to be taken to be. Quite simply, they had to decide which observations to keep and which to throw out in order that it could be said that the observations had given rise to any numbers at all.

Ten more eclipse observations were conducted between 1922 and 1952. Only one, in 1929, managed to observe a star that was closer than two solar radii from the edge of the sun, and this suggested that the displacement at the edge would be 2.24 seconds of arc. Most of the other nine results were also on the high side. Although there are other reasons to believe the Einstein value, the evidence on the bending of visible star light by the sun, at least up to 1952, was either indecisive or indicated too high a value to agree with the theory. And yet 1919 remains a key date in the story of relativity. Is this because science needs decisive moments of proof to maintain its heroic image?

CONCLUSION TO PARTS 1 AND 2

None of this is to say that Einstein was wrong, or that the eclipse experiments were not a fascinating and dramatic element in the great change which our understanding of nature has undergone in the twentieth century. But we should know just what the experiments were like. The picture of a quasi-logical deduction of a prediction, followed by a straightforward observational test is simply wrong. What we have seen are the theoretical and experimental contributions to a cultural change, a change which was just as much a licence for observing the world in a certain way as a consequence of those observations.

The way that the 1919 observations fit with the Michelson–Morley experiment should be clear. They were mutually reinforcing. Relativity gained ground by explaining the Michelson–Morley anomaly. Because relativity was strong, it seemed the natural template through which to interpret the 1919 observations. Because these observations then supported relativity further, the template was still more constraining when it came to dealing with Miller's 1925 observations.

While all this was going on, there were still other tests of relativity that had the same mutually reinforcing relationship to these tests as they had to each other. For example, there were observations of the 'red-shift'. It followed from Einstein's theory that light coming from the sun should be affected by the sun's own gravitational field in such a way that all wavelengths would be shifted slightly toward the red end of the spectrum. The derivations of the quantitative predictions were beset with even more difficulties than the calculations of the bending of light rays. The experimental observations, conducted both before and after 1919, were even more inconclusive. Yet after the interpretation of the eclipse observations had come firmly down on the side of Einstein, scientists suddenly began to see confirmation of the red-shift prediction where before they had seen only confusion. Just as in the example of gravitational radiation discussed in chapter 5, the statement of a firm conclusion elicited firm grounds for reaching that conclusion. Once the seed crystal has been offered up, the crystallisation of the new scientific culture happens at breathtaking speed. Doubt about the red-shift turned into certainty. John Earman and Clark Glymour, from whom we have borrowed much of our account of the Eddington observations, put it this way:

> There had always been a few spectral lines that could be regarded as shifted as much as Einstein required; all that was necessary to establish the red-shift prediction was a willingness to throw out most of the evidence and the ingenuity to contrive arguments that would justify doing so. The eclipse results gave solar spectroscopists the will. Before 1919 no one claimed to have obtained spectral shifts of the required size; but within a year of the announcement of the eclipse results several researchers reported finding the Einstein effect. The red-shift was confirmed because reputable people agreed to throw out a good part of the observations. They did so in part because they believed the theory; and they believed the theory, again at least in part, because they believed the British eclipse expeditions had confirmed it. Now the eclipse expeditions confirmed the theory only if part of the observations were thrown out and the discrepancies in the remainder ignored ...   (*Earman and Glymour, 1980, p. 85*).

Thus, Eddington and the Astronomer Royal did their own throwing out and ignoring of discrepancies, which in turn licensed another set of ignoring and throwing out of discrepancies, which led to conclusions about the red-shift that justified the first set of throwing out still further. What applies in the relationship in any two of these sets of observations applies, *a fortiori* to all the tests of relativity that were taking place around the same time. No test viewed on its own was decisive or clear cut, but taken together they acted as an overwhelming movement. Thus was the culture of science changed into what we now count as the truth about space, time and gravity. Compare this process with, say, political direction of scientific consensus from the centre – which is close to what once happened in the Soviet Union – and it is admirably 'scientific', for the scientists enter freely into their consensual position, leaving only a small minority of those who will not agree. Compare it, however, to the idealised notion of scientific 'method' in which blind tests prevent the observer's biasses entering into the observations, and it is much more like politics.

We have no reason to think that relativity is anything but the truth – and a very beautiful, delightful and astonishing truth it is – but it is a truth which came into being as a result of decisions about how we should live our scientific lives, and how we should licence our scientific observations; it was a truth brought about by agreement to agree about new things. It was not a truth forced on us by the inexorable logic of a set of crucial experiments.

Appendix to chapter 2 part 2

In history, as in science, facts do not speak for themselves – at least not exactly. The interpretation that Professors Earman and Glymour would put on their data might not entirely match the conclusion of this book. It is because Earman and Glymour cleave to rather different views of the nature of science than we do that we have been particularly careful to stay close to their account. We have popularised and clarified wherever we can but we have done our best to avoid any possibility of seeming to distort their material.

The section of this chapter which is most close to Earman and Glymour's original starts at the sub-heading 'The nature of the experiment', and finishes around page 51 at the paragraph which ends with the sentence: 'It appears, however, that at the time he was unable to educe any convincing evidence to show that this was the case'. In other places, other sources, and more of our own interpretation creep in.

It is, perhaps, only fair to Earman and Glymour to quote their own conclusion:

> This curious sequence of reasons might be cause enough for despair on the part of those who see in science a model of objectivity and rationality. That mood should be lightened by the reflection that the theory in which Eddington placed his faith because he thought it

beautiful and profound – and, possibly, because he thought that it would be best for the world if it were true – this theory, so far as we know, still holds the truth about space, time and gravity. (p. 85).

Appropriately understood, we ourselves see no reason to disagree with this.

3

The sun in a test tube: the story of cold fusion

When two chemists working at the University of Utah announced to the world's press on 23 March 1989 that they had discovered fusion, the controlled power of the hydrogen bomb, in a test tube, they launched the equivalent of a scientific gold rush. And the gold was to be found everywhere – at least in any well-equipped laboratory. The two scientists were Martin Fleischmann and Stanley Pons.

The apparatus was simple enough (see figure 3.1): a beaker of heavy water (like ordinary water but with the hydrogen atoms replaced by 'heavy hydrogen', otherwise known as deuterium); a palladium 'electrode' known as the cathode, and a platinum electrode, known as the anode. A small amount of the 'salt', lithium-deuteroxide, was added to the heavy water to serve as a conductor. Though these substances are not in everyday use, and are rather expensive, they are quite familiar to any modern scientist; there is nothing exotic about the apparatus. Put a low voltage across this 'cell' for a period of up to several hundred hours, and out should come the gold: fusion power. The heavy hydrogen atoms should fuse together into helium, releasing energy; this is the way the sun is powered. The telltale signs of fusion were heat and nuclear bypro-ducts such as neutrons – sub-atomic particles – and traces of the super-heavy hydrogen atom, tritium.

Pons and Fleischmann added an intriguing tease to the account of their success. They warned that the experiment was only to be attempted on a small scale. An earlier cell had mysteriously exploded

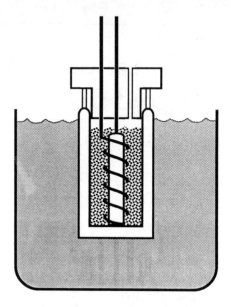

Figure 3.1. Cold fusion cell (redrawn by Steven W. Allison from Close, 1991, p.76).

vaporising the palladium and producing a large hole in the concrete floor of the laboratory. Luckily it had happened during the night and no-one was hurt.

The experiment seemed straightforward and there were plenty of scientists willing to try it. Many did. It was wonderful to have a simple laboratory experiment on fusion to try after the decades of embarrassing attempts to control hot fusion. This effort required multi-billion dollar machines whose every success seemed to be capped with an unanticipated failure. 'Cold fusion' seemed to provide, as Martin Fleischmann said during the course of that famous Utah press conference, 'another route' – the route of little science.

Scientists the world over immediately started scrambling for information about the experiment. Details were hard to come by. Faxes, electronic mail networks, newspapers and television all played a role. Some scientists did not wait for details. That same night enterprising students at MIT started the first attempted replications based on a video of a television news programme on which the apparatus had briefly been shown. Such experiments had little chance of success because the exact conditions employed by Pons and Fleischmann were not yet known. Like the worm-running experiments discussed in chapter 1, cold fusion experiments were to suffer from their apparent simplicity – at least in the early days before scientists recognised just how complicated a palladium–deuterium electrolytic cell could be. Within a week a photocopied manuscript showing the technical details of the experiment became available. Now replication started with a vengeance. Scarce supplies of palladium were bought up and pieces of equipment were scavenged from everywhere. Many stayed up all night nursing their electrolytic cells. Science had seen nothing like it; neither had the world's press which ran continuous news items and updates of progress. It was 'science by press conference' as scientists queued up to announce their latest findings and predictions to the media.

And for a while it looked as if cold fusion was real. Amazingly, in the week following the first announcement it became clear that there was not just one Utah cold fusion group, but two. The second independent group was located at nearby Brigham Young University and they too had been getting positive results for the previous three years. This group, headed by physicist Steven Jones, had not found excess heat, but had detected neutrons from a cold fusion cell (although at a much lower level than claimed by Pons and Fleischmann). Both groups had submitted their results to the prestigious scientific journal *Nature*.

Texas A&M University soon announced to the waiting media that they too were seeing excess heat from a cold fusion cell, and then came an announcement from Georgia Tech that they were seeing neutrons. Positive results were reported from Hungary and elsewhere in Eastern Europe. Rumours of positive results came in from all over the scientific world. The Japanese were supposed to be launching their own massive detection programme.

Patents had been filed on behalf of Pons and Fleischmann by the University of Utah. Indeed part of the reason for the press release before the results were published in a scientific paper (a breach of scientific etiquette which was to be held against the scientists) was the University of Utah's concern to ensure priority over the nearby group at Brigham Young University. Utah seemed set to become the Gold Rush State with the State Legislature meeting and voting $5 million towards the cold fusion effort. Congress was approached for a possible further $25 million. Even President Bush was being kept appraised of developments.

But then doubts started to surface. It transpired that Georgia Tech had made a mistake; their neutron detector turned out to be heat sensitive. The Texas A&M excess heat measurements were explained away by an improperly earthed temperature sensitive device. Groups at MIT and national laboratories such as Lawrence Livermore and Oak Ridge were not yet seeing anything. Pons and Fleischmann's paper was mysteriously withdrawn from *Nature*. Congress decided to put the $25 million on hold.

At the American Physical Society meeting that May in Baltimore, with the ever-present media circus in attendance, criticism reached a crescendo. An MIT group claimed that Pons and Fleischmann had incorrectly interpreted their evidence for neutrons; a prestigious California Institute of Technology (Cal Tech) group reported detailed replication attempts, all negative, and cast doubt upon the correctness of the Utah measurements of excess heat; and finally a Cal Tech theorist pronounced that cold fusion was impossible theoretically and accused Pons and Fleischmann of delusion and incompetence. The University of Utah pair were not at the meeting to defend themselves, but Steven Jones from the other Utah cold fusion group was there. Unfortunately, even Jones distanced himself from Pons and Fleischmann's work, claiming that he too had doubts about the measurements of excess heat.

For most of the gathered community of physicists, already sceptical about whether chemists could overturn cherished assumptions about fusion physics, enough was enough. Gold became fool's gold, or that at least is how the story goes. As we shall see, like most of the episodes examined in this book, there is more to be said; much more.

The little science route to fusion

One can chart the rise and decline of cold fusion from the price of palladium. On 23 March, 1989, just before the announcement of the discovery, the price was $145.60 an ounce. By May 1989 at the height of the cold fusion frenzy the price had risen to $170.00 an ounce. Prices plummeted following the Baltimore APS meeting. As of today (October 1992) the price has fallen back to $95.00 an ounce.

It is palladium, or rather one property of palladium, which provided the impetus to the search for cold fusion. It is known that palladium has a surprising ability to absorb vast quantities of hydrogen. If a piece of palladium is 'charged' with as much hydrogen as it can absorb, then the pressure inside the crystal lattice dramatically increases. Perhaps at such high pressures the normal barrier of positive charge (known as the Coulomb barrier) preventing nuclei coming together to fuse could be overcome. It was a long-shot but scientists before Pons and Fleischmann had actually tried to produce fusion between hydrogen nuclei this way.

In the 1920s, soon after the discovery of the atomic structure of matter, two German chemists working at the University of Berlin attempted to produce fusion of hydrogen using palladium. Fritz Paneth and Kurt Peters were not interested in fusion as a source of energy but in the product, helium, which was used in airships. New ways to make helium were urgently sought by German industry because the USA, the main commercial supplier, refused to sell helium to Germany after the First World War. Paneth and Peters, knowing of palladium's affinity for hydrogen, set up an experiment in which they passed hydrogen over red-hot palladium. They claimed to detect the presence of small amounts of helium. Unfortunately they later discovered that the probable source of the helium was gas already absorbed in the glass walls of their apparatus. However, their work was taken up another scientist and inventor: John Tandberg, a Swede who worked at the Electrolux Corporation Laboratory in Stockholm.

Tandberg had remarkably similar ideas to those of Pons and Fleischmann 60 years later, or so it seems with hindsight. In 1927 he had applied for a patent for a device to manufacture helium by the electrolysis of water with a palladium cathode. In his device hydrogen produced at the cathode entered the palladium lattice and there, with the huge pressures induced by absorption, underwent fusion to produce helium. That at least was the claim. The only substantial difference between Tandberg's device and the later set-up of Pons and

Fleischmann was the use of light water as the electrolyte. Tandberg's patent was rejected because the description was said to be too sketchy. However, after the discovery of deuterium (in the 1930s) Tandberg pursued the work further by attempting to create fusion in a wire of palladium which had been saturated with deuterium by electrolysis. It seems he met with little success, at least in regard to the production of helium.

Pons and Fleischmann were unaware of the earlier work when they started their experiments in 1984. Martin Fleischmann is one of Britain's most distinguished electrochemists. Stanley Pons (an American), visited the University of Southampton to study for his PhD in 1975 and that is where the two met. Fleischmann, who was Faraday Professor of Electrochemistry at Southampton, had a reputation for being the sort of scientist who liked to carry out high-risk science, pursuing bold and innovative ideas and approaches. Indeed he had built his career with such work and some of the risks had paid off. Fleischmann had made a number of important discoveries, as recognised by his election as a Fellow of the Royal Society in 1986.

The reason for Fleischmann being in Utah in 1989 had to do with British Prime Minister, Margaret Thatcher. The Thatcher cutbacks of funding to British universities in 1983 meant that Fleischmann was forced to take early retirement from the University of Southampton (where he retained an un-paid position). He became a freelance researcher teaming up with Pons who was by now a productive scientist in his own right, and chair of the University of Utah Chemistry Department. Pons was aged 46 and Fleischmann 62 when the discovery was announced. Pons, too, had a reputation for successful high-risk science. Pons and Fleischmann were well aware that cold fusion was a long-shot. They initially funded experiments with $100 000 of their own money, expecting to see at most tiny traces of tritium and perhaps some neutrons. The levels of excess heat they detected were a complete surprise.

Jones' involvement

The announcement of 23 March 1989 cannot be understood without reference to the work of the other Utah group, led by Steven Jones at

Brigham Young University. While the scientific community were unfamiliar with Pons and Fleischmann's work on cold fusion, they had been following Jones' progress for several years. In 1982 Jones and his colleagues had undertaken a major experimental effort looking for fusion triggered by sub-atomic particles produced at the Los Alamos particle accelerator. They had found far more evidence of such fusions than theory would have led them to expect, but not enough to make a source of viable energy. Like hot fusion research, particle-induced fusion was a frustrating step away from the excess energy output needed for commercial exploitation.

Jones had moved on to consider how very high pressures might encourage hydrogen isotopes to fuse. The key breakthrough in his thinking came in 1985 when Brigham Young geophysicist Paul Palmer drew his attention to the anomaly of excess heavy helium (helium-three) found near volcanoes. Palmer and Jones thought this could be explained by deuterium contained in ordinary water undergoing geologically induced cold fusion inside the earth.

The Brigham Young group pursued the idea, attempting to reproduce the geological processes in the laboratory. They were searching for a metal, traces of which in rock might serve as a catalyst for fusion. They built an electrolytic cell essentially similar to that of Tandberg and tried various materials for the electrodes. Soon they too decided that palladium, with its ability to absorb hydrogen, was the most likely candidate. The group built a low-level neutron detector to measure any fusion which was occurring. In 1986 they started to observe neutrons at a rate just above background levels. By 1988, using an improved detector, they felt confident that they had found definite evidence of neutron production.

Jones had carried out this research unaware of the similar efforts being carried out at the nearby University of Utah. He first heard of Pons and Fleischmann's experiments in September 1988 when he was sent their research proposal to referee by the Department of Energy (Pons and Fleischmann had at last decided that their work merited funding from public sources).

It was unfortunate for both groups that such similar work was being pursued in such close proximity. In view of the obvious commercial payoff which might result from cold fusion and the need for patent protection it meant that a certain amount of rivalry and suspicion arose between the two groups. Exactly what they agreed regarding the joint publication of their results is still disputed.

It seems that in early 1989 Pons and Fleischmann were hoping that Jones would hold off from publishing for a period (up to eighteen months), giving time for them to refine their measurements. Pons and Fleischmann were, it appears, confident that they were seeing excess heat, but had no firm evidence for its nuclear origins. Some crude measurements indicated that neutrons were coming out, but more exact measurements were desirable. Fleischmann even tried to arrange to have a cold fusion cell flown out to the Harwell Laboratory in England where he was a consultant and where very sensitive neutron detectors were available. Unfortunately the cell was declared a radiation risk and could not be taken across international boundaries. In the event Pons and Fleischmann claimed they could indirectly detect neutrons by observing interactions in a water shield surrounding the cell. It was these hastily carried out measurements which were later to be challenged by the MIT group; they turned out to be the Achilles heel in the Utah body.

Pons and Fleischmann were under pressure from Jones' impending announcement. Although Jones cancelled one seminar in March, he planned to announce his results at the meeting of the American Physical Society on 1 May. Pons and Fleischmann, in order not to lose their priority claim, reached an agreement with Jones to dispatch separate papers from both groups to *Nature* on 24 March.

In March, however, communication between the two groups broke down. Although Jones was going to speak in May his abstract was made public beforehand. Pons and Fleischmann, it seems, took this as licence to go public themselves. Also, the University of Utah group were worried that Jones might be stealing their ideas on excess heat, having had access to their work via the Department of Energy research proposal. A further complicating factor was a request in March to Pons from the editor of the *Journal of Electroanalytical Chemistry* for a paper on his latest work. Pons quickly wrote up an account of the cold fusion experiments which he submitted to the journal. It was this paper (published in April 1989), which would eventually be widely circulated, and provided the first technical details of the experiments.

Under growing pressure from the Utah administration, Pons and

Fleischmann decided to go ahead with a press conference on 23 March, the day before the planned joint submission to *Nature*. A leak from Fleischmann to a British journalist meant that the first report of the discovery appeared in the British *Financial Times* on the morning of 23 March. Thus the world's press were primed to descend on Utah. At the press conference no mention was made of the other Utah group.

Jones, who was by now infuriated both by the press conference and the revelation that a paper had already been submitted, considered the agreement to have been broken and immediately dispatched his own paper to *Nature*. Nothing could be more symbolic of the mis-communication which had arisen between the two Utah groups than the lone figure of Marvin Hawkins (a graduate student who worked with Pons and Fleischmann), waiting at the Federal Express office at Salt Lake City Airport at the appointed hour on 24 March for someone from Jones' group to appear. No-one arrived and the Pons and Fleischmann paper was mailed alone.

The controversy

It was Pons and Fleischmann's results that gave rise to the cold fusion controversy. The levels of neutrons detected by Jones were of lower orders of magnitude and he has never claimed to observe excess heat. Jones' results also did not pose the same theoretical challenge. Furthermore, Jones, unlike Pons and Fleischmann, made a point of playing down the commercial application angle.

The detrimental effect on the credibility of scientists' findings when they get caught up in a scientific controversy not of their own choosing is revealed by the reception of Jones' results. Few would doubt, given his previously established reputation in the field, the minimal theoretical consequences his results posed, and the modest manner in which he presented them, that, if it had not been for Pons and Fleischmann, Steve Jones would by now have quietly established an interesting fact about the natural world: fusion of small amounts of deuterium in palladium metal.

Despite his attempts to distance himself from the other Utah group, Jones has inevitably been subject to the same suspicions. The reality of his neutron measurements has come into question, and there is no consensus as to whether he has observed fusion.

Pons and Fleischmann, unlike Jones, had no established reputation in the field of fusion research; they were chemists not physicists. Moreover they were claiming something which to most physicists was theoretically impossible. Not only did it seem extremely unlikely that fusion could be occurring, but also, if all the heat excess was caused by *fusion*, then the levels of neutrons produced should have been more than enough to have killed Pons and Fleischmann and anyone else who happened to be in the close proximity of one of their cells. In short, fusion could not occur and, if it did, then they should be dead. This is what one might refer to as a 'knockdown' argument!

There is little doubt that when fusion researchers heard the news on 23 March they were sceptical. The reaction was:

'Suppose you were designing jet airplanes and then you suddenly heard on CBS news that somebody had invented an antigravity machine.' (Quoted in Mallove, 1991, p. 41).

Another remarked at the time:

'I'm willing to be open-minded, but it's really inconceivable that there's anything there.' (Ibid., p. 41).

Part of the scepticism came from fusion researchers being only too familiar with grandiose claims for breakthroughs which shortly afterwards turn out to be incorrect. There had been many such episodes in the history of the field and thus fusion scientists were wary of extravagant claims. For them, solving the world's energy problems via a breakthrough in fusion had about as much chance of being true as the perennial claims to have superseded Einstein's theory of relativity.

Though fusion researchers, well-used to spectacular claims, and with their own billion-dollar research programs to protect, were incredulous, other scientists were more willing to take the work seriously. Pons and Fleischmann have fared better with their colleagues in chemistry where, after all, they were acknowledged experts. Early on Pons presented his findings to a meeting of the American Chemical Society where he was given a rapturous reception. For most, the prejudices of the scientific community probably mattered less than the fact that the experiment seemed easy to perform. If there was anything to it, most scientists reckoned, then all should soon become clear. Pons and Fleischmann had two sorts of evidence to back up their claims: excess heat and nuclear products. These had to be tested.

Excess heat

Testing for excess heat was in essence no more than a high-school physics problem. A careful account of the power input and output of the cell was kept, including all the known chemical reactions that are capable of transforming chemical energy into heat. This accounting needs to be carried out over a period of time because at any one moment the books might not balance as energy might get stored in the cell (turning it into a heat bank, as one might say). It is a fairly straightforward procedure to establish the power output by measuring the temperature rise, the cell first having been calibrated using a heater of known power. In practice the experiment took some time to perform because the palladium electrodes had to be fully charged with deuterium (for 8 mm diameter electrodes this could take several months).

The heat excess varied between cells. Some cells showed no heat excess at all. The power sometimes came in surges; in one case four times as much power was recorded coming out as went in. However, more routinely the heat excess was between 10% and 25%.

Despite the capricious nature of the phenomenon, Pons and Fleischmann were confident that the heat excess could not be explained by any known chemical process or reaction.

Nuclear products

The most direct proof of fusion would be the production of neutrons correlated with the excess heat. The first neutron measurements attempted by Pons and Fleischmann were relatively crude. The output from a cell was compared with the background as measured at a distance of 50 metres from the cell. A signal three times the background was recorded for this one cell. This was a suggestive result, but as neither the energy of the neutrons was known, nor whether the background was the same close to the cell as at 50 metres distance, it was far from conclusive. A more satisfactory procedure was to measure the gamma-ray bursts produced by neutrons captured by protons in the water bath surrounding the cell. These measurements were made over a two-day period by Bob Hoffman, a Utah radiologist. The numbers of neutrons detected if any were billions less than would be expected if all the heat was produced by the deuterium fusion reaction.

Another piece of evidence for fusion having taken place would be the presence of its products, such as tritium. Pons and Fleischmann found traces of tritium in the palladium cathode of one cell. The difficulty with this finding – a problem which has beset all the claims – is that tritium is a known contaminant of heavy water.

Replication

As mentioned already, after the announcement on 23 March attempts to repeat the experiments followed fast and furious. Although they got much media attention, these early results (both positive and negative) counted for little. The embarrassment caused by the premature announcements from Georgia Tech and Texas A&M cautioned those scientists who were seriously trying to repeat the experiment that they faced a long struggle. Many were taken in by the seeming ease of the experiment only to discover that a palladium electrolytic cell was a deal more complicated than expected.

Part of the difficulty facing scientists trying to repeat the experiment was that Pons and Fleischmann's account of what they had done was insufficiently detailed. There was discussion of the exact size of the electrodes to be used, the current densities at which to operate the cells, whether the lithium salt was crucial or could be substituted by another salt, whether the cathode was 'poisoned' and with what, and for how long the experiment should run. None of these were clear. Following on from their initial announcement, Pons and Fleischmann were inundated with requests for information. In the frenetic atmosphere at Utah it is no wonder that scientists did not always find it easy to get the crucial information.

Some have accused Pons and Fleischmann of deliberate secrecy in order to secure patent rights or (later on, when many became disillusioned) to hide their own incompetence. However, given the commercial importance of the discovery, securing the patent rights is no small matter; it is routine in areas of biotechnology. Also it seems that Pons and Fleischmann were initially hesitant because of their own uncertainties and their fears about the dangers of the experiment. They were also worried about creating a cheap source of tritium, since tritium is one of the crucial ingredients of a hydrogen bomb.

The elusive details of the experiments were soon spreading through an informal network of electronic mail and telephone contacts. Indeed, electronic mail may have been important in this controversy in producing the rapid consensus against cold fusion which developed after the Baltimore American Physical Society meeting. For instance, Douglas Morrison, a CERN (European Organisation for Nuclear Research) physicist and early enthusiast of cold fusion, set up an electronic newsletter which seems to have been widely read. Morrison soon became sceptical of the claims and referred scientists to Irving Langmuir's notorious talk on 'pathological science', where a number of cases of controversial phenomena (including N-Rays and ESP) in science were dismissed as a product of mass delusion. (Langmuir's talk was reproduced in *Physics Today* in October 1989.) Cold fusion was, according to Morrison, the most recent case of pathological science.

What became clear early on was that, while most groups saw nothing, a few had positive results. The classic problem of replication during a scientific controversy was surfacing. Negative results could be explained away by the believers as being due to differences in the replicating experiment. To those who failed to find anything, however, this was simply confirmation that there was nothing to be found. Fleischmann and Pons's own attitude, as expressed in their testimony to Congress in April 1989, was that they were not surprised by the negative results as many cells were being set up with incorrect parameters and dimensions.

Of the early positive replications reported, one of the most important came from Robert Huggins, a materials scientist at Stanford University. Huggins had run two cells, one with ordinary water and one with heavy water, and found that only the heavy water cell produced excess heat. This answered a long-running criticism of Pons and Fleischmann for not setting up a 'control' cell with ordinary water. Huggins has consistently found positive results over the years.

Another criticism of the Pons and Fleischmann work was that the cells they used were open cells from which the gases produced in electrolysis (deuterium and oxygen) could escape. The worry here was whether the energy balance was affected by the possible chemical recombination of deuterium and oxygen to form heavy water, thereby adding heat to the system. This objection was finally overcome when John Appleby of Texas A&M (*not* the same Texas A&M group which prematurely announced positive results) performed closely controlled calorimetry experiments using closed cells. Heat excesses were again found.

Of the negative results, one of the most influential came from a Cal Tech group headed by chemist Nathan Lewis and physicist Charlie Barnes. The Cal Tech team had tried a variety of combinations of conditions and had found nothing. As mentioned already, Lewis reported the negative results to the Baltimore American Physical Society meeting to dramatic effect. His results had extra impact since he implied that Pons and Fleischmann were guilty of an elementary oversight. They had neglected to stir the electrolyte thus allowing hot spots to develop and produce spurious temperature readings.

However, it seems that Lewis' charges were misplaced. Pons and Fleischmann claimed that there was no need to stir the electrolyte because the deuterium bubbles produced by the reaction did the job sufficiently well. In order to demonstrate the error Lewis had tried to make an exact copy of Pons and Fleischmann's cell. He had taken as his source a photograph of a cell in the *Los Angeles Times*. It turns out that this cell was only used by Pons and Fleischmann for demonstration purposes and was of much larger dimensions than the cells used in actual experimental runs. Pons and Fleischmann were later able to demonstrate with a simple experiment placing a few drops of dye in the electrolyte that the bubbles acted as an adequate stirring mechanism.

As in other controversies what was taken by most people to be a 'knockdown' negative result turns out, on closer examination, to be itself subject to the same kinds of ambiguities as the results it claims to demolish. If Lewis' measurements had been unpacked in the same kind of detail reserved for Pons and Fleischmann they might not have seemed as compelling as they did at the time. In the atmosphere of the Baltimore meeting, where physicists were baying for the blood of the two chemists, and where a whole series of pieces of negative evidence was presented (see below), Lewis was able to deliver the knock-out blow.

The classic problem of replication has surfaced with another set of highly influential negative findings, those reported by Harwell. As a result of Fleischmann's contact with Harwell, David Williams, an ex-graduate student of Fleischmann's, actually started his experiments *before* the March announcement. The results obtained to all intents and purposes killed off cold fusion in Britain. Again on the face of it the experiments look impressive with a number of cells being checked for excess heat and neutrons over lengthy periods.

The results, however, are not compelling for proponents of cold fusion such as Eugene Mallove, who claim that almost half the cells were run at currents below the threshold for cell activity. Other criticisms have been made of the Harwell methods of heat estimation. Despite the differing interpretations of the Harwell experiment, for many scientists it was the last word on cold fusion.

As well as attempts to replicate the phenomenon by setting up electrolytic cells, new experiments have searched for cold fusion by other methods. One such is cooling and reheating the palladium so that it becomes supersaturated with deuterium. Bursts of neutrons have been detected in such experiments.

The difficulty which the proponents face in getting positive results accepted is well illustrated by the fate of the tritium measurements. It will be recalled that Pons and Fleischmann had themselves found traces of tritium. More evidence came from other experimenters, including a group in India with a long history of making tritium measurements, a group at Los Alamos and a third group at Texas A&M University. However, since tritium is a known contaminant of heavy water there is a ready-made 'normal' explanation for all such results. It has proved to be impossible to satisfy the critics that no contamination has occurred, because they can always think of ways in which tritium might get into the cell.

It has even been suggested that the affair has involved fraud. In 1990, an article in the journal *Science* puts forward fraud as a factor in the Texas A&M tritium measurements. The impasse between proponents and critics, an impasse made worse by each side accusing the other of 'unscientific' behaviour, is typical of scientific controversies. The critics cite a preponderance of negative results as grounds to dismiss the controversial phenomenon and any residual positive results are explained away as incompetence, delusion or even fraud. The proponents, on the other hand, account for the negative results as having arisen from the failure to reproduce exactly the same conditions as used to obtain positive results. Experiments alone do not seem capable of settling the issue.

Cold fusion: a theoretical impossibility?

Most of the debate has been fought out against a background in which cold fusion has been held to be impossible on theoretical grounds. Although Pons and Fleischmann, like Tandberg beforehand, hoped that the extreme pressures inside the palladium lattice would help enhance fusion of deuterium, there was little theoretical justification that this would be the case.

One of the responses of nuclear physicists to the cold fusion claims has been a detailed re-examination of the theoretical possibilities. Cal Tech theorist Steve Koonin has devoted considerable time and energy to this problem. Although in reworking the calculations Koonin discovered errors which increased the rate of deuterium–deuterium fusion by a factor of over 10 billion compared with earlier calculations, the main thrust of his work has been to show why deuterium fusion in palladium in the amount needed to produce excess heat is extremely unlikely. Koonin has pointed out that the increased pressure inside palladium was not enough to bring about fusion. Indeed, in a palladium lattice the deuterium nuclei would actually be further apart than in ordinary heavy water. His calculations for the likelihood of deuterium–deuterium fusion showed that the rate would be extremely slow. In a telling comparison Koonin described it this way: 'A mass of cold deuterium the size of the Sun would undergo one fusion per year.'

Thus Koonin, in reviewing all the theoretical possibilities at the May meeting of the American Physical Society, was able to make theoretical justifications seem preposterous. As Koonin told a *New York Times* reporter: 'It is all very well to theorize about how cold fusion in a palladium cathode might take place ... one could also theorize about how pigs would behave if they had wings. But pigs don't have wings!' (quoted in Mallove, 1991, p. 143).

In a context where the experimental evidence was fast vanishing it was little wonder that most physicists were happy to go along with the accepted wisdom.

There is no doubt that Koonin represents the standard view. As is typical for a scientific controversy where experiment seems to go against prevailing theory, however, there is more to say than this. Indeed throughout the cold fusion episode a number of suggestions have been made as to how fusion might occur on the necessary scale and furthermore how it might occur without neutrons being produced. Some of the more serious suggestions have come from physics Nobel Laureate Julian Schwinger and the MIT laser physicist who helped invent the X-ray laser, Peter Hagelstein. One idea has been to think of ways whereby a rare neutronless fusion reaction could be the source of the excess heat, with energy being transferred into the palladium lattice. Hagelstein, drawing upon ideas in laser physics, has also proposed 'coherent fusion', whereby chains of fusion reactions occur in a kind of domino effect.

With the experimental results under a cloud, most theorists see little reason to entertain such exotic ideas. One is reminded of the solar-neutrino case (see chapter 7), where many speculative theories were produced to explain the discrepancy between standard theory and the experimental results. Even though the discrepancy there was only a matter of a factor of 3 none of the alternative theories gained widespread acceptance. It seems unlikely that, in a case where the discrepancy is a factor of 57 orders of magnitude (10 with 56 0s after it) and where the experimental results have much less credibility, conventional theory is going to be over-thrown. There is no doubt that Hagelstein himself takes these alternative theories very seriously – he has even applied for patents for devices based upon his theories. The risks in pursuing such theories beyond the mere 'what if' stage (i.e. treating such theories as serious candidates rather than mere speculations) are well illustrated by the Hagelstein case: there have been persistent rumours that his tenure at MIT was in jeopardy after he started to produce theoretical explanations of cold fusion.

Credibility

The struggle between proponents and critics in a scientific controversy is always a struggle for credibility. When scientists make claims which are literally 'incredible', as in the cold fusion case, they face an uphill struggle. The problem Pons and Fleischmann had to overcome was that they had credibility as electrochemists but not as nuclear physicists. And it was nuclear physics where their work was likely to have its main impact.

Any claim to observe fusion (especially made in such an immodest and public manner), was bound to tread upon the toes of the nuclear physicists and fusion physicists who had already laid claim to the area. A vast amount of money, expertise, and equipment had already been invested in hot fusion programs and it would be naive to think that this did not affect in some way the reception accorded Pons and Fleischmann.

This is not to say that the fusion physicists simply rejected the claims out of hand (although a few did), or that it was a merely a matter of wanting to maintain billion-dollar investments (although with the Department of Energy threatening to transfer hot fusion funding to cold fusion research there was a direct threat to their interests), or that this was a matter of the blind prejudice of physicists over chemists (although some individuals may have been so prejudiced); it was simply that no scientists could hope to challenge such a powerfully established group without having his or her own credibility put on the line. As might be expected, the challenge to Pons and Fleischmann has been most acute in the area where the physicists feel most at home, the area of the neutron measurements.

Neutron measurements

For many physicists it was the neutron measurements which provided the best evidence for fusion. Yet paradoxically these measurements formed the weakest link in Pons and Fleischmann's claims. As we have seen, the measurements were carried out belatedly and under pressure from others. Worse, neither Pons nor Fleischmann had any special expertise in such measurements.

It was at Harwell, at a seminar given by Fleischmann shortly after the March announcement, that the first inkling of difficulties was to arise. Fleischmann presented the evidence of neutrons and showed a graph of the gamma-ray peak obtained by Hoffman from the water shield. To physicists in the audience who were familiar with such spectra, the peak looked to be at the wrong energy. The peak was at 2.5 MeV whereas the expected peak for gamma-rays produced by neutrons from deuterium should have been at 2.2 MeV. It looked as if something had gone awry with the calibration of the gamma-ray detector, but it was impossible to tell for certain because Fleischmann did not have the raw data with him and had not made the measurements himself. In any event by the time the graph appeared in the *Journal of Electroanalytical Chemistry* the peak was given at the correct value of 2.2 MeV.

Whether the two versions arose from 'fudging' or genuine errors and doubt over what had been measured is unclear. Frank Close, in his much publicised sceptical book about the cold fusion controversy, *Too Hot To Handle*, suggests that the graph was deliberately doctored – a charge taken up by science journalist William Broad in an article in the *New York Times*, of March 17, 1991. Such accusations should, however, be treated with caution. Close, in particular, falls into the trap of exposing all the gory detail of the proponents' experiments, leaving the critics' experiments to appear as clear-cut and decisive. Such a one-sided narrative merely serves to reaffirm the critics' victory.

The neutron measurements soon came under further scrutiny. Richard Petrasso, of the MIT Plasma Fusion Center, also noticed that the shape of the gamma-ray peak looked wrong. The difficulty in taking this observation further was that Pons and Fleischmann had not yet released their background gamma-ray spectrum. What the

MIT scientists did was to pull off something of a scientific scoop. They obtained a video of a news programme which showed the inside of Pons and Fleischmann's laboratory including a VDU display of their gamma-ray spectrum. Petrasso concluded that the claimed peak could not exist at 2.2 MeV and that furthermore it was impossible to see such a slim peak with the particular instrument used. The absence of a Compton edge also eliminated the peak as a viable candidate for neutron capture. The conclusion of the MIT group was that the peak was 'probably an instrumental artefact with no relation to γ-ray interactions'.

Preliminary reports of the work were given by Petrasso at the Baltimore meeting to maximum rhetorical effect. In tandem with the Cal Tech negative results they were to have the decisive impact on the course of the controversy which we have already charted.

The criticism of the neutron measurements was eventually published in *Nature* along with a reply from Pons and Fleischmann. Although they made much of MIT's resort to a news video as a source of scientific evidence (pointing out that what had been referred to by Petrasso as a 'curious structure' was none other than an electronic cursor and denying that the video had shown a real measurement), the Utah pair were now placed on the defensive. They published their full spectrum showing no peak at 2.2 MeV but claiming evidence for a new peak at 2.496 MeV. Although they could not explain this peak in terms of a known deuterium fusion process they maintained the peak was produced by radiation from the cell. In an ingenious move they tried to turn Petrasso's argument around by saying that if indeed their instrument was not capable of detecting such peaks then the lack of a peak at 2.2 MeV should not in itself be taken as evidence against fusion. MIT replied in turn claiming that the peak at 2.496 MeV was actually at 2.8 MeV.

Many scientists have taken this episode as showing that the main argument in favour of fusion had collapsed. However, another interpretation is possible. This is that the best evidence for cold fusion always came from the excess heat measurements – the experimenters' own strength. The hastily performed nuclear measurements had always been puzzling because too few neutrons were observed. In trying to 'come clean' on the difficulties of interpreting their nuclear measurements Pons and Fleischmann were attempting to draw attention back to the main thrust of their argument – the excess heat measurements. Indeed, when Pons and Fleischmann finally published their full results in July 1990, the paper was almost entirely about calorimetry – no nuclear measurements were reported.

The trouble was that for many physicists the nuclear data were what had got them excited in the first place and the weakness of the neutron evidence left the excess heat measurements as mere anomalies, possibly of chemical origin. Furthermore, the problems over the nuclear measurements could easily be taken to demonstrate Pons and Fleischmann's incompetence as experimenters. Despite the Utah pair being widely acknowledged as experts in electrochemistry, this kind of 'guilt by association' seems to have paid off for the critics and has helped discredit the experiment as a whole.

Conclusion

In our account we have focussed mainly on the early stages of the controversy, pointing in particular to the role of the Baltimore American Physical Society meeting where the tide turned against Pons and Fleischmann. Today scientists still continue to work on the phenomenon, some positive results are reported, and conferences are held on such topics as 'Anomalous Phenomena in the Palladium–Deuterium Lattice'. Indeed, the very labelling of the phenomena in this way reflects a feature familiar from other controversies where, in order to try to get the controversial phenomenon accepted, proponents play down its implications for other scientists. Gone are the bold claims that the phenomenon is definitely fusion and gone is the prospect of a new source of commercial energy just around the corner (although Japanese companies continue to invest money). It may eventually be established that there is something unusual going on in the palladium–deuterium lattice but that something is unlikely to be cold fusion as it appeared *circa* March 1989. The failure in 1989 to attract significant Department of Energy funding means that, compared with its initial promise, cold fusion research is in decline. The Utah National Cold Fusion Institute was finally wound up in June 1991.

In the cold fusion controversy the stakes were very high and the normally hidden working of science has been exposed. The cold fusion episode is often taken to show that there is something wrong with modern science. It is said that scientists claimed too much, based on too little, and in front of too many people. Press review is said to have replaced peer review. False hopes of a new age of limitless energy were raised, only to be dashed.

Such an interpretation is unfortunate. Pons and Fleischmann appear to have been no more greedy or publicity seeking than any prudent scientists would be who think they have on their hands a major discovery with a massive commercial payoff. The securing of patents and the fanfare of press conferences are inescapable parts of modern science, where institutional recognition and funding are ever more important. There is no turning the clock back to some mythical Golden Age when scientists were all true gentlemen (they never were anyway, as history of science has taught us in recent years). In cold fusion we find science as normal. It is our image of science which needs changing, not the way science is conducted.

4

The germs of dissent: Louis Pasteur and the origins of life

Spontaneous generation

'Spontaneous generation' is the name given to the doctrine that, under the right circumstances, life can form from dead matter. In a sense, nearly all of us believe in spontaneous generation, because we believe that life grew out of the primeval chemical slime covering the newly formed earth. This, however, is taken to be something that happened slowly, by chance, and once only in the history of the earth; it ought never to be seen in our lifetimes.

The question of the origin of life is, of course, as old as thought but, in the latter half of the nineteenth century, the debate raged within the scientific community. Could new life arise from sterile matter over and over again, in a few minutes or hours? When a flask of nutrients goes mouldy, is it because it has become contaminated with existing life forms which spread and multiply, or is it that life springs anew each time within the rich source of sustenance? It was a controversial issue, especially in nineteenth-century France because it touched upon deeply rooted religious and political sensibilities.

Our modern understanding of biochemistry, biology and the theory of evolution is founded on the idea that, aside from the peculiar conditions of pre-history, life can only arise from life. Like so many of our widespread scientific beliefs we tend to think that the modern view was formed rapidly and decisively; with a few brilliant experiments conducted in the 1860s, Louis Pasteur speedily defeated outright those who believed in spontaneous generation. But the route, though it might have been decisive in the end, was neither speedy nor straightforward. The opposition were crushed by political manoeuvering, by ridicule, and by Pasteur drawing farmers, brewers, and doctors to his cause. As late as 1910, an Englishman, Henry Bastian, believed in the spontaneous generation heresy. He died believing the evidence supported his view.

As in so many other scientific controversies, it was neither facts nor reason, but death and weight of numbers that defeated the minority view; facts and reasons, as always, were ambiguous. Nor should it be thought that it is just a matter of 'those who will not see'. Pasteur's most decisive victory – his defeat of fellow Frenchman Felix Pouchet, a respected naturalist from Rouen, in front of a commission set up by the French Academie des Sciences – rested on the biasses of the members and a great stroke of luck. Only in retrospect can we see how lucky Pasteur was.

The nature of the experiments

The best-known experiments to test spontaneous generation are simple in concept. Flasks of organic substances – milk, yeast water, infusions of hay, or whatever – are first boiled to destroy existing life. The steam drives out the air in the flasks. The flasks are then sealed. If the flasks remained sealed, no new life grows in them – this was uncontested. When air is readmitted, mould grows. Is it that the air contains a vital substance that permits the generation of new life, or is it that the air contains the already living germs – not metaphorical, but literal – of the mould. Pasteur claimed that mould would not grow if the newly admitted air was itself devoid of living organisms. He tried to show that the admission of sterile air to the flasks had no effect; only contaminated air gave rise to putrescence. His opponents claimed that the admission of even pure air was sufficient to allow the putrefaction of the organic fluids.

The elements of the experiment are, then:

1.   one must know that the growth medium is sterile but has nutritive value;

2.   one must know what happens when the flasks are opened; is sterile air being admitted or is contamination entering too?

Practical answers to the experimental questions

Nowadays we believe we could answer those questions fairly easily, but in the nineteenth century the techniques for determining what was sterile and what was living were being established. Even what counted as life was not yet clear. It was widely accepted that life could not exist for long in a boiling fluid, so that boiling was an adequate means of sterilisation. Clearly, however, the medium could not be boiled dry without destroying its nutritive value. Even where the boiling was more gentle it might be that the 'vegetative force' of the nutrient might have been destroyed along with the living organisms. What counted as sterile air was also unclear. The distribution of micro-organisms in the world around us, and their effect on the air which flowed into the flasks, was unknown.

Pasteur made attempts to observe germs directly. He looked through the microscope at dust filtered from the air and saw egg-like shapes that he took to be germs. But were they living, or were they merely dust? The exact nature of dust could only be established as part of the same process that established the nature of putrescence.

If germs in the air could not be directly observed, what could be used to indicate whether air admitted to a flask was contaminated or not? Air could be passed through caustic potash or through sulphuric acid, it could be heated to a very high temperature or filtered through cotton wool in the attempt to remove from it all traces of life. Experiments in the early and middle part of the nineteenth century, using air passed through acids or alkalis, heated or filtered, were suggestive, but never decisive. Though in most cases admission of air treated in this way did not cause sterilised fluids to corrupt, putrescence occurred in enough cases to allow the spontaneous generation hypothesis to live on. In any case, where the treatment of the air was extreme, it might have been that the vital component which engendered life had been destroyed, rendering the experiment as void as the air.

Air could have been taken from different places – high in the

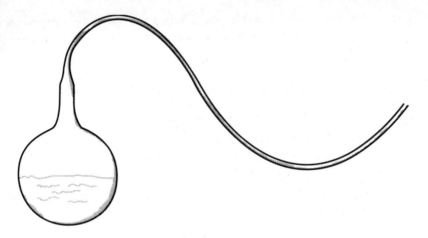

Figure 4.1. One of Pasteur's swan-neck flasks.

mountains, or low, near to cultivated fields – in the expectation that the extent of microbial contamination would differ. To establish the connection between dust and germs, other methods of filtration could be used. Pasteur used 'swan neck flasks' (see figure 4.1). In these the neck was narrowed and bent so that dust entering would be caught on the damp walls of the orifice. Experiments were conducted in the cellars of the Paris Observatoire, because there the air lay sufficiently undisturbed for life-bearing dust to have settled. Later on, the British scientist, William Tyndall, stored air in grease-coated vessels to trap all the dust before admitting it to the presence of putrescible substances. For each apparently definitive result, however, another experimenter would find mould in what should have been a sterile flask. The kinds of arguments that the protagonists would make can be set out on a simple diagram.

Box 1 is the position of those who think they have done experiments that show that life *does* grow in pure air and believe in spontaneous generation. They think these experiments prove their thesis. Box 2 is the position of those who look at the same experiments but do not believe in spontaneous generation; they think there must have been something wrong with the experiment, for example, that the air was not really pure.

Box 4 represents the position of those who think they have done

Possible interpretations of spontaneous generation experiments

Believe in spontaneous generation

		Yes	No
		(1) Proves thesis	**(2)** Air accidentally contaminated
Life grows in apparently pure air	Yes		
	No	**(3)** Air spoiled by treatment	**(4)** Proves thesis

experiments showing that life *does not* grow in pure air and do not believe in spontaneous generation. They think the experiments prove their hypothesis. Box 3 is the position of those who look at the same experiments but do believe in spontaneous generation. They think there must have been something wrong with the air, for example, that its vital properties were destroyed in the purifying process.

There was a period in the 1860s when arguments of the type found in box 3 were important but this phase of the debate was relatively short-lived; it ended as the experimenters ceased to sterilise their air by artificial means and instead sought pure sources of air, or room temperature methods of 'filtration'. Arguments such as those found in box 2 were important for a longer time. They allowed Pasteur virtually to define all air that gave rise to life in the flasks as contaminated, whether he could show it directly or not. This is especially obvious in that part of his debate with Felix Pouchet concerning experiments using mercury, as we shall see.

The Pasteur–Pouchet debate

One episode of the long debate between Pasteur and those who believed in spontaneous generation illustrates clearly many of the themes of this story. In this drama, the elderly (60-year-old) Felix Pouchet appears to serve the role of 'foil' for the young (37-year-old) Pasteur's brilliant role as experimental scientist. Pasteur, there is no doubt, defeated Pouchet in a series of celebrated trials, but the retrospective and triumphalist account glosses over the ambiguities of the trials as they took place in real time.

As with all such experimental controversies, it is the details that are crucial. The argument between Pasteur and Pouchet concerned what happens whan an infusion of hay – 'hay tea', as one might say – which is sterilised by boiling, is exposed to the air. It is undisputed that the infusion goes mouldy – microscopic life forms grow upon its surface – but the usual question remained. Was this because air has life-generating properties or because air contains living 'seeds' of mould?

Experiments 'under mercury'

Pouchet was a believer in spontaneous generation. In his early experiments he prepared sterilised infusions of hay 'under mercury' – to use the jargon. The method was to do the work with all vessels immersed in a mercury trough so that ordinary air could not enter. Specially prepared air could be introduced into the flask by bubbling through the mercury trough. This was the standard way of admitting various experimental gases into experimental spaces without admitting the ordinary air. In Pouchet's case it was purified air that was bubbled through the mercury. It was considered that purified air could be made by heating ordinary air, or by generating oxygen through the decomposition of an oxide; coincidentally this was often mercury oxide which gives off oxygen when heated. Invariably Pouchet found that when purified hay infusions were prepared under mercury, and exposed to pure air, organic life grew. It appeared then that, since all sources of existing life had been eliminated, the new life must have arisen spontaneously.

Pouchet started the debate with Pasteur by writing to him with the results of these experiments. Pasteur wrote back to Pouchet that he could not have been cautious enough in his experiments. "... in your recent experiments you have unwittingly introduced common [contaminated] air, so that the conclusions to which you have come are not founded on facts of irreproachable exactitude' (quoted in Farley and Geison, 1974, p. 19). Here, then, we see Pasteur using an argument of the type that is found in box 2 above. If Pouchet found life when he introduced sterilised air to sterilised hay infusions, then the air *must* have been contaminated.

Later, Pasteur was to claim that, although the hay infusion was sterile in these experiments, and the artificial air was equally devoid of life, it was the mercury that was contaminated with micro-organisms – they were in the dust on the surface of the mercury – and this was the source of the germ.

This is interesting because it seems that the contaminated mercury hypothesis was necessary to explain some of Pasteur's own early results. He reported that in his own attempts to prevent the appearance of life by preparing infusions under mercury, he succeeded in only 10% of his experiments. Though, at the time, he did not know the source of the contamination, he did not accept these results as evidence in support of the spontaneous generation hypothesis. In his own words, he '... did not publish these experiments, for the consequences it was necessary to draw from them were too grave for me not to suspect some hidden cause of error in spite of the care I had taken to make them irreproachable' (quoted in Farley and Geison, 1974, p. 31). In other words, Pasteur was so committed in his opposition to spontaneous generation that he preferred to believe there was some unknown flaw in his work than to publish the results. He *defined* experiments that seemed to confirm spontaneous generation as unsuccessful, and vice versa. Later the notion of contaminated mercury replaced the 'unknown flaw'.

Looking back on the incident we must applaud Pasteur's foresight. He was right, of course, and had the courage of his convictions in sufficient degree to refuse to be swayed by what, on the face of it, was a contrary experimental indication. But it *was* foresight. It was not the neutral application of scientific method. If Pasteur, like Pouchet, had been supporting the wrong hypothesis we would now be calling his actions 'dogged obstinacy in the face of the scientific facts'. Perfect hindsight is a dangerous ally in the history of science. We shall not understand the Pasteur–Pouchet debate as it was lived out unless we cut off our backward seeing faculty.

Flasks exposed at altitude

The business of the experiments under mercury was just the preliminary skirmish. The main debate began with Pasteur's experiments on flasks opened to the air at altitude, and Pouchet's rebuttal.

Pasteur prepared flasks with necks drawn out in a flame. He boiled an infusion of yeast and sealed the neck once the air had been driven out. If unopened, the contents would remain unchanged. He could then take the flasks and break the neck at various locations, allowing air to re-enter. To admit air in what ought to be germ-free locations, Pasteur would break the neck with a long pair of pincers which had been heated in a flame, while the flask was held above his head so as to avoid contamination from his clothes. Once the air from the chosen location had entered, Pasteur could once more seal the flask with a flame. Thus he prepared a series of flasks containing yeast infusions together with samples of air taken from different locations. He found that most flasks exposed in ordinary locations became mouldy, whereas those exposed high in the mountains rarely changed. Thus, of 20 flasks exposed at 2000 metres on a glacier in the French Alps, only one was affected.

In 1863, Pouchet challenged this finding. With two collaborators he travelled to the Pyrenees to repeat Pasteur's experiments. In their case, all eight of the flasks exposed at altitude were affected, suggesting that even uncontaminated air was sufficient to begin the life-forming process. Pouchet claimed that he had followed all of Pasteur's precautions, except that he had used a heated file instead of pincers to open the flasks.

Sins of commission

In the highly centralised structure of French science in the mid-nineteenth century, scientific disputes were settled by appointing commissions of the Paris-based Academie des Sciences to decide on the matter. The outcomes of such commissions became the quasi-official view of the French scientific community. Two successive commissions looked into the spontaneous generation controversy. The first, set up before Pouchet's Pyrenean experiments, offered a prize to 'him who by well-conducted experiments throws new light on the question of so-called spontaneous generation'. By accident or design, all members of the commission were unsympathetic to Pouchet's ideas and some announced their conclusions before even examining the entries. Two of its members had already responded negatively to Pouchet's initial experiments and the others were well-known opponents of spontaneous generation. Pouchet withdrew from the competition, leaving Pasteur to receive the prize uncontested for a manuscript he had written in 1861, reporting his famous series of experiments demonstrating that decomposition of a variety of substances arose from air-borne germs.

The second commission was set up in 1864 in response to Pouchet's experiments in the Pyrenees. These experiments had aroused indignation in the Academie, most of whose members had considered the matter to be already settled. The new commission started out by making the challenging statement: 'It is always possible in certain places to take a considerable quantity of air that has not been subjected to any physical or chemical change, and yet such air is insufficient to produce any alteration whatsoever in the most putrescible fluid' (quoted in Dubos, 1960, p. 174). Pouchet and his colleagues took up the challenge adding: 'If a single one of our flasks remains unaltered, we shall loyally acknowledge our defeat' (quoted in Dubos, 1960, p. 174).

The second commission too was composed of members whose views were known to be strongly and uniformly opposed to those of Pouchet. When he discovered its composition, Pouchet and his collaborators attempted to alter the terms of the test. They wanted to expand the scope of the experimental programme while Pasteur insisted that the test should depend narrowly upon whether the smallest quantity of air would always induce putrescence. All Pasteur was required to show, according to the original terms of the competition, was that air could be admitted to some flasks without change to their content. After failing to change the terms of reference, Pouchet withdrew, believing that he would be unable to obtain a fair hearing given the biasses of the members of the commission.

Pouchet's position could not be maintained in the face of his twice withdrawing from competition. That the commissions were entirely one-sided in their views was irrelevant to a scientific community already almost uniformly behind Pasteur.

Retrospect and prospect on the Pasteur–Pouchet debate

Pouchet's position was rather like that of an accused person whose fate hangs on forensic evidence. Granted, the accused was given the chance of producing some evidence of his own, but the interpretation was the monopoly of the 'prosecution' who also acted as judge and jury. It is easy to see why Pouchet withdrew. It is also easy to understand how readily Pasteur could claim that Pouchet's Pyrenean experiments were confounded by his use of a file rather than pincers to cut the neck of the flasks. We can imagine the fragments of glass, somehow contaminated by the file even though it had been heated, falling into the infusion of hay and seeding the nutrients therein. We can imagine that if Pouchet had been forced by the commission to use sterilised pincers after the fashion of Pasteur then many of the flasks would have remained unchanged. We may think, then, that Pouchet's understandable failure of nerve in the face of this technical strait-jacket merely saved him from a greater embarrassment. Although the two commissions were disgracefully biassed, surely this was merely a historical contingency that would not have affected the accurate scientific conclusion they reached?

Interestingly, it now seems that if Pouchet had not lost his nerve he might not have lost the competition. One difference between Pouchet and Pasteur was the nutritive medium they used for their experiments, Pasteur using yeast and Pouchet hay infusions. It was not until 1876 that it was discovered that hay infusions support a spore that is not easily killed by boiling. While the boiling of a yeast infusion will destroy all life, it does not sterilise a hay infusion. Modern commentators, then, have suggested that Pouchet might have been successful if he had stayed the course – albeit for the wrong reasons! It is worth nothing that nowhere do we read of Pasteur repeating Pouchet's work with hay. In fact, except to complain about the use of a file instead of pincers, he hardly ever mentioned the Pyrenean experiments, expending most of his critical energy on the earlier mercury-trough experiments for which he had a ready-made explanation. The Pyrenean experiments, of course, were carried out without mercury, the supposed contaminant in the earlier work. As one of our sources remarks: 'If Pasteur ever did repeat Pouchet's experiments without mercury, he kept the results private' (quoted in Farley and Geison, 1974, p. 33). The conclusion to the debate was reached, then, as though the Pyrenean experiments had never taken place.

The difference between hay and yeast, as we now understand it, adds a piquant irony to the results of the commission. We, however, do not think that Pouchet would have been wiser to go ahead with the challenge, and that scientific facts speak for themselves. The modern interpretation suggests that the facts of hay infusions would have spoken, even to a biassed commission, in the unmistakable voice of spontaneous generation. We don't believe it. The commission would have found a way to explain Pouchet's results away.

Postscript

It is interesting that the defenders of Pasteur were motivated in part by what now seems another scientific heresy. It was thought at the time that Darwinism rested upon the idea of spontaneous generation. In an attack on Darwinism, published in the same year as the second commission was constituted, the secretary of the Academie des Sciences used the failure of spontaneous generation as his main argument. he wrote 'spontaneous generation is no more. M. Pasteur has not only illuminated the question, he has resolved it' (quoted in Farley and Geison, 1974, p. 23). Pasteur, then, was taken to have dealt a final blow to the theory of evolution with the same stroke as he struck down the spontaneous generation of life. One heresy destroyed another. Those who feel that because 'it all came out right in the end', science is vindicated, should think again.

Finally, let us note that we now know of a number of things that might have stopped Pasteur's experiments working if he had pushed them a little further. There are various spores in addition to those found in hay that are resistant to extinction by boiling at 100°C. In the early part of the twentieth century, Henry Bastian was supporting the idea of spontaneous generation by, unknowingly, discovering more of these heat-resistant spores. Further, the dormancy of bacteria depends not only on heat but also on the acidity of the solution. Spores which appear dead in acid solution can give rise to life in an alkaline environment. Thus experiments of the type that formed the basis of this debate can be confounded in many ways. To make sure that a fluid is completely sterile it is necessary to heat it under pressure to a temperature of about 160 °C, and/or subject it to a cycle of heating and cooling repeated several times at the proper intervals. As we now know, there were many ways in which Pasteur's experiments could, and should, have gone wrong. Our best guess must be that they did, but Pasteur knew what he ought to count as a result and what he ought to count as a 'mistake'.

Pasteur was a great scientist but what he did bore little resemblance to the ideal set out in modern texts of scientific method. It is hard to see how he would have brought about the changes in our ideas of the nature of germs if he had been constrained by the sterile model of behaviour which counts, for many, as the model of scientific method.

5

A new window on the universe: the non-detection of gravitational radiation

Detecting gravity waves

In 1969, Professor Joseph Weber, of the University of Maryland, claimed to have found evidence for the existence of large amounts of gravitational radiation coming from space. He used a new type of detector of his own design. The amount of radiation he saw was far greater than the theoretical predictions of astronomers and cosmologists. In the years that followed, scientists tried to test Weber's claims. No-one could confirm them. By 1975, few, if any, scientists believed that Weber's radiation existed in the quantities he said he had found. But, whatever it looks like now, theory and experiment alone did not settle the question of the existence of gravitational radiation.

Gravitational radiation can be thought of as the gravitational equivalent of electromagnetic radiation such as radio waves. Most scientists agree that Einstein's general theory of relativity predicts that moving massive bodies will produce gravity waves. The trouble is that they are so weak that it is very difficult to detect them. For example, no-one has so far suggested a way of generating detectable amounts of gravitational radiation on Earth. Nevertheless, it is now accepted that some sensible proportion of the vast amounts of energy generated in the violent events in the universe should be dissipated in the form of gravitational radiation, and it is this that may be detectable on Earth. Exploding supernovae, black holes and binary stars should produce sizeable fluxes of gravity waves which would show themselves on Earth as a tiny oscillation in the value of 'G' – the constant that is related to the gravitational pull of one object on another. Of course, measuring 'G' is hard enough in itself.

It was a triumph of experimental science when, in 1798, Cavendish measured the gravitational attraction between two massive lead balls. The attractive force between them comprised only one 500 millionth of their weight. Looking for gravitational radiation is unimaginably more difficult than looking for this tiny force because the effect of a gravity wave pulse is no more than a minute fluctuation within the tiny force. To exemplify, one of the smaller gravitational antennae in operation in 1975 (the detectors are often referred to as antennae) was encased in a glass vacuum vessel. The core consisted of, perhaps, 100 kilograms of metal yet the impact of the *light* from a small flashgun on the mass of metal was enough to send the recording trace off scale.

The standard technique for detecting gravitational radiation was pioneered by Weber (pronounced 'Whebber') in the late 1960s. He looked for changes in the length (strains) of a massive aluminium alloy bar caused, effectively, by the changes in gravitational attraction between its parts. Such a bar, often weighing several tons, could not be expected to change its dimensions by more than a fraction of the radius of an atom as a pulse of gravitational radiation passed. Fortunately, the radiation is an oscillation and, if the dimensions of the bar are just right, it will vibrate, or 'ring' like a bell, at the same frequency as the radiation. This means that the energy in the pulse can be built up into something just measurable.

A Weber-bar antenna comprises the heavy bar with some means of measuring its vibrations. Most designs used strain-sensitive 'piezo-electric' crystals glued, or otherwise fixed, to the bar. When these crystals are distorted they produce an electrical potential. In a gravity wave detector the potential produced by the deformation of the crystals is so small as to be almost undetectable. This means that the impulse from the crystals must be amplified if it is to be measured. A critical part of the design is, then, the signal amplifier. Once amplified, the signals can be recorded on a chart recorder, or fed into a computer for immediate analysis.

Such devices don't really detect gravity waves, they detect vibrations in a bar of metal. They cannot distinguish between vibrations

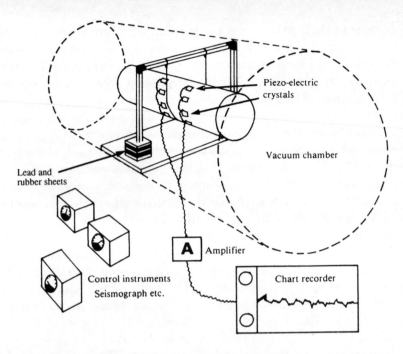

Figure 5.1. Weber-type gravity wave antenna. Compare Weber's method of seismic insulation with the heavy concrete foundations used in the Michelson–Morley experiments (see chapter 2). Heavy foundations actually link the apparatus firmly to the ground thus making certain that vibrations will be channelled through to the apparatus. Remember that Michelson (chapter 2) discovered this his apparatus would be disturbed by stamping on the ground 100 metres from the laboratory. Weber-type detectors are much less sensitive than this due to the ingenious insulation and the narrow waveband of the radiation.

due to gravitational radiation and those produced by other forces. Thus to make a reasonable attempt to detect gravity waves the bar must be insulated from all other known and potential disturbances such as electrical, magnetic, thermal, acoustic and seismic forces. Weber attempted to do this by suspending the bar in a metal vacuum chamber on a thin wire. The suspension was insulated from the ground in an original and effective way by using a stack of lead and rubber sheets.

In spite of these precautions the bar will not normally be completely quiescent. So long as it is at a temperature above absolute zero there will be vibrations caused by the random movements of its own atoms; the strain gauges will, then, register a continual output of 'thermal noise'. If this is recorded on graph paper by a pen recorder (as it was in many experiments), what will be seen is a spiky wavy line showing random peaks and troughs. A gravity wave would be represented as, perhaps, a particularly high peak, but a decision has to be made about the threshold above which a peak counts as a gravity wave rather than unwanted 'noise'. However high the threshold it must be expected that occasionally a peak due entirely to noise would rise above it. In order to be confident that some gravity waves are being detected it is necessary to estimate the number of 'accidental' peaks one should obtain as a result of noise alone, then make certain that the total number of above-threshold peaks is still greater. In 1969 Weber claimed to be detecting the equivalent of about seven peaks a day that could not be accounted for by noise.

Current status of Weber's claims and of gravitational radiation

Weber's claims are now nearly universally disbelieved. Nevertheless the search for gravitational radiation goes on. Weber's findings were sceptically received because he seemed to find far too much gravitational radiation to be compatible with contemporary cosmological theories. If Weber's results were extrapolated, assuming a uniform universe, and assuming that gravitational radiation was not concentrated into the frequency that Weber could best detect, then the amount of energy that was apparently being generated would mean that the cosmos would 'burn away' in a very short time – cosmologically speaking. These calculations suggested that Weber must be wrong by a very long way. The apparatuses now under development are designed to detect the much lower fluxes of radiation that cosmologists believe might be there. The new antennae are 1000 million times more sensitive; they should detect fluxes 1000 million times smaller than Weber said he had found.

Though Weber's first results were not believed because of the amount of radiation he claimed to see, he eventually managed to persuade others to take him more seriously. In the early 1970s he developed his work in a number of ingenious ways, leading other laboratories to attempt to replicate his findings. One of the most important new pieces of evidence was that above-threshold peaks could be detected simultaneously on two or more detectors separated by a thousand miles. At first sight it seemed that only some extra-terrestrial disturbance, such as gravity waves, could be responsible for these simultaneous observations. Another piece of evidence was that Weber discovered peaks in the activity of his detector which happened about every 24 hours. This suggested that the source of the activity had something to do with the rotation of the earth. As the earth rotated, carrying the detector with it, the sensitivity would be expected to vary if the radiation came mostly from one direction in space. The 24 hour periodicity thus indicated that his detectors were being vibrated by an extra-terrestrial source rather than some irrelevant earth-bound disturbance.

What is more, the periodicity at first seemed to relate to the earth's disposition with regard to the galaxy, rather than with regard to the sun – the periodicity related to the astronomical day. This was important, because as the earth moves in orbit round the sun, one would expect the time of day when the detector was most sensitive to change with the seasons. (The geometry is just the same as in the Michelson–Morley experiment; see chapter 2.) This suggested that the source must be outside the solar system – again a strong indicator that it was cosmic events that were causing the gravity wave detector to vibrate rather than something local and uninteresting. This effect became known as the 'sidereal correlation', meaning that the peak periods of activity of the detector were related to the earth's relationship to the stars rather than to the sun.

Persuading others

It is worth noting at this point that with an unexpected claim like Weber's it is necessary to do much more than report experimental results in order to persuade others to take the work sufficiently seriously even to bother to check it! To have any chance of becoming an established result it must first 'escape' from the laboratory of its originator. Persuading other scientists to try to *disprove* a claim is a useful first step. In Weber's case different scientists were convinced by different experimental developments. Some thought one feature was convincing whereas others thought the opposite. For instance, the first of Weber's elaborations was the demonstration of coincident signals from two or more detectors separated by large distances. Some scientists found this convincing. Thus, at the time (1972) one scientist said to Collins:

> [ ] wrote to him specifically asking about quadruple and triple coincidences because this to me is the chief criterion. The chances of three detectors or four detectors going off together is very remote.

On the other hand some scientists believed that the coincidences could quite easily be produced by the electronics, chance, or some other artefact. Thus:

> ... from talking it turns out that the bar in [ ] and the bar in [ ] didn't have independent electronics at all. ... There was some very important common contents to both signals. I said ... no wonder you see coincidences. So all in all I wrote the whole thing off again.

Another elaboration adopted by Weber involved passing the signal from one of the detectors through a time delay before comparing it with the signal from a distant detector. Under these circumstances there should be no coincidences – that is to say, any coincidences would be purely a product of accident. Weber showed that the number of coincident signals did indeed go down when one signal was delayed with respect to the other, suggesting that they were not an artefact of the electronics or a matter of chance. Several scientists made comments such as '... the time delay experiment is very convincing', whereas others did not find it so.

Weber's discovery of the correlation of peaks in gravity wave activity with star time was the outstanding fact requiring explanation for some scientists, thus:

> ... I couldn't care less about the delay line experiment. You could invent other mechanisms which would cause the coincidences to go away ... The sidereal correlation to me is the only thing of that whole bunch of stuff that makes me stand up and worry about it ... If that sidereal correlation disappears you can take that whole ... experiment and stuff it someplace.

Against this, two scientists remarked:

> The thing that finally convinced a lot of us . . . was when he reported that a computer had analysed his data and found the same thing.
> The most convincing thing is that he has put it in a computer . . .

But, another said:

> You know he's claimed to have people write computer programmes for him 'hands off'. I don't know what that means. . . . One thing that me and a lot of people are unhappy about, is the way he's analysed the data, and the fact that he's done it in a computer doesn't make that much difference . . .

Picking the right experimental elaboration to convince others requires rhetorical as well as scientific skills.

The experimenter's regress

By 1972 several other laboratories had built or were building antennae to search for gravitational radiation. Three others had been operating long enough by then to be ready to make tentative negative reports. Now we must imagine the problems of a scientist attempting to replicate Weber's experiment. Such a scientist has built a delicate apparatus and watched over it for several months while it generated its yards and yards of chart recorder squiggles. The question is: are there peaks among the squiggles which represent real gravity wave pulses rather than noise? If the answer seems to be 'no' then the next question is whether to publish the results, implying that Weber was wrong and that there are no high fluxes of gravity waves to be found. At this point the experimenter has an agonising decision to make; it could be that there really are gravity waves but the negative experiment is flawed in some way. For example, the decision about the threshold for what counts as real peaks might be wrong, or the amplifier might not be as sensitive as Weber's, or the bar might not be appropriately supported, or the crystals might not be well enough glued to allow the signals to come through. If such is the case, *and* if it turns out that there are high fluxes of gravity waves, then in reporting their non-existence, the scientist will have revealed his own experimental incompetence.

Here the situation is quite unlike that of the school or university student's practical class. The student can have a good idea whether or not he or she has done an experiment competently by referring to the outcome. If the outcome is in the right range, then the experiment has been done about right, but if the outcome is in the wrong range, then something has gone wrong. In real time, the question for difficult science, such as the gravity wave case and the others described in this book, is, '*What is the correct outcome?*'. Clearly, knowledge of the correct outcome cannot provide the answer. Is the correct outcome the detection of gravity waves or the non-detection of gravity waves? Since the existence of gravity waves is the very point at issue, it is impossible to know this at the outset.

Thus, what the correct outcome is depends upon whether there are, or are not, gravity waves hitting the earth in detectable fluxes. To find this out we must build a good gravity wave detector and have a look. But we won't know if we have built a good detector until we have tried it and obtained the correct outcome. But we don't know what the correct outcome is until ... and so on *ad infinitum*.

This circle can be called the 'experimenter's regress'. Experimental work can only be used as a *test* if some way is found of breaking into the circle of the experimenter's regress. In most science the circle is broken because the appropriate range of outcomes is known at the outset. This provides a universally agreed criterion of experimental quality. Where such a clear criterion is not available, the experimenter's regress can only be avoided by finding some other means of defining the quality of an experiment; and the criterion must be independent of the output of the experiment itself.

Scientists at their work

What should the consequences of the experimenter's regress be? Because no-one knows what counts as the correct result, it is not easy to see who has done a good experiment. We might, then, expect gravity wave scientists to disagree about who had done their experiment well. We might think they would disagree about whether a particular result was the outcome of incompetence on the part of the experimenter and/or flaws in the apparatus. Some scientists would think that Weber saw gravity waves because his methods, or his apparatus, were faulty. Others would think that *failure* to see the radiation must be a consequence of lack of skill, insufficient persever-ance, or bad luck. One of the authors of this book, Collins, interviewed most of the scientists involved in the gravity wave work in Britain and America. Such disagreement was precisely what he found. The following set of comments, taken from inter-views conducted in 1972, show how scientists' views about others' work varied. In each case, three scientists who come from three different laboratories are commenting on the experiment of a fourth.

Comments on the experiment conducted at W

Scientist (a): . . . that's why the W thing, though it's very complicated, has certain attributes so that if they see something, it's a little more believable . . . They've really put some thought into it . . .

Scientist (b): They hope to get very high sensitivity but I don't believe them frankly. There are more subtle ways round it than brute force . . .

Scientist (c): I think that the group at . . . W . . . are just out of their minds.

Comments on the experiment conducted at X

Scientist (i): . . . he is at a very small place . . . [but] . . . I have looked at his data, and he certainly has some interesting data.

Scientist (ii): I am not really impressed with his experimental capabilities so I would question anything he has done more than I would question other people's.

Scientist (iii): That experiment is a bunch of shit!

Comments on the experiment conducted at Y

Scientist (1): Y's results do seem quite impressive. They are sort of very business-like and look quite authoritative . . .

Scientist (2): My best estimate of his sensitivity, and he and I are good friends ... is ... [low] ... and he has just got no chance [of detecting gravity waves].

Scientist (3): If you do as Y has done and you just give your figures to some ... [operator] and ask them to work that out, well, you don't know anything. You don't know whether those [operators] were talking to their [friends] at the time.

Comments on the experiment conducted at Z

Scientist (I): Z's experiment is quite interesting, and shouldn't be ruled out just because the ... group can't repeat it.

Scientist (II): I am very unimpressed with the Z affair.

Scientist (III): Then there's Z. Now the Z thing is an out and out fraud!

Not only do scientists' opinions about the same experiment differ, but every experiment differs from every other in countless ways. Indeed, it is hard to know what it means to do an experiment that is *identical* to another. As one scientist put it:

> Inevitably in an experiment like this there are going to be a lot of negative results when people first go on the air because the effect is that small, any small difference in the apparatus can make a big difference in the observations. ... I mean when you build an experiment there are lots of things about experiments that are not communicated in articles and so on. There are so called standard techniques, but those techniques, it may be necessary to do them in a certain way.

It is easy, then, to find a difference that will explain and justify a scientist's views about the work of another. Variations in signal processing techniques, in design of the amplifier, in the material of the bar (did it suffer from 'creep'?), in the method of attachment of the piezo-electric crystals, and in many other factors were cited in defence and criticism of the various experiments. Technical arguments, however, were not the only sources of judgement of others' experiments. Other grounds for doubt extended beyond what are usually thought of as science. In 1972, experimenters were casting around for non-technical reasons for believing or disbelieving the results of the various experiments. The list of reasons they provided at the time included the following:

1.   Faith in a scientist's experimental capabilities and honesty, based on a previous working partnership.
2.   The personality and intelligence of experimenters.
3.   A scientist's reputation gained in running a huge lab.
4.   Whether or not the scientist worked in industry or academia.
5.   A scientist's previous history of failures.
6.   'Inside information'.
7.   Scientists' style and presentation of results.
8.   Scientists' 'psychological approach' to experiment.
9.   The size and prestige of the scientist's university of origin.
10.   The scientist's degree of integration into various scientific networks.
11.   The scientist's nationality.

As one scientist put it, in explaining why he disbelieved Weber's results:

> You see, all this has very little to do with science. In the end we're going to get down to his experiment and you'll find that I can't pick it apart as carefully as I'd like.

The competence of experimenters and the existence of gravity waves

These arguments over whose work is well done are part and parcel of the debate about whether or not gravity waves exist. When it is decided which are the good experiments, it becomes clear whether those that have detected gravity waves, or those that have not been able to see them, are the good ones. Thus whether gravity waves are there to be detected becomes known. On the other hand, when we know whether gravity waves are there to be detected we know which detectors are good ones. If there are gravity waves a good apparatus is one that detects them; if there are no gravity waves the good experiments are those which do not see them. Thus, defining what counts as a good gravity wave detector, and determining whether gravity waves exist, are the same process. The scientific and the social aspects of this process are inextricable. This is how the experimenter's regress is resolved.

Gravitational radiation: 1975

After 1972, events favoured Weber's claims less and less. In July 1973 negative results were published by two separate groups (two weeks apart), in the scientific journal, *Physical Review Letters*. In December 1973, a third group published negative results in the journal, *Nature*. Further articles claiming that there was nothing to be seen even as the sensitivity of the apparatus was increased were published by these groups and also by three other groups. No-one has since concluded that they found anything that would corroborate Weber's findings.

In 1972, a few scientists believed in the existence of high fluxes of gravity waves, and very few would *openly commit* themselves to their non-existence. By 1975, a number of scientists had spent time and effort actively prosecuting the case against Weber. Most of the others accepted that he was wrong and only one scientist other than Weber thought the search for high fluxes still worth pursuing. One might say that the problem posed by the experimenter's regress had been effectively solved by 1975 – it was now 'known' (by nearly everyone) that an antenna that detected high fluxes of gravity waves was a dud, and one that did not had every chance of being a well-designed experiment. How did this come to pass?

Weber, it seems, was not very surprised at the flood of negative results. A respondent reports that Weber felt that, since a negative result is the easiest thing to achieve, then negative results were to be expected:

> ... about that time [1972] Weber had visited us and he made the comment, and I think the comment was apt, that 'it's going to be a very hard time in the gravity wave business', because, he felt that he had worked for ten or twelve years to get signals, and it's so much easier to turn on an experiment and if you don't see them, you don't look to find out why you don't see them, you just publish a paper. It's important, and it just says, 'I don't see them'. So he felt that things were going to fall to a low ebb ...

But it is hard to have complete confidence in an experiment that found nothing. It is hard to see what made scientists so confident that their negative results were correct as long as Weber was still claiming to see gravity waves. Why were they not more cautious? As one scientist remarked:

> ... [a major difference between Weber and the others is that Weber] spends hours and hours of time per day per week per month, living with the apparatus. When you are working with, and trying to get the most out of things you will find that, [for instance] a tube that you've selected, say one out of a hundred, only stays as a good noise tube for a month if you are lucky, but a week's more like it. Something happens, some little grain falls off the cathode and now you have a spot that's noisy, and the procedures for finding this are long and tedious. Meanwhile, your system, to the outside, looks just the same.
>
> So lots of times you can have a system running, and you think it's working fine, and it's not. One of the things that Weber gives his system, that none of the others do, is dedication – personal dedication – as an electrical engineer which most of the other guys are not ...
>
> Weber's an electrical engineer, and a physicist, and if it turns out that he's seeing gravity waves, and the others just missed it, that's the answer, that they weren't really dedicated experimenters ... Living with the apparatus is something that I found is really important. It's sort of like getting to know a person – you can, after a while, tell when your wife is feeling out of sorts even though she doesn't know it.

This feature of experimental work must make scientists wary about drawing clear conclusions from a set of negative results. It is another way of expressing the experimenter's regress. How did they gain enough confidence to damn Weber's findings?

How the debate closed

By 1975 nearly all scientists agreed that Weber's experiment was not adequate but their reasons differed markedly. Some had become convinced because at one point Weber had made a rather glaring error in his computer program; others thought that the error had been satisfactorily corrected before too much damage was done. Some thought that the statistical analyses of the level of background noise and the number of residual peaks was inadequate; others did not think this a decisive point.

Weber had also made an unfortunate mistake when he claimed to have found coincident signals between his own detector and that of an entirely independent laboratory. These coincidences were extracted from the data by comparing sections of tape from the two detectors. Unfortunately for Weber it turned out that because of a confusion over time zones, the two sections of tape he compared had been recorded more than four hours apart so that he was effectively conjuring a signal out of what should have been pure noise. Once more though, it was not hard to find scientists who thought that the damage had not been too great since the level of signal reported was scarcely statistically significant.

Another factor considered important by some was that Weber did not manage to increase the signal-to-noise ratio of his results over the years. It was expected that as he improved his apparatus the signal would get stronger. In fact, the net signal seemed to be going down. This, according to many scientists, was not how new scientific work ought to go. What is more, the correlation with star time that Weber first reported faded away. Again, however, these criticisms were only thought to be decisive by one or two scientists; after all there is no guarantee that a cosmic source of gravity waves should remain stable.

It goes almost without saying that the nearly uniform negative results of other laboratories were an important point. Nevertheless, all of the, roughly, six negative experiments were trenchantly criticised by Weber and, more important, five of them were criticised by one or more of Weber's critics! This should come as no surprise given the analysis in earlier sections of this paper. The one experiment that remained immune to criticism by Weber's critics was designed to be as near as possible a carbon-copy of the original Weber design. No-one thought it was crucial.

What seems to have been most important in the debate was the trenchant criticism, careful analysis, and confrontational style of one powerful member of the physics community Richard Garwin. As one scientist put it:

> ... as far as the scientific community in general is concerned, it's probably Garwin's publication that generally clinched the attitude. But in fact the experiment they did was trivial – it was a tiny thing ... But the thing was, the way they wrote it up ... Everybody else was

awfully tentative about it ... It was all a bit hesitant ... And then
Garwin comes along with this toy. But it's the way he writes it up you
see.

Another scientist said:

Garwin ... talked louder than anyone and he did a very nice job of
analysing his data.

And a third:

[Garwin's paper] ... was done in a very clear manner and they sort of
convinced everybody.

When the first negative results were reported in 1972, they were
accompanied with a careful exploration of all the logical possibilities
of error. Understandably, the first scientists to criticise Weber hedged
their bets. Following closely came the outspoken experimental report
by Garwin with careful data analysis and the uncompromising claim
that the results were 'in substantial conflict with those reported by
Weber'. Then, as one respondent put it, 'that started the avalanche
and after that nobody saw anything'.

As far as *experimental results* are concerned, the picture that
emerges is that the series of negative experiments made strong and
confident disgreement with Weber's results openly publishable but
that this confidence came only after, what one might call, a 'critical
mass' of experimental reports had built up. This mass was 'triggered'
by Garwin.

Garwin believed from the beginning that Weber was mistaken. He
acted on that belief as he thought proper. Thus he made certain that
some of Weber's errors were given wide publicity at a conference and
he wrote a 'letter' to a popular physics journal which included the
paragraph:

[it was shown] that in a ... [certain tape] ... nearly all the so-called
'real' coincidences ... were created individually by this single pro-
gramming error. Thus not only some phenomenon besides gravity
waves *could*, but in fact *did*, cause the zero-delay excess coincidence
rate [in this data]. [Garwin's stress]

and the statement:

... the Weber group has published no credible evidence at all for their claim of detection of gravitational radiation.

Concerning some of their later work, a member of Garwin's group remarked to me:

At that point it was not doing physics any longer. It's not clear that it was ever physics, but it certainly wasn't by then.

and

We just wanted to see if it was possible to stop it immediately without having it drag on for twenty years.

Thus, without the actions of Garwin and his group it is hard to see how the gravity wave controversy would have been brought to a close. That such a contribution was needed is, once more, a consequence of the experimenter's regress.

Conclusion

We have indicated how the experimenter's regress was resolved in the case of gravity waves. The growing weight of negative reports, all of which were indecisive in themselves, were crystallised, as it were, by Garwin. After he had spoken, only experiments yielding negative results were counted and there just were no more high fluxes of gravity waves. All subsequent experiments that produced positive results must, by that very fact, be counted as flawed.

Reporting an experimental result is itself not enough to give credibility to an unusual claim. If such a claim is to be taken sufficiently seriously for other scientists even to try to refute it then it must be presented very clearly and with great ingenuity. Weber had to make a long series of modifications before his claims were given significant notice. Then, once the controversy was under way, a combination of theory and experiment alone was not enough to settle matters; the experimenter's regress stands in the way. We have seen some of the ways in which such issues actually are resolved. These resolving, or 'closure', mechanisms are not normally thought of as 'scientific' activities yet, without them, controversial science cannot work.

It is important to notice that the science of gravity waves after the resolution of the controversy does not look at all like the science of gravity waves before the resolution. *Before* the resolution there was real and substantial uncertainty, and it was very reasonable uncertainty. In spite of the large amount of scientific work that had been done and the large number of experimental and theoretical results that were available, things were not clear. At that point no-one could be blamed for thinking that there were two possibilities open and for being reluctant to plump for one side or the other. *After* the resolution everything is clarified; high fluxes of gravity waves do not exist and it is said that only incompetent scientists think they can see them.

Of course, the model also shows that a controversy once closed may, in principle, be re-opened. Professor Joseph Weber has never ceased to believe that his results were correct and, especially since 1982, after our story ends, has been publishing papers which provide new arguments and evidence in support of his view. The question is, will they gain the attention of the scientific community?

The, pre-resolution, gravity wave science of 1972 is the sort of science that is rarely seen or understood by the science student. Nevertheless, to stress a point that will be made again in the conclusion to the whole book, it is the sort of science that the research scientist may one day face and it is the sort of science that the public are asked to consider when, say, they listen to forensic evidence as members of a jury, or when they attend to public inquiries on technical matters, or when they vote for policies, such as defence or energy policies, which turn on technical matters. For many reasons then, it is as important to understand this unfamiliar face of science as it is to understand its more regular counterpart.

6

The sex life of the whiptail lizard

Introduction

David Crews, a professor of zoology and psychology at the University of Texas, might be thought of as a sexual voyeur. This is because he spends much of his time observing the bizarre sex lives of reptiles such as lizards and snakes. His work is of great interest to biologists. It is sometimes controversial. Our focus in this chapter is on one particular set of observations which Crews made of the mating behaviour of a particular genus of whiptail lizard. However, by way of introduction to the sexual world of reptiles which Crews studies, we will first look at his less controversial work on the red-sided garter snake.

The Arctic environment of western Canada provides perhaps the harshest conditions encountered by any vertebrate on the planet. It is here that the red-sided garter snake lives. In order to survive the long Arctic winter, snakes have learnt the trick of cryopreservation. Their blood becomes extremely thick, and crucial bodily organs stop functioning almost completely, exhibiting barely detectable levels of activity. However, when Spring arrives, they undergo rapid transformation in preparation for mating.

Mating occurs over a short, intense period. The males emerge first from their long winter deep-freeze and spend from three days to three weeks basking in the sun near the entrance to the den. When the females emerge, either alone or in small groups, the males are

attracted by a pherome (a messenger substance) on their backs. Up to
100 males converge and form a 'mating ball'. Once a male succeeds in
mating, the others immediately disperse. The mated female, who has
been rendered unattractive to other males as a result of a pherome
which she has received from the mating male, now leaves the locale.
The males regroup, waiting by the entrance of the den for the
emergence of other females with which to mate.

Why are biologists interested in such a curious ritual? Crews is a
behavioural neuroendocrinologist. He studies the evolution of the
systems in the body that control reproduction and sexual behaviour.
He uses a variety of techniques, including observations of behaviour,
examination of organs, and analyses of substances in the blood.
Comparisons are made with other species. The garter snake is of
particular interest to Crews because of the way that its sexual
behaviour and its physiology are synchronised with the demands of
the environment. The snakes' sexual activities may seem strange to
us, but they have adapted perfectly to the extreme conditions under
which they live. For Crews the behaviour of the garter snakes was a
particularly powerful illustration of how environmental factors may
influence the evolution and development of various aspects of
reproduction. By emphasising the role of the environment Crews can
be thought of as taking sides in one of the oldest debates in biology:
nature versus nurture.

Crews' interest in reproductive physiology is somewhat at odds
with the traditional fields of reptile study. His work falls between the
interests of herpetologists who study snakes and lizards from a
natural history standpoint and neuroendocrinologists who compare
various hormonal control systems without necessarily linking their
work to the sexual behaviour of the species. With his interest in
evolution and in comparing more than one species, Crews also finds
audiences for his work among evolutionary theorists, comparative
biologists, zoologists and psychologists. Like many scientific innovators, Crews brings together approaches from a variety of areas that
traditionally have gone their separate ways. It is partly because of this
that his work has been tinged with controversy. By asking new
questions of aspects of the behaviour and physiology of species that
have already been well studied, Crews was posing a challenge to the
established experts.

Of course, just because a scientist's work challenges that of his or her colleagues, does not mean that it will necessarily lend itself to controversy. Many contentious findings or approaches within science are simply ignored. For instance, numerous papers have been published challenging the foundations of quantum mechanics or relativity theory which scarcely cause a ripple on the surface of physics. Turning a blind eye in the no-nonsense way to deal with potentially troublesome ideas. Indeed, obtaining a controversial status for a set of ideas such that other scientists feel compelled to reject them in an explicit manner is a substantial achievement in itself.

By the time Crews produced his controversial work on the whiptail lizard he was too important a figure to ignore. In the early stages of his career at Harvard there was no inkling of the controversy to come. His approach and findings did not challenge the fundamentals of his field. By the time he moved to Texas University (after seven years at Harvard) he was a highly respected, visible, and well-connected scientist. It was only now, after having established himself, that he started to stress the radical quality of his ideas. The most sharply focussed controversy in which Crews has become involved has not centred on the grander issues of evolutionary theory but on some rather specific claims that he made concerning the sexual behaviour of the whiptail lizard. It is his observations of this vertebrate and their reception which form the backbone of our story.

In what follows we shall be particularly concerned to follow the twists and turns of this one scientific controversy. It may seem perverse to go into such detail. However, we would remind the reader that it is exactly in the detailed arguments that we find the rough diamond of science.

'Leapin' lesbian lizards'

This heading was used by *Time* magazine to introduce Crews' observations of the sexual habits of *Cnemidophorus*, the whiptail lizard. *Cnemidophorus* is unusual in the reptile world because it breeds 'parthenogenetically'. That is to say it can reproduce from the eggs of the female without needing a male to fertilise them. This makes the species ideal for studying aspects of the evolution of

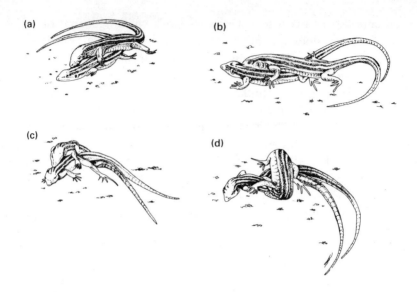

Figure 6.1. Sexual behaviour in *C. uniparens* (redrawn by Steven W. Allison from Myers, 1990, p. 273).

sexuality that cannot be separated and analysed in normal sexual species, where the complicating factor of male heredity is always present.

As soon as Crews started work on *Cnemidophorus* he noticed what at first sight was a bizarre pattern of behaviour. These non-sexual lizards, who did not need to mate, sometimes mounted each other, behaving just like other sexual lizards. It was this observation which previous researchers had ignored, or chosen to ignore, which lies at the heart of the controversy.

The behaviour of significance to our story is reproduced in the series of illustrations shown in figure 6.1. The sequence appears to be simple enough. One active female climbs onto the back of another passive female, curves its tail around its partner's body so that their sexual organs come into contact, strokes the neck and back, and rides on top of the other for one to five minutes. All biologists agree that this is what happens. They disagree over the meaning to be given to the observations.

For Crews and his co-worker Fitzgerald, the lizard's strange behaviour (repeatedly observed with different lizards) was clearly sexually related. Indeed, they thought that what they had seen was so significant that they presented it as a new and important scientific discovery about parthenogenetic species. The courtship routine followed by the copulatory behaviour seemed remarkably similar to ordinary mating which Crews had observed in other closely related sexual species. Furthermore, dissection and palpation (examining by touch), of the lizards revealed its sexual significance. The courted animal appeared to be reproductively active, 'having ovaries containing large, preovulatory follicles, while the courting animal was either reproductively inactive or postovulatory, having ovaries containing only small undeveloped follicles'. This difference raised general questions about the function of the pseudo-copulatory behaviour for sexuality, such as its possible role in priming reproductive mechanisms.

If Crews thought he had made a major discovery, other biologists were not so sure. Some were outright sceptics. Two of the best-known researchers into this genus of lizard, Orlando Cuellar of the University of Utah, who in the early 1970s had shown the chromosomal mechanisms of parthenogenesis, and C. J. Cole of the American Museum of Natural History, who pioneered the physiological study of the genus, soon disputed Crews' claims. For these scientists, who had spent years studying *Cnemidophorus* and in particular learning how to maintain them in captivity, Crews was an inexperienced upstart. Rather than carefully observing the lizards over lengthy periods, he had, in their view, immediately seized upon a peculiar piece of behaviour, noticed in a very few animals, and blown it up into a sensational claim. Cuellar and Cole may have been particularly irked that *Time* magazine had picked up on the story; the sexual exploits of lizards made for compelling media coverage.

The first response of Cuellar and Cole was to attempt to play down the aberrant behaviour. They claimed that there was nothing particularly novel or surprising going on, since others (including themselves) had observed such activity among lizards before. Also Crews was simply wrong in claiming any general significance for the study of parthenogenetic species. The behaviour he had observed was trivial: it was unnatural and a product of captivity. Moreover a more experienced worker would not have been led astray and would have chosen to ignore it for the artefact it undoubtedly was. The key issue, then, was whether the lizard's behaviour was an artefact, produced by the overcrowded conditions of captivity, as the critics asserted, or an essential and previously neglected part of reproductive behaviour.

One feature of scientific controversies is that they bring into sharp focus the competence of the protagonists. Normally in science ability is taken for granted. However, in a controversy the specific scientific issues at stake and the abilities of the scientists involved are difficult to disentangle. In the ensuing debate between Crews and his critics the need for all the researchers to establish their skill became paramount.

Much of the controversy has taken place in the published scientific literature and one indication of the increasing importance attached to the establishment of competence is the expansion of the normally brief 'methods' sections of the papers. In Crews and Fitzgerald's original paper the method section was simply a few lines which accompanied photographs of the lizards. However, by the time it comes to rebutting their critics five years later, there is a remarkable amount of detail concerning the regimen of care of the lizards, the observational procedures followed and so on. As the controversy develops, the skills and competence necessary to make these sorts of observation also become an issue. For instance, in his published attack on Crews, Orlando Cuellar refers to his own long experience (over a decade) observing captive *Cnemidophorus* produce eggs, and his 'precise knowledge' of the reproductive cycle. He states that, although he has seen behaviour such as that observed by Crews sporadically on and off for fifteen years in the laboratory, it is insignificant.

In the same way, Cole and Townsend, in a rebuttal of Crews and Fitzgerald, emphasise their own skills as observers, stressing the detail and duration of their observations (in contrast to the short period of Crews and Fitzgerald's work), and the fine-grained nature of their behaviour categorisation system. They even mention where the lizards were kept (in their offices), and that they cared for the animals personally. Again such details never normally appear in routine research reports.

Such personal appeals to a scientist's own skills and reconstructions of the details of everyday work in the lab produce, however, an unintended effect. They make science look more like other areas of activity which are carried out in the mundane world of offices and which depend on skill.

It is no accident that the routine scientific paper plays down such factors. It is the absence of these discussions which makes science look like a special activity; scientists become merely mediators or passive observers of Nature. Because the establishment of skill and competence becomes important during a controversy we start to see better what goes into the making of science. Processes which are normally hidden become visible.

Ironically when Crews and his colleagues responded to Cuellar they made his appeal to his own diligence and experience count against him. They took his admission that he had indeed seen the pseudo-copulatory behaviour as a confirmation of their own observations. They then went on to treat his failure to realise its significance as stemming from his own preconceptions. This is part of a general strategy which Crews has used against his critics whereby he portrays them as being stick-in-the-mud, paradigm bound, and caught up in the old traditions, rather than seeing what is there to be seen. This 'young Turks' strategy is not unfamiliar in scientific controversy.

Part of the argument concerning competence centres on the carefulness of the observers. In this case the critics claim that Crews and Fitzgerald simply have not been careful enough in their observations. The argument about carefulness, however, like most arguments in a controversy, can cut both ways. This line is taken by Crews and his group in their response to Cole and Townsend; they pick upon an apparent lack of rigour in the methods followed. They note that Cole and Townsend assess the reproductive state of the lizards from a visual inspection of abdominal distension. This, they claim, is inadequate as it is well known that palpation is also needed. In an ingenious move, they actually cite Crews' other critic, Cuellar, in support of this requirement.

Accusations of carelessness are ineffective in resolving disputes because they tend to circularity. Everyone knows that the careful scientist will find the 'truth', while the careless observer gets it wrong. But what there is to find is exactly the point at issue. If you believe pseudo-copulation is a genuine phenomenon then Crews appears to have been careful and his critics careless; conversely if pseudo-copulation is taken to be an artefact then it is his critics who have been careful and Crews careless. Care, in and of itself, like most such factors in a controversy, cannot provide an independent means to settle the issue. We are back in the experimenter's regress with a vengeance.

If general attributions of skill and competence cannot settle the controversy, what about matters of fact? As we have argued above, matters of fact are inseparable from the skills of the scientist used to produce them. Thus when the critics make a specific claim in an attempt to refute Crews, it is no surprise to find again that issues of competence are never far from the surface. The claim made by Cuellar, and Cole and Townsend, that the copulatory-like behaviour of the lizards stems from overcrowded conditions lies at the core of the controversy. It is answered by Crews in the following way. In his later articles, as mentioned above, he goes into great detail concerning his methods. The exact conditions under which his lizards are kept are given. Having done this, he is able to turn the tables on his critics by claiming that they present no specific data themselves to show that crowded conditions will lead to the artefactual copulation. 'They do not give the dimensions of the cages used, nor the number of animals housed per cage' (quoted in Myers, 1990, p. 125). With this move, it is Crews who appears to have been painstakingly careful in the very area where his critics have chosen to make their attack; the critics, on the other hand, are made to look cavalier in their accusation.

One way in which this controversy in biology appears to differ from the controversies in physics examined in this book is that very few new data are generated during the course of the controversy. The grounds of the debate seem to be constantly switching in the process of trying to find the right interpretation for previous observations. In physics, experiments serve as a way of focussing the debate. In this area of biology, experiments are seldom possible. Rather, attention is constantly drawn to evidence that is missing from the rival side's position – such as the evidence on crowded conditions leading to pseudo-copulation as mentioned by Crews in response to Cole and Townsend.

The most salient piece of negative evidence in the whole debate is simply that no-one, including Crews and Fitzgerald, has ever seen pseudo-copulation of lizards in the field. Cole and Townsend make much of this point, mentioning that the most thorough study of *Cnemidophorus* in the wild does not include it. As might be expected, Crews' and his group's response is up to the job. Again they turn the tables on the critics. They point out that such behaviour might well occur, but are observations in the wild capable of documenting it? It is well known that *Cnemidophorus* is a very shy species and that even matings in the ordinary sexual lizard are observed infrequently. So where better to observe such delicate phenomena than in captivity!

Love bites and hand waving

Often in the course of a scientific controversy previously ignored minutiae become highly relevant and hotly debated. As both sides try to cast doubt upon the others' arguments, more and more additional pieces of evidence get brought in. In the present case the number of 'love bites' the lizards underwent and whether or not they wave their hands as a sign of sexual submission both became important.

Cuellar argued that in species he had collected in the wild he had rarely seen any 'copulation bites' and more would be expected if pseudo-copulation was routine. The answer Crews and his group gave was again to reverse the argument by pointing out that if Cuellar was right then it would mean that normal sexual lizards were not mating either! The answer, they suggested, was that such bites are not a natural inscription of mating. To try to substantiate their point they examined the corpses of 1000 dead female lizards from a sexual species and found only 3% had marks on their backs and sides and, further, that the same frequency of males possessed such marks. So in this way Crews managed to turn the evidence produced by Cuellar back against him. Marks are most certainly found on dead lizards, but as they are found on males as well they are probably produced by aggressive behaviour.

Hand waving became significant in a postscript added by Cole and Townsend to their rebuttal of Crews. They criticise Crews for 'erroneously' relying on the lizards' lifting of the hand as an indication of submissiveness. Instead, according to them, it is merely a sign that the lizard is basking. Again it is the competence of the researchers which is under attack. A researcher who cannot tell basking from hand waving has a credibility problem. Although Crews does not seem to have responded in public to this particular criticism, from what has gone above the reader can speculate about the possible lines of argument Crews could have adopted in defence.

An honorable draw

So where does this controversy stand today? The current consensus is that Crews and his critics have battled to an honorable draw. Both sides have given their version of the endocrinology of *Cnemidophorus* in separate articles in the *Scientific American* and both continue to work within their rather different approaches.

The even-handed view which we have presented as we have followed the twists and turns of the debate is not likely to be shared by the protagonists. Their own arguments and positions are, of course, compelling, indeed irresistible to them. In presenting a neutral account we risk disappointing both sides.

Many scientists are wary of getting entangled in controversies and perceive them to be the repository of shoddy science. This can mean that denying you are party to a controversy can itself be a tactic in such disputes. We see it happening in the lizard controversy. In writing their articles in *Scientific American* both sides avoided any explicit reference to the controversy at all.

One way to close down a controversy is to rewrite history such that the dispute seems premature: an over-reaction of an under-developed field. Crews, in particular, in his later writing has presented his first paper and the reaction to it as having this character. For Crews it was an unfortunate debate which was characterised by a lack of firm experimental tests and decisive evidence. By appealing to the rhetoric of experiment and testing, something to which his methodology of working with lizards in captivity is ideally suited, Crews can appear to have found a way to have advanced beyond the earlier controversy. Whether this rhetoric succeeds remains to be seen.

One question has been left unanswered. Do *Cnemidophorus*

lizards indeed exhibit pseudo-copulatory behaviour which is relevant to their reproduction? Despite five years of research and debate the answer appears to be that we do not know. According to one group of respected scientists they do; according to another group they do not. As always the facts of nature are settled within the field of human argument.

Set the controls for the heart of the sun: the strange story of the missing solar neutrinos

The many stars we see burning in the night sky have one thing in common. They all convert matter into energy by a process known as nuclear fusion. This is the same process that occurs in hydrogen bombs. Because stars are continually eating up their own mass of hydrogen over time, they slowly change. The process of change or evolution is usually gradual, but can have dramatic moments such as the cataclysmic end of a star in a huge explosion, a supernova. The changing history of stars, including our own sun, is described by stellar evolution theory: one of the most fundamental theories in modern astrophysics. This theory successfully explains the different transitions undergone by most stars. For astronomers and astrophysicists, stellar evolution theory is taken for granted as much as Darwin's theory of evolution is for biologists.

Yet, despite the undoubted successes of the theory, its central assumption – that nuclear fusion is the source of a star's energy – has only recently been directly tested.

In 1967, Ray Davis, of the Brookhaven National Laboratory tried to detect solar neutrinos: sub-nuclear particles produced by nuclear fusion in our own sun. This was the first direct experimental test of stellar evolution theory. All other radiation coming from the sun is the result of processes that took place millions of years earlier. For example, light rays take millions of years to escape from the sun's core as they work their way to the surface. Neutrinos, because they interact so little with matter, travel straight out of the sun. Their detection on the earth would tell us what was happening in the core of the sun only 8 minutes earlier (the time the neutrinos take to travel from the sun to the earth). Solar neutrinos thus provide a direct test of whether our nearest star, the sun, has fusion as its energy source.

Precisely because neutrinos interact so little with matter, they are very very hard to detect. On average a neutrino can travel through a million million miles of lead before it is stopped. Detecting neutrinos was always going to be a difficult project! Davis' experiment is rather unusual. He used a vast tank of chlorine-rich cleaning fluid, the size of an Olympic swimming pool, buried deep underground in a disused mine shaft. Every month Davis dredges this tank searching for a radioactive form of argon, produced by the reaction of incoming neutrinos with chlorine. Unfortunately particles from outer space, known as cosmic rays, also trigger the reaction and this is why the experiment must be located deep underground to provide enough shielding to absorb the unwanted rays. The radioactive argon, once extracted from the tank, is placed in a very sensitive radioactive detector (a form of geiger counter), where the exact amount formed can be measured.

This experiment, which must be one of the most peculiar of modern science, has had a baffling outcome. The predicted neutrino fluxes are not there. A test which was intended as the crowning glory of stellar evolution theory has instead produced consternation. It is scarcely imaginable that stars do not have nuclear fusion as their energy source, so what has gone wrong? The experiment has been checked and rechecked, theories have been juggled, and models and assumptions have been carefully probed for errors. Thus far, however, no-one is sure what has gone wrong. Even today, with second-generation experiments 'coming on the air' (or more accurately 'going underground' since all such experiments need shielding from cosmic rays), it is by no means clear what the outcome will be.

This then is a classic case of a confrontation between experiment and theory. The theoretical realm and the experimental realm cannot, however, be so easily separated. In the solar-neutrino case, theorists and experimentalists have been collaborating for years to reach a conclusion.

In the first part of our story we will examine how the scientists built the partnership from which the experiment was born. The reception of the results of Davis' experiment, which we deal with in the second part, can only be understood against this background.

Just as the solar-neutrino experiment is supposed to give us a glimpse into the heart of the sun, the solar-neutrino *episode* gives us a glimpse of what happens in the heart of science when things do not turn out as expected. Strangely, we shall encounter science become 'unmade'.

Although the theoretical models used to calculate the solar-neutrino flux are complex (they are run on large computers), and the experiment is mind-boggling in its sensitivity (a handful of argon atoms are searched for in a tank containing billions upon billions of atoms), when the experiment was first thought of, the procedures were considered routine. Ray Davis, who is a chemist, perhaps over-modestly describes his experiment as merely a matter of 'plumbing'. Indeed, in the early 1960s, so confident was the physics community that Davis would confirm stellar evolution theory that a whole series of underground 'telescopes' were planned to detect neutrinos from a range of different cosmic sources. Such plans were shelved after Davis' first results became known. What were formerly taken to be well-understood areas of science became problematic and contentious. The robust became fragile, the closed open, and the certain uncertain. The intricate network of ties between theory and experiment was threatened with rupture. That the rupture has thus far been contained; that the experimental results have stood the test of time; and that the structure of stellar evolution theory remains in place, is a puzzle. We are *not* witnessing the collapse characteristic of a scientific revolution, yet, on the other hand, it is not quite 'business as usual'.

PART 1. BUILDING EXPERIMENTS AND PARTNERSHIPS

Experiments, like any outcome of human activity, do not arrive *de novo*. When Ray Davis 'switched on' his apparatus in the summer of 1967 to look for the expected flux of neutrinos, the previous 20 years of hard work by himself and others was at stake. Of particular importance was a unique partnership between Davis and a group of nuclear astrophysicists (nuclear astrophysics is nuclear physics applied to astronomy), at the Kellogg Radiation Laboratory of the California Institute of Technology, headed by William Fowler.

The neutrino has always held a special fascination for experimenters because it is one of the most elusive and therefore challenging particles to detect. First postulated by Wolfgang Pauli in 1930 as a purely theoretical entity needed to make theories of radioactive decay consistent, the neutrino was thought to have zero mass and zero electric charge. A kind of reverse radioactivity reaction was one of the few ways to detect this elusive particle. In such reactions a neutrino is absorbed by the nucleus of an atom to form a new element which is unstable and in turn decays. Separating out the few atoms of the newly formed element from the billions upon billions of target atoms is a technically daunting task. Carrying out this task is what Davis, who had long been interested in neutrino detection, set out to do.

The experimental technique Davis used came from the hybrid field of radioactivity and chemistry, known as radio-chemistry. The idea was to use chemistry to separate out the newly formed radioactive element (argon) from the target material. Davis achieved this by having the target in liquid form and purging it with helium gas, thus sweeping out the accumulated argon atoms. The exact quantity of argon formed could then be measured by counting its characteristic decays. In order to help separate argon decays from the background radiation Davis shielded his counter in a First-World-War gun barrel made of steel with low natural radioactivity.

The use of the chlorine–argon reaction for neutrino detection was first suggested by physicists Bruno Pontecorvo and Louis Alvarez. Alvarez's involvement was particularly important. As was the case for so much post-war physics, the idea stemmed from war-time work. Alvarez had devised a new method to determine whether the Germans were building an atomic bomb. This was a mobile radio-chemical detector which could be placed in a bomber and could be used to search for radioactive emissions from smoke-stacks when flown over Germany (none were found).

Davis took over Alvarez's ideas and by 1955 he had built a small working detector using 550 gallons of cleaning fluid. Of course, he could not detect anything unless he had a source of neutrinos. One of the most likely sources was thought to be nuclear power plants and thus Davis installed his detector at the Savannah River nuclear power reactor. At the same time and place Frederick Reines and Clyde Cowan were making their now historic measurements which provided the first detection of the free neutrino. Unfortunately for Davis it turned out that his apparatus was not sensitive to the types of neutrino produced in nuclear reactors. Davis now faced a dilemma. He had developed a promising detection system, but he had no neutrinos to detect. It was William Fowler who provided the way out of the dilemma.

Collaboration with Cal Tech

At Cal Tech, William Fowler was watching Davis's work closely. Nuclear astrophysics as a discipline had taken off in the 1930s following on from Eddington and Jean's pioneering achievement in identifying nuclear reactions as the most likely source of the sun's energy (this is the same Eddington as encountered in chapter 2). By the end of the 1950s, after many laboratory measurements of nuclear reactions, the detailed cycles of nuclear reactions in our own sun had been determined. In 1957 a comprehensive theory of how lighter elements are synthesised into heavier elements in stars was outlined by Fowler and his co-workers at Cal Tech. This was one of the highpoints of the discipline – it appeared to explain how all familiar substances were formed from the lightest element of all, hydrogen.

In 1958 one of the reaction rates crucial to the nuclear reaction cycle in the sun was remeasured and found to have been in error. It looked as if the sun produced some fairly high-energy neutrinos, which Davis should be able to detect. Fowler immediately alerted Davis to the possibility and from then on the two collaborated in order to bring the detector plans to fruition. At the time Fowler considered the detection of solar neutrinos to be the 'icing on the cake' of stellar evolution theory.

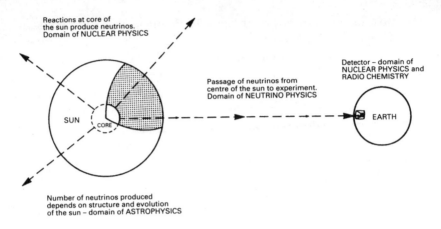

Figure 7.1. The different domains of solar-neutrino science.

Bahcall: a house theorist away from home

The Cal Tech end of the partnership with Davis centred upon a young post-doctoral student of Fowler's, John Bahcall. If solar neutrinos were to be Fowler's icing on the cake, they proved to be John Bahcall's bread and butter. Solar neutrinos became a dominant theme of Bahcall's subsequent career. By the time Davis was ready to make measurements it was Bahcall's career as much as Davis' that was at stake. The need for scientists to act in a concerted manner over a period of time as they pursue their careers is well illustrated by Bahcall's involvement.

Bahcall was a theoretical physicist and, as well as providing theoretical expertise, his job was to coordinate the Cal Tech effort. The prediction of the number of neutrinos Davis should expect to measure was a complex task requiring a variety of different sorts of knowledge. When Bahcall did not have the requisite expertise himself, he proved very adept (with Fowler's support) at recruiting others to help him.

The detailed prediction involved nuclear physics, astrophysics, neutrino physics, as well as radio-chemistry. The different domains of solar-neutrino physics are shown in figure 7.1.

Nuclear physics was needed both to measure the nuclear reaction rates in the sun and to calculate the interaction between neutrinos and chlorine in the detector. Since all the relevant nuclear reaction rates are measured in the laboratory at much higher energies than occur in the core of the sun, extrapolations to lower energies have to be made. These measurements and consequent estimates are often uncertain, and throughout the history of the solar-neutrino problem reaction rates have been revised as different measurements and calculations have been made. The Kellogg Radiation Laboratory housed some of the leading nuclear physicists. Bahcall soon enlisted their help in remeasuring many of the crucial nuclear parameters.

Another key element in calculating the neutrino fluxes is astrophysics. This is required to produce a detailed model of the sun's structure and evolution. The solar evolution is modelled on a computer over the equivalent of the 4.5 billion years life of the sun. Many data about the sun, such as the composition of its constituent elements, have to be fed into the model. Such input data were constantly revised. The solar model was constructed by specialists at Cal Tech. The largest component of the neutrino flux which Davis was expected to detect came from one sub-branch of the main hydrogen fusion chain of nuclear reactions in the sun. These high-energy neutrinos turned out to be extraordinarily temperature sensitive and critically dependent on the details of the solar-model. Expertise in neutrino physics was also required in order to determine what happened to the neutrinos in their passage through the sun and on their long journey to the earth.

As well as working on the prediction of the neutrino fluxes, Bahcall helped Davis with theoretical problems that arose in connection with the design of the experiment, such as, for instance, what the likely cosmic ray background might be, when best to take samples from the tank, and so on. In his own words he became the 'house theorist'. He eventually became a consultant to the Brookhaven National Laboratory where Davis worked and thus was paid for his services by the same 'house'.

Funding the experiment

Davis estimated the cost of the experiment to be approximately $600 000. In the 1960s this was a large sum to obtain for one experiment which, unlike particle accelerators, could be used to produce only one sort of measurement. Fowler was extremely influential in the process of obtaining the funding. He constantly advised Davis and Bahcall and elicited support from his own colleagues. Soundings were taken with all likely sources of support: the Atomic Energy Commission, the National Science Foundation and NASA.

It is naive to think that scientists obtain funding merely by writing a compelling grant proposal. To get funding for a major facility scientists have to engage in political lobbying and other forms of persuasion. In raising the money for Davis' experiment the following were important: the publication by Davis and Bahcall of their results and plans in the leading physics journal, *Physical Review Letters*; the use of the highly influential Kellogg Radiation Laboratory 'Orange and Lemon Aid' Preprint series in circulating information to the scientific community about what was happening; and coverage in the scientific and popular press – articles about solar neutrinos appeared in both *Time* and *Newsweek*. Of most importance was a letter to the Atomic Energy Commission which Fowler wrote at the bidding of Davis' departmental chairman, Richard Dodson. In this letter Fowler strongly urged that the experiment be funded. Dodson and Fowler were old friends and former colleagues at Cal Tech. It seems that at the time the Atomic Energy Commission did not use formal peer review, and Fowler's 'fine letter' (Dodson's words) provided the needed technical acclaim to ensure funding.

Of course, all these efforts to raise funding turned on the scientific merits of the case. The experiment was widely billed as a 'crucial' direct test of stellar evolution theory. Two things about the rhetoric used at the time are worth noting. Firstly, although undoubtedly more direct than other ways of measuring radiation from the sun's core, the neutrinos Davis expected to detect came from one highly temperature-sensitive sub-branch of the chain of hydrogen reactions. A more direct test would be of the fundamental hydrogen fusion reaction itself. The second-generation experiments now starting to produce results are sensitive to neutrinos from this reaction. Yet, in the effort to obtain funding, these new experiments too have been billed as 'crucial'. The rhetoric of 'cruciality' is clearly context dependent. There can be little doubt that when seeking hard-pressed dispensers of funds for large sums of money it helps to be doing something crucial.

The second thing to note is that many of the scientists whose support was needed for the experiment were nuclear and particle physicists. Such physicists, brought up on 'hard-nosed' laboratory science, were sceptical of astrophysics which they regarded as being much less precise. Many physicists were cautious about funding an experiment based upon astrophysics. One such sceptic was nuclear physicist Maurice Goldhaber, the Director of the Brookhaven National Laboratory. His support was crucial. Bahcall paid a special visit to Brookhaven to add his voice to the effort to persuade Goldhaber that the predictions were reliable and the experiment feasible.

In order to convince sceptics such as Goldhaber it was in Bahcall's interests to have a clear-cut prediction of a large signal which Davis could detect without ambiguity. There is some evidence that the predictions of the flux of solar neutrinos varied with physicists' need for funding. Figure 7.2 shows the predicted solar neutrino flux in SNUs (solar neutrino units) over time. It reveals that at the moment when the experiment was funded in 1964 the predicted flux was high (40 SNU). It can also be seen that immediately afterwards the predicted flux started to come down, and that by the time Davis got his first results in 1967 it had fallen to a much lower figure (19 SNU). Happily Davis managed to obtain greater sensitivity by improvements in the detection process, but several scientists commented that the experiment would never have been funded if the smaller levels of fluxes predicted in 1967 had been predicted earlier, in 1964 when the experiment was funded.

Many of the changes in the predicted flux came from parameters beyond Bahcall's immediate control, such as remeasurements of nuclear reaction rates and changes in other parameters. However, the timing of the push for funding, and the realisation (only after funding had been awarded) that one of the most important nuclear reaction rates had been incorrectly extrapolated to low energies, tended to work in favour of an overly optimistic prediction in 1964. The interdependence of theory and experiment could scarcely be clearer.

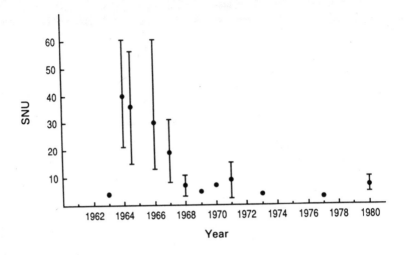

Figure 7.2. Solar neutrino flux (redrawn by Steven W. Allison from Pinch, 1986, p. 39).

Building the experiment

If Bahcall was engaged in unconventional activities for a theoretical physicist, Davis too faced some unusual tasks. Having obtained the necessary funding, he needed to find a deep mine shaft in which to locate his experiment. This proved to be far from easy, not only because of physical constraints such as the depth and stability of rock, but also because most mine owners could see little merit in housing an inconvenient and possibly dangerous experiment in their mines. Davis spent much of 1964 in negotiation with mine owners. Finally the Homestake Mining Company agreed to go ahead with the project once they realised that it was sponsored by the Atomic Energy Commission. It was no accident that the Atomic Energy Commission were consumers of the product of another important Homestake mining venture: uranium.

The building of the experiment involved Davis in extensive liaisons with the mining company and other commercial companies who helped fabricate the tank and associated equipment and deliver the cleaning fluid to the mine. (The cleaning fluid is actually on loan and may one day be returned for its more usual purpose!) In the end the local miners became enthusiastic about the experiment and several issues of the Homestake newspaper were devoted to the story.

It is a very impoverished view of science which treats theorists simply as producers of new ideas, and experimenters as the people who test or verify such ideas. As we have seen, doing theory and experiment are far more interesting than that. Theory and experiment are not independent activities. They are linked through and through, and form part of a wider network of ties between scientists. If it had not been for the collaboration of theoreticians and experimenters, and in particular the influence of the powerful group of Cal Tech scientists under William Fowler's leadership, the solar-neutrino experiment would never have happened.

PART 2. SCIENCE UNMADE

We will now turn to examine what happened when, against all expectations, Davis reported his negative result. Unlike some of the other cases discussed in this volume which involve a clash between theory and experiment, Davis' experiment has not lost credibility. For a while severe doubts were raised about his experimental method – perhaps somewhere in the vast tank of cleaning fluid he was losing a few atoms of argon. Davis, however, was able to survive such criticism and indeed eventually emerge with an enhanced reputation as a careful experimenter. The theorists too, and Bahcall in particular, have by-and-large managed to live with the result, although, as we shall see, Bahcall for a time felt that any contradiction between theory and experiment was not compelling.

The main feature of the period, once it was widely recognised that the solar-neutrino problem did indeed exist, has been a process of questioning and examination; just about every assumption upon which the scientific basis of the project was based has come under challenge. It is in such challenges that we can catch a glimpse of science as it becomes 'unmade'.

The first results

Davis' first results were obtained in August 1967. They indicated a very low signal, that is, a very low flux of neutrinos. Indeed the signal was so low that it could not be reported as a number (of neutrinos detected) with a possible error, but only as the upper limit: 6 SNU. In other words the signal was no greater than 6 SNU and this signal might result from background radiation alone. Improvements in the detection technique meant that by early 1968 Davis could set an even lower limit on the neutrino fluxes of 3 SNU. Davis, who had been working with this detection technique for most of his career, did not doubt that his result was correct. In view of its importance, however, he invited two fellow Brookhaven chemists to check his work. They could find nothing wrong. As an added precaution Davis calibrated his experiment by irradiating his tank with a neutron source which also produced the same isotope of argon as he detected. He recovered the expected number of argon atoms which seemed again to indicate that all was working well. However, this test was not taken to be compelling by everyone, as we shall see below. By this stage (May 1968) Davis felt confident enough to publish his result. In preliminary reports of his findings he stressed that his result was five times below the predicted signal of 19 SNU.

Bahcall's reaction

Davis' confidence that his result was out of line with theory was not shared by Bahcall. As soon as Bahcall learnt of Davis' low result (he was, of course, in continual contact), he went to work with yet more 'fine-tuning' of the theoretical 'prediction'. New measurements of various parameters were included which reduced the prediction to 7.5 SNU (with an error bar of 3 SNU). This enabled Bahcall to report by May 1968 that the 'present results of Davis . . . are not in obvious conflict with the theory of stellar structure'.

At this point Bahcall very much wanted Davis' experiment to be in agreement with his 'prediction'. With Davis reporting ever lower results, Bahcall became more and more depressed. Most of the other theorists shared Bahcall's concerns and were hoping against hope that the conflict would go away. A lot had been invested in this experiment. There was even talk of a Nobel Prize in the offing if only Davis' experiment would 'come out right'.

Iben's reaction

That a contradiction between theory and experiment existed was first and most forcefully recognised not by Bahcall, but by an old colleague of his from Cal Tech days, Icko Iben. Iben was a solar model specialist who had been part of the Cal Tech team which made the 1964 prediction. Iben now took a rather jaundiced view of what Bahcall was doing. For him, Bahcall was being disingenuous, abandoning the previously bold predictions of a high flux and using rather arbitrary values for parameters in order to try and lower the flux. In Iben's mind there was little doubt that there was a conflict and he used his own solar models to demonstrate its extent. A potentially acrimonious dispute between the two theorists was avoided, however, when shortly afterwards (in 1969) Bahcall, too, went on record proclaiming there to be a discrepancy. The solar-neutrino problem was now officially born.

The disagreement between Bahcall and Iben reminds us once more how flexible the 'prediction' with its many inputs could be. This episode also shows that judging the outcome of a test of a theory is not always straightforward. It is not simply a matter of inspecting theoretical prediction and experimental result as some philosophers believe. Interpretation is always involved. Bahcall and Iben were both highly competent theorists who were well-acquainted with the relevant scientific issues, yet in 1967 they drew rather different conclusions.

Bahcall now became one of the leading advocates of the view that there was a discrepancy – so much so that he has even fought battles with other scientists who were less enthusiastic about the extent and importance of the solar-neutrino problem. Although it is hazardous imputing strategies to individual scientists, and we should be wary of any simple-minded models of scientists as rational calculators who always try to promote what is in their best career interests, we can nevertheless speculate as to what rationale Bahcall might have had for his dramatic change in position.

His initial resistance to the idea that there was a conflict can be understood as a response to his previous involvement with the experiment. In 1967 Bahcall rightly or wrongly believed that further progress in his career depended upon Davis getting the right answer. However, the longer he held to the view that there was no conflict, while other theorists such as Iben who had less at stake in the project drew opposite conclusions, the more tenuous his position became. An indication of the kind of pressure he was under at the time comes from a conversation which Bahcall recalls having had with the famous Cal Tech physicist, Richard Feynman. Feynman apparently advised the young Bahcall that he had done nothing wrong and that if there was a contradiction this made the result *more* rather than less important. It seems Bahcall took Feynman's advice to heart. Furthermore, it seems to have been good advice. Bahcall has managed to continue to make a career out of solar neutrinos by stressing the scientific importance of the problem. His career does not seem to have suffered either; he has won prizes for his work on solar neutrinos and currently holds the highly prestigious post of Professor of Astronomy and Astrophysics at the Princeton Institute for Advanced Study.

Ray Davis: an ideal experimenter

With the conflict between theory and experiment now publicly recognised by the theorists, the heat was back on Davis to make sure that the problem did not reside with him. In most controversies of this type, as we have seen elsewhere in this volume, other scientists become involved in attempts to repeat the original experiment; in this case the experiment was too daunting and costly. This placed a special onus on Davis. Although he felt further tests of his procedures were largely a waste of time in terms of learning any new science, he saw the need to convince the more sceptical community of astrophysicists.

Throughout, Davis has made a point of following up and carrying out their suggestions, no matter how out-landish they might appear.

The strategy seems to have paid off because over the years Davis has acquired something of a reputation as the ideal experimenter. Indeed at one meeting in 1978 he was heralded as an unsung 'scientific hero' and he is widely regarded as one of the best experimenters in modern science. The ideal experimenter's profile which Davis cultivated is that of openness, caution, and modesty. There can be little doubt that acquiring such a profile helps an experimenter to maintain credibility. That Davis had already built a partnership with the theoreticians can now be seen to go some way towards explaining why his result has been taken so seriously. Having invested so much in him and his experiment, and having worked with him over the years, the theoreticians could not easily abandon him.

Among the new tests Davis agreed to perform was the introduction of 500 atoms of argon directly into his tank. Davis went on to recover the argon with the expected efficiency. He also persuaded some Brookhaven chemists to look for an anomalous form of argon which might remain trapped in the tank. They could find none. However, to repeat a familiar theme from other parts of this book, no experiment is alone definitive, and loop-holes can always be found by a determined critic. In 1976 such a determined critic appeared in the shape of a sceptical astrophysicist, Kenneth Jacobs.

Argon trapping

Jacobs was worried that Davis' experiment had never been repeated and he drew analogies with other experiments, such as Weber's gravity wave detector (discussed in chapter 5), where a signal near the noise was used as a basis to challenge established theories, and where in the long run the experiment had become discredited. Jacobs maintained that it was most likely that argon was being trapped somewhere, thus explaining the low result. He proposed a possible mechanism for such trapping in the form of weak 'polymerisation' which liquid hydro-carbons similar to Davis' cleaning fluid were known to undergo. He remained unconvinced that all the previous tests ruled out this possibility.

Jacobs' doubts could always be raised because of the logic of the types of calibration experiment Davis was forced to undertake.

Calibration tests by their very nature always involve differences when compared with what happens in an actual experimental run. For example, the calibration Davis used relied on ready-made argon atoms rather than atoms formed by neutrino interaction. Even when argon atoms were deliberately formed by fast neutron bombardment the chains of reaction were quite different from those involved in the case of neutrinos from the sun. Differences between a calibration and an experiment itself always exist. A compelling calibration is one where the importance of such differences seems small so that calibration is as much like the 'real thing' as possible, but 'seeming small' is a variable phenomenon.

Differences between experiments, as we see in other chapters of this book, always give grounds for doubt. Whether or not such doubts are raised depends on how far a scientist is prepared to challenge the conventional wisdom which holds such differences to be insignificant. Jacobs, as we have seen, was prepared to challenge that wisdom and for him the differences revealed a chink through which his argon-trapping hypothesis could sneak.

There was a complex test which was widely regarded as ruling out trapping. Davis eventually performed this test successfully. We do not know if Jacobs could have questioned this as well, because he failed to get tenure at his university and quit science altogether. Although the matter has rested here, if someone else as determined as Jacobs were to appear on the scene . . .

Solutions to the problem

Radio-chemistry aside, the overwhelming response to Davis' results has been to question one or more of the complicated chain of assumptions in the nuclear physics, astrophysics or neutrino physics which form the basis of the predicted neutrino fluxes. By 1978 over 400 papers had been published proposing 'solutions' to the solar-neutrino problem. Perhaps unsurprisingly it is in the area of astrophysics that most solutions have been canvassed. We have already remarked on the extraordinary temperature sensitivity of the neutrinos Davis sought to detect and many solutions have involved modifications to the solar model which lower the sun's central temperature. For instance, mixing of cooler material from the exterior of the sun into the hot core (like a giant cauldron) would reduce the neutrino fluxes. A reduction would also be obtained if the sun had become contaminated by heavy elements early on in its history, perhaps as a result of a collision with another celestial body. In the area of nuclear physics it has been suggested that the extrapolations of reaction rates to low energies are not sound. One of the strongest candidate solutions is that of 'neutrino oscillation'. Over the years Davis' result has consistently been about one third less than the best theoretical prediction. Since there are three types of neutrino and Davis' experiment is only sensitive to one sort, the proposal is that the neutrinos are produced in one state in the sun but oscillate between their three states in the long journey to the earth, and Davis only picks up a third of his expected signal.

Some of the proposed solutions have been almost bizarre: the sun is not burning hydrogen at all; or a fundamental theory, such as weak interaction theory, which governs the interaction between neutrinos and chlorine, is in error. Many solutions have not been rebutted and remain unremarked upon in the literature. Others have been given careful consideration and rejected on a variety of grounds. Often such solutions have proved difficult to rule out altogether and scientists have had to resort to notions such as that they are *ad hoc*, or 'aesthetically unappealing'. Overall none of the solutions has yet gained universal assent. On the other hand, stellar evolution theory has not been overthrown. The solar-neutrino result has been treated as an anomaly; something to be put aside for the time being.

An experiment into the nature of science

Although no challenge has yet gained consensus as *the solution* to the solar-neutrino problem, such challenges are interesting because they reveal a world of doubt and uncertainty which lies behind even the most well-established areas of knowledge. Before 1967, the project to detect solar neutrinos seemed to rest upon a solid structure of theoretical and experimental assumptions – it was at least solid enough for a large amount of funding and scientific time to be devoted to it. No doubt, once an agreed solution is reached, all the current uncertainties will vanish and scientists will again have the greatest confidence in these areas of science. What now has become 'unmade' will be 'remade'.

One way of thinking about what has happened is to treat Ray Davis' result itself as an experiment into the nature of science. It is as if Davis' result cuts a knife of uncertainty through the normal taken-for-granted ideas and practices. For a moment scientists could think the unthinkable, explore the unexplorable and cut loose from the shackles of normal science and just see 'what if . . .'. But if we take every suggestion seriously then nearly everything we take for granted is challenged. In this world the sun no longer has nuclear fusion as its source of energy; neutrinos oscillate, decay or stay within the sun; the sun experiences periods of mixing which correlate with ice ages; argon is trapped; weak interaction theory does not work; and so forth.

We have Ray Davis to thank for giving us this thought experiment in the plasticity of scientific culture. Of course, 'what-if science' is not conventional science; in ordinary science a million flowers most decidedly do not bloom. The puzzle the solar-neutrino problem leaves us with is the following: if scientists can in some circumstances think the unthinkable, what stops them doing it most of the time? If the answer does not lie in recalcitrant Nature, and throughout this book we have suggested that Nature imposes much less of a constraint than we normally imagine, this leaves scientific culture. Science works the way it does, not because of any absolute constraint from Nature, but because we make our science the way that we do.

Postscript 1992

The scientific jury on the solar-neutrino case is still out. Two second-generation experiments have reported results. SAGE is the Soviet–American Gallium Experiment using a detector containing 30 tonnes of pure gallium metal located under a mountain in the North Caucasus. GALLEX is an international collaboration using a huge tank of gallium chloride located under the Apennine Mountains in Italy. Both experiments should see between 124 and 132 SNU. SAGE has found only 20 SNU, whilst GALLEX has found 83 SNU. The

GALLEX result can be incorporated within standard solar models by 'severe stretching', but the SAGE result would need a more radical explanation such as neutrino oscillation. The conflicting results are explained by some scientists as being due to the difficulties of operating the pure gallium detector as opposed to the gallium chloride detector. Negotiations are in progress!

Conclusion: putting the golem to work

Looking forward and looking back

We have followed several episodes of science as they have unfolded. We have described not only the work of the most revered scientists, the Einsteins, Newtons and Pasteurs, but also work which it appears will not be acclaimed: Joseph Weber's high fluxes of gravity waves and Ungar and McConnell's memory transfer. In some of the cases examined – the solar-neutrino problem and the sexual behaviour of the whiptail lizard – the jury is still out. Will they make it into the scientific canon or will they be scientific cannon fodder? It remains to be seen, but don't expect to find the answer in the experiments and theories alone.

It is no accident that we have chosen to look at high science and low science together. We have tried to level out the scientific mountain range which rises up as a result of the forces of celebratory history. Look back whence we came in science and there are what seem to be unconquerable peaks – Mount Newton, Mount Pasteur, Mount Einstein – a mountain range of truth. But look forward and the terrain is flat. A few new foothills wrench themselves from the plain every time we glance backwards. What are those new peaks? Were they there yesterday? To understand how science works we must examine how we cause these foothills and mountains to emerge. To do this we must understand science which fails as well as science which succeeds. Only in this way will we have the courage to climb the forbidding mountains of yesterday, and those which are newly forming behind us. What our case studies show is that there is no logic of scientific discovery. Or, rather, if there is such a logic, it is the logic of everyday life.

Human error

It is impossible to separate science from society, yet preserving the idea that there are two distinct spheres is what creates the authoritarian image so familiar to most of us. How is it made to seem that the spheres are separate?

When something goes wrong with science, the scientific community reacts like a nest of ants with an intruder in their midst. Ants swarm over an intruder giving their lives for the nest; in the case of science it is human bodies that are sacrificed: the bodies of those responsible for the 'human error' that allowed the problem to arise. The space shuttle explodes because of human error; Chernobyl explodes because of human error. Finding the human error is the purpose of post-accident inquiries. By contrast, our conclusion is that human 'error' goes right to the heart of science, because the heart is made of human activity. When things go wrong, it is not because human error could have been avoided but because things will always go wrong in any human enterprise. One cannot ask of scientists and technologists that they be no longer human, yet only mythical automata – quite unlike the constituents of a golem – could deliver the sort of certainty that scientists have led us to expect of them.

As things stand, we have, as we remarked in the introduction, only two ways of thinking about science; it is all good or all bad. Unstable equilibrium – flip-flop thinking – is the inevitable consequence of a model of science and technology which is supposed to deliver complete certainty. The trouble is that both states of the flip-flop are to be feared. The overweening claims to authority of many scientists and technologists are offensive and unjustified but the likely reaction, born of failed promises, might precipitate a still worse anti-scientific movement. Scientists should promise less; they might then be better able to keep their promises. Let us admire them as craftspersons: the foremost experts in the ways of the natural world.

Public understanding of science

How does this view of science make a difference? The first point to stress, if it is not already clear, is that this is not an anti-science attitude. It should make very little difference to the way scientists act when they are doing their work at, metaphorically speaking, the laboratory bench. There is a sense in which the social view of science is useless to scientists – it can only weaken the driving force of the determination to discover. The impact of our redescriptions should be on the scientific method of those disciplines which ape what they take to be the way of going on in the high-prestige natural sciences, and on those individuals and organisations who would destroy fledgling sciences for their failure to live up to a misplaced ideal.

Notoriously, the social sciences suffer from the first malaise – physics envy, as it is known – with areas of experimental psychology and quantitative sociology, all pedantically stated hypotheses, and endless statistical manipulation of marginal data, being the most clear-cut examples of this kind of 'scientism'.

The second malaise is more worrisome. The favourable public reception of unusual sciences such as parapsychology – the study of 'mind over matter', 'telepathy', and the like – has given rise to fears that fringe sciences are taking over. An anti-fringe science movement has been spawned whose members take it on themselves to 'debunk' all that is not within the canon, in the name of proper scientific method. Where this effort is aimed at disabusing the public about unsupported claims, it is admirable, but the zeal of these self-appointed vigilantes carries over into areas where they have no business.

Recently, on British television, the public at large was able to witness a stage magician informing a prestigious scientist, head of a famous Paris institute, that his ideas were ridiculous. The motive for this attack was not the professor's methods but the topic he had chosen to research – homeopathy; the instrument of the attack was, nevertheless, an idealised version of what scientific method ought to be. It is no coincidence that those who feel most certain of their grip on scientific method have rarely worked on the frontiers of science themselves. There is a saying in love 'distance lends enchantment'; it is true of science too. It is important that these vigilante organisations do not become so powerful that they can stamp out all that is strange in the scientific world. Saving the public from charlatans is their role, but scientists must not use them to fight their battles for them. If homeopathy cannot be demonstrated experimentally, it is up to scientists, who know the risks of frontier research, to show why. To leave it to others is to court a different sort of golem – one who might destroy science itself.

Science and the citizen

The debate about the public understanding of science is equally confounded by confusion over method and content. What should be explained is methods of science, but what most people concerned with the issues want the public to know about is the truth about the natural world – that is, what the powerful believe to be the truth about the natural world. The laudable reason for concern with public understanding is that scientific and technological issues figure more and more in the political process. Citizens, when they vote, need to know enough to come to some decision about whether they prefer more coal mines or more nuclear power stations, more corn or clearer rivers, more tortured animals or more healthy children, or whether these really are the choices. Perhaps there are novel solutions: wave power, organic farming, drug testing without torture. The 'public understanders', as we might call them, seem to think that if the person in the street knows more science – as opposed to more *about* science – they will be able to make more sensible decisions about these things.

How strange that they should think this; it ranks among the great fallacies of our age. Why? – because PhDs and professors are found on all sides in these debates. The arguments have largely been invented in universities. Thus, all sides have expertise way beyond what can ever be hoped of the person in the street, and all sides know how to argue their case clearly and without obvious fallacies. Why such debates are unresolvable, in spite of all this expertise, is what we have tried to show in the descriptive chapters of this book. That is, we have shown that scientists at the research front cannot settle their disagreements through better experimentation, more knowledge, more advanced theories, or clearer thinking. It is ridiculous to expect the general public to do better.

We agree with the public understanders that the citizen needs to be informed enough to vote on technical issues, but the information needed is not about the content of science; it is about the relationship of experts to politicians, to the media, and to the rest of us. The citizen has great experience in the matter of how to cope with divided expertise – isn't this what party politics is? What the citizen cannot do is cope with divided expertise pretending to be something else. Instead of one question – 'Who to believe?' – there are two questions – 'Who to believe?' and 'Are scientists and technologists Gods or charlatans?'. The second question is what makes the whole debate so unstable because, as we have argued, there are only two positions available.

What we have tried to do here is dissolve the second question – scientists are neither Gods nor charlatans; they are merely experts, like every other expert on the political stage. They have, of course, their special area of expertise, the physical world, but their knowledge is no more immaculate than that of economists, health policy makers, police officers, legal advocates, weather forecasters, travel agents, car mechanics, or plumbers. The expertise that *we* need to deal with them is the well-developed expertise of everyday life; it is what we use when we deal with plumbers and the rest. Plumbers are not perfect – far from it – but society is not beset with anti-plumbers because being anti-plumbing is not a choice available to us. It is not a choice because the counter-choice, plumbing as immaculately conceived, is likewise not on widespread offer.

To change the public understanding of the political role of science and technology is the most important purpose of our book and that is why most of our chapters have revealed the inner workings of science.

Forensic science

It is not only where science and politics meet that there are implications for the understanding of science developed here. Wherever science touches on another institution things change when we learn to see science as expertise rather than as certain knowledge. Consider what happens when science and the law meet. In the courtroom scientific experts provide evidence touching upon a suspect's guilt or innocence. Was the hair found at the scene of the crime the same as the hair on the suspect's head? Were there fabric fibres in common? Could body fluids found on the victim have come from the accused, and how likely is it that they came from someone else? Had the accused handled explosives recently? At the time of writing, the British legal system is being rocked by a series of overturned legal verdicts in cases concerning bombs planted by the Irish Republican Army. Men and women have been locked up for many years, only for it to be discovered that the 'evidence' on which they were convicted was, to use the legal jargon 'unsafe'. Typically, the crucial evidence has been forensic science tests purporting to show that the accused had recently been handling nitroglycerine, indelible traces remaining on his or her hands. The trouble is, as it now turns out, the test is not infallible.

Other objects, such as playing cards, are made with chemicals related to nitroglycerine, and handling such objects might give rise to a positive test result. The forensic scientists involved in the trials did not report the possibility of these false positive readings, nor how likely they were to come about. The British forensic science profession, indeed the whole legal system, has lost credibility through these miscarriages of justice. Worse, it is probably the case that a number of innocent citizens suffered many years of unjust incarceration.

Comparing the analysis of method offered here with the conventional picture of science, it is easy to see how this disaster came about. As long as it is thought that science produces certainty, it seems inappropriate to treat scientific evidence like other legal evidence, so that disagreement *must*, once more, be blamed on human error. But it is the institutions in which forensic evidence is embedded that must take the blame. The problem is that it has not been seen to be necessary to have two versions of the evidence: a defence version and a prosecution version. Typically, in a British court, the Home Office alone supplies the scientists and the scientific conclusions. They present their seemingly neutral results to the court without prior detailed analysis by the defence. The scientific evidence should be neutral, so an alternative view is redundant – it is bound to come to the same conclusions! (To put it another way, scientists are not seen as *re*presenting, merely presenting.) But, as we have seen in the bombing scandals, contested forensic evidence is like contested scientific evidence everywhere; it is like the science described in this book. It is contestable.

The cost of having contested forensic evidence will be that science will no longer put a speedy end to legal trials. Instead of the law passing its responsibility over to the scientific experts, the scientific experts would be just one part of the contested legal process. But this is what *ought* to happen – it is unjust for it to be any other way. What is more, if scientific evidence is subject to the same contestation as other kinds of evidence, it cannot suffer the embarrassment of misplaced certainty.

Interestingly enough, in the American legal system things seem to have gone too far the other way. In the hands of a clever lawyer any piece of forensic evidence can be taken apart. Often forensic evidence carries no weight at all because lawyers have become so adept at finding so-called 'expert witnesses' who will 'deconstruct' each and every piece of scientific evidence. The new way of looking at science throws light upon what is happening here too.

In the first place we should not be surprised that any piece of evidence can be examined and doubted – this is what we should expect given the new understanding of science. It is not a matter of one side having an adequate grasp of the scientific facts and the other side being in error. Doubts about evidence can always be raised. But it does not follow from this that forensic evidence should carry no weight. In judging the merits of forensic evidence we have to apply the normal rules which we would apply if we were judging any argument between experts. For instance, some experts will have more credibility than others and some will have no credibility at all. What has happened in the American legal system seems to draw on only one lesson from the new view of science. Just because scientists disagree, and because experiments and observation alone cannot settle matters, does not mean that scientists do not reach agreement. Consider: gravity waves are not facts of the natural world, while the bending of star light by the sun is a fact.

What has to be thought about in the American legal system is how to bring about closure of debate now that scientists have lost so much credibility. Mechanisms will have to be found so that the influence of non-expert voices is not as great as that of experts. Of course, this will not be easy, especially when expertise is for hire to special interest groups. But solving such problems is the stuff of political and institutional life. American governmental agencies such as the Food and Drug Administration and the Environmental Protection Agency, and the American legal system as a whole, will only maintain credibility if they realise that science works by producing agreement among experts. Allowing everyone to speak is as bad as allowing a single group alone to speak. It is as bad as having no-one speak at all.

The trouble over forensic science can be seen as a microcosm of the whole debate. Claim too much for science and an unacceptable reaction is invited. Claim what can be delivered and scientific expertise will be valued or distrusted, utilised or ignored, not in an unstable way but just as with any other social institution.

Public inquiries

If we apply this new analysis everywhere that science touches on another social institution then a more useful understanding will emerge. What is happening when there are public enquiries about the building of a new nuclear power station? On the one hand there are experts producing complex calculations that seem to make the probability of an accident negligible. On the other hand, there are experts who consider the risk too awful to contemplate. One must take one's choice. Quasi-legal institutions, or Federal agencies, can help to sift and filter expert evidence but in the end the citizen can do no better than listen to both sides and decide in just the same way as one decides on where to buy a house; there is no way of being certain that one is not making a mistake.

Experiments or demonstrations in the public domain

When the Federal Aviation Authority crashed a plane filled with anti-misting kerosene to find out if it was a safer aviation fuel, and when

British Rail crashed a train into a nuclear fuel flask to find out whether it could be broken in an accident, they were not doing science. Experiments in real science hardly ever produce a clear-cut conclusion – that is what we have shown. What these agencies were doing were 'demonstrations' set up to settle a political debate. The role of science in such demonstrations is as dubious as it is in the one-sided British legal system.

At the very least, be suspicious if one interpretation of such a test is treated as though it were inevitable. Listen for interpretations from different interest groups, and make sure those groups are happy that they each had some control over how the test was set up, and what the result was taken to mean. If they do not agree on this, listen to the nature of their complaints.

Science on television

When science is described on television, watch out for the model of science that is implied. One television programme that came near to the sort of account we have given here revealed the trials and tribulations of the CERN team who discovered the fundamental 'Z' particle. The programme described the messiness of the apparatus, the false starts and the rebuildings, the uncertainties that attended the first results, the statistical calculations that were used to bolster certainty that something was being seen, the decision of the director to 'go public' in spite of the deep doubts of members of his team, and then the press conference in which a discovery announcement was made to the world. All this was wonderfully portrayed, but the last phrases of the narrator gave the game away. The programme was entitled, with a hint of self-conscious irony, let us hope, 'The Geneva Event', and the narrator looked back on what he had described as one of the greatest discoveries since the experiments of Faraday. Even here, then, the mess was not allowed to be the message. At the end triumphalism ruled. All too few television programmes offer the picture of science portrayed in these pages.

Accident inquiries

When public inquiries take place after accidents, as in the case of the space shuttle disaster, if they discover nothing but human error, beware. Discovering human error is attributing blame to something outside of science. It would be better if the blame were attributed to something inside – of course it will be humans who are to blame, but also not to blame. No-one is perfect. If the officials who allowed the frozen shuttle to fly that fateful morning had listened to every warning they were offered at every launch, then the space plane would never have flown. Science and technology are inherently risky. When responsibility for trouble is attributed to particular individuals it should be done in the same spirit as political responsibility is attributed; in politics, responsibility is not quite the same as fault. We may be sure that there are many accidents waiting to happen and many more heads will roll, but there is simply nothing we can do about it.

Science education

Finally we come to science education in schools. It is nice to know the content of science – it helps one to do a lot of things such as repair the car, wire a plug, build a model aeroplane, use a personal computer to some effect, know where in the oven to put a soufflé, lower one's energy bills, disinfect a wound, repair the kettle, avoid blowing oneself up with the gas cooker, and much much more. For that tiny proportion of those we educate who will go on to be professional research scientists, knowledge of the content of science must continue to be just as rigorous and extended, and perhaps blinkered, as it is now. But for most of our children, the future citizens of a technological society, there is another, and easier, lesson to be learned.

Every classroom in which children are conducting the same experiment in unison is a microcosm of frontier science. Each such multiple encounter with the natural world is a self-contained sociological experiment in its own right. Think about what happens: the teacher asks the class to discover the boiling point of water by inserting a thermometer into a beaker and taking a reading when the water is steadily boiling. One thing is certain: almost no-one will get 100 °C unless they already know the answer, and they are trying to please the teacher. Skip will get 102 °C, Tania will get 105 °C, Johnny will get 99.5 °C, Mary will get 100.2 °C, Zonker will get 54 °C, while Brian will not quite manage to get a result; Smudger will boil the beaker dry and burst the thermometer. Ten minutes before the end of the experiment the teacher will gather these scientific results and start the social engineering. Skip had his thermometer in a bubble of super-heated steam when he took his reading, Tania had some impurities in her water, Johnny did not allow the beaker to come fully to the boil, Mary's result showed the effect of slightly increased atmospheric pressure above sea-level, Zonker, Brian and Smudger have not yet achieved the status of fully competent research scientists. At the end of the lesson, each child will be under the impression that their experiment has proved that water boils at exactly 100 °C, or would have done were it not for a few local difficulties that do not affect the grown-up world of science and technology, with its fully trained personnel and perfected apparatus.

That ten minutes renegotiation of what really happened is the important thing. If only, now and again, teachers and their classes would pause to reflect on that ten minutes they could learn most of what there is to know about the sociology of science. For that ten minutes illustrates better the tricks of professional frontier science than any university or commercial laboratory with its well-ordered predictable results. Eddington, Michelson, Morley, Weber, Davis, Fleischmann, Pons, Jones, McConnell, Ungar, Crews, Pasteur and Pouchet are Skips, Tanias, Johnnys, Marys, Zonkers, Brians, and Smudgers with clean white coats and 'PhD' after their names. They all come up with wildly varying results. There are theorists hovering around, like the schoolteacher, to explain and try to reconcile. In the end, however, it is the scientific community (the head teacher?) who brings order to this chaos, transmuting the clumsy antics of the collective Golem Science into a neat and tidy scientific myth. There is nothing wrong with this; the only sin is not knowing that it is always thus.

References and further reading

Atkinson, P. and Delamont, S. (1977) 'Mock-ups and Cock-ups: The Stage Management of Guided Discovery Instruction', in P. Woods, and M. Hammersley (eds.) *School Experience: Explorations in the Sociology of Education*, London: Croom Helm

Bennett, E. L. and Calvin, M. (1964) 'Failure to Train Planarians Reliably', *Neurosciences Research Program Bulletin*, July–August, 3–24

Bijker, W., Hughes, T. P. and Pinch, T. J. (1987) (eds.) *The Social Construction of Technological Systems*, Cambridge, Mass.: MIT Press

Bloor, D. (1991) *Knowledge and Social Imagery*, 2nd edition, Chicago and London: University of Chicago Press

Byrne, W. L., Samuel, D., Bennett, E. L., Rosenzwieg, M. R., Wasserman, E., Wagner, A. R., Gardner, F., Galambos, R., Berger, B. D., Margoulis, D. L., Fenischel, R. L., Stein, L., Corson, J. A., Enesco, H. E., Chorover, S. L., Holt, C. E. III, Schiller, P. H., Chiapetta, L., Jarvik, M. E., Leaf, R. C., Dutcher, J. D., Horovitz, Z. P. and Carlton, P. L. (1966) 'Memory Transfer', *Science*, 153, 658–9

Close, F. (1991) *Too Hot to Handle: The Race for Cold Fusion*, Princeton University Press

Collins, H. M. (1981) (ed.) *Knowledge and Controversy*, special issue of *Social Studies of Science*, 11, No. 1

Collins, H. M. (1985), *Changing Order: Replication and Induction in Scientific Practice*, London and Beverley Hills: Sage; second edition with a new afterword published by Chicago University Press, 1992

Collins, H. M. (1990) *Artificial Experts: Social Knowledge and Intelligent Machines*, Cambridge, Mass.: MIT Press

THE GOLEM

Collins, H. M. and Pinch, T. J. (1982) *Frames of Meaning: the Social Construction of Extraordinary Science*, London: Routledge.

Collins, H. M. and Shapin, S. (1989) 'Experiment, Science Teaching and the New History and Sociology of Science', in M. Shortland and A. Warwick (eds.) *Teaching the History of Science*, London: Blackwell

Corning, W. C. and Riccio, D. (1970) 'The Planarian Controversy', in W. L. Byrne (ed.) *Molecular Approaches to Learning and Memory*, New York: Academic Press, pp. 107–49

Dubos, R. (1960) *Louis Pasteur: Free Lance of Science*, English edition: New York: Charles Scribner's

Earman, J. and Glymour, C. (1980) 'Relativity and Eclipses: The British Eclipse Expeditions of 1919 and their Predecessors', *Historical Studies in the Physical Sciences*, 11 (1), 49–85

Einstein, A. and Infeld, L. (1938) *The Evolution of Physics: From Early Concepts to Relativity and Quanta*, New York: Simon and Schuster

Farley, J. and Geison, G. L. (1974) 'Science Politics and Spontaneous Generation in Nineteenth-Century France: the Pasteur–Pouchet Debate', *Bulletin for the History of Medicine*, 48, 161–98. (Referenced page numbers are from the version of this paper reprinted in Collins, H. M. (1982) (ed.) *The Sociology of Scientific Knowledge: A Sourcebook*, Bath University Press)

Fleck, L. (1979) *Genesis and Development of a Scientific Fact*, Chicago and London: University of Chicago Press

Gieryn, T. (1992) 'The Ballad of Pons and Fleischmann: Experiment and Narrative in the (Un)Making of Cold Fusion', in Ernan McMullin (ed.) *The Social Dimensions of Science*, Notre Dame University Press

Goldstein, A. (1973) 'Comments on the "Isolation, Identification and Synthesis of a Specific-Behaviour-Inducing Brain Peptide" ', *Nature*, 242, 60–2

Goldstein, A., Sheehan, P. and Goldstein, P. (1971) 'Unsuccessful Attempts to Transfer Morphine Tolerance and Passive Avoidance by Brain Extracts', *Nature*, 233, 126–9

Gooding, D., Pinch, T. and Schaffer, S. (1989) *The Uses of Experiment*, Cambridge University Press

Haraway, D. (1989) *Primate Visions: Gender, Race, and Nature in the World of Modern Science*, London and New York, Routledge

Hawking, S. (1988) *A Brief History of Time: From the Big Bang to Black Holes*, Bantam Books

Jasanoff, S. (1991) *The Fifth Branch*, Cambridge, MA: Harvard University Press

Kuhn, T. S. (1972) *The Structure of Scientific Revolutions*, Chicago: University of Chicago Press

Latour, B. (1984) *Science in Action*, Milton Keynes and Cambridge, Mass.: Open University Press and Harvard University Press

Latour, B. and Woolgar, S. (1979) *Laboratory Life*, London and Beverley Hills: Sage

Lewenstein, B. (1992) 'Cold Fusion and Hot History', *Osiris*, 7 (in press)

Mallove, E. (1991) *Fire From Ice: Searching for the Truth Behind The Cold Fusion Furore*, New York: John Wiley

McConnell, J. V. (1962) 'Memory Transfer Through Cannibalism in Planarians', *Journal of Neurophysiology*, 3, 42–8

McConnell, J. V. (1965) 'Failure to Interpret Planarian Data Correctly: A Reply to Bennett and Calvin', unpublished manuscript, Ann Arbor: University of Michigan

Miller, D. C. (1933) 'The Ether Drift Experiment and the Determination of the Absolute Motion of the Earth', *Reviews of Modern Physics*, 5, 203–42

Myers, G. (1990) *Writing Biology: Texts in the Social Construction of Scientific Knowledge*, Madison: University of Wisconsin Press

Pickering, A. (1984) *Constructing Quarks*, Chicago: University of Chicago Press

Pinch, T. J. (1986) *Confronting Nature: The Sociology of Solar-Neutrino Detection*, Dordrecht: Reidel

Richards, E. (1991) *Vitamin C and Cancer: Medicine or Politics*, London: Macmillan

Shapin, S. and Schaffer, S. (1985) *Leviathan and the Air-Pump: Hobbes, Boyle and the Experimental Life*, Princeton University Press

Swenson, L. S. (1972) *The Ethereal Aether: A History of the Michelson-Morley-Miller Aether-Drift Experiments, 1880–1930*, Austin and London: University of Texas Press

Travis, G. D. L. 'Memories and Molecules: A Sociological History of the Memory Transfer Phenomenon', PhD Thesis, University of Bath, 1987

Ungar, G. (1973) 'The Problem of Molecular Coding of Neural Information: A Critical Review', *Naturwissenschaften*, 60, 307–12

Ungar, G, Desiderio, D. M., and Parr, W. (1972) 'Isolation, Identification and synthesis of a specific-behaviour-inducing Brain Peptide. *Nature*, 238, 198–202

Von Kluber, H. (1960) 'The Determination of Einstein's Light-deflection in the Gravitational Field of the Sun', *Vistas of Astronomy*, 3, 47–77

Index

skill 7, 9, 11, 14, 18, 114–16
  versus *ad hocery* 12
slime trails, importance to worms 10, 11
sobral eclipse observations 48, 51
'social engineering' 151
social sciences 143
sociology of science 151
solar eclipse 43–55
solar model 127, 136
solar neutrino problem xi, 73, 121–39
solar system 34, 95
Soviet Union 54
Soviet–American Gallium Experiment 138, 139
space shuttle 142, 150
specificity argument, in memory transfer controversy 21
speed of light 29, 30
spontaneous generation 79–90
spurious effects 47
standard works of science 51
Stanford University 18–20, 70
State Legislature 60
statistics 7, 11, 103
stellar evolution theory 121, 123, 125, 128, 137
sterilisation 81
stirring mechanism in cold fusion cell 70
strange results; *see* unusual claims in science
submissiveness in lizards 118
sustaining myth of science 42
Swenson, L. xii, 155
systematic errors 51

Tandberg, T. 61, 62
technological society 150
television 149
temperature sensitivity
  affecting worm running 12
  of gravity wave detectors 94
  of neutrino detectors 136
  of telescopes 34, 35, 46
tenure 74, 136
Texas A&M University 59, 60, 68, 70–72
Thatcher, M. 62
The Journal of Biological Psychology 13
The Worm Runner's Digest 12
theoretical explanations 74
theoretical impossibility 66, 72
theoretical justifications 73
theoretical models 123

theoretical possibilities 72
theoreticians 122, 131, 133, 135, 151
  and experimenters, collaboration between 122, 123, 129, 131, 135
theory
  of evolution 89
  and measurement 44
  of stellar structure 132
thermal noise 93, 94
Thomson, J. 50
threshold, of noise in gravity wave detection 94
time delay experiment, in gravitational wave detection 96
Time magazine 111, 113, 128
time zones, confusion over, in gravity wave controversy 104
Townsend, C. 114, 115, 116, 117
transfer experiments 5–25
  in mammals 17–25
transplantation versus chemical transfer of memory 8
transverse arm problem in Michelson–Morley experiment 36
Travis, D. xii, 155
tritium 68, 71, 72
triumphalism in science 149
triumphalist account of scientific history 84
trouble; *see* anomalies
Tyndall, W. 82

uncertainty in science 107, 137, 138
uncompromising rejection of gravity waves 105
'undisplaced' stars 47
unexpected claims *see* unusual claims
unfamiliar face of science 107
Ungar, G. 5–25, 155
University of Berlin 61
University of Southampton 62
University of Texas 109, 111
University of Utah 57, 59, 63, 64, 113
unorthodox science *see* unusual claims
unresolvable debates 144
unusual claims in science 16, 18, 95, 106
Utah National Cold Fusion Institute 77
Utah press conference 58

variables in worm running experiments 10–12